# Bioterrorism and Biocrimes

## The Illicit Use of Biological Agents Since 1900

**W. Seth Carus**

Center for Counterproliferation Research
National Defense University
Washington, D.C.

Bioterrorism and Biocrimes:
The Illicit Use of Biological Agents Since 1900

by
W. Seth Carus
For
Center for Counterproliferation Research
National Defense University

ISBN: 1-4101-0023-5

Copyright © 2002 by Fredonia Books

Reprinted from the original edition

Fredonia Books
Amsterdam, The Netherlands
http://www.fredoniabooks.com

All rights reserved, including the right to reproduce
this book, or portions thereof, in any form.

# Table of Contents

# Preface

This is the eighth revision of a working paper on biological terrorism first released in August 1998. The last version was released in April 2000. As with the earlier versions, it is an interim product of the research conducted by the author into biological terrorism at the National Defense University's Center for Counterproliferation Research. It incorporates new cases identified through December 31, 2000, as well as a considerable amount of new material on older cases acquired since publication of the previous revision.

The working paper is divided into two main parts. The first part is a descriptive analysis of the illicit use of biological agents by criminals and terrorists. It draws on a series of case studies documented in the second part. The case studies describe every instance identifiable in open source materials in which a perpetrator used, acquired, or threatened to use a biological agent. While the inventory of cases is clearly incomplete, it provides an empirical basis for addressing a number of important questions relating to both biocrimes and bioterrorism. This material should enable policymakers concerned with bioterrorism to make more informed decisions.

In the course of this project, the author has researched over 270 alleged cases involving biological agents. This includes all incidents found in open sources that allegedly occurred during the 20th Century. While the list is certainly not complete, it provides the most comprehensive existing unclassified coverage of instances of illicit use of biological agents. Research into the cases is ongoing, and additional information will be incorporated as further information is uncovered.

# Acknowledgements

This working paper could not have been prepared without the assistance of a large number Most important were my colleagues at the Center for Counterproliferation Research at the National Defense University. Ambassador Robert Joseph, director of the Center when the bulk of the work was conducted, provided the author with the opportunity to work at the Center, which provided the time needed to research and write this manuscript. He showed extraordinary forbearance and support for this project. In addition, his careful editing substantially strengthened the manuscript.

Writing this study would have been impossible without the expert guidance provided by many people who took the time to explain the arcana of biological warfare. To all of them, I express my appreciation. In particular, I have benefited from the willingness of several people who have had first hand experience in the development of biological agents to spend time explaining the esoteric art of biological warfare. This includes the late Thomas Dashiell, William J. Patrick III, and Ken Alibek.

Detailed research into two of the bioterrorism incidents was supported in part by Jonathan Tucker and the Monterey Institute for International Studies. Case studies based on that research were published in Jonathan B. Tucker, editor, *Toxic Terror: Assessing Terrorist Use of Chemical and Biological Agents* (Cambridge, Massachusetts: MIT Press, 2000). In addition, the author benefited considerably from interactions with his fellow authors, although the conclusions reached here sometimes differ from theirs.

The author is grateful for the assistance provided by the staff of the National Defense University Library. In particular, the author is indebted to Jeannemarie Faison, Lorna Dodt, and Bruce Thornlow for their expertise in performing electronic searches. Especially appreciated is the expert assistance of Katrina Elledge provided valuable research assistance while serving as an intern at the Counterproliferation Center.

A considerable number of people have provided useful suggestions that corrected errors and otherwise improved the manuscript. My thanks to Kathleen Bailey, Ph.D., Gordon Burck, LTC George W. Christopher, USAF, MC, Joseph Goldberg, Ph.D., Ambassador Read Hanmer, Dave Huxsoll, D.V.M., Ph.D., Noreen A. Hynes, M.D., M.P.H., Ambassador Robert Joseph, Ph.D., Shellie A. Kolavic, DDS, Cornelius G. McWright, Ph.D., Dennis Perrotta, Ph.D., and Brad Roberts, Ph.D. I am indebted to them all. Any remaining errors are the fault of the author.

Finally, the research and writing of this study was guided in many ways, more than she may realize, by the sage advice and expert assistance of my wife, Noreen.

# Part I: Bioterrorism in Perspective

# Chapter 1: Introduction

During the past five years, the threat of bioterrorism has become a subject of widespread concern. Journalists, academics, and policy analysts have considered the subject, and in most cases found much to alarm them. Most significantly, it has captured the attention of policy makers at all levels of government in the United States. Unfortunately, bioterrorism remains a poorly understood subject. Many policymakers and policy analysts present apocalyptic visions of the threat, contending that it is only a matter of time before some terrorist uses biological agents to cause mass casualties. In contrast, other analysts argue that the empirical record provides no basis for concern, and thus largely dismiss the potential threat.

Neither approach is helpful. Imagining catastrophic threats inevitably leads to a requirement for impossibly large response capabilities. In contrast, denying the potential danger altogether leads to the kind of tunnel vision that led U.S. intelligence officials to totally ignore the emergence of Aum Shinrikyo in Japan, despite its overtly hostile attitude towards the United States. This study takes an intermediate course. It provides empirical evidence to support the views of those who argue that biological agents are difficult to use. It also provides abundant evidence that some people have desired to inflict mass casualties on innocent populations through employment of biological agents. Fortunately, these accounts also suggest that such people lacked the capability to follow through with their plans. The research also casts considerable doubt on our ability to predict which biological agents a perpetrator might employ. While some analysts assume that terrorists will use those agents that proved of most interest to state weapons programs, bioterrorists and biocriminals have acquired and used agents of little or no value as weapons of war. Ultimately, the evidence supports the view that bioterrorism is a low probability, potentially high consequence event.

## What is Bioterrorism?

There is no commonly accepted definition of bioterrorism. For purposes of this study, bioterrorism is assumed to involve the threat or use of biological agents by individuals or groups motivated by political, religious, ecological, or other ideological objectives. This definition, which emerged from the research recorded in this volume, differs in several significant ways from many of the widely accepted definitions of terrorism. Official definitions of terrorism generally emphasize that terrorism is intended to intimidate governments or societies.[1] In essence, the core of terrorism is the ability to terrorize. The definition of bioterrorism adopted here does not require such a motivation, although it also does not exclude it. A definition that focuses on political intimidation fails to capture two significant motivations for bioterrorism.

First, some terrorists are attracted to biological weapons because they understand that pathogens could cause mass casualties on an unprecedented scale. Official definitions appear to exclude groups with apocalyptic visions who are uninterested in influencing governments and seek instead to inflict mass casualties. Traditional terrorists use violence as a means to an end. In contrast, proponents of catastrophic terrorism view mass killing as the desired end. Groups of this type are not common, yet they do exist.

Second, other terrorists are attracted to unique features of bioterrorism that have nothing to do with the intended psychological impact of biological weapons use. They see biological agents as a tool for achieving specialized objectives not necessarily intended to directly influence government actions. Virtually all bioterrorists seek to keep their use of biological agents a secret, because in many instances success depended on the lack of appreciation that a disease outbreak was intentional.

A bioterrorist can include any non-state actor who uses or threatens to use biological agents on behalf of a political, religious, ecological, or other ideological cause without reference to its moral or political justice.

---

[1] There are multiple definitions of terrorism. The Department of Defense defines terrorism as "the calculated use of violence or threat of violence to inculcate fear; intended to coerce or to intimidate governments or societies in the pursuit of goals that are generally political, religious, or ideological." See Joint Publication 1-02, *DOD Dictionary of Military and Associated Terms*, as found at *http://www.dtic.mil/doctrine/jel/doddict/*. In contrast, the FBI defines terrorism as "the unlawful use of force or violence against persons or property to intimidate or coerce a Government, the civilian population, or any segment thereof, in furtherance of political or social objectives." See Federal Bureau of Investigation, *Terrorism in the United States 1995*, as found at *http://www.fbi.gov*.

This includes non-state actors who operate in organized military units (as with guerillas) if biological agent use was undertaken with covert, improvised delivery means.

## Studying Bioterrorism

Despite all the attention devoted to bioterrorism, it remains surprisingly misunderstood. In part, this reflects a lack of information about bioterrorism. Relatively little effort was devoted to its study, and the focus of the small literature on the subject was largely theoretical.[2] Virtually nothing was written about past examples of bioterrorism. Indeed, the first unclassified effort to systematically identify all bioterrorism incidents was not conducted until 1995.[3] Given this apparent lack of interest, it is perhaps not surprising that the first official account of the 1984 use of biological agents by the Rajneeshees was published only in 1997.[4] In the late 1990s, the gaps in our understanding of past terrorist interest in biological agents have been reduced by several initiatives to explore the history of bioterrorism. The Monterey Institute for International Studies has played a significant role in this process. It has created a comprehensive database of chemical and biological terrorism incidents and has sponsored teams of scholars who have produced detailed case studies analyzing terrorist resort to chemical and biological weapons.[5] In addition, several researchers have examined specific instances of bioterrorism.

### Study objectives

This volume reflects the result of a study initiated in early 1997 to address the lack of information about bioterrorism. Part I provides a descriptive analysis of what is known about past instances of bioterrorism, based on the comprehensive survey of all known bioterrorism incidents provided in Part II. Each of the incidents included in Part II is described to the extent possible with the available information. In addition, the data provided in this volume provides some insights useful for the debates about bioterrorism that erupted in the late 1990s. In particular, it provides some insight into possible motivations for resort to bioterrorism and the technical hurdles that face anyone attempting to use biological agents.

The result is a description and analysis of 54 alleged terrorist cases. The quality of the available information, however, is such that only 27 of the cases can be substantiated.[6] Because it was clear that it would be possible to identify few confirmed cases involving terrorist groups, the research included other types of perpetrators, including criminals and covert use by governments.[7] These inclusions led to the addition of 82 criminal cases, of which there was confirmation on 56, and 113 cases where the perpetrators cannot be characterized clearly as either criminals or terrorists (only 97 confirmed). Almost all of the confirmed cases where a perpetrator cannot be identified are anthrax hoaxes. Most of these cases probably would be classified as criminal incidents if more information about the perpetrators were available.[8] In addition, 20 of the cases

---

[2] Among the past studies of bioterrorism are Jeffrey D. Simon, *Terrorists and the Potential Use of Biological Weapons: A Discussion of Possibilities*, RAND report R-3771-AFMIC, December 1989, p. 8, Jessica Eve Stern, "Will Terrorists Turn to Poison?," *Orbis*, Vol. 37, No. 3 (Summer 1993), pp. 393-410, and Raymond Allan Zilinskas, "Terrorism and Biological Weapons: Inevitable Alliance?," *Perspectives in Biology and Medicine*, Vol. 34, No. 1 (Autumn 1990), pp. 44-72. See also the essays in Brad Roberts, editor, *Terrorism with Chemical and Biological Weapons* (Alexandria, Virginia: Chemical and Biological Arms Control Institute, 1997).

[3] The major exception was the survey of bioterrorism incidents by Ron Purver, *Chemical and Biological Terrorism: The Threat According to the Open Literature*, Canadian Security Intelligence Service, June 1995.

[4] Thomas J. Török, et al., "A Large Community Outbreak of Salmonellosis Caused by Intentional Contamination of Restaurant Salad Bars," *JAMA*, August 6, 1997, pp. 389-395.

[5] The case studies are contained in Jonathan B. Tucker, editor, *Toxic Terror: Assessing Terrorist Use of Chemical and Biological Agents* (Cambridge, Massachusetts: MIT Press, 2000). They provide a more detailed look at several of the cases included in this volume. However, the conclusions in this volume sometimes differ from those of the authors of the *Toxic Terror* case studies..

[6] The criteria for inclusion are discussed in Chapter 4, while the individual cases are described in Chapters 5 through 8. The cases are listed in Appendix A.

[7] Criminals are distinguished from terrorists by motivation and objective. Criminals are motivated by objectives such as personal revenge or financial gain. They may be driven by psychological pathologies. They do not have larger ideological objectives.

[8] In some instances, it is difficult to determine if perpetrators were motivated by political or criminal motivations. Several perpetrators who tried to extort money from governments also made political demands. Since such political demands could have been a cover for financial motivations, when little is known about the perpetrator's true objectives it is impossible to determine whether an incident should be considered terrorist or criminal. Some widely reported cases fall into this category. For example, Thomas Lavy, a survivalist living in Arkansas, was arrested in 1995 on charges related to the possession of the toxin ricin. His motivations for acquiring the ricin were never clarified before he committed suicide. Nor is it clear why Larry Wayne Harris purchased *Yersinia pestis*, the organism that causes plague. Although Harris had links to white supremacist groups, including the Aryan Nation and the Christian Identity movement, he

involve allegations of covert state activities, although the evidence is compelling in only 11 of then. In all, 269 cases were researched involving allegations that terrorists, criminals, or covert state operators used, acquired, threatened use, or took an interest in biological agents.

Although there are differences between terrorist and criminal uses of biological agents, the biocriminal faces many of the same obstacles as the bioterrorist. Both must acquire, develop, and employ biological weapons, so the technical constrains that appear in criminal cases are likely to apply for terrorist cases. In addition, it is possible that criminal cases will be a leading indicator of possible terrorist interest in biological agents. Nevertheless, the differences between terrorists and criminals suggest caution needs to be exercised in extrapolating from the experience of criminals to that of terrorists.

---

claimed that the cultures were needed to support research on the development of medical treatments for the disease. The law enforcement investigation uncovered no evidence that he had a more nefarious objective.

# Chapter 2:
# The Practice

The unique characteristics of biological agents make bioterrorism fundamentally different from other forms of terrorism. Not only do biological agents differ radically from other weapons available to the terrorist, but biological weapons also are substantially different from other weapons of mass destruction, such as chemical and nuclear weapons. Assessing the prospects for bioterrorism requires an appreciation of how biological agents can be acquired and how they are disseminated. Because terrorists are likely to be confronted with many of the same obstacles faced by criminals in the acquisition and use of biological agents, both types of actors are included in this discussion.

## Experience of Bioterrorism

A starting point for evaluating the challenge posed by bioterrorism is an examination of the evidence regarding the extent to which terrorists have used or thought about using biological agents. Some caution must be exercised in evaluating the empirical data, because it is possible that future patterns will differ significantly from past patterns of behavior. Hence, the following should be considered in the context of the subsequent discussion of the factors that might affect the propensity of terrorists to resort to biological weapons.

### Bioterrorism or Biocrimes

Interest in biological agents is not confined to groups with known political agendas. Indeed, most individuals and groups who have used biological agents had traditional criminal motives. Hence, it is essential to separate the clearly criminal perpetrators from those with political agendas, whether the motive is sectarian, religious, or ecological. The available evidence, in fact, suggests that the vast majority of cases involve criminal motives.

### Extent of interest

To date, few terrorists have demonstrated an interest in bioterrorism, and fewer still tried to acquire biological agents. As mentioned previously, open source accounts mention at least 54cases in which a terrorist group allegedly had an interest in biological agents, but there is little evidence to confirm most of the cases. Thus, there are only 27 cases in which there is more than minimal evidence that a terrorist group possessed, attempted to acquire, threatened to use, or expressed interest in biological agents. Even in some of confirmed cases, there is no way to determine the seriousness of the interest in biological agents. Terrorist groups apparently acquired biological agents in only eight cases.

Terrorists have used biological agents, but rarely and with relatively little effect. A review of the cases researched for this study confirms only five groups that used or tried to use biological agents. Although there may be other examples that have never been publicly identified, only one of these cases is known to have resulted in harm to people.

*Rajneeshees*: According to the FBI, there is only one instance in which a terrorist group operating in the United States actually employed a chemical or biological agent.[9] This incident took place in September 1984. The perpetrators were members of the Rajneeshee, a religious cult that established a large commune in Wasco County, a rural area east of Portland, Oregon. The Rajneeshees used *Salmonella typhimurium*, which causes salmonellosis or food poisoning, to contaminate restaurant salad bars. An estimated 751 people became ill because of that attack, including about 45 who were hospitalized. There were no fatalities. This is the only bioterrorism incident in which human illness has been verified.

---

[9] Testimony of John P. O'Neill, Supervisory Special Agent, Chief, Counterterrorism Section, Federal Bureau of Investigation, p. 238, in Committee on Governmental Affairs, U.S. Senate, *Global Proliferation of Weapons of Mass Destruction*, Part I.

**Table 1: Confirmed cases of illicit biological agent activity**

| Type | Terrorist | Criminal | Other/Uncertain | Total Cases |
|---|---|---|---|---|
| Acquire and Use | 5 | 16 | 0 | 21 |
| Acquire | 3 | 7 | 2 | 12 |
| Interest | 6 | 4 | 0 | 10 |
| Threat/Hoax | 13 | 29 | 95 | 137 |
| Total Cases | 27 | 56 | 97 | 180 |

Source: Based on cases reviewed in Part II. A brief explanation for the decision to include or exclude each specific case is provided in Appendix A.

*Aum Shinrikyo*: In addition to using sarin nerve gas in the Tokyo subway system, Aum Shinrikyo produced biological agents and tried to use them. According to press reports, the Japanese police discovered that the Aum's membership included skilled scientists and technicians, including some with training in microbiology. The Aum expressed an interest in several biological agents, allegedly including *B. anthracis*, botulinum toxin, *C. burnetii* (Q-fever), and even Ebola. The Aum tried to disseminate biological agents, including *B. anthracis* and botulinum toxin, but there is no evidence that they actually managed to produce any pathogens or toxins. The group allegedly targeted the U.S. Navy base at Yokosuka in one of its attempted attacks.[10]

*Dark Harvest*: This little known group protested the continued anthrax contamination of Gruinard Island, which is where the British military tested an anthrax bomb during World War Two. The group took anthrax-contaminated soil, apparently from the island, and dumped it on the grounds of Porton Down, the site of Britain's biological and chemical weapons research establishment. The anthrax was in a form that was highly unlikely to cause harm.

*Mau Mau*: The British believe that in late 1952 individuals associated with the Mau Mau African independence movement were responsible for using a plant toxin to poison livestock in what is now Kenya. The full extent of these activities is not known.

*Polish Resistance*: Multiple reports suggest that Polish resistance organizations used biological agents against German forces during the early part of the World War Two. At least one Polish official claimed that 200 Germans were killed in this fashion, but the claim was never confirmed.

## Motives for use

The review of cases identifies a number of reasons that led terrorists and criminals to become interested in biological agents:

[10] Sheryl WuDunn, Judith Miller, and William J. Broad, "How Japan Germ Terror Alerted World," *New York Times*, May 26, 1998, pp. A1, A10, provides the most thorough reporting of Aum's biological warfare activities. See page 47 for additional details.

**Mass murder**: At least two terrorist groups, motivated by apocalyptic, millenarian visions of creating a better society, clearly wanted to kill large numbers of people. In principle, such groups also could be motivated by desires for revenge against a specific political or ethnic group. Steven Pera and Allan Schwander formed a group, which they called R.I.S.E., with the intention of killing most of the human race so that mankind could start over again. Aum Shinrikyo also wanted to murder large numbers of people as part of their efforts to seize control of Japan.

**Murder**: Several terrorist groups are known to have considered biological agents as weapons to kill specific individuals. In general, the perceived attractiveness of biological agents results from the belief that the victim will appear to have died a natural death. The perpetrators hoped that it would prove impossible either to detect the biological agent (especially if it was a toxin) or to determine that the victim was deliberately infected (especially if it was a pathogen).

**Incapacitation**: In at least two instances, the perpetrators wanted to incapacitate large numbers of people without necessarily killing anyone. According to press accounts, the Weathermen attempted to obtain biological agents to infect water supplies. They hoped the repressive reaction of the government to such an incident would radicalize the general population and create additional supporters for their cause. The

**Table 2: Objectives for using biological agents**

| Type | Terrorist | Criminal | Other/ Uncertain | Total Cases |
|---|---|---|---|---|
| Murder | 4 | 17 | 0 | 21 |
| Terrorize | 6 | 9 | 22 | 37 |
| Extortion | 0 | 13 | 3 | 16 |
| Disruption | 0 | 5 | 0 | 5 |
| Anti-animal/crops | 1 | 2 | 0 | 4 |
| Mass Murder | 4 | 0 | 0 | 3 |
| Revenge | 0 | 3 | 0 | 3 |
| Incapacitation | 2 | 0 | 0 | 2 |
| Political statement | 1 | 0 | 0 | 1 |
| Unknown | 9 | 7 | 72 | 88 |

Note: Because some perpetrators had multiple objectives, the totals in this table may exceed the total number of cases.

Rajneeshees also wanted to incapacitate the citizens of The Dalles, Oregon, so that the people of the community could not vote in an upcoming election. While the circumstances of that attack are unlikely to reappear, the case demonstrated that biological agents have utility as mass incapacitants.

**Political statement**: In one case, the perpetrators used biological agents to make a political statement. This was the objective of Dark Harvest, a group that apparently was uninterested in causing harm to people or property, but was willing to "use" of biological agents to send a political message.

**Anti-agriculture**: This can mean either targeting livestock or crops.[11] As previously mentioned, the Mau Mau apparently used a plant toxin to kill cattle as part of a concerted campaign that involved known use of other poisons, including arsenic. Besides this instance, there are no confirmed cases of threats against

[11] Lester C. Caudle III, "The Biological Warfare Threat," pp. 459-461, Frederick R. Sidell, et al., *Medical Aspects of Chemical and Biological Warfare* (Washington, D.C.: Office of the Surgeon General, Department of the Army, 1997), provides a summary of the biological warfare threat to animals and crops.

agriculture.[12] Numerous biological agents can be used to target crops and livestock. The viability of the threat is demonstrated by the efforts by several countries to develop biological agents for use against crops. The United States Army weaponized several agents for use against crops prior to the 1969 decision to dismantle the U.S. offensive BW program.[13] The Soviet Union had a substantial program to agents for use against crops and animals.[14] Iraq admits that during the 1980s it was developing at least one biological agent for use against crops, wheat cover smut, which kills the affected plants.[15]

**Criminal motives**: An examination of criminal use of biological agents reveals additional motives. Many of the criminal uses of biological agents involved extortion. Extortion was the motive in about 9 per cent of the confirmed cases. Generally, the target was a food or grocery company. In only one of these cases is the perpetrator known to have had the capability to undertake the threatened contamination. There is no documented case of a terrorist group using biological agents to extort money. However, several unidentified individuals tied political agendas to extortion plots involving threats of biological weapons use. Many of the cases appear to involve deliberate efforts to terrorize the victims. In most of these cases, the perpetrator appeared to want to accomplish nothing more than to make the victims worry about their health. At least one case, involving the Japanese physician Dr. Mitsuru Suzuki, appears to have been motivated by the desire for revenge. Suzuki was angry about the treatment he was receiving as a resident in his medical training, and allegedly retaliated by infecting other health care providers and patients. Suzuki's motivations are complicated by suggestions that he may have been creating clinical cases to further his academic research into *S. typhi*.

## Trends in Bioterrorism

The available evidence indicates that there is an explosion of interest by criminals in biological agents. Forty of the 56 confirmed criminal cases occurred in the 1990s. Similarly, 19 of 27 confirmed terrorist cases occurred in the 1990s. This suggests growing interest in biological agents.[16] The most extensive official comment on terrorist and criminal interest in biological weapons comes from 1997 testimony given by Director Louis Freeh. At that time, he made the following observations:

> The FBI has also investigated and responded to a number of threats which involved biological agents and are attributed to various types of groups or individuals. For example, there have been apocalyptic-type threats which actually advocate destruction of the world through the use of WMD [weapons of mass destruction]. We have also been made aware of interest in biological agents by individuals espousing white-supremacist beliefs to achieve social change; individuals engaging in criminal activity, frequently arising from jealousy or interpersonal conflict; individuals and small anti-tax groups, and some cult interest. In most cases, threats have been limited in scope and have targeted individuals rather than groups, facilities, or critical infrastructure. Threats have surfaced which advocate dissemination of a chemical agent through air ventilation systems. Most have made little mention of the type of device or delivery system to be employed, and for this reason have been deemed technically not feasible. Some threats have been validated.[17]

According to 1997 testimony by DCI George Tenet, the intelligence community also has found evidence that foreign terrorist groups are showing greater interest in biological weapons. "We are increasingly seeing terrorist groups looking into the feasibility and effectiveness of chemical, biological, and radiological weapons."[18] Overall, the CIA concluded, "The current WMD terrorist threat is considered low but

---

[12] There are documented instances of chemical contamination of food to prevent sale of agricultural produce. For example, mercury was injected into oranges exported from Israel in 1978, causing a dramatic reduction in demand for its citrus crop. See Purver, *Chemical and Biological Terrorism*, pp. 87-88, for a review of the literature discussing this event.

[13] Specifically, the United States weaponized and stockpiled rice blast, rye stem rust and wheat stem rust. See Table 1 in George W. Christopher, et al., "Biological Warfare: A Historical Perspective," *JAMA*, Vol. 278, No. 5 (August 6, 1997), p. 412. The rice blast was aimed at China, while the other two were targeted at the Soviet Union. For one view on the utility of such attacks, see J.H. Rothschild, *Tomorrow's Weapons* (New York: McGraw-Hill, 1964), pp. 121-131.

[14] Judith Miller, "U.S. to Use Lab for More Study Of Bioterrorism," *New York Times*, September 22, 1999, p. A25.

[15] R. A. Zilinskas, "Iraq's Biological Weapons: The Past as Future?," *JAMA*, Vol. 278, No. 5 (August 6, 1997), p. 419.

[16] This conclusion differs significantly from the author's original views, when it appeared that only three of 12 terrorist cases took place in the 1990s. New cases and additional research on old cases have resulted in an increase in the number of identified terrorist cases from three to eight.

[17] Statement of Louis J. Freeh, Director, Federal Bureau of Investigation, before the United States Senate Appropriations Committee Hearing on Counterterrorism, May 13, 1997.

[18] United States Senate, Select Committee on Intelligence, *Current and Projected National Security Threats to the United States* (Washington, D.C.: Government Printing Office, 1997), p. 8.

**Table 3: Trends in bioagent cases**

| | Terrorist | Criminal | Other/ Uncertain | Total |
|---|---|---|---|---|
| 1990-1999 | 19 | 40 | 94 | 153 |
| 1980-1989 | 3 | 6 | 0 | 9 |
| 1970-1979 | 3 | 2 | 3 | 8 |
| 1960-1969 | 0 | 1 | 0 | 1 |
| 1950-1959 | 1 | 0 | 0 | 1 |
| 1940-1949 | 1 | 0 | 0 | 1 |
| 1930-1939 | 0 | 3 | 0 | 3 |
| 1920-1929 | 0 | 0 | 0 | 0 |
| 1910-1919 | 0 | 3 | 0 | 3 |
| 1900-1909 | 0 | 1 | 0 | 1 |
| Totals | 27 | 56 | 97 | 180 |

increasing."[19] In April 1998, Clinton Administration officials reportedly testified during a classified hearing before the Senate Intelligence Committee that there was a "high degree of likelihood that such an attack would occur in 10 years."[20]

There is also reason for concern that future bioterrorism attacks may be more deadly than past incidents. Three factors account for the change. First, an increasing number of terrorist groups—foreign and domestic—are adopting the tactic of inflicting mass casualties to achieve ideological, revenge, or "religious" goals, often hard to understand. If such groups acquired an effective aerosol dissemination capability for anthrax, for example, they could potentially kill tens or hundreds of thousands of people. The World Trade Center and Oklahoma City bombings both were conducted by people who had no compunction about mass killing and, in fact, sought to kill large numbers of civilians.[21] Second, the technological sophistication of the terrorist groups is growing. We now know that some terrorists have tried to master the intricacies of aerosol dissemination of biological agents. Perhaps more disturbing for the future, some terrorists might gain access to the expertise generated by a state-directed biological warfare program. Finally, Aum Shinrikyo demonstrated that terrorist groups now exist with resources comparable to some governments. Therefore, it is seems increasingly likely that some group will become capable of using biological agents to cause massive casualties.

---

[19] United States Senate, Select Committee on Intelligence, *Current and Projected National Security Threats to the United States*, p. 94.

[20] As characterized by Senator Carl Levin, reported by "Reno, FBI Head Warn Of Terrorism," *Associated Press*, April 23, 1998, 4:44 A.M. feed. The FBI has issued some statistics that appear to indicate a trend towards greater use of nuclear, biological, and chemical weapons. In testimony before the same committee, Louis Freeh reported that the Bureau investigated 114 cases involving chemical, biological, or other weapons of mass destruction during the last year. See Tim Weiner, "U.S. May Stockpile Medicine for Terrorist Attack," *New York Times*, April 23, 1998.

The significance of that figure is difficult to interpret. The Department of Defense defines a weapon of mass destruction to include nuclear, biological, and chemical weapons, but the legal definition is different. "The Violent Crime Control and Law Enforcement Act of 1994," defines a WMD to include "any destructive device as defined in section 921" of Title 18 of the U.S. Code. According to section 921, a destructive device is "any gun with a barrel larger than half an inch, any bomb, any grenade, any "rocket having a propellant charge of more than four ounces." In other words, to the FBI, a weapon of mass destruction is basically any destructive device, including a great many that clearly cannot cause mass destruction and that have nothing to do with nuclear, biological, or chemical weapons. Nevertheless, the Director's statement apparently refers only to nuclear, biological, and chemical weapons cases.

[21] Bruce Hoffman, *Inside Terrorism* (London: Victor Gollancz, 1998), pp. 92-94.

## Acquiring Biological Agents

Biological agents are organisms or toxins produced by organisms that can be used against people, animals, or crops. In contrast, chemical agents, poisonous substances that can kill or incapacitate, are man-made materials.[22]

**Pathogens:** Pathogens are naturally occurring microorganisms that cause disease. There are hundreds of pathogens, including bacteria, viruses, fungi, and parasites. Among the pathogens often mentioned as potential biological agents are *Bacillus anthracis*, the organism that causes anthrax, and *Yersinia pestis*, the organism that causes plague.[23] Because pathogens are living organisms, they are self-replicating. Exposure to even a small number of organisms can produce severe symptoms or even death. Thus, it is believed that the $ID_{50}$ for pneumonic plague is fewer than 100 *Y. pestis* organisms, while 8-10,000 *B. anthracis* spores will cause inhalation anthrax.[24]

Only some pathogens are transmissible from person to person. For example, someone suffering from pneumonic plague can transmit *Y. pestis* organisms to others, creating a serious risk of epidemic spread. In contrast, bubonic plague is communicable generally only if someone is exposed to pus from an infected

---

[22] There is no standard definition of a biological agent. The definition used here follows the definition in Frederick R. Sidell and David R. Franz, "Overview: Defense Against the Effects of Chemical and Biological Warfare Agents," pp. 4-5, in Frederick R. Sidell, et al., *Medical Aspects of Chemical and Biological Warfare* (Washington, D.C.: Office of the Surgeon General, Department of the Army, 1997): "Biological agents are either replicating agents (bacteria or viruses) or nonreplicating materials (toxins or physiologically active proteins or peptides) that can be produced by living organisms. Some of the nonreplicating biological agents can also be produced through either chemical synthesis, solid-phase protein synthesis, or recombinant expression methods."

The Department of Defense officially defines a biological agent as "a microorganism that causes disease in personnel, plants, or animals or causes the deterioration of materiel." It separately defines a toxin agent as "a poison formed as a specific secretion product in the metabolism of a vegetable or animal organism as distinguished from inorganic poisons. Such poisons can also be manufactured by synthetic processes." See Joint Publication 1-02, *DOD Dictionary of Military and Associated Terms*, as found at *http://www.dtic.mil/doctrine/jel/doddict/*. A slightly different definition of toxins was offered in *Medical Management of Biological Casualties* (Fort Detrick, Frederick, Maryland: U.S. Army Medical Research Institute of Infectious Diseases, March 1996), p. 75: "Toxins are defined as any toxic substance of natural origin produced by an animal, plant, or microbe. They are different from chemical agents such as VX, cyanide, or mustard in that they are not man-made."

The Biological Weapons Convention provides no specific definition. Article I requires adherents not to "develop, produce, stockpile or otherwise acquire or retain: Microbial or other biological agents, or toxins whatever their origin or method of production, of types and in quantities that have no justification for prophylactic, protective or other peaceful purposes." Thus, the convention really provides little guidance as to what is prohibited.

[23] There is considerable misunderstanding of biological agents. In February 1998, federal officials alleged that some perpetrators had "military grade anthrax", a meaningless statement. There are many different strains of *B. anthracis*, but there is no uniquely "military" type. Rather, biological agents used in biological weapons have been strains of naturally occurring organisms. Similarly, there is considerable confusion about plague. *Y. pestis*, the plague bacillus, causes several different diseases, including bubonic plague and pneumonic plague, but there is no bubonic plague or pneumonic plague organism.

[24] The $ID_{50}$ is the dose (D) at which 50 per cent of those exposed will become infected (I). The $LD_{50}$ is the dose (D) that is lethal (L) to 50 per cent of those exposed. With some diseases, the $ID_{50}$ might be identical to the $LD_{50}$. The figures are from *Medical Management of Biological Casualties*, Appendix.

According to one estimate, there are $10^{10}$ *B. anthracis* spores (or 10 billion) in a milligram, which is one-thousandths of a gram or one-millionth of a kilogram. Thus, a milligram contains roughly one million infective doses. Because the agent cannot be disseminated perfectly, it could not infect anywhere near that number of people. According to one estimate, the accidental release of *B. anthracis* spores from the Soviet biological weapons facility at Sverdlovsk killed at least 66 people and involved somewhere between a few milligrams and a gram of agent. It appears that 1-3 per cent of those in the area covered by the *B. anthracis* cloud died. Thus, if only 6 milligrams were disseminated, the agent cloud would have contained at least 6 million lethal doses, which is nearly 100,000 times the number of people who actually died. See Matthew Meselson, Jeanne Guillemin, Martin Hugh-Jones, Alexander Langmuir, Ilona Popova, Alexis Shelokov, and Olga Yampolskaya, "The Sverdlovsk Anthrax Outbreak of 1979," *Science*, Volume 266, Number 5188 (November 18, 1995), pp. 1202-1208. See also, Matthew Meselson, "Note Regarding Source Strength," November 21, 1994.

Estimates of $LD_{50}$ should be treated cautiously. Generally, they are based on extrapolation of animal data. A recent review of the published anthrax research reached the following conclusion on the susceptibility of humans to infection from anthrax.

> The data available on human exposure to *B. anthracis* spores do not allow us to establish the minimum critical dose required to establish any of the forms of the disease. From the information available, it can be said that man appears to be moderately resistant to anthrax. It is crucial to note that any critical dose will depend very heavily on the strain of *B. anthracis*, particularly the presence of the virulence factors, and on the health of the individual host.

See A. Watson and D. Keir, "Information on which to base assessments of risk from environments contaminated with anthrax spores," *Epidemiology and Infection*, 113(1994), pp. 479-490.

person. Anthrax is not contagious, and only those exposed to the released *B. anthracis* spores are likely to become infected.[25]

Pathogens require an incubation period before symptoms of infection appear. For some diseases, the incubation period is only a few days, while for others it might be several weeks. Typically, 3-5 days pass before the acute symptoms of inhalation anthrax appear, while for Q fever (caused by the *Coxiella burnetii* organism) the incubation period is two to three weeks, depending on the size of the dose.[26]

**Toxins:** Toxins are poisonous chemicals produced by living organisms. Among the best known are botulinum toxin, which is produced by the bacteria *Clostridium botulinum*, and ricin, which is extracted from the seed of the castor bean plant. Unlike pathogens, toxins are not self-replicating, so their physical effects are solely a result of the agent released.

While toxins share many characteristics with chemical agents, they also have some significant differences.[27] Many toxins are more toxic than the most lethal of chemical agents. Thus, the $LD_{50}$ for botulinum toxin when injected is 0.001 micrograms per kilogram of body weight. In contrast, VX, perhaps the most lethal of the chemical agents, has an $LD_{50}$ of 15 micrograms per kilogram of bodyweight.[28] Toxins are not volatile, unlike many chemical agents, and thus do not naturally generate a persistent threat. Generally, toxins are not dermally active, meaning that contact with the skin is insufficient to produce disease. Rather, the agent must be brought into the body, either by ingestion, inhalation, or through an opening in the skin.[29]

The quantity of toxin required to achieve a desired effect is dependent on the lethality of the agent. According to one estimate, eight tons of ricin would be needed to blanket an area to achieve the same effect accomplished using only eight kilograms of botulinum toxin. For many toxins, the quantities of agent required to produce a given effect are similar in size to that for the more lethal chemical agents.[30]

## Sources of agent

Only 33 of non-state cases involved actual acquisition of agent. Four different methods were used: purchase from legitimate suppliers, theft, self-production, and use of material of natural origin contaminated with biological agents. The data on acquisition routes are summarized in Table 4.

Gaining access to biological agents never appears to have been a significant limiting factor. In fact, acquiring biological agents has usually proven to be relatively easy. In a few cases, pathogens were acquired from culture collections, usually legitimately but sometimes not, while the perpetrators usually produced toxins. Culture collections were a preferred source for pathogens even when the terrorists or criminals possessed the skills to culture organisms acquired in nature. Reliance on such collections may be a result of the relative ease with which the cultures can be obtained. Alternatively, perpetrators may prefer to obtain cultures from standardized sources to ensure purity and avoid cross-contamination of cultures with unwanted organisms. In addition, the effectiveness of biological agents depends heavily on the specific strain of the organism, and it may be difficult to acquire the more dangerous strains relying on natural sources.

---

[25] Abram S. Benenson, editor, *Control of Communicable Disease Manual*, 16th edition (Washington, DC: American Public Health Association, 1995), pp. 20, 355.

[26] Benenson, *Control of Communicable Disease Manual*, pp. 19, 380. Note, however, that in Sverdlovsk the incubation period was 4 to 43 days and that a 9 to 10 day period was most common. See Meselson, et al., "The Sverdlovsk Outbreak of 1979," pp. 1206-1207.

[27] A useful comparison of chemical and toxin agents is provided by David R. Franz, "Defense Against Toxin Weapons," pp. 604-608, in Sidell, et al., *Medical Aspects of Chemical and Biological Warfare.*

[28] *Medical Management of Biological Casualties*, Table 1, Appendix. At least one authority argues that the $LD_{50}$ is significantly greater than commonly reported. According to William Patrick, who developed biological weapons for the U.S. Army in the 1950s and 1960s, the $LD_{50}$ for botulinum toxin through the inhalation route is 4.88 micrograms (a microgram is one millionth of a gram) for a 70 kilogram man (assuming 50% pure toxin). This translates to about 0.035 micrograms of pure toxin per kilogram of body weight, not 0.001 micrograms as usually reported. See Frederick R. Sidell, William C. Patrick, III, and Thomas R. Dashiell, *Jane's Chem-Bio Handbook* (Alexandria, Virginia: Jan's Information Group, 1998), p. 179, and William C. Patrick III, "Potential Incident Scenarios," p. I-60, in *Proceedings of the Seminar on Responding to the Consequences of Chemical and Biological Terrorism*, July 11-14, 1995, sponsored by the U.S. Public Health Service, Office of Emergency Preparedness, Uniformed Services University of Health Sciences, Bethesda, Maryland. Other authorities cite a figure of 0.003 micrograms per kilogram of body weight for inhaled botulinum toxin. See John L. Middlebrook and David R. Franz, "Botulinum Toxin," p. 647, in Sidell, et al., *Medical Aspects of Chemical and Biological Warfare.*

[29] At least one class of toxins, mycotoxins (the substances allegedly involved with the "yellow rain" attacks in Southeast Asia), pose a dermal hazard because they can penetrate the skin. See *Medical Management of Biological Casualties*, pp. 75 and 100, and Robert W. Wannemacher, Jr., and Stanley L. Weiner, "Tricothecene Mycotoxins," pp. 658-659, in *Medical Management of Biological Casualties.*

[30] Figure 30-1 in Franz, "Defense Against Toxin Weapons," p. 606, in Sidell, et al., *Medical Aspects of Chemical and Biological Warfare.*

Despite efforts to restrict the illicit acquisition of biological agents, it is likely that terrorists and criminals will be able to obtain the agent that they want when they want it. If unable to acquire from a legitimate culture collection or a medical supply company, they can steal it from a laboratory. If unable to steal it, a group with the right expertise could culture the agent from samples obtained in nature. Many biological agents are endemic, and a skilled microbiologist would have little difficulty culturing an agent from material taken from nature.

**Table 4: Acquisition of biological agents**

| Type | Terrorist | Criminal | Other/ Uncertain | Total Instances |
|---|---|---|---|---|
| Legitimate supplier | 1 | 9 | 1 | 11 |
| Theft | 1 | 3 | 0 | 4 |
| Self-manufactured | 1 | 4 | 1 | 6 |
| Natural source | 2 | 4 | 0 | 6 |
| Unknown | 3 | 3 | 0 | 6 |
| Total instances | 8 | 23 | 2 | 33 |

Note: This table reflects the predominant method of acquisition; some individuals or groups acquired agent through multiple paths.

**Culture Collections**: In 11 of the 33 cases involving acquisition, the non-state actors obtained biological agents or toxins from legitimate suppliers. The American Type Culture Collection (ATCC) was the source of the agent in at least two cases. Larry Wayne Harris obtained *Y. pestis*, while Kevin Birch and James Cahoon acquired *Clostridium botulinum* and *Clostridium tetani* from this source. Benoyendra Chandra Pandey obtained the *Y. pestis* from the stocks of a medical research institute that he used to murder his brother, but only after several failed attempts to obtain it illicitly from the same source. The Rajneeshees purchased their seed stock of *Salmonella typhimurium* from a medical supply company. Significantly, another group could do the same today under current regulations, because the organism involved is not on any control list.[31] In any case, the Rajneeshees had a state certified clinical laboratory, which gave them a legitimate reason to acquire agents like the one that they used.

**Theft**: In four cases of the 33 cases involving acquisition, the perpetrators acquired their biological agents by stealing them from research or medical laboratories. Almost all of the thefts involved people who had legitimate access to the facilities where the biological agents were kept. J.A. Kranz, a graduate student in parasitology, took the *Ascaris suum* eggs that he used against his roommates from the collections in the university laboratory where he studied. Law enforcement officials believe that a laboratory technician removed the *Shigella dysenterlae* Type 2 used to infect hospital laboratory technicians from the culture collection of the hospital where she worked. Similarly, Dr. Suzuki stole *S. typhi* cultures from the Japanese National Institute of Health, and reportedly used those cultures in preference to the ones he cultured himself from specimens taken from typhoid patients. In only one of the reported incidents was an attempt made to infiltrate a laboratory to steal a biological agent. It is alleged that the Weathermen group attempted to suborn an employee at the U.S. military research facility at Ft. Detrick in order to obtain pathogens.

**Self-manufacture**: In six of the cases involving acquisition, the perpetrators manufactured the agent themselves. In every reported case, the perpetrators produced ricin toxin by extracting it from castor beans. The Minnesota Patriots Council, which produced a small quantity of ricin toxin, made it from a recipe found in a book. In contrast, there were no successful attempts to grow *C. botulinum* to produce botulinum toxin.

Several readily available "how-to" manuals purport to describe techniques for producing botulinum toxin or extracting ricin from castor beans. A considerable number of perpetrators have used *The Poisoner's Handbook* and *Silent Death*. Maynard Campbell's *Catalogue of Silent Tools of Justice*, which is apparently no

[31] The United States has implemented regulations that control the transfer of biological agents on a control list.

**Table 5: Type of agent involved**

| Type | Terrorist | Criminal | Other/ Uncertain | Total Cases |
|---|---|---|---|---|
| Pathogen | 15 | 38 | 83 | 136 |
| Toxin | 9 | 15 | 2 | 26 |
| Unknown | 4 | 1 | 1 | 6 |

Note: Because some perpetrators considered multiple agents, the totals in this table exceed the total number of cases.

longer in print, was used by the Minnesota Patriots Council in their ricin production. Long before the Internet, perpetrators found it easy to obtain information about biological agents.

**Natural**: In six cases involving acquisition the biological agent was obtained from a natural reservoir and transmitted without any processing. Some perpetrators apparently used castor beans, the seed containing ricin, to poison people without attempting to extract the ricin from the bean. Similarly, in several cases the perpetrators injected the victims with HIV-contaminated blood.

## Types of agent actually acquired

Terrorists and criminals have shown an interest in both pathogens and toxins. In 129 of the 150 non-state cases, the perpetrators threatened to use or considered pathogens. Note that few of these cases involved actual possession. Some perpetrators considered multiple pathogens. In one instance, at least seven different pathogens were involved.

Terrorists and criminals may not use the same agents as those selected by military biological weapons programs. A comparison between the biological agents commonly considered suitable for military use and those actually adopted by the perpetrators of the cases studied here is shown in Table 6. The objectives of the terrorists will influence the selection of an agent, as will agent availability and the resources at the disposal of the group for producing and disseminating the agent. This may lead to selection of unusual agents not associated with state-sponsored biological weapons programs. Fortunately, many of the alternative agents are unlikely to result in mass fatalities, even if they affect large numbers of people.

**Bacterial agents**: Approximately 125 of the cases focused on bacterial agents. *B. anthracis* appears most often, and is associated with at least 113 cases, largely due to the growing popularity of anthrax threats. Note that only three of cases involved possession of anthrax. Aum Shinrikyo may have had a stolen vaccine anthrax strain incapable of causing harm to humans. Dark Harvest had anthrax-contaminated soil, but never possessed the agent in a form likely to cause harm to people. Finally, the Polish Resistance apparently used cultures stolen from laboratories with legitimate uses for the organism. *Yersinia pestis*, *S. typhi*, and *Shigella dysenteriae* strains appear several times, while seven other pathogens appear no more than once.

**Viral agents**: Few perpetrators have considered viral agents, except when they can use it in a natural state. HIV appears in 15 cases, including at least four murder cases. Six of the HIV cases involved extortion threats in which in which there is no evidence of actual possession. In one case, the perpetrators employed a viral agent, rabbit hemorrhagic disease.

**Other pathogens**: In only one case involved use of a parasite. In that case, the perpetrator contaminated food with *Ascaris suum*, a worm that infects pigs and does not normally infect humans.

**Toxins**: In 27 of the 180 non-state cases, the perpetrators considered toxins. Ricin was considered in 14 cases. The next most common choice was botulinum toxin, which was an agent of choice in 9 cases. Significantly, there is no reported example of successful production of botulinum toxin, despite claims that it is easy to produce.[32] Other toxins include tetrodotoxin, an unknown mushroom poison, and an unspecified snake toxin. In most cases, only a single toxin was involved. In one case, a group of murderers acquired the toxins produced by *Corynebacterium diphtheria* and *Vibrio cholerae*.

---

[32] Uncle Fester, *Silent Death*, Revised and Expanded 2nd Edition (Port Townsend, Washington: Loompanics Unlimited, 1997), pp. 93-106.

**Table 6: Biological agents involved**

| | Traditional Biological Warfare Agents | Agents associated with biocrimes and bioterrorism |
|---|---|---|
| Pathogens | ***Bacillus anthracis****<br>*Brucella suis*<br>***Coxiella burnetii****<br>*Francisella tularensis*<br>Smallpox<br>Viral encephalitides<br>**Viral hemorrhagic fevers***<br>***Yersinia pestis**** | *Ascaris suum.*<br>***Bacillus anthracis****<br>***Coxiella burnetii****<br>*Giardia lamblia*<br>HIV<br>*Rickettsia prowazekii* (typhus)<br>*Salmonella typhimurium*<br>*Salmonella paratyphi*<br>*Salmonella typhi*<br>*Shigella* species<br>*Schistosoma* species<br>*Vibrio cholerae*<br>**Viral hemorrhagic fevers (Ebola)***<br>Yellow fever virus<br>*Yersinia enterocolitica*<br>***Yersinia pestis**** |
| Toxins | **Botulinum***<br>**Ricin***<br>Staphylococcal enterotoxin B | **Botulinum***<br>Cholera endotoxin<br>Diphtheria toxin<br>Nicotine<br>**Ricin***<br>Snake toxin<br>Tetrodotoxin |
| Anti-crop agents | Rice blast<br>Rye stem rust<br>Wheat stem rust | |

* These agents appear in both lists.

**Combinations**: In six cases, the perpetrators considered use of both pathogens and toxins. In three of the cases, the perpetrator was interested in both *B. anthracis* and botulinum toxin. In another case, the perpetrators thought about HIV and tetanus in addition to both *B. anthracis* and botulinum toxin. The last two cases involved combinations that are more unusual: tetanus and botulinum toxin in one case, and *S. typhi* and an unknown mushroom poison in another instance. In only two of these cases did the perpetrator acquire a viable biological agent.

# Employing Biological Agents

A biological agent is not necessarily a biological weapon. Only if there is a mechanism for spreading the agent is it transformed into a weapon. Thus, a pathogen growing on a petri dish is not a weapon, or even a threat, because it is unlikely to infect anyone. In some cases, the release method need not be very sophisticated. If the agent is highly contagious, infecting a single person or animal may be sufficient to start an epidemic.

## Disseminating biological agents in theory

When the agent is not contagious, as with many pathogens and all toxins, it is necessary to have a dissemination mechanism that spreads the agent to the intended target. While it is possible to infect people by injecting them one by one with biological agents, such a method is unlikely to prove attractive to most terrorists. More likely, a terrorist will seek a technique to infect the entire target, whether people, livestock, or crops, at one time.

**Aerosol dissemination**: Of greatest concern is the possibility that a terrorist might disseminate biological agents as an aerosol cloud. In the context of biological warfare, the aerosol cloud should consist of particles of 1-5 microns (one-millionth of a meter) in size. Particles much larger than 5 microns do not penetrate into the lungs, since they are filtered out by the upper respiratory tract. In addition, they tend to settle out of the air relatively quickly. In contrast, smaller particles do not remain in the lungs, but tend to be breathed out.[33]

Several considerations account for the concern about aerosol delivery. Many diseases are most dangerous when contracted in this fashion. Thus, cutaneous anthrax, which is contracted through the skin, has a case fatality rate of 5 to 20 per cent, though antibiotic treatment is highly effective. In contrast, inhalation anthrax is usually fatal, and if not detected early there is no effective treatment. Similarly, *Y. pestis* is responsible for substantially different diseases, including both bubonic and pneumonic plague. Bubonic plague,

**Table 7: Biological Agent Attack on City of 1,000,000 people**

| Disease Caused by Agent | Number of People at Risk | Deaths | Incapacitated Only |
|---|---|---|---|
| **Anthrax** | 180,000 | 95,000 | 30,000 |
| **Brucellosis** | 100,000 | 400 | 79,600 |
| **Epidemic typhus** | 100,000 | 15,000 | 50,000 |
| **Plague** | 100,000 | 44,000 | 36,000 |
| **Q fever** | 180,000 | 150 | 124,850 |
| **Tularemia** | 180,000 | 30,000 | 95,000 |
| **Venezuelan equine encephalitis** | 60,000 | 200 | 19,800 |

Source: World Health Organization, *Health Aspects of Chemical and Biological Weapons* (Geneva: World Health Organization, 1970), pp. 95-99. The WHO model assumes a city of 1,000,000 people in a developed country, and makes assumptions regarding the population distribution around a high density urban core that may no longer be appropriate. The model also makes certain assumptions about the agent (50 kilograms of dried powder containing $6 \times 10^{15}$ organisms disseminated in a line 2 kilometers long at a right angle to the wind direction. The model nominally illustrates dissemination from an aircraft, but none of the calculations appears to depend on the type of the delivery vehicle involved. As an example, the model assumes that the Venezuelan equine encephalitis will survive for only about 5-7 minutes, during which time it will travel about 1 kilometer. About 60,000 people will be exposed to the agent. About 20,000 people will become incapacitated, including 200 who will die. In contrast, anthrax will survive for more than two hours and will travel for more than 20 kilometers. At least 180,000 people will be exposed to the agent, including 30,000 who will become incapacitated and 95,000 who will die.

generally acquired from the bite of an infected flea, has a case fatality rate of 50 to 60 per cent if untreated, but generally responds to medical treatment. Pneumonic plague is also generally fatal if untreated. Early treatment is essential to save those infected. Pneumonic plague is considered highly contagious, while bubonic plague is not.[34]

Aerosol transmission also makes it possible to spread biological agents over a large area and thus affect a large number of people in one attack. The Office of Technology Assessment calculated that 100 kilograms of anthrax spread over Washington could kill from one to three million people if disseminated effectively under the right environmental conditions. In contrast, a one-megaton nuclear warhead would kill

[33] Edward M. Eitzen, "Use of Biological Weapons," p. 440, in Sidell, et al., *Medical Aspects of Chemical and Biological Warfare*.

[34] Benenson, *Control of Communicable Disease Manual*, pp. 18-19, 353. A recent review of the anthrax threat, however, notes that the survival data predates the creation of hospital intensive care units, and suggests that more people might survive under contemporary conditions than usually stated. See James C. Pile, John D. Malone, Edward M. Eitzen, and Arthur M. Friedlander, "Anthrax as a Potential Biological Warfare Agent," *Archives of Internal Medicine*, Vol. 158 (March 9, 1998), pp. 429-434. Significantly, there were 11 identified survivors of inhalation anthrax from the Sverdlovsk release, suggesting a case fatality rate of only 85 per cent.

from 750,000 to 1.9 million people.[35] An alternative set of calculations was prepared for a study by the World Health Organization (WHO). According to estimates prepared by WHO's expert panel, 50 kilograms of dry anthrax used against a city of one million people would kill 36,000 people and incapacitate another 54,000.[36]

**Water contamination:** Many pathogens that have had a significant impact on human life, such as *Vibrio cholerae* (which is the organism responsible for cholera) and *Salmonella typhi* (which causes typhoid fever), are water-borne. It is also possible to inject toxic substances into water systems, including toxins. Thus, it is not surprising that some terrorist groups interested in biological agents have targeted municipal water systems.[37]

Fortunately, water systems are less vulnerable than often thought. Municipal water systems are designed to eliminate impurities, especially pathogens. As part of this process, communities use filters to remove particles from the water and add chlorine to kill any organisms that remain. In addition, the $ID_{50}$ for diseases spread through water is often extremely high. One test indicated that only half of persons who ingested $10^7$ (10 million) *S. typhi* organisms became ill.[38] According to a Department of Defense biological warfare analyst, it would require "trainloads" of botulinum toxin to contaminate the New York City water supply to cause problems, simply because of the extent to which the toxin is diluted.[39] For all these reasons, infecting a large population through deliberate contamination of water supplies is difficult to accomplish.

**Food contamination:** Terrorists also have spread biological agents by contaminating food. In general, only uncooked or improperly stored food is vulnerable, because the heat generated during cooking readily destroys most pathogens and toxins. This implies that a terrorist would need to target foods that are commonly eaten uncooked, or that can be contaminated after being cooked. Alternatively, the terrorists would need to rely on a toxin that survives cooking.

The dangers from deliberate contamination of food have probably grown due to fundamental changes in food distribution systems. The food processing industry has become increasingly centralized, so that contamination introduced at a single facility can affect large numbers of people. In addition, an increasing amount of food is imported, raising the prospect that perpetrators operating in a foreign country might be able to contaminate food eaten in the United States.[40]

**Direct application:** The most reliable way to infect someone is to inject the victim with the organisms responsible for causing a disease. This technique avoids most of the technical problems associated with the dissemination of biological agents. Similar techniques can be used with toxins. In addition, some toxins can cause harm even if applied on the skin.

---

[35] U.S. Congress, Office of Technology Assessment, *Proliferation of Weapons of Mass Destruction: Assessing the Risks*, OTA-ISC-559 (Washington, DC: Government Printing Office, August 1993), pp. 53-54.

[36] This calculation assumes a 50 per cent reduction in fatalities due to prompt administration of antibiotics. It also excludes people who might be infected more than two hours after agent release. World Health Organization, *Health Aspects of Chemical and Biological Weapons* (Geneva: World Health Organization, 1970), pp. 98-99.

[37] For a review of the risk to municipal water systems, see World Health Organization, *Health Aspects of Chemical and Biological Weapons*, pp. 113-120.

[38] World Health Organization, *Health Aspects of Chemical and Biological Weapons*, p. 115.

[39] Testimony by Dr. Barry Erlick, p. 38, in United States Senate, Committee on Governmental Affairs, Permanent Subcommittee on Investigations, *Global Spread of Chemical and Biological Weapons* (Washington, D.C.: Government Printing Office, 1990).

[40] Janice Rosenberg, "Attack of the killer shellfish, raspberries, hamburgers, milk, poultry, eggs, vegetables, potato salad, pork…." *American Medical News*, May 4, 1998, pp. 12-15.

**Table 8 : Dissemination techniques**

| Type | Terrorist | Criminal | Other/ Uncertain | Total Cases |
|---|---|---|---|---|
| Aerosol dissemination | 2 | 0 | 0 | 2 |
| Direct injection/Topical application | 6 | 10 | 0 | 16 |
| Contaminate food | 1 | 20 | 1 | 22 |
| Contaminate water | 4 | 0 | 2 | 6 |
| Insect/Natural vectors | 0 | 1 | 1 | 2 |
| None | 10 | 13 | 79 | 102 |
| Unknown | 5 | 10 | 2 | 17 |
| Total Cases | 28 | 54 | 85 | |

Note: Because some perpetrators considered multiple agents, the totals in this table exceed the total number of cases.

**Insect vectors**: Many diseases are naturally transmitted by insects. For example, plague is transmitted by certain flea species, yellow fever is carried by one specific mosquito species, *Aedes aegypti*, and typhus is spread by the body louse, *Pediculus humanus corporis*. It is thus not surprising that biological warfare experts have considered insects as potential vectors for biological agents. The Japanese biological warfare program devoted considerable effort to this dissemination route. On at least a few occasions, the Japanese to have used infected fleas to spread plague.[41] The United States considered use of mosquitoes to disseminate certain agents, and established a facility to breed the needed mosquitoes.[42] Insect vectors posed problems: they were difficult to control, and their use was likely to create disease reservoirs in the area where the insects were released.

## Dissemination in practice

There is a substantial difference between the theory and practice of bioterrorism. The technical obstacles associated with the use and dissemination of biological agents are considerable, and should not be underestimated. Even individuals with considerable technical expertise often find that it is difficult to work with biological agents, even when using relatively simple dissemination techniques.

**Aerosolization**: Only two groups are known to have considered aerosolization of biological agents: Aum Shinrikyo and R.I.S.E. Neither group mastered the requisite technology. According to published accounts, the Aum Shinrikyo attempted to disseminate both *B. anthracis* and botulinum toxin on multiple occasions. They are not known to have caused any casualties.

**Water contamination:** In six instances, the perpetrators threatened or planned to contaminate water supplies. The quasi-Green group R.I.S.E. wanted to put *S. typhi* into the Chicago water supply with the objective of killing hundreds of thousands of people. In contrast, it is alleged that the Weatherman organization conceived of biological agents as something that could be used to contaminate water supplies to make a great many people sick.

**Food contamination:** Ten of the 17 cases in which people were harmed by use of biological agents involved contamination of food. The use of biological agents to contaminate food has resulted in the largest

[41] Ed Regis, *Biology of Doom: The History of America's Secret Germ Warfare Project* (New York: Henry Holt and Company, 1999), pp. 18-19, 112-113.

[42] Jeffery K. Smart, "History of Chemical and Biological Warfare: An American Perspective," p. 50, in Frederick R. Sidell, et al., *Medical Aspects of Chemical and Biological Warfare* (Washington, D.C.: Office of the Surgeon General, Department of the Army, 1997)

number of casualties. The Rajneeshee spread *S. typhimurium* at salad bars and other places to affect a large number of people. Several of the criminal cases also involved contamination of food to make multiple people ill, including one case of contamination of donuts and muffins with shigella organisms.

**Direct application**: In 16 cases the perpetrators planned to directly apply a biological agent, either by parenteral delivery (injection) or topical application. Injection has been used to deliver both toxins and pathogens. Dr. Suzuki injected *S. typhi*, as did the French murderer Henri Girard. Several perpetrators have injected their victims with HIV-contaminated blood. Topical application generally involves use of toxins, although the Rajneeshees attempted to spread *S. typhimurium* by contaminating objects that people handle in the hope that the intended victims would transfer the organisms to their mouth. The Minnesota Patriots Council planned to use a mixture of ricin and DMSO, apparently hoping that the DMSO would transport the ricin. More plausibly, Thomas Leahy mixed DMSO with pure nicotine to achieve the same result.

**Insect vectors**: In at least two cases, the threatened dissemination technique involved insects. In one case, an individual sent letters containing ticks, threatening to spread infection in that way. There is no evidence, however, that the ticks carried any pathogens. In any event, the insects were dead on delivery.

## Consequences of use

Bioterrorism differs significantly from other forms of terrorism. In the typical terrorist attack, there is immediate evidence that something has happened. In contrast, a biological agent attack is unlikely to generate any visible signatures, and the first evidence of a biological attack is likely to be the onset of disease.[43] Thus, it might be days or even weeks before the consequences of a biological attack become evident. It might be impossible to determine that an outbreak resulted from an intentional act.

Numerous efforts have been made to calculate the potential impact that biological weapons might have on population centers. In general, such estimates should be used with considerable caution. Models used to calculate agent effects rely on numerous assumptions regarding the movement and infectiveness of the agent, and the results may be extremely sensitive to changes in those variables. At best, the models provide an illustration of the potential consequences of bioterrorism.

The World Health Organization has prepared the most authoritative estimates of the casualties likely to result from the biological weapon use.[44] Although these estimates are highly dependent on the assumptions built into the calculations, they provide a basis for understanding the potential consequences of biological agent use. The impact depends heavily on the nature of the attack, including the method of dissemination, the particular agents involved, the concentration of agent, and (in the case of aerosol dissemination) atmospheric conditions.

Some of the WHO estimates are summarized in Table 7, which shows the potential impact on a city of one million people of aerosol releases. In all cases, the attacks assume a release of 50 kilograms of dried powder along a two-kilometer line at a right angle to the wind direction. As is evident, the impact varies considerably depending on the agent involved. If the agent causes a disease resulting in few fatalities, such as Q-fever, only a few hundred people might be killed, although tens of thousands of people might be incapacitated. In contrast, a high lethality agent, such as anthrax, could kill 95,000 people and incapacitate another 30,000.

---

[43] Dan Crozier, William D. Tiggertt, and Joseph W. Cooch, "The Physician's Role in the Defense Against Biological Weapons," *JAMA*, January 7, 1961, p. 99.

[44] World Health Organization, *Health Aspects of Chemical and Biological Weapons* (Geneva: World Health Organization, 1970).

**Table 9: Casualties from use of bioagents**

| | Total Casualties | Deaths |
|---|---|---|
| Bioterrorism | 751 | 0 |
| Biocrimes | 130 | 10 |
| Totals | 881 | 10 |

There has never been a biological warfare attack of the type modeled by the WHO team of experts. Therefore, it is not surprising that the consequences of biological agent use have been far less severe than shown in Table 7. There are only 21 confirmed bioterrorism and biocrime cases involving use or attempted use of biological agents. In 20 of these cases, there were human casualties, including deaths in seven cases. In all, there were 881 victims, including 10 deaths. The outbreak caused by the Rajneeshees caused an estimated 751 casualties. Dr. Suzuki's activities resulted in an estimated 66 victims. In other words, two cases accounted for

**Table 10: Confirmed deaths using biological agents**

| Perpetrator | Victims | Date/ Location | Number of Deaths | Agent Employed |
|---|---|---|---|---|
| Arthur Warren Waite | Mrs. Hannah Peck | New York City, 1916 | 1 | Uncertain |
| O'Brien de Lacy and Dr. Pantchenko | Captain Buturlin | Russia, 1910 | 1 | Direct injection of diphtheria toxin |
| Henri Girard | M. Pernotte<br>Mme. Monin | France, 1909-1918 | 2 | Food contamination and direct injection using pathogen ***Salmonella typhi*** and unknown poisonous mushroom |
| Benoyendra Chandra Pandey | Amarendra Pandey | India, 1933 | 1 | Direct injection of the pathogen ***Yersinia pestis*** |
| Tei-Sabro Takahashi | Hisako Inukai<br>Yoshiko Yanagida<br>Yorinobu Nakayama | Japan 1936 | 3 | Pastries contaminated with ***Salmonella typhi*** |
| Kikuko Hirose | Ritsuo Kato | Japan, 1939 | 1 | Pastries contaminated with ***Salmonella typhi*** and ***S. paratyphi*** (types A and B) |
| Graham Farlow | Geoffrey Pearce | July 1990 | 1 | Injection of HIV-infected blood |

nearly 93 per cent of all the confirmed victims of biological weapons use. This information is summarized in Table 9. The incidents leading to death are listed in Table 10.

The diseases inflicted by biological agents are not the only potential consequences of their use. Threats of use also can cause considerable disruption. This was demonstrated during the B'nai B'rith incident in Washington, D.C., which resulted in the shut down of a large part of Washington's downtown. Thus, even in cases where no agent was present, the perpetrators can achieve a disproportionate impact. The costs of the required medical and public health response to an attack also could be disproportionate to the actual effects of the dissemination. A single case of smallpox in Yugoslavia in 1972 eventually required the quarantine of 10,000 people for periods of at least two weeks, and the government was forced to immunize 20,000,000 people. The neighboring countries closed their borders with Yugoslavia, disrupting normal commerce. It was nine weeks before the outbreak was over. This illustrates how even a small outbreak can have huge economic and social consequences.[45] Finally, the psychological impact of even a small agent release should not be underestimated. The concern that developed over the relatively small plague outbreak in India in 1996 is indicative of the fear that certain infectious diseases can generate. Experience with Aum use of chemical agents suggests that there will be lasting psychological consequences for many of the victims and initial responders.[46]

## Technical constraints on use

There is considerable disagreement among experts concerning the extent of the technical impediments that may constrain use of biological agents.[47] Some argue that terrorists face few if any technical hurdles in employing bioagents. For example, DCI George Tenet told Congress, "Terrorist interest in chemical and biological weapons is not surprising, given the relative ease with which some of these weapons can be produced in simple laboratories...."[48] In contrast, Dr. David Franz, formerly Commander of the U.S. Army Medical Institute for Infectious Diseases (USAMRIID), argued that "an effective, mass-casualty producing attack on our citizens would require either a fairly large, very technically competent, well-funded terrorist program or state sponsorship."[49]

Empirical evidence suggests that effective dissemination of some agents, and especially aerosolization of agents such as anthrax, can pose significant technical hurdles. Every case discussed in Part II of this study in which an individual became sick due to use of a biological agent was perpetrated by someone (a criminal or a terrorist) who had basic scientific or medical training. In general, the level of expertise required appears to depend on two factors: the quantity of agent involved and the dissemination technique.

As previously noted, access to bioagents has rarely posed a problem for terrorists or criminals. More skill was necessary if the perpetrators sought to grow larger quantities of an agent, depending on the agent involved. Some pathogens are easy to culture, while others are extremely difficult. For this reason, perpetrators who adopted objectives that required significant quantities of agent usually selected biological agents easy to culture. None of the perpetrators examined in this study successfully cultured any agent that required technical skill to grow. Thus, there is no evidence that any managed to culture a virus, although several had success with bacteria. Nor is there any evidence to suggest that any individual or group ever successfully cultured a virulent strain of *C. botulinum*, although several have tried. In fact, one recent criminal perpetrator, Thomas Leahy, may have inadvertently grown a non-virulent strain of the organism.

If a simple dissemination technique is employed, relatively little technical expertise is needed. For example, limited skill is required if the perpetrators can inject agent directly into their victims or if they seek to contaminate food. Moreover, dissemination of a highly communicable disease like smallpox would require limited expertise. The use of highly contagious diseases may be the easiest way to cause mass casualties from a technical perspective. However, such agents pose risks for the group using them and could have an impact on people that the perpetrators do not want to affect. In contrast, spreading an agent through the air poses

---

[45] D.A. Henderson, "Biological Terrorism," *Emerging Infectious Diseases*, Vol. 4, No. 1 (July-September 1998), p. 400.

[46] Harry C. Holloway, et al., "The Threat of Biological Weapons: Prophylaxis and Mitigation of Psychological and Social Consequences," *JAMA*, 278 (August 6, 1997), pp. 425-427.

[47] Statement of Richard Davis, Director, National Security Analysis, National Security and International Affairs Division, *Combating Terrorism: Observations on Crosscutting Issues*, Testimony Before the Subcommittee on National Security, International Affairs and Criminal Justice, Committee on Government Reform and Oversight, House of Representatives, General Accounting Office, GAO/T-NSIAD-98-164, April 23, 1998.

[48] Prepared Statement of George J. Tenet, Acting Director, Central Intelligence, p. 8, in United States Senate, Select Committee on Intelligence, *Current and Projected National Security Threats to the United States* (Washington, D.C.: Government Printing Office, 1997). Similarly, Richard Danzig, former Under Secretary of the Navy, argued, "Biological weapons are inexpensive and accessible. A small pharmaceutical industry or even moderately sophisticated university or medical research laboratory can generate a significant offensive capability." See "Biological Warfare: A Nation at Risk—A Time to Act," *Strategic Forum*, Institute for National Strategic Studies, Number 58, January 1996.

[49] Posture Statement by Colonel David Franz, Deputy Commander, United States Army Medical Research and Development Command for the Joint Committee on Judiciary and Intelligence, United States Senate, "International Biological Warfare Threat in CONUS," March 4, 1998.

formidable difficulties. There is no known example of a terrorist or criminal successfully spreading a disease through the aerosol route, at least one group—the Aum Shinrikyo—reportedly tried, and R.I.S.E. intended to do so.

The central technical problems for bioterrorism arise when the objective is to cause mass casualties through the aerosolization of an agent. The apparent failure of the Aum Shinrikyo to develop a biological warfare capability is suggestive. The Aum drew on the skills of a relatively large cadre of trained people, and apparently devoted considerable resources to their biological warfare efforts. It appears that the Aum failed to produce an effective biological weapon. Unfortunately, too little is known about the Aum's activities to determine why they failed.[50]

Aerosolization is a complicated process, and is subject to factors that are difficult to assess. Agents that can be spread through the air can be in either liquid or dry form. The liquid form is relatively easy to produce, but must be processed into a form suitable for dissemination. The processing must address both physical issues (to ensure that the sprayer nozzles do not become clogged) and biological issues (to ensure that the organisms survive once aerosolized). An agent in liquid form can be aerosolized using a modified commercially available sprayer, but problems remain. Most of the agent dies during the spraying process (estimates range as high as 99 per cent). In contrast, a dry agent is relatively simple to disseminate, but most experts agree producing it is a dangerous process almost certainly beyond the capabilities of non-state actors.[51]

As previously noted, biological agents disseminated through the air must be released in particles 1-5 microns in size. Smaller particles are not retained in the lungs. Particles larger than 10 microns fall out of the air relatively quickly. In addition, the body filters large particles so that they do not reach the lungs. Moreover, the size of the dose required to induce illness climbs substantially as the size of the particles grows. Producing aerosol particles of the wrong size might reduce an attack to complete ineffectiveness.[52] In addition, the particles must be released in the correct location to have the desired effect. Particles 1-5 microns in size act like a gas. They settle from the air very slowly. If the agent is not released in an enclosed space, like a building or subway, then considerable operational skill is needed to ensure that the agent infects the intended victims.[53]

Finally, technical skills are required to overcome environmental conditions hostile to agent survival.[54] Biological agents die or lose virulence once released into the atmosphere. Thus, some disease-causing bacteria lose virulence at a rate of 10 per cent per minute, while some viruses would decay at a rate of 30 per cent per minute. A few organisms, such as the spores of *B. anthracis*, decay extremely slowly when not exposed to ultraviolet radiation.

The implications of these variables will differ from one organism to the next. Perpetrators need to be familiar with the factors that affect the agents they are using.[55] The rate of biological decay depends on a host of factors, including ultraviolet radiation, temperature, humidity, and a phenomenon known as the Open Air Factor (believed to be the presence of certain air pollutants).[56] There are other potential difficulties in effective

---

[50] According to a press report, Japanese authorities believe that Aum may have used a "relatively harmless vaccine strain" of *B. anthracis*. Similarly, it appears that Aum may have used a *C. botulinum* strain that was not prolific in the production of toxin. See Broad, Miller, and WuDunn, "How Japan Germ Terror Alerted World," *New York Times*, May 26, 1998, p. A10.

[51] Franz, "International Biological Warfare Threat in CONUS." See also World Health Organization, *Health Aspects of Chemical and Biological Weapons*, pp. 93-95.

[52] One study reported that guinea pigs became infected by only 3 tularemia organisms when the particles were of 1 micron. When the particle size was increased to 7 microns, 6,500 organisms were needed. At 22 microns, 170,000 organisms were necessary. Research reported in William D. Sawyer, "Airborne Infection," *Military Medicine*, February 1963, pp. 90-92.

[53] Aerosols consisting of particles of 1-5 microns have certain characteristics of significance for biological weapons use. Such aerosol clouds tend to act as a gas, meaning that the particles will enter buildings. The particles also remain airborne for extended periods. According to one calculation, a 1-micron particle settles out of the air at a rate of 0.21 centimeters per minute. This means that the particle will take about 500 minutes, or more than 8 hours, to drop just 1 meter. In contrast, a 5-micron particle has a settling rate of 4.7 centimeters per minute, so would take only 20 minutes to drop 1 meter. Charles L. Punte, "Some Aspects of Particle Size in Aerosol Studies," *Armed Forces Chemical Journal*, March-April 1968, p. 28.

[54] A survey of our knowledge in this area is provided by Alan Jeff Mohr, "Fate and Transport of Microorganisms in Air," pp. 641-650, in Christon J. Hurst, editor in chief, *Manual of Environmental Microbiology* (Washington, D.C.: ASM Press, 1997). See also Linda D. Stetzenbach, "Introduction to Aerobiology," pp. 619-626, in the same volume.

[55] The WHO experts estimated that an aerosol cloud containing the organisms that cause Q fever would decay at a rate of 10 percent per minute. They estimated the decay rate for the organism responsible for yellow fever at 30 percent per minute, the rate decay for the agents causing plague and tularemia at only 2 percent per minute, and the decay rate for anthrax is a mere 0.1 percent per minute. All these figures assume that the agents were produced using special stabilizers to protect against adverse environmental conditions. World Health Organization, *Health Aspects of Chemical and Biological Weapons*, p. 94. *B. anthracis* survives only in the spore form; the vegetative organisms are not very hardy and die quickly in the outdoors.

dissemination of biological agents. Weather is particularly important. Poor atmospheric conditions can make it virtually impossible to release an agent cloud likely to cause casualties.

These comments suggest that aerosolization of pathogens can be extremely difficult. Thus, while aerosolization is the most dangerous way to disseminate agent, it is significantly more difficult to accomplish than by the alternative methods. This is an important factor in assessing the sources of potential threats from biological agents.[57]

Yet, this threat is not theoretical. The potential was demonstrated during studies conducted by the United States Army's Chemical Corps in the 1950s and 1960s, before the United States abandoned its offensive biological warfare program. These tests demonstrated—to the extent possible with the technology then available—that biological agents could be disseminated as an aerosol cloud and cover a large area with potentially lethal doses.[58] Particularly disturbing are the results of tests in the New York City subway conducted during the 1960s. The U.S. Army released a simulant for *B. anthracis, Bacillus globigii*, into the subway system. Based on the distribution patterns of the agent, Army experts estimated that 10,000 people would have died if *B. anthracis* had been released.[59]

---

[56] Open Air Factor, which remains a poorly understood phenomenon, was first identified by British researchers in the late 1960s. They found that when *E. coli* organisms were exposed to air from outdoors the decay rate went from 0.2 per cent per minute to between 1.5 and 20 per cent per minute, but normally between 3-10 per cent per minute. This effect was noted with many organisms, including some with biological warfare potential, such as the organisms responsible for tularemia and brucellosis. See K.R. May, et al., "Toxicity of Open Air to a Variety of Microorganisms," *Nature*, 221(March 22, 1969), pp. 1146-1147. Significantly, spore-forming organisms such as *B. anthracis* were unaffected. Some researchers believe that the Open Air Factor is related to the presence of ozone and certain kinds of hydrocarbons. See G. de Mik and Ida de Groot, "The germicidal effect of the open air in different parts of the Netherlands," *Journal of Hygiene*, 78(1977), pp. 175-187.

[57] Some of the perpetrators of anthrax hoaxes have included powders in the packages sent to their victims. As this discussion indicates, if the particles are larger than 10 microns they are unlikely to pose a risk to large numbers of people. In most cases, the descriptions suggest the particles were considerably larger than 10 microns. Such large particles will fall out of the air relatively quickly, so even if it turned out that the powder was composed of *Bacillus anthracis* spores few people would get exposed

[58] These tests are reviewed in Leonard A. Cole, *Clouds of Secrecy: The Army's Germ Warfare Tests over Populated Areas* (Savage, Maryland: Littlefield, Adams Quality Paperback, 1990).

[59] Pile, et al., "Anthrax as a Potential Biological Warfare Agent," pp. 429-434. A retired Army biological warfare expert has calculated that as many as 3 million people would have been affected if *F. tularemia* had been used instead. See Patrick, "Potential Incident Scenarios," p. I-60, in *Proceedings of the Seminar on Responding to the Consequences of Chemical ad Biological Terrorism.*

# Chapter 3:
# The Practitioners

In this chapter, the characteristics of perpetrators who employed, acquired, or considered use of biological agents are examined. The perpetrators included in this study were both terrorists and criminals. Terrorists were groups who were motivated primarily by political objectives, while criminals were driven by motives of financial gain, personal revenge, or some other non-political consideration.

## Nature of the Perpetrators

### Size of the perpetrating group

The size of the perpetrating groups was examined to gain some insight into the number of people required to exploit biological agents. Anyone participating in the acquisition or use of biological agents, whether in the planning, production, or distribution, was counted.

In three of the 180 confirmed non-state cases, the perpetrating group consisted of five or more people. All of these groups attempted use. There were 19 cases in which small groups of two to four people were involved. Generally, it appears that in small groups there was a single person with scientific or technical skills. Other members directed or supported the efforts of the sole expert.

A single individual was responsible for perpetuating plots in 43 cases. Significantly, the lone perpetrators successfully acquired biological agents in 19 of those cases, and used the agent in 12 of them. In 115 of 180 cases, there is not enough information available to estimate the number of people involved. In most such cases, the alleged perpetrators have never been identified.

**Table 11: Size of perpetrating group**

| Type | Terrorist | Criminal | Other/ Uncertain | Total Cases |
|---|---|---|---|---|
| Lone | 0 | 37 | 6 | 43 |
| Small group (2–4) | 5 | 12 | 2 | 19 |
| Large group (5+) | 3 | 0 | 0 | 3 |
| Unknown | 19 | 7 | 89 | 115 |
| **Totals** | 27 | 56 | 97 | 180 |

### Geographical distribution

The perpetrators involved with biological agents have been located in countries around the globe. About 82 percent (147 of 180) of the cases took place in North America, all but one in the United States. Europe was the next most common location with 17 cases. Incidents occurred in Britain, France, Germany, Poland, and Russia.

**Table 12: Geographic distribution**

| Type | Terrorist | Criminal | Other/ Uncertain | Total Cases |
|---|---|---|---|---|
| North America | 14 | 37 | 96 | 147 |
| Europe | 6 | 10 | 1 | 17 |
| Asia | 5 | 6 | 0 | 11 |
| Africa | 2 | 0 | 0 | 2 |
| Australia/New Zealand | 0 | 3 | 0 | 3 |
| Totals | 27 | 56 | 97 | 180 |

## Scientific and technical expertise

The range of perpetrator expertise varies considerably. Technical expertise could include background in medicine, microbiology, or pharmaceutics.

The perpetrators had some scientific or medical training in 23 cases. In 16 of the cases, a physician or a Ph.D.-level microbiologist was involved. In several cases, individuals with medical training instigated use of biological agents. A nurse, Ma Anand Puja, created the Rajneeshee biological warfare capability. She relied on the expertise of a trained laboratory technician to culture the *Salmonella typhimurium* used to contaminate the salad bars. Dr. Suzuki, a Japanese physician and bacteriologist with considerable laboratory experience, infected at least 66 people with typhoid and dysentery before he was arrested in 1966.

In a few cases, the person who conceived the notion of using biological agents lacked the requisite skills, and so enlisted the services of unscrupulous physicians. Benoyendra Chandra Pandey drew on the medical skills of Dr. Taranath Bhatacharya, who was responsible for culturing the *Y. pestis* that was used in the 1933 murder of Pandey's brother. Similarly, in 1910 Patrick O'Brien de Lacy's brother-in-law was murdered by an injection of diphtheria toxin given by a physician, Dr. Pantchenko, who obtained the agent from a research laboratory in Russia.

The available evidence suggests that in 36 cases the perpetrators had no scientific or medical expertise. Significantly, in only six cases is there any evidence that the perpetrators actually acquired biological agents. Equally significant, there is only a single case of use involving perpetrators with no known technical training, although this number might grow when more is known about some of the other perpetrators. In that case, Graham Farlow, a prison inmate, murdered a guard by injecting him with HIV-tainted blood. A perpetrator with no known professional training obtained a biological agent in only five cases. In three instances they extracted ricin toxin from castor beans, in one case used HIV-infected blood, and in the last case acquired the agent from a legitimate supplier. Eight of the 36 cases were extortion plots. Interestingly, only one extortion case involved a perpetrator who actually possessed a biological agent. The perpetrator in that case, Michael Just, had a Ph.D. in microbiology. He was convicted in 1996 for threatening to contaminate milk with *Yersinia enterocolitica*.

**Table 13: Perpetrator expertise**

| Type | Terrorist | Criminal | Other/ Uncertain | Total Cases |
|---|---|---|---|---|
| Medical or scientific expertise | 4 | 17 | 2 | 23 |
| No Known expertise | 6 | 24 | 6 | 36 |
| Unknown | 17 | 15 | 89 | 121 |
| Totals | 27 | 56 | 97 | 180 |

In 121 cases, the available evidence makes it impossible to assess the expertise of the perpetrators. Given that 91 of them were anthrax threats, all those cases probably involve people with no technical expertise.

## Terrorist Group Characteristics

A number of studies have attempted to identify the characteristics of terrorist groups that could lead them to consider acquisition and use of biological agents. A study by Jeffrey Simon argues that a terrorist group inclined to use biological agents would demonstrate certain attributes:

- A general, undefined constituency whose possible reaction to a biological-weapons attack does not concern the terrorist group.
- A previous pattern of large-scale, high-casualty-inflicting incidents.
- Demonstration of a certain degree of sophistication in weaponry or tactics.
- A willingness to take risks.[60]

These criteria are largely consistent with the characteristics of groups inclined to inflict mass casualties using biological agents. Simon's list may be less useful in identifying groups with alternative motives, such as harming agriculture, who may believe that they can deal with the risk of using biological agents that do not cause loss of life.

Another effort to consider the types of groups potentially attracted to the use of biological agents appears in a draft report on the threat of chemical and biological weapons prepared by the North Atlantic Assembly. That report gave the following list of terrorist groups likely to resort to biological weapons.

- Those whose goals include vague notions about world revolution, universalistic goals such as the Japanese Red Army and certain European radical left-wing groups.
- Those unconcerned with the effects of public opinion such as neo-Nazi groups in Europe and North America.
- Those with a history of high-casualty, indiscriminate attacks, such as Sikh extremists, pro-Iranian Shiite fundamentalist groups such as Hezbollah, and extremists within the Palestinian movement such as the Abu Nidal Organization.
- Those ideologically opposed to Western society in general.
- Those noted for their sophistication in weaponry or tactics, such as the Popular Front for the Liberation of Palestine-General Command.
- Those with state sponsors, especially where the sponsor is known to possess chemical or biological weapons.[61]

---

[60] Simon, *Terrorists and the Potential Use of Biological Weapons*, p. 17.

[61] Draft report of the North Atlantic Assembly, *Chemical and Biological Weapons: the Poor Man's Bomb*, AN253 STC(96)8, October 4, 1996.

This list is too inclusive to identify potential users of biological agents. It refers to groups that are not known to have considered use of biological agents, yet provides no basis for predicting under what circumstances a group might decide to adopt biological agents.

More recently, Professor Walter Laqueur has argued that terrorism is undergoing a profound change. In contrast to the politically motivated terrorists who predominated in the 1970s, many of today's terrorists define their objectives in ethnic or religious terms. Many of these groups are infected by millenarian ideas, believing that the world as we have known it is ending. Such groups may have few if any scruples about using weapons to cause mass casualties.[62]

Other terrorism experts believe that the perpetrators most likely to employ biological agents are religiously motivated terrorists. Significantly, the two most significant bioterrorism incidents, involving the Rajneeshees and the Aum Shinrikyo, were undertaken by religious cults with political agendas. A former Chief of Counter-Terrorism at the FBI expressed a similar view of Middle East groups influenced by radical Islam.

> The danger originating from Middle East terrorist groups infused with the dogma of Radical Islamic Fundamentalism cannot be minimized. One of the principal concerns is the potential for their use of weapons of mass destruction. Given their demonstrated disregard for limiting casualties, indeed their apparent desire to inflict maximum damage, this scenario is one that has occupied much of the thinking of counter-terrorism planners at all levels of government. Biological and chemical weapons are certainly available to sophisticated terrorist organizations, especially those, like many of the Middle East groups, that operate with the support of governments. These weapons are both relatively easy to acquire and lethal in their application.[63]

The essential consideration seems to be a combination of group's interest in causing mass casualty coupled with an ideology that would justify such operations. Such views are not necessarily unique to religiously motivated groups.

## Domestic groups

There is considerable evidence to suggest that terrorist groups based in the United States have actively explored resort to biological agents. Experience suggests that interest in biological agents can come from a broad range of terrorist groups espousing radically different political philosophies. In the 1960s, the leader of the right-wing Minuteman group openly discussed the possibilities of biological agents, although there is no evidence that there was any substance behind the rhetoric. In the 1970s, several left wing groups considered bioterrorism. As noted earlier. The quasi-Green group R.I.S.E. was on the verge of disseminating several biological agents when the Chicago police arrested the ringleaders. The left-wing Weather Organization may have initiated a plot to acquire biological agents for use against municipal water systems. In the1980s, a religious cult, the Rajneeshees, acquired and used biological agents. More recently, it appears that right wing groups, many affiliated with the militia movement, have expressed the most interest in biological terrorism. In some cases, the groups have acquired biological agents.

Fortunately, in the past there was more interest in bioterrorism than actual use. From this perspective, an important question becomes the extent to which domestic terrorists might decide to resort to biological agents. This involves two related considerations: to what extent could they acquire the capability to employ biological agents, and under what circumstances might they decide to use them?

Although domestic groups could acquire some bioterrorism capability with little or no outside assistance, as demonstrated by the experience of the Rajneeshees, there is reason to doubt the ease with which such groups could cause mass casualties. For reasons discussed above, aerosol dissemination of biological agents may be beyond the capabilities of groups developing their own dissemination technology. Such groups would need to develop a considerable range of expertise, and it is likely that it would take some time before they could effectively undertake wide area dissemination of agent of highly lethal agents. Consequently, the initial uses of biological agents will probably involve small-scale actions with limited consequences. This suggests that effective public health surveillance of unusual disease outbreaks coupled with vigilant law enforcement activity could detect and respond to bioterrorism before the responsible groups develop a mass casualty capability.

The ability of terrorists to employ biological agents effectively would be greatly enhanced if such groups received external assistance from state-sponsored biological weapons programs. Such assistance could

---

[62] Walter Laqueur, "Postmodern Terrorism," *Foreign Affairs*, September-October 1996, pp. 24-36.

[63] Steve Pomerantz, "Counterterrorism in a Free Society," *Journal of Counterterrorism & Security International*, Spring 1998, p. 24.

come directly from a state biological weapons program, or from individuals formerly associated with such a program.

## State-sponsorship

A number of countries with records of supporting terrorist organizations also are believed to have biological weapons programs. The Department of State names seven countries as state supporters of terrorism: Cuba, Iran, Iraq, Libya, North Korea, Sudan, and Syria.[64] Published reports issued by the Department of Defense and the Arms Control and Disarmament Agency suggest that five of these countries, Iran, Iraq, Libya, North Korea, and Syria, possess biological warfare programs.[65] Press reports have suggested that some Iraqi scientists associated with biological weapons research may be working in Sudan, and that the Sudanese have created a research institute for chemical and biological warfare funded by Osama bin Laden. Bin Laden is the former Saudi citizen who has become a major financial supporter for international terrorism.[66] U.S. intelligence officials have reported that bin Laden has provided support for a Sudanese biological weapons program. This allegation was confirmed by the British Minister of State for Defence, George Robertson, in an on-the-record interview.[67]

Since at least the late 1980s, press reports have claimed that Cuba has a biological weapons program.[68] In early 1998, the Department of Defense expressed concern about Cuba's potential for creating biological weapons.[69] Thus, almost all the countries associated with support for international terrorism also support efforts to develop biological weapons.

Relatively little publicly available information is available on the biological warfare programs of these countries, except for Iraq.[70] What is known suggests that the sophistication of these programs varies considerably. Iraq certainly had a relatively sophisticated program, and probably retains a capability to develop biological weapons within a few weeks. Less is known about North Korea's activities, but it has been conducting research in the area of biological warfare for more than thirty years and probably has capabilities equal to or greater than Iraq's. Iran likely comes next in competence, followed by Syria and Libya.[71] If it exists, Sudan's program is certainly the least developed.

---

[64] U.S. Department of State, *1996 Patterns of Global Terrorism Report*, as found at *http://www.state.gov.*

[65] Arms Control and Disarmament Agency, *Adherence To and Compliance With Arms Control Agreements, 1996*, as found at *http://www.acda.gov*, and Office of the Secretary of Defense, *Proliferation: Threat and Response*, November 1997.

[66] Al J. Venter, "North Africa faces new Islamic threat," *Jane's Pointer*, March 1998, p. 11. Based on an October 31, 1997 report that appeared in an Arabic language newspaper published in Paris, *Al-Watan al-'Arabi*. For official confirmation of bin Ladin's role in supporting terrorism, see the testimony of Assistant Secretary of State Toby T. Gadi, United States Senate, Select Committee on Intelligence, *Current and Projected National Security Threats to the United States*, p. 21, and the reply for the record appearing on p. 128 of that report.

[67] Background briefing on "Terrorist Camp Strikes," August 20, 1998, as found at *http://www.defenselink.mil*, and "Britain Has Bin Laden Evidence," *Associated Press*, August 23, 1998,11:00 a.m. EDT.

[68] John Barron, "Castro, Cocaine and the A-Bomb Connection," *Reader's Digest*, March 1990, p. 70, and Harvey McGeorge, "Chemical Addiction," *Defense and Foreign Affairs*, April 1989, p. 17. The allegation was repeated by Congressman Lincoln Diaz-Balart (R-Florida), "Under the guise of genetic, biological and pharmaceutical research, Castro is developing a serious germ and chemical warfare capability." See, George Gedda, "U.S. Gen. Supports Some Cuba Ties," *Associated Press*, April 25, 1998, 12:06 p.m. EDT.

[69] The DIA assessment is that "Cuba's current scientific facilities and expertise could support an offensive BW program in at least the research and development stage. Cuba's biotechnology industry is one of the most advanced in emerging countries and would be capable of producing BW agents." See DIA, "The Cuban Threat to U.S. National Security," May 6, 1998. Secretary of Defense William S. Cohen noted, "I remain concerned about Cuba's potential to develop and produce biological agents, given its biotechnology infrastructure." See his transmittal letter to Strom Thurmond, Chairman, Armed Services Committee, May 6, 1998. This material was taken from the Department of Defense public affairs web site at *http://www.defenselink.mil.*

[70] Zilinskas, "Iraq's Biological Weapons: The Past as Future?," *JAMA*, pp. 418-424, provides an excellent overview of the Iraqi program.

[71] Office of the Secretary of Defense, *Proliferation: Threat and Response*, November 1997, pp. 6, 27, 32-33, 34, 37, for reporting on Iran, Iraq, Libya, and North Korea. See also the comments by DCI John Deutch, at the Conference on Nuclear, Biological, Chemical Weapons Proliferation and Terrorism, May 23, 1996, regarding North Korea, Iran, Iraq, and Libya.

**Table 14: State Supporters of Terrorism and BW Programs**

| State Supporters of Terrorism | BW Program |
|---|---|
| **Cuba** | Suspected |
| **Iraq** | Confirmed |
| **Iran** | Confirmed |
| **Libya** | Confirmed |
| **North Korea** | Confirmed |
| **Sudan** | Suspected |
| **Syria** | Confirmed |

Sources: U.S. Department of State, *1996 Patterns of Global Terrorism Report;* Arms Control and Disarmament Agency, *Adherence To and Compliance With Arms Control Agreements, 1996*, as found at *http://www.acda.gov*, and Office of the Secretary of Defense, *Proliferation: Threat and Response*, November 1997. Also, see the text.

Under what circumstances might a hostile state provide biological warfare expertise to a terrorist group? There is no evidence that such an exchange has ever taken place. In 1996, the Defense Intelligence Agency made the following points.

> Most of the state sponsors have chemical or biological or radioactive material in their stockpiles and therefore have the ability to provide such weapons to terrorists if they wish. However, we have no conclusive information that any sponsor has the intention to provide these weapons to terrorists.[72]

Moreover, the Department of Defense asserted in 1997, "The likelihood of a state sponsor providing such weapons to a terrorist group is believed to be low."[73]

In addition, it appears that terrorists now rely less on state-sponsorship than was true in the 1980s. According to an unclassified CIA assessment, the primary threat increasingly comes from transient groups not necessarily dependent on any particular country for support

> International terrorist groups have developed large transnational infrastructures, which in some cases literally circle the globe. These networks may involve more than one like-minded group, with each group assisting the others. The terrorists use these infrastructures for a variety of purposes, including finance, recruitment, the shipment of arms and material, and the movement of operatives.[74]

Potentially, the emergence of such transient groups has considerable significance. Such groups are less tied to the strategic interests of any particular country, and thus are less likely to act in a manner that reflects the guidance of specific countries. This makes them difficult to deter by exerting pressure on a state sponsor. While the groups may have substantial resources, they usually lack a permanent infrastructure, which may make it harder for them to generate an effective biological warfare capability. From this perspective, reports that bin Laden has financed a Sudanese biological warfare facility becomes a source of serious concern.

## Political and moral constraints

Some analysts have argued that moral constraints are likely to inhibit use of biological weapons, either because the terrorists subscribe to moral tenets or because their supporters do. This is based on the

[72] United States Senate, Select Committee on Intelligence, *Current and Projected National Security Threats to the United States and its Interests Abroad*, p. 213.

[73] Office of the Secretary of Defense, *Proliferation: Threat and Response*, p. 49.

[74] *Current and Projected National Security Threats to the United States*, p. 7. Some additional elaboration is provided in the reply for the record on p. 93.

argument, as articulated by terrorism expert Bryan Jenkins, that terrorists are usually not interested in mass murder.

> Simply killing a lot of people has seldom been a terrorist objective. Terrorists want a lot of people *watching*, not a lot of people *dead*. Most terrorists operate on the principle of minimum force necessary. Generally, they do not attempt to kill many, as long as killing a few suffices for their purposes.[75]

Thus, Jenkins appears to argue that combinations of political and moral considerations have affected the willingness of terrorists to employ weapons that could cause massive harm. The implication is that they would be unwilling to employ biological weapons for the same reasons.

The Rajneeshees, for example, specifically rejected the use of a more dangerous pathogen, *S. typhi*, which causes typhoid fever. However, in this case, the primary factor that militated against use of the agent was not moral qualms, but rather concern that an outbreak of typhoid fever would attract too much attention. The group believed that it could accomplish its intended objective, incapacitation, using a generally non-lethal agent, *S. typhimurium*, which causes a common form of food poisoning.

In fact, in recent years there has been growing evidence that terrorist groups are interested in causing mass casualties. This is reflected in the publicly expressed views of the CIA.

> The emphasis on high casualty operations and the frequency of attacks on nonofficial targets have been significant trends in international terrorism in recent years. These trends are reflected in the statistics on international terrorism, which show that the number of terrorist incidents has declined during the 1990s but casualties from terrorist attacks lately have been on the increase.
>
> We expect these trends to continue. The newer breed of international terrorist, who seeks revenge more than carefully defined political objectives, is interested in inflicting mass casualties.[76]

Thus, there are growing concerns of erosion in the political and moral constraints that in the past kept most terrorist groups from resorting to weapons of mass murder.

In general, however, the most serious constraint on the use of biological agents has probably been operational rather than moral. For many purposes, biological agents are more difficult to use and less effective than other weapons. Guns and bombs are probably more than sufficient if the objective is to murder one or even several hundred people.[77] The fact that so many individuals and groups have considered using biological agents is an indication of the fragility of the moral barriers.

## Operational Considerations

The research highlights certain operational aspects in the use of biological agents. While these observations should be considered tentative, because they are based on a small sample, they are derived from real world experience.

Terrorists or criminals who possess or use biological agents almost never advertise their intent. In only one case is it clear that perpetrators known to have possessed biological agents sent communiqués or otherwise made known the fact of possession. In contrast, those who claimed to possess biological agents almost never did. This tends to suggest that individuals or groups who do not claim credit will undertake most cases involving actual use of biological agents.

This experience adds weight to the views of some experts that terrorists are increasingly unlikely to claim credit for their actions. According to Bruce Hoffman, "Terrorists now deliberately seek to conceal their responsibilities for attacks in hopes of avoiding identification and subsequent arrest."[78] In Hoffman's view,

---

[75] Brian Michael Jenkins, *Future Trends in International Terrorism*, RAND Paper P-7139, December 1985, p. 4. For another articulation of this statement, see Brian Michael Jenkins, *The Future Course of International Terrorism*, RAND Paper P-7139, September 1985, p. 4.

[76] United States Senate, Select Committee on Intelligence, *Current and Projected National Security Threats to the United States*, p. 94.

[77] An unnamed intelligence official made these comments on this point: "The fertilizer bomb has demonstrated its capacity on numerous occasions to inflict ... mass casualties. We would consider those tried-and-true low-tech means of operation still to be the main type of attack about which we have to worry." See Jim Wolf, "First terrorist cyber-attack reported by U.S.," *Reuters*, May 4, 1998, 3:17 PDT.

[78] Bruce Hoffman, "Why Terrorists Don't Claim Credit," *Terrorism and Political Violence*, Vol. 9, No. 1 (Spring 1997), p. 4.

terrorists can obtain the publicity that they seek even without claiming credit for specific acts of terror. Significantly, he argues that this anonymity may make them more likely to commit increasingly lethal acts.[79]

Hiding biological weapons programs is easy. The efforts of the Rajneeshees to develop biological agents were detected only when the cult fell apart and law enforcement agencies developed informers among former members of the group. An intensive public health investigation of the outbreak failed to determine the cause of the outbreak. In fact, an Oregon State official issued a report claiming that unsanitary practices by restaurant workers caused the outbreak and dismissed allegations that intentional contamination was a factor. It was only a year after the outbreak that law enforcement officials developed credible evidence that intentional contamination was responsible.

The available evidence suggests that intelligence and law enforcement agencies are unlikely to learn that a particular terrorist group is interested in acquiring and using biological agents. This is a concern of the intelligence community, as reflected in the publicly stated views of the State Department's Bureau of Intelligence and Research.

> The involvement of terrorist groups in WMD would be difficult to detect. This is particularly true with regard to chemical and biological materials since the agents can be obtained fairly easily and the production can be hidden.[80]

There is no evidence that Japanese authorities were aware of Aum Shinrikyo's interest in biological agents. Only after the subway attack did Japanese law enforcement officials learn of the biological warfare program and hear the allegations that Aum actually attempted to use biological agents. Moreover, the Aum was virulently anti-American, and repeatedly accused the United States of waging chemical and biological warfare on the cult.[81] Yet, the U.S. intelligence community was completely unaware of its activities. Neither the CIA nor the FBI appears to have believed at the time that they had any responsibility for tracking such activities on the part of groups like the Aum.[82]

---

[79] Hoffman, "Why Terrorists Don't Claim Credit," p. 5.

[80] United States Senate, Select Committee on Intelligence, *Current and Projected National Security Threats to the United States*, p. 129.

[81] See Staff Statement, "Global Proliferation of Weapons of Mass Destruction: A Case Study on the Aum Shinrikyo," pp. 52-54 in United States Senate, Committee on Governmental Affairs, *Global Proliferation of Weapons of Mass Destruction*, Part I.

[82] United States Senate, Committee on Governmental Affairs, *Global Proliferation of Weapons of Mass Destruction*, Part I, pp. 275-276.

# Part II:
# Cases

# Chapter 4: Case Definition

The survey included all publicly reported instances in which a non-state actor, either a terrorist or a criminal, or an operative acting on behalf of a state, allegedly used, threatened to use, acquired, attempted to acquire, or even expressed an interest in biological agents.[83]

## Agent involvement

The primary characteristic of the cases is the involvement of biological agents, as defined in the first chapter of this study. This means that the agents can include a variety of microorganisms, such as bacteria, viruses, fungi, and parasites.

- The involvement of biological agents can include use, threatened use, acquisition, attempted acquisition, or an expression of interest in biological agents.
- The target of the biological agents can be people, animals, crops, or processed foods. If animals or crops are targeted, the action or planned action must either violate the laws of the jurisdiction involved or otherwise involve a prohibited activity.
- Cases that involve animals, such as insects or poisonous snakes, are excluded unless the animals were used as a vector for a pathogen.
- Cases involving transmission of disease directly from an infected person are not included.[84]
- Cases involving only chemical agents are excluded.

## Perpetrators and activities

The perpetrators must meet one of several criteria.

---

[83] Several cases discussed below do not meet the criteria for inclusion in the study. Such cases were researched based on published claims that they involved biological agents. Descriptions of these cases are provided to explain the rationale for excluding them.

[84] This excludes instances in which people deliberately engage in risky behavior, such as HIV carriers engaging in unprotected sex. It also excludes cases where the perpetrators deliberately introduce infected individuals into the target population.

There are a surprising number of instances in which HIV-infected people have tried to deliberately infect others. According to one account, by 1991 there had been more than 200 prosecutions of AIDS-related criminal cases, mostly for attempted murder. See Jennifer Grishkin, "Knowingly Exposing Another to HIV," *Yale Law Review*, 106(March 1997), p. 1617, citing sources dated to 1990 and 1991.

On January 15, 1998, George Howard Stewart was arrested by the Denver Police Department for violating an order to stay away from his wife's house. After being arrested, Stewart, who was HIV positive, reportedly spit at the arresting officer, including into his mouth. Stewart is alleged to have had a history of threatening to infect people with his HIV. A District Judge ruled that he had to stand trial for second degree assault. See Howard Pankratz, "Man with HIV to stand trial in assault case," *Denver Post*, April 29, 1998, as found at the newspaper's World Wide Web site, *http://denverpost.com*. Similarly, in April 1998, a Clinton, Louisiana, jury convicted James Houston of attempted intentional exposure to HIV. The incident occurred on October 15, 1997, when Houston, who had been diagnosed as HIV positive in July 1997, was being moved to a new cell block. Houston tried to resist, and spat on the officers who were attempting to control him. Louisiana has a law prohibiting the "throwing of blood or other bodily substances" to spread HIV. See James Minton, "Man convicted in AIDS exposure case," *Advocate* (Baton Rouge), April 14, 1998, as found at the newspaper's World Wide Web site, *http://www.theadvocate.com*.

Also relatively common are convictions of HIV-infected individuals who put others at risk of contracting the disease through unsafe sexual practices. For example, in late October 1998, Swedish police were searching for an HIV-infected man who called himself James Patrick Kimball who had unprotected sex a large number of women. Swedish courts have convicted eight people for such behavior. See "Sweden looks for American with HIV," *Associated Press*, October 20, 1998, 5:45 p.m. EDT.

- If the perpetrators are non-state actors, then any involvement of biological agents merits inclusion. Both terrorists, who use biological agents to further political agendas, and criminals, who are motivated by more personal considerations, are included.
- If the perpetrators are employed by a nation state, then the involvement of biological agents must be outside the context of a declared or undeclared war with another nation state.
- Excluded from the study are incidents in which health care providers poison patients using biological agents with common medicinal uses, such as digitalis or curare.[85] Also excluded are instances of suicide.[86]

## Timeframe

The incident must have occurred on or after January 1, 1900.

## Geographic scope

The incident could have occurred anywhere in the world.

## Case identification numbers

The case identification numbers consist of the year in which the incident occurred and a sequence number assigned as each newly identified case was researched. A case is dated to the point either when the earliest date when the activity involving biological agents is known to have occurred, or, if that date is not known, to the date when the activity way was discovered. Thus, the number 1996-05 indicates that the incident took place in 1996 and that it was the fifth case from that year investigated. This means that the cases are not necessarily numbered in chronological order. In many instances, a case was uncovered long after earlier cases were researched. In such instances, the original case numbers were retained, and the new case inserted into the working paper in the correct chronological order.

In some instances, the sources do not identify the exact year in which the incident took place. Such cases are arbitrary assigned to the first year belonging to the same decade, which is defined to include every year that has the same first three digits. Thus, cases believed to have occurred in the 1970s are assigned to 1970 and are given a sequence number for that year. When it is impossible to assign a case to a specific decade, it was assigned to 1900. To indicate that the date is approximate, such cases are also marked with an X at the end of the number.

Cases that have an M at the end of their identification number involve illicit use of a biological agent with legitimate medicinal uses by a health care provider in a medical setting. While these cases are excluded from the analysis for the reasons discussed above, several were researched during the course of the study.

---

[85] This is an admittedly arbitrary exclusion. Health care providers have opportunities for using certain toxins not available to other perpetrators. They often have legitimate access to toxins, or can easily steal it from facilities that have a legitimate need for the substances. In addition, health care providers have routine access to victims that other perpetrators do not have. There are few other settings in which people willingly allow a stranger to stick them with a needle. Thus, the activities of health care providers give little insight into what a terrorist might be able to accomplish. Finally, there appear to be a significant number of cases of this type, so that including them in the study would distort analysis of the data.

The drugs of choice today are rarely biological agents. According to Eric W. Hickey, *Serial Murderers and Their Victims*, 2nd edition (Washington: Wadsworth Publishing Company, 1997), pp. 219, 248-250, commonly used drugs are potassium chloride, pavulon, succinylcholine, and digoxin. Only one of these could be considered a biological agent, digoxin, which is one of the active ingredients of digitalis. See John Mann, *Murder, Magic, and Medicine* (New York: Oxford University Press, 1992), pp. 170-171. While the true incidence of murder by health care providers in medical settings is unknown, Hickey suggests that it is a growing problem. Three cases are discussed in the text, case 1977-02M, Arnfinn Nesset, on page 60, case 1994-03M, Orville Lynn Majors, on page 76, and case 1966-01M, Mario Jascalevich, on page 86.

[86] Two cases of suicidal use of pathogens are discussed in the case studies: the first involves a physician who injected himself with rabies (see Case 1930-02X on page 90); the second involves a woman who injected herself with HIV-infected blood (see Case 1990-05X on page 77). Such cases are excluded from the analysis because the motivations and actions of such individuals differs significantly from that of other perpetrators more relevant to the study of bioterrorism.

## Comments on the case definition

The case definition was generated in order to serve the research needs of the project. Specifically, the objective was to study incidents involving terrorists. Preliminary research indicated that there were few instances in which terrorist groups used, acquired, or even considered using biological agents. In fact, the author has been able to identify only 30 cases in which a terrorist group is thought to have been involved with biological agents. In almost all of those cases, the perpetrators never actually possessed or used a biological agent. This apparent lack of interest in biological agents is significant, and will be discussed further.

The small number of bioterrorism cases led the author to extend the study to cover other illicit activities that might shed some insight into bioterrorism. Many of these added cases are criminal in character (biocrimes). Such cases show what an individual or small group can accomplish using biological agents, and thus provide some insight into what a terrorist group might be able to accomplish. Certain state-sponsored activities also are discussed as well, including assassinations involving biological agents and sabotage operations. The state-sponsored cases also provide some insight into the complexities of undertaking covert biological activities, as well as giving some insights into what state support might mean for a terrorist group.

None of the cases involved use of biological agents by military organizations or other state entities in the context of wars with other countries. Japanese use of biological weapons during the Second World War, alleged Soviet use of biological agents in Southeast Asia, and other claimed instances of biological warfare in the context of conventional military operations are excluded. In contrast, German use of biological agents during World War One is included because of the covert use of such agents in neutral countries.

# Sources of information

## Identifying cases for research

This survey is as comprehensive as possible. It includes every case that the author has been able to identify in the unclassified literature that meets the case definition of a biological incident. Several sources were used to identify potential cases. An important source was the open source literature on biological terrorism, which describes numerous incidents involving biological agents. Especially useful were the lists of biological terrorism incidents compiled in 1995 by Ron Purver and in 1987 by Joseph D. Douglass, Jr., and Neil C. Livingstone.[87] Bruce Hoffman shared data from the *RAND-St. Andrews Terrorism Chronology*, an electronic database of international terrorism incidents, by providing an extract of "All Chemical/Biological Incidents, 1968-1995." Jason Pate of the Chemical and Biological Weapons Project at the Center for Nonproliferation Studies, Monterey Institute for International Studies, kindly shared a working copy of a similar list that he was in the process of compiling. Finally, in 1971 the Stockholm International Peace Research Institute (SIPRI) compiled a comprehensive survey of allegations of use of biological agents in connection with wars, including several instances that appear to meet the case definition used here.[88] These earlier studies identified approximately half the cases.

Several other sources also played an important role in uncovering cases. First, the author identified additional cases through a survey of press reports, books, and other published accounts. Much of this effort focused on regional newspapers, because the major national newspapers ignored most of the cases discussed here. Books discussing the criminal use of poisons also were consulted, primarily to identify old cases. Second, other analysts brought a number of cases to the attention of the author. The sources are credited in the notes.

## Researching the cases

Five main sources of information were used to describe the cases. First, the bulk of the information came from press reports. Most of the incidents received little coverage in major newspapers, such as *the New*

[87] The primary source was Ron Purver, *Chemical and Biological Terrorism: The Threat According to the Open Literature*, Canadian Security Intelligence Service, June 1995, supplemented by Joseph D. Douglass, Jr., and Neil C. Livingstone, *America the Vulnerable: The Threat of Chemical and Biological Warfare* (Lexington, Massachusetts: Lexington Books, D.C. Heath and Company, 1987), pp. 183-187. Not all cases mentioned by these sources are included in this review. For example, Purver mentions cases involving acquisition of some toxic fungi by a foreign scientist, which have been excluded here since they appear to refer to acquisition of biological agents by a state biological weapons program. Similarly, Purver mentions some incidents involving people infected with infectious diseases who were allegedly used as vectors to infect target populations.

[88] SIPRI, *The Problem of Chemical and Biological Warfare, Volume I: The Rise of CB Weapons* (New York: The Humanities Press, 1971), pp. 214-230.

*York Times*, the *Washington Post*, or the London *Times*. For this reason, it was necessary to rely on regional newspapers, such as the *Chicago Tribune*, the *Columbus Dispatch* (Ohio), the *Dallas Morning News*, the Las Vegas *Sun* and the Las Vegas *Review-Journal*, the Portland *Oregonian*, and the Seattle *Times*. Second, some of the accounts rely on descriptions that came from the bioterrorism literature. In a few cases, it appears that these sources had access to intelligence or law enforcement information not available elsewhere. Third, a few of the cases have been described in detail in the medical literature, including specialized forensic medicine publications. Fourth, in some cases court records and other legal or law enforcement documents were used. Finally, the author interviewed individuals associated with some of the cases, usually public health or law enforcement officials.

## Assessing the data

Because the data used in this research is of uneven reliability, a careful assessment of the quality of data supporting the allegations associated with individual cases is essential. Research for this study identified more than 100 instances in which it is alleged that terrorists, criminals, or state actors used, acquired, attempted to acquire, or considered acquisition of biological agents. Reviewing the data presented in Part II of this study reveals problems with at least half the cases. At the same time, any analysis may be skewed by the exclusion of cases.

### Criteria for inclusion

Each case was evaluated to determine if the supporting evidence met the case definition. Because information about the activities of many of the alleged perpetrators is scanty, the quality of the supporting material was carefully reviewed. With one exception, cases were included in the analysis only if verified by an authoritative source, such as an official government document, or if at least two apparently independent unofficial sources were found. The only exception applies to anthrax hoaxes, which are included if only a single source refers to them. In most cases, those hoaxes are insufficiently serious to merit more extensive press coverage. Cases are not included if controversy surrounds essential data related to the inclusion criteria. Whenever there were serious questions concerning the accuracy of the allegations, the case was treated as unconfirmed.

**Lack of data**: Many of the cases were excluded because there was insufficient evidence to confirm the allegations. In some cases, the reports are extremely tenuous. Thus, the RAND-St. Andrews database includes a report that an otherwise unknown organization calling itself the "Legion of Nabbil Kadduri Usur" threatened to release bacteria if its demands were not met. The original source of the report is unknown, and all that is known of the allegation is what appears in the database.[89] Under the circumstances, the data is too weak to merit inclusion.

**Faulty data interpretation**: In some cases, it appears that allegations were made based on misunderstanding of the available data. Thus, one source lists as a biological terrorism incident a 1973 case involving contamination of the Naples water supply. A closer reading of the available data, however, indicates that the episode involved criminal charges resulting from negligence on the part of municipal officials who failed to prevent the spread of cholera-contaminated water. The episode had nothing to do with intentional contamination. (See page 173 for details.)

**False accusations**: In a number of cases, authoritative sources erroneously believed that some illicit activity had occurred. This is true for the well-publicized incident (discussed on page 167) in which the FBI wrongly accused Larry Wayne Harris and William Leavitt of possessing a biological weapon. Such cases are interesting to study as part of an effort to understand responses to biological terrorism threats, but do not satisfy the case definition.

**Fabrications**: Some incidents appear to be without any foundation. Thus, Steve Quayle, a survivalist who produces a shortwave radio broadcast known as "Blueprint for Survival," claimed that unspecified "Middle East terrorists" had tried to mount a biological warfare attack on Ames, Iowa. The available evidence, reviewed starting on page 110, suggests that there was no basis for the story.

**Gaps in evidence**: The difficulties entailed in identifying cases are exemplified by the allegations that a Florida dentist, Dr. David Acer, deliberately infected at least six of his patients with HIV in the late 1980s (see page 79). Despite an extensive investigation, the Centers for Disease Control and Prevention (CDC) has been unable either to exonerate Dr Acer or to confirm his culpability. Thus, while CDC believes that Acer's patients contracted HIV from him, it cannot demonstrate that the transmission was intentional rather than

[89] For a description of this incident, see page 122.

accidental.[90] For this reason, the Acer case is excluded from the analysis, although it is possible that Acer deliberately infected his patients.

**Alternative case definition**: The definition of a biological agent used in this study excludes insects, unless they are a vector for a pathogen. For this reason, cases involving the deliberate spread of insects do not meet the case definition used for this study. This leads to the exclusion of incidents such as the one reviewed on page 173 involving "The Breeders", a California group that allegedly was deliberately releasing Medflies. Others, however, treat such cases as instances of biological terrorism.[91]

## How complete is the survey?

Despite efforts to make the research as comprehensive as possible, the list of incidents is clearly not complete. Indeed, it is virtually a certainty that there are additional instances of biological agent use not included in the study. It is impossible to ascertain, however, how many cases are not included. Nor is it possible to estimate the number of people who might have been affected by bioagent use.

The circumstances surrounding the discovery of some of the cases reinforces the view that there are additional unidentified cases. Several of the incidents became known only because of information obtained by law enforcement agencies or other authoritative sources well after the event. The Japanese military reportedly attempted to infect members of the League of Nations' Lytton Commission in 1932, but information about the incident did not become public until 1994, sixty-two years later. (See page 67.) It was a year after the salmonellosis outbreak in The Dalles, Oregon, before law enforcement officials obtained information linking the outbreak to use of biological agents by the Rajneeshees. (This episode is discussed starting on page 50.) Similarly, Japanese authorities (see page 47) only learned of the efforts by Aum Shinrikyo to employ biological agents after the cult collapsed and former members confessed to police.

In addition, the sources used in researching the cases also necessarily limit the comprehensiveness of the study. Most of the sources consulted during the research originated in the United States, and almost all are English language. It is likely that a thorough exploration of foreign language material would uncover additional cases. In addition, the research relied on searches of electronic databases available in full text form. Additional cases may be identified by searching through sources currently not on-line. At present, publications in the United States are more readily available on-line than those published elsewhere, which probably leads to over-representation of incidents that occurred in the United States. Finally, some cases have been described in publicly available sources. Consequently, there is little doubt but that additional cases could be identified and added to the list in the study.

Although it is difficult to estimate the impact of missing cases, the overall data set is so small that even a few additional cases might significantly skew the results reported below. This is particularly true for assessments of the consequences of biological agent use. The number of casualties associated with these cases is relatively small, so that even a few additional cases involving illness would make a substantial difference in the reported data. For this reason, caution should be exercised in using this data.

# Organization of cases

The cases described in the following sections are divided into four categories: use of biological agents, threatened use, possession, and other. These categories are then subdivided into sub-categories.

### 1. Use of biological agents

- **Confirmed use**: The use of a biological agent was confirmed by some authoritative source, either a court, a law enforcement agency, or by a credible government official in these cases.
- **Probable or possible use**: In these cases, the perpetrators may have used a biological agent, but there is no authoritative confirmation. It also includes some cases in which a biological agent was used, but there is no information to indicate whether the perpetrator knowingly caused the infection. The probability of intentional contamination for these cases ranges from highly likely to highly unlikely.

---

[90] Dennis L. Breo, "The dental AIDS cases—Murder or an unsolvable mystery," *JAMA*, December 8, 1993, p. 2732.

[91] Robert S. Root-Bernstein, "Infectious Terrorism," *Atlantic*, May 1991, p. 48.

2. **Threatened use**

- **Threatened use (confirmed possession):** This category includes cases in which the perpetrators threatened to use biological agents, and subsequent investigations confirmed that they possessed or probably possessed biological agents. This category includes cases in which the perpetrators never implemented planned attempts to use biological agents, even if their intentions were kept secret.
- **Threatened use (no confirmed possession):** This category includes cases in which the perpetrators threatened to use biological agents, but subsequent investigations determined that they did not possess biological agents. This category also includes cases in which it was never determined whether the perpetrator possessed a biological agent.
- **Threatened use (anthrax hoaxes):** This category includes cases in which the perpetrators threatened use of anthrax, or in which the recipient interpreted the threat to involve anthrax. These cases were separated from those in the previous category because of the substantial number of anthrax hoaxes.

3. **Possession of biological agents (no use or threat to use)**

- **Confirmed possession**: Cases in which authoritative sources confirmed that the perpetrators possessed biological agents. In these cases, no attempt was made to use the agents, and there was no known threat to use the agents.
- **Probable or possible possession**: There is no authoritative confirmation that the perpetrators possessed biological agents. In these cases, no attempt was made to use the agents, and no threats of use were made.

4. **Others**

- **Interest in acquisition**: The perpetrators expressed an interest in acquiring biological agents, but never actually acquired the agent in these cases. In some cases, the interest was slight, while in other cases the perpetrators actually attempted to acquire the agent. In these cases, the perpetrators also never made threats to employ biological agents.
- **False cases**: Some source incorrectly identified a case as an example of biological agent use. In some instances, it is unclear if the alleged event ever took place. In other cases, something may have happened, but a biological agent was not involved. In yet other cases, law enforcement officials believed that perpetrators were engaged in illegal activity, but the evidence failed to support the accusations.

The cases are discussed in reverse chronological order, starting with the most recent.

# Chapter 5: Use of Biological Agents

## Confirmed Use

In these cases, the use of a biological agent was confirmed by some authoritative source, either a court, a law enforcement agency, or by a credible government official.

***Case 1997-06: Unknown New Zealand farmers, August 1997***

On August 26, 1997, New Zealand's Ministry of Agriculture and Forestry (MAF) confirmed that it had identified the presence of rabbit hemorrhagic disease (RHD) in areas of the country's South Island. According to MAF's Chief Veterinary Officer, "It appears that this disease has been deliberately and illegally introduced by people wanting to use it as a biocontrol tool."[92] Australian farmers use RHD to kill feral rabbits as an animal control tool.

Earlier in 1997, a group of agricultural organizations mounted an effort to gain MAF approval to import RHD from Australia and use it to reduce the feral rabbit population on farms in New Zealand. This application was rejected on July 2, 1997, after considerable scientific review.[93] An appeal was turned down on August 19, 1997.

New Zealand authorities believe that someone smuggled RHD into New Zealand, probably from Australia, and introduced it into rabbit population. Farmers apparently told journalists that the RHD had been brought into the country two months before the release.[94] Some farmers indicated that introduction of RHD into New Zealand was inevitable, whatever the government decided.[95] Government officials apparently believed that illegal introduction was likely, and took steps to deal with such an eventuality. Significantly, no attempts were made to address farmers' concerns about the need for effective rabbit control that would motivate such an illegal act.[96]

Although it is not known who originally introduced the RHD, other farmers admitted to further propagating the disease. According to press reports, farmers spent six weeks prior to the identification of the outbreak perfecting their dissemination techniques. They mixed in a blender the liver, spleen, and hearts of infected rabbits with 100 milliliters of water. Initially, the farmers injected this mixture into rabbits, but found

---

[92] New Zealand Ministry of Agriculture and Forestry, "RCD Confirmed in South Island," August 26, 1997, as it appears in the ministry's World Wide Web site, *http://www.maf.govt.nz/*. An interesting discussion of this episode is provided in notes prepared for a presentation given at Plum Island by Graham Mackereth, "Rabbit Haemorrhagic Virus (RHDV)—The New Zealand experience," National Centre for Disease Investigation, New Zealand, August 1998. The author is grateful to Terrance M. Wilson, D.V.M., Ph.D., for providing a copy of this paper.

Rabbit hemorrhagic disease (RHD) or rabbit hemorrhagic viral disease (RHVD) was called rabbit calicivirus disease (RCD) in Australia and New Zealand. The Australian government adopted the name RCD because it claimed that the pathogen involved technically did not cause a hemorrhagic disease. The government of New Zealand followed the Australian example. Others rejected RCD as a name because this disease is not the only calicivirus known to infect rabbits, and thus lacks specificity. Australia has invested considerable effort into a program to use RCD as a rabbit control tool, and some critics claim that the disease was renamed to make its use more palatable to the public. For a description of the use of RCD as a rabbit control tool, see the web site maintained by the Australia and New Zealand Rabbit Calicivirus Disease Program at *http://www.csiro.au/communication/rabbits/qarabbit.htm*. In 1999, governments decided to revert to the name RHD after some European scientists discovered another organism that causes similar symptoms and named it rabbit calicivirus disease. See "A disease by any other name," *The Press* (New Zealand), February 11, 1999, as found at the newspaper's World Wide Web site, "The Press On-Line: New Zealand News," at *http://www.press.co.nz*. All newspaper references were taken from this web site.

[93] New Zealand Ministry of Agriculture and Forestry, "MAF Says "No" To RCD As Rabbit Control in New Zealand," July 2, 1997, as it appears on the ministry's World Wide Web site, *http://www.maf.govt.nz/*.

[94] Michael Rentoul, "Govt likely to abandon RCD fight," *The Press* (New Zealand), August 30, 1997.

[95] "Farmers' reaction," *The Press* (New Zealand), July 3, 1997.

[96] Mackereth, "Rabbit Haemorrhagic Virus (RHDV)."

that the disease spread too slowly. They then put the mixed the material with carrots and oats to attract rabbits, and then spread the infected bait in areas heavily infested with rabbits.[97]

After the presence of the disease was discovered, MAF made a largely ineffective effort to prevent the organism from spreading. For about a week the ministry attempted to quarantine the infected area. The MAF deployed 15 of its people to the area, and 30 police supported them. Roadblocks were established to prevent the movement of any "rabbits or rabbit-related material" from the quarantine zone.[98] This effort collapsed, however, as the ministry found that the disease was spreading more quickly than it could be contained. This appears to have led to a reevaluation of government policy towards RHD.

The response of the New Zealand government to the illegal introduction of RHD was extremely confused. There were substantial divisions within the New Zealand government. Some ministers wanted to eradicate the disease. Others accepted that the disease had been introduced and advocated adopting it as an animal control measure. There also appear to have been disagreements within the government over interpretations of the laws that regulated biological agents.

Initially, the government threatened to prosecute anyone involved in the introduction or spread of the disease. Subsequently, however, the government adopted a softer line. The MAF took the position that under the terms of the Biosecurity Act, New Zealand could not prosecute those involved in spreading the disease by using agent obtained from New Zealand rabbits. Consequently, the government decided to change its regulations and legalize use of the disease under the terms of the Biosecurity Act.

MAF initially took the position that the government had no authority to prevent someone from spreading a pathogen by using infected animal parts, as the farmers had admitted to doing. However, the Crown Law Office reportedly determined that provisions of the Animals Act made any possession of RHD illegal. In addition, the Crown Law Office also determined that the Biosecurity Act prohibited intentional spreading of RHD. However, because of the contrary advice given by MAF, the government determined that it could not prosecute violators of the laws.

MAF continued its efforts to identify the perpetrators, and signaled its intent to prosecute anyone involved either in smuggling RHD into the country or in releasing the original agent.[99] To determine who was responsible for introducing the agent into the country, MAF staff began interviewing "every rabbit-plagued farmer" in the areas where the disease first appeared.[100]

Despite the introduction of the disease into New Zealand, MAF continued to oppose importing RHD from Australia. The ministry argued that the strains of the disease already present in New Zealand were proving effective in killing rabbits. It also claimed that there was no evidence indicating that the RHD in New Zealand could lose its virulence. Finally, the government asserted that it was impractical to rely on imported Australian seed stock for logistics reasons.[101] In February 1998, however, the New Zealand government decided to legalize the use of RHD for rabbit control.[102]

As of late 1997, the government of New Zealand had not identified those responsible for introducing the RHD virus into the country.[103] According to one press report, apparently relying on the statements of New Zealand farmers, the person responsible for importing the disease was not from New Zealand.[104]

***Case 1996-05: Diane Thompson, October 1996***

On October 29, 1996, twelve people who worked in the laboratory of the St. Paul Medical Center hospital in Dallas, Texas, were deliberately infected with *Shigella dysenteriae* type 2, a rare strain of shigella that causes diarrhea. Another person became ill after consuming a pastry brought home by one of the

---

[97] John Keast, "Rabbit smoothies help spread virus," *The Press* (New Zealand), August 30, 1997. These accounts are confirmed by New Zealand government officials. See Mackereth, "Rabbit Haemorrhagic Virus (RHDV)."

[98] "Outbreak dispatches from the RCD zone," *The Press* (New Zealand), September 6, 1997.

[99] New Zealand Ministry of Agriculture and Forestry, "MAF Clarified Legal Stance on RCD Prosecutions," September 5, 1997, as found on the ministry's World Wide Web site at *http://www.maf.govt.nz/*. See also New Zealand Government, "Government Response To The Outbreak of RCD," September 9, 1997.

[100] "MAF still investigating RCD," *Southland Times*, September 17, 1997.

[101] New Zealand Government, "Government Response To The Outbreak of RCD," September 9, 1997, as found at *http://www.maf.govt.nz/*.

[102] Ministry of Agriculture and Forestry, "Pesticides Board Grants Experimental Use Permit for RCD," February 26, 1998, as found at *http://www.maf.govt.nz/*.

[103] "Introduction Probe Continues," *The Southland Press*, November 12, 1997.

[104] John Keast, "Silence of the rabbits," *The Press*, July 25, 1998.

laboratory workers. Four people became sufficiently sick to be hospitalized and five other victims went to emergency rooms for treatment. There were no fatalities.[105]

Reportedly, an e-mail message was sent to the laboratory personnel inviting them to eat some pastries that were available in the laboratory's lunchroom. There were two boxes of pastries with blueberry muffins and an assortment of doughnuts. The lunchroom was always locked and was accessible only to those with the combination. Eleven of the workers ate pastries between 7:15 a.m. and 1:30 p.m. The twelfth victim took a muffin home and shared it at 7:00 p.m. The victims started to become sick at 9:00 p.m. All were ill by 4:00 a.m. on November 1. Everyone who ate a pastry became ill.[106]

Clinical tests revealed that eight of the victims were infected with *S. dysenteriae*. Tests of a muffin saved by one of the victims revealed that it was contaminated with the same pathogen. The muffin was given to police investigating the case, and taken to a laboratory at the Texas Department of Health. Comparisons indicated that there was an extremely high probability that the victims had the same strain of the organism as was identified in the muffin. Investigators learned that the laboratory had a vial containing beads impregnated with *S. dysenteriae* type 2 of the same strain. Some of the beads apparently were missing.[107]

In addition to the epidemiological study, the St. Paul Medical Center Police also launched an investigation into the incident. Their attention was focused on a 25-year old laboratory technician, Diane Thompson, who had ready access to the laboratory's shigella culture.[108]

During the investigation in the shigella outbreak, hospital police learned that a year before a boyfriend of Thompson, John P. Richey, had suffered from similar symptoms.[109] Richey met Diane Thompson in January 1994, when the two worked at the Harris Methodist Hospital in Ft. Worth, Texas. The two began dating. Although Richey tried to end the relationship in September 1995, he continued to see Thompson because his parents were fond of her. The next month, Richey became ill with what his physician diagnosed as strep throat. He was treated with an antibiotic and initially seemed to get better. A few days later, however, he developed diarrhea and a fever, and, on the night of October 20, he went to the emergency room at St. Paul's Medical Center after developing severe chest pains. Richey's condition continued to worsen. On October 26, he was admitted to the hospital suffering from severe dehydration. According to information subsequently uncovered by investigators, Thompson falsified Richey's laboratory tests. She apparently went to the hospital's microbiology laboratory and replaced Richey's stool sample with one from someone who was not infected. In this way, she hoped to ensure that the physicians treating Richey would not learn of his infection.

According to Richey's statements to investigators, he became suspicious of Thompson's behavior at this time. She apparently brought him a glass of water while he was in the hospital, and became agitated when he refused to drink it. After being released from the hospital, she brought him a bottle of Gatorade, which he refused to use when he came to suspect that Thompson was trying to conceal that she had previously opened it. A few days later, Thompson gave Richey some lasagna to take to work for lunch. Sometime after eating it, Richey again became sick. As before, he was treated with antibiotics. The next night, Thompson convinced Richey to allow her to take a blood sample so that she could analyze it at the hospital. Approximately an hour later, his arm began to get sore. Later that evening Thompson's hospital supervisor called to tell him that his blood was filled with bacteria and that he should go to the emergency room. He was again treated with

---

[105] The primary sources used in preparing this account are the Affidavit of Warrant for Arrest, St. Paul Medical Center Police, November 8, 1996, as provided by Nancy J. Cutler, Assistant District Attorney, Dallas County District Attorney's Office, and S. A. Kolavic, et al., "An Outbreak of *Shigella dysenteriae* Type 2 Among Laboratory Workers Due to Intentional Food Contamination," *JAMA* (Journal of the American Medical Association), August 6, 1997, pp. 396-398. An earlier presentation of the *JAMA* study was given in "Outbreak of *Shigella dysenteriae 2* among Hospital Laboratory Workers—Texas," a presentation by Dr. Shellie A. Kolavic at the 46th Annual Epidemic Intelligence Service Conference, April 18, 1997, Centers for Disease Control and Prevention, Atlanta, Georgia. The hospital's name is not given in the CDC reports, but is identified as the St. Paul Medical Center in the affidavit and multiple press accounts. See "Spiking of doughnuts with rare bacteria probed by FBI," *San Diego Union-Tribune*, November 12, 1996, p. A4, and the *Houston Chronicle*, November 11, 1996. The *Houston Chronicle* citation was drawn from the newspaper's World Wide Web site at *http://www.chron.com.*

[106] The e-mail was sent from a supervisor's computer at a time when the supervisor was out of the office. See Kolavic, et al., "An Outbreak of *Shigella dysenteriae* Type 2 Among Laboratory Workers Due to Intentional Food Contamination," p. 397.

[107] Kolavic, et al., "An Outbreak of *Shigella dysenteriae* Type 2 Among Laboratory Workers Due to Intentional Food Contamination," pp. 397-398, and the Affidavit of Warrant for Arrest. The origin of the laboratory's *S. dysenteriae* type 2 culture is not known. Investigators believe that it may have been obtained from a patient and then used for training purposes at a time when the laboratory was used as a training facility.

[108] Published accounts do not indicate why investigators focused on Thompson.

[109] The details of Richey's involvement are taken from Affidavit of Warrant for Arrest, St. Paul Medical Center Police, November 8, 1996.

antibiotics. Richey believed that Thompson contaminated a syringe with bacteria before using it to draw his blood.

During the next month and a half, Richey had his tires slashed five times and sugar was put into his car's fuel tank. At that point, Richey moved to Corpus Christie to get away from Thompson. He told investigators that he made the move to get away from Thompson, and that he was extremely afraid of her. Richey claimed that Thompson subsequently admitted to him that she was responsible for his illnesses. This statement was corroborated by statements made by two of Thompson's co-workers at the hospital.[110]

Because of the police investigation, Thompson was arrested on November 8, 1996 for allegedly falsifying documentation related to the laboratory.[111] A Dallas County grand jury indicted her on counts of tampering with a government document and aggravated assault on January 14, 1997.[112] At the time, authorities claimed that she intentionally contaminated food eaten by her boyfriend with the shigella organisms. She was released from jail after paying bail set at $15,000.[113]

On August 28, 1997, Thompson was indicted by the State of Texas on three charges of tampering with a food product. She was accused of infecting 12 people with *Shigella dysenteriae* Type 2. The maximum penalty for each charge is life imprisonment. According to press reports, a federal criminal investigation was also launched.[114]

Thompson was found guilty on five felony assault charges and to falsifying documents related to the infection of her boyfriend. She was sentenced to twenty years in prison.[115]

***Case 1995-02: Debora Green, August 1995***

On April 17, 1996, Dr. Debora Green pleaded no contest to two charges of murder and two charges of attempted murder. One of the attempted murder charges was based on a claim that she had tried to use ricin to poison her estranged husband, Dr. Michael Farrar.[116] She had earlier pleaded not guilty to those charges. After prosecutors indicated that they would seek the death penalty, she negotiated a plea bargain that eliminated any chance she would be sentenced to death. Instead, she was sentenced to life with a provision that she will be eligible for parole only after serving 40 years.[117]

Farrar is a cardiologist, who was then in the process of getting a divorce from Green, an oncologist. The two had three children. Green apparently was a heavy drinker, and appeared to suffer from a severe psychiatric disorder. A psychologist who examined Green claimed that she was "a very, very immature person" who had "the emotional capability of a 1-year-old."[118]

On August 17, 1995, Farrar was hospitalized with a mysterious illness that almost killed him. He had come down with the symptoms about a week earlier. Initially, his physicians thought he might have contracted an unusual tropical disease during a July 1995, trip to Peru, perhaps an unusual form of typhoid. He was hospitalized twice more in the next few weeks.[119]

---

110 Affidavit of Warrant for Arrest.

111 Charles Ornstein, "Lab bacteria put in pastry caused illnesses," *Dalles Morning News*, November 11, 1996, p. 20A, and *Houston Chronicle*, November 11, 1996.

112 "Grand jury indicts ex-lab worker in poisoning case," *Dallas Morning News*, January 28, 1997, p. 14A.

113 Steve Scott, "Ex-hospital worker indicted: She's accused of tainting muffins, doughnuts that made co-workers ill," *Dallas Morning News*, August 29, 1997, p. 28A.

114 Steve Scott, "Ex-hospital worker indicted: She's accused of tainting muffins, doughnuts that made co-workers ill," *Dallas Morning News*, August 29, 1997, p. 28A.

115 "Ex-lab worker tainted food," *Houston Chronicle*, September 12, 1998, p. A48. The sentence information comes from Nancy Cutler in a telephone communication.

116 "Mother pleads in children's murder," *St. Louis Post-Dispatch*, April 18, 1996, as found on the newspaper's web site, *http://www.stlnet.com*. For a lengthy account of this case, see Ann Rule, *Bitter Harvest: A Woman's Fury, A Mother's Sacrifice* (New York: Simon & Schuster, 1997).

117 Tony Rizzo, "Green gets life sentence," *Kansas City Star*, May 31, 1996. These articles were found at *http://www.kcstar.com*.

118 Tony Rizzo, "Green gets life sentence," *Kansas City Star*, May 31, 1996.

119 Tony Rizzo, "Fire inquiry examined possible poisoning," *Kansas City Star*, November 9, 1995, Richard Espinoza, "Mother accused of arson is moved," *Kansas City Star*, November 25, 1995. Additional details appear in Rule, *Bitter Harvest*, pp. 74-78. According to Rule's account, the first poisoning incident apparently occurred on August 11, when Green fed Farrar a chicken salad sandwich that tasted "a little bitter." Farrar became extremely ill, but appeared to be getting better until his symptoms worsened on August 18, when he was hospitalized. He remained in the hospital until August 25. The second incident apparently occurred that same day after he ate a spaghetti dinner served by Green. He was hospitalized again three or four hours after eating the meal. Finally, on the evening of September 4 he was again put into the hospital after the symptoms returned.

The cause of his illness was only clarified in late September. After a bitter argument with his wife, during which she became extremely abusive, Farrar called police. She was taken into custody at that time, and Farrar tried to have her committed. She was released after voluntarily spending four days at the Menninger Institute.

At the time of her detention, Farrar gave the police eight packages of castor beans, which he had removed from her purse. Some of the packages were empty. Only a few days before, on September 20 or 22, a garden store sold her ten identical packages of castor beans. The store's assistant manager remembered the transaction because of the need to special order the beans. Because castor plants are quick-growing annuals, they must be replanted every year. Normally, the seeds are purchased only at the start of the growing season, and to obtain the seeds so late in the year meant getting them from the store's main office.[120]

On the night of October 24, after Farrar informed Green that he was seeking custody of their three children, Green set fire to their house to kill the children. Two died in the fire, and the third escaped only by climbing out of a second story window. Believing that the fire was arson, an investigation was launched, and Green was arrested for killing her children. She also was charged with attempting to poison her husband. Analysis by the FBI laboratory found antibodies in Farrar's blood that proved he had been poisoned with ricin.[121] Police apparently believe that he was poisoned on three occasions when Green served him meals during August and September.[122]

Farrar was hospitalized after each suspected poisoning. In addition, he required additional hospitalization in the months following the attacks. According to Farrar's doctors, the ricin perforated his gastrointestinal tract, leading to metastatic infections of the heart (endocarditis) and brain (abscesses), both of which required surgical intervention.[123]

It is not known how Green prepared the beans prior to contaminating Farrar's food. Despite pleading guilty, Green has refused to describe how Farrar was poisoned. In fact, she now blames the poisoning on her dead son.[124] The poisoning could have been done in one of two ways. If castor beans are eaten intact, they are not poisonous, since the shell does not contain ricin and is sufficiently rugged to survive a passage through the digestive tract.[125] Accordingly, either Green must have prepared the beans in a way that exposed the ricin inside or she extracted the ricin from the beans and then added the toxin to the food. Any evidence of her activities might have been destroyed when she set her house on fire.

---

[120] From the testimony of Kyle Shipps and Leighann Stahl during Green's preliminary hearing, State of Kansas vs. Debora Green – 95CR5387, pp. 207-265. Paul J. Morrison, District Attorney, Tenth Judicial District, and his executive assistant, Terri L. Issa, provided selected transcripts from these hearings. See also Tony Rizzo, "Green to stand trial in children's death," *Kansas City Star*, February 2, 1996.

Green must have made at least one previous purchase of caster beans to use in August and early September when she apparently poisoned Farrar. There is no indication that law enforcement officials were able to identify such purchases.

[121] See the testimony of FBI supervisory special agent Drew Campbell Richardson at Dr. Green's preliminary hearing, pp. 395-402. According to Richardson (pp. 417-418), this may have been the first time that the FBI laboratory did an immunoassay of a blood sample. He noted that during the 1980s, the laboratory did gain some experience in assaying solid ricin samples, but that different techniques are needed to detect the antibodies created in response to an exposure to ricin. The FBI laboratory received technical advice from the Naval Medical Research Institute, Bethesda, Maryland.

[122] Tony Rizzo, "Fire inquiry examined possible poisoning," *Kansas City Star*, November 9, 1995.

[123] Richard Espinoza, "Mother accused of arson is moved," *Kansas City Star*, November 25, 1995, Tony Rizzo, "Green gets life sentence," *Kansas City Star*, May 31, 1996.

[124] Telephone interview with Paul Morrison, Johnson County District Attorney, September 15, 1997. Green repeated this allegation in her interview with Ann Rule. See Rule, *Bitter Harvest*, p. 343.

[125] Julia F. Morton, "Poisonous and Injurious Higher Plants and Fungi," p. 1502, in C.G. Tedeschi, William G. Eckert, and Luke G. Tedeschi, editors, *Forensic Medicine: A study in trauma and environment, Volume III: Environmental Hazards* (Philadelphia: W. B. Saunders, 1977). According to "Castor Beans (*Ricinus Communis L*)," pp. 1847-1849, in Matthew J. Ellenhorn, et al., editors, *Ellenhorn's Medical Toxicology: Diagnosis and Treatment of Human Poisoning*, 2nd Edition (Baltimore: Williams & Wilkins, A Waverly Company, 1997), the lethal dose of ricin is about 1 microgram per kilogram (µg/kg) of body weight. This corresponds to about eight beans, depending on the size of the beans. Other sources give different doses. Thus, *Medical Management of Biological Casualties*, Appendix, estimates 3-5 µg/kg.

A distinctly different perspective on castor bean toxicity is offered by Albert Rauber and Julia Heard, "Castor Bean Toxicity Reexamined: A New Perspective," *Veterinary and Human Toxicology*, Vol. 27 (December 1965), pp. 498-502. These authors reviewed the available data on castor bean poisoning, drawing on data from poison control centers. They collected reports discussing 751 cases, and calculated that there was a 1.8 per cent fatality rate. Excluding the oldest cases, from a study published in 1906 that identified a 6 per cent case fatality rate, leads to a fatality rate of only 0.8 per cent. Modern standards of medical treatment probably account for much of the discrepancy. They conclude that while "capable of causing severe disease … a pessimistic prognosis will rarely be warranted."

***Case 1994-04: Richard J. Schmidt, August 1994***

On October 23, 1998, a Lafayette, Louisiana, jury voted 10-2 to convict Richard J. Schmidt of attempted second-degree murder. Schmidt could have received a prison sentence of between 10 and 50 years.[126] The trial judge sentenced Schmidt to 50 years in prison.[127]

Schmidt was accused of injecting a former lover, Janice Trahan, with HIV-infected blood. Schmidt, a married gastroenterologist, resisted efforts by the victim to end a ten-year-old affair. According to authorities, Schmidt gave the injection on the night of August 4, 1994. Schmidt regularly gave vitamin B-12 injections to Trahan. According to the prosecution, Schmidt made a quick visit that evening to the victim's house after first calling to determine that she was home. He found her already in bed, and offered to give her a vitamin injection. She refused. District Attorney Michael Hanson gave the following account of what happened next. "Before she could do anything more, he jab her in the left arm. She has never even sees the hypodermic. Next thing, he's leaving almost immediately." That was the last time that the two had physical contact. Trahan developed symptoms about a month later. Laboratory tests confirmed that she was infected with HIV. The accused denied the charges and claimed that the alleged victim was trying to "ruin his life with this charge."[128]

The prosecution argued that laboratory tests demonstrated that Trahan contracted the same strain of HIV as found in one of Schmidt's patients. The defense attempted to keep the scientific data concerning the DNA typing of the HIV strains out of the trial. Louisiana courts rejected the defense request, and allowed the prosecutors to make use of it.[129]

***Case 1993-03: "Iwan E.", June 1992***

In May 1994, a Dutch man, identified in court only as "Iwan E." was given a ten-year prison sentence for injecting his former girlfriend, identified only as "Gina O.", with 2-5 milliliters of HIV-contaminated blood. The blood was drawn from an HIV-positive friend of the perpetrator. According to prosecutors, "Iwan E." acted in June 1992 after "Gina O." broke up with him. The defense argued that the defendant was acting in self-defense, because "Gina O." had threatened to stab him with a knife during an argument. Three months after the injection, she was diagnosed as HIV-positive. Following the trial, the District Court issued a statement that said, "The defendant has attacked the victim's life in an extremely aggressive way and has violated her physical and mental integrity."[130]

***Case 1992-05: Brian T. Stewart, February 1992***

On April 22, 1998, Brian T. Stewart was arrested on charges of deliberately infecting his own son with HIV. He was arraigned the next day in St. Charles County, Missouri, charged with first-degree assault, and ordered to post a $500,000 bond to be released from jail. Stewart pleaded innocent to the charges, which could result in a life sentence.[131]

Prosecutors believe that Stewart injected the boy with HIV-contaminated blood on February 6, 1992, when the then 11 month-old baby was being treated for a respiratory ailment at the St. Joseph's Medical Center-West in Lake Saint Louis. According to press accounts, he was seen carrying a lab coat into his son's room. It is alleged that he then injected the blood into his son. The coat was of a type not typically worn at that time of year. According to St. Charles County Prosecutor Tim Braun, "The inference that we would have is that he had blood in there, and if somebody looked in the pocket of the coat, he would say, 'Oh, I had that left over from my other job' or 'I forgot to take that out'." Stewart allegedly told one witness something like, "You don't have to worry about me paying child support because the child won't live long enough."[132]

---

[126] Bruce Schultz, "Jury says physician tried to kill lover with HIV injection," *Baton Rouge Advocate*, October 24, 1998, pp. 1-b, 3-b [Acadiana edition].

[127] Bruce Schultz, "Judge sentences Lafayette doctor to 50 years in HIV case," *Advocate* (Baton Rouge, Louisiana), February 18, 1999, as found at the newspaper's World Wide Web site, *http://www.theadvocate.com.*

[128] "Doctor accused of Injecting His Girlfriend with HIV," *Los Angeles Times*, July 25, 1996, p. A17.

[129] "Appeals Court Takes HIV Case Under Advisement," *Sun Herald* (Biloxi, Mississippi), May 5, 1997.

[130] A medical account of the case appears in Jan Veenstra, et al., "Transmission of Zidovudine-Resistant Human Immunodeficiency Virus Type 1 Variants Following Deliberate Injection of Blood from a Patient with AIDS: Characteristics and Natural History of the Virus," *Clinical Infectious Diseases*, Vol. 21 (September 1995), pp. 556-560. "Man Jailed For 10 Years For Injecting Girlfriend with HIV Virus," *Associated Press, AP Worldstream*, May 26, 1994, 9:50 a.m. Eastern Time. See also, "Aids attack," *Times* (London), May 12, 1994, p. 10.

[131] Michele Munz, "Stewart arraigned on charges of injecting son," *St. Louis Post-Dispatch*, April 23, 1998. Articles were taken from the newspaper's web site at *http://www.stlnet.com.*

[132] "Mother in HIV case pleads for privacy," *CNN*, April 24, 1998, as found at *http://www.cnn.com.*

Stewart worked as a phlebotomist, a medical technician who draws blood from patients. At the time of the alleged incident, Stewart was working at Barnes Hospital in St. Louis, Missouri. Authorities apparently believe that he obtained blood from an HIV-infected patient, and took that blood to the hospital where his son was being treated.[133]

The boy was born thirteen months after Stewart met the mother in January 1990. The two were married in July 1993, and divorced in 1996. Stewart apparently refused to pay child support for the boy after the two separated, claiming that he had not fathered the boy. Subsequently, the courts were convinced by laboratory tests that he was the father, and ordered him to pay child support.[134]

The boy was extremely sick as a baby, but his physicians were unable to determine the cause. Finally, in May 1996, when he was five years old and in extremely ill health, they determined that he was suffering from AIDS. At that point, social workers at St. Louis Children's Hospital informed police of the case, and an investigation was launched. According to St. Charles County Sheriff Douglas Saulters, law enforcement officials spent two years investigating the case. They ruled out alternative causes, but admitted that the evidence was largely circumstantial.[135]

At the end of a two-day hearing, held May 26-27, 1998, Judge Jon Cunningham ruled that the prosecution had sufficient evidence to proceed with a trial. The defense attorney argued that the boy could have contracted AIDS either because of the medical treatments that he received or by coming into contact with an infected needle.[136]

On December 8, 1988, a jury found Stewart guilty of the charges after deliberating for only seven hours.[137] In early January 1999, the trial judge sentenced Stewart to life imprisonment, the maximum sentence for first-degree assault. The case is currently under appeal.[138]

***Case 1990-04: Graham Farlow, July 1990***

In July 1990, an Australian prison warder, Geoffrey Pearce, was injected with HIV-contaminated blood by Graham Farlow, an inmate in a prison in New South Wales. Pearce was treated with zidovudine, also known as AZT. Nevertheless, four weeks after the attack laboratory tests detected the presence of HIV in Pearce's blood. Farlow was asymptomatic at the time he injected Pearce. Nine months later, however, Farlow was diagnosed with AIDS. He died two months later. Soon after the assault, Farlow was charged with assault and malicious wounding. He could not be charged with murder because the then-existing law required the victim to die within one year and one day of the alleged assault. Farlow died before he could be tried. Pearce died in 1997.[139]

***Case 1990-01: Aum Shinrikyo, April 1990-March 1995***

The Japanese group responsible for the 1995 dissemination of sarin nerve gas in the Tokyo subway system, a religious cult known as the Aum Shinrikyo, also produced biological agents and tried to use them.[140] In fact, it appears that the group attempted to master biological agents before focusing on chemical agents.

---

133 Kristina Sauerwein, "Someone with access, intent can defy lab security," *St. Louis Post-Dispatch*, April 26, 1998.

134 William C. Lhotka and Lance Williams, "Man Accused of Giving Son HIV is Described as a Drifter," *St. Louis Post-Dispatch*, April 26, 1998.

135 Jim Salter, "Dad May have Injected Son with AIDS," *Associated Press*, April 24, 1998, 2:29 a.m.

136 Michele Munz, "Trial is ordered for man accused of giving son AIDS," *St. Louis Post-Dispatch*, May 28, 1998, Michele Munz, "Lawyer suggests other ways boy could have gotten AIDS," *St. Louis Post-Dispatch*, May 27, 1998, Jim Salter, *Associated Press*, May 28, 1998, 12:57 a.m. EDT, and Jim Salter, *Associated Press*, May 26, 1998, 10:27 p.m. EDT.

137 Michele Munz, "Father is found guilty of giving his son an HIV-tainted injection," ," *St. Louis Post-Dispatch*, December 6, 1998.

138 Jim Salter, "Father of AIDS-infected child is sentenced," Associated Press, January 9, 1999.

139 Philip D. Jones, "HIV transmission by stabbing despite zidovudine prophylaxis" [letter], *Lancet*, Vol. 338 (October 5, 1981), p. 884. According to Jones, he could find no previous reports in which the "malicious transmission" of HIV occurred through use of HIV-infected blood in a syringe. For other press accounts, see "Prison Guard says he got AIDS virus after attack," *Los Angeles Times*, September 1, 1990, p. A24, "Prisoner charged with AIDS-poisoning of warder dies from AIDS," *Reuters North American Wire*, April 27, 1991, PM cycle, Robert Milliken, "Sydney warders strike over HIV needle attacks," *Independent* (London), September 17, 1990, p. 14, "AIDS-attack victim prison officer dies in Australia," Deutsche Presse-Agentur, September 2, 1997, BC cycle, 02:42 Central European Time, and Rob Taylor, "Prison officer dies after seven year AIDS battle," *AAP*, September 1, 1997.

140 This account is based primarily on David E. Kaplan and Andrew Marshall, *The Cult at the End of the World* (New York: Crown Publishers, 1996), supplemented by Sheryl WuDunn, Judith Miller, and William J. Broad, "How Japan Germ Terror Alerted World," *New York Times*, May 26, 1998, pp. A1, A10, which provides new details of alleged Aum activities. See also D.W. Brackett, *Holy Terror: Armageddon in Tokyo* (New York: Weatherhill, 1996) and Staff Statement, "Global Proliferation of Weapons of Mass Destruction:

A charismatic guru who called himself Shoko Asahara founded Aum Shinrikyo. Asahara built the cult into a massive empire with a membership of approximately 10,000 with financial assets of at least US $300 million.[141] Aum was organized into Ministries and Departments, mimicking the structure of the Japanese government. Of particular importance for the biological warfare activity was the Ministry of Science and Technology, headed by Hideo Murai, and the Ministry of Health and Welfare, headed by Seichi Endo. Murai had graduated from Osaka University with a degree in astrophysics, and then worked for Kobe Steel doing research and development. Endo had researched genetic engineering at Kyoto University's Viral Research Center.[142]

According to one report, Endo first investigated *Clostridium botulinum*, which they obtained from environmental samples acquired near the Tokachi River on Hokkaido, the northern-most of the main Japanese islands.[143] By early April 1990, the Aum thought that it had made considerable progress in its efforts to develop botulinum toxin as a biological agent. A production facility was built at the cult's Mount Fuji facility. Unfortunately, when Endo tested the toxin, it failed to affect test rats. Aum's researchers also were attempting to produce an antitoxin using horse sera. This work was conducted by the group's Mount Aso laboratory. A stable was built for the horses used in the research.[144]

Sometime in mid-1993, the cult completed work on a new biological research facility, which was located on the highest floor of an eight-story office building that Aum owned in the eastern part of Tokyo. At this location, Aum worked on *Bacillus anthracis*. On the adjacent roof of the building, a larger industrial sprayer was built to disseminate the anthrax.[145]

In addition to botulinum toxin and anthrax, the Aum also was believed to have experimented with Q fever and the spores from a poisonous mushroom.[146] In 1992, Aum sent a team of 40 people to Zaire to acquire Ebola. Led by Asahara himself, the team included doctors and nurses. During an outbreak of Ebola in Zaire, a Japanese tourist visiting that country may have contracted the hemorrhagic fever. This report, which received considerable publicity in Japan, apparently inspired Asahara to mount the expedition to Zaire in October 1992. Ostensibly, this trip was intended as a humanitarian mission, called the "African Salvation Tour." It is not known if Aum actually obtained Ebola cultures. A Japanese magazine quoted a former member of the group, "We were cultivating Ebola, but it needed to be studied more. It can't be used practically yet."[147]

Press accounts suggest that Aum attempted to use aerosolized biological agents against nine targets, two with anthrax and seven with botulinum toxin.[148]

- In April 1990, the Aum Shinrikyo outfitted three vehicles to disseminate botulinum toxin. One vehicle was driven through central Tokyo, spraying the toxin, with the Japan's parliament, the Diet, the main target. Another vehicle reportedly was directed against two targets: the town of Yokohama and the Yokosuka naval base, the U.S. Navy's most important facility in the east Pacific. The third vehicle allegedly was used in the area of the Narita International Airport, one of Japan's most important airports.
- In early June 1993, the cult attempted to disrupt the planned wedding of Prince Naruhito, Japan's Crown Prince, by spreading botulinum toxin in downtown Tokyo using a specially equipped automobile.

---

A Case Study on the Aum Shinrikyo," pp. 47-102, in Permanent Subcommittee on Investigations, Committee on Governmental Affairs, U.S. Senate, *Global Proliferation of Weapons of Mass Destruction*, Part I (Washington, D.C.: Government Printing Office, 1996).

[141] Kevin Sullivan, "Japan Cult Survives While Guru Is Jailed," *Washington Post*, September 28, 1997, p. A21. Other sources provide much larger estimates. According to Staff Statement, "Global Proliferation of Weapons of Mass Destruction: A Case Study on the Aum Shinrikyo," pp. 54, 57-58, puts the membership at 40,000 to 60,000, including an estimated 30,000 to 50,000 in Russia, and the total financial resources at about US $1 billion.

[142] Kaplan and Marshall, *Cult at the End of the World*, pp. 51-53.

[143] WuDunn, Miller, and Broad, "How Japan Germ Terror Alerted World," p. A10.

[144] Kaplan and Marshall, *Cult at the End of the World*, p. 97.

[145] Kaplan and Marshall, *Cult at the End of the World*, pp. 94-95.

[146] Kaplan and Marshall, *Cult at the End of the World*, p. 151.

[147] Kaplan and Marshall, *Cult at the End of the World*, p. 97. Staff Statement, "Global Proliferation of Weapons of Mass Destruction: A Case Study on the Aum Shinrikyo," pp. 63-64, indicates that the Endo mentioned Ebola as a biological agent in a December 1994 radio broadcast from Moscow.

[148] Kaplan and Marshall, *Cult at the End of the World*, pp. 58-59, 93-94, 94-96, and pp. 234-236, and WuDunn, Miller, and Broad, "How Japan Germ Terror Alerted World," p. A10.

- In late June 1993, the cult attempted to spread anthrax in Tokyo using a sprayer system on the roof of an Aum-owned building in east Tokyo.
- Sometime in July 1993, an attempt was made to contaminate the area around the Diet in central Tokyo using a truck modified to disseminate anthrax.
- Later in July 1993, another attempt was made to disseminate anthrax in the area around the Imperial Palace in Tokyo. A truck-based system was used in this operation as well.
- On March 15, 1995, the Aum planted in the Tokyo subway three briefcases designed to release botulinum toxin.[149] Apparently, the individual responsible for filling the botulinum toxin had qualms about the planned attack and substituted a non-toxic substance. The failure of this attack led the cult to use sarin in its March 20, 1995 subway attack.

The Aum scientists apparently made mistakes either in the way they produced or disseminated the agents, and all the attacks failed. Aum may have relied on a strain of C. botulinum that produced little or no toxin, and thus may have been incapable of producing the desired effects. The quantities of toxin disseminated may have been too small to cause lethal effects. The Aum also had problems with their anthrax. According to Japanese officials, Endo discovered that Aum was using a vaccine strain of the organism, which was "relatively harmless." The Aum also had problems with the nozzles on their sprayers clogging. As far as is known, no one became ill or died from the Aum attempts.[150]

Finally, it is reported that the cult murdered some of its own members by feeding them food contaminated with toxins and pathogens from Endo's laboratory.[151]

***Case 1984-02: The Rajneeshees, August-September 1984***

In August and September of 1984, a religious cult, known as the Rajneeshees, employed biological agents against the inhabitants of The Dalles, a small town in Oregon.[152] Consequently, 751 people became sick. According to an FBI official, this is the only confirmed instance of chemical or biological terrorism to occur in the United States.[153] Despite its uniqueness, surprisingly little is known of this incident. While often mentioned in the terrorism literature, the accounts are often inaccurate and always incomplete.[154] For these reasons, an extended account of the incident is provided here.

---

[149] Staff Statement, "Global Proliferation of Weapons of Mass Destruction," p. 100, shows a drawing of the botulinum dissemination system. The design appears relatively simple. A vent was cut into the side of the briefcase. There were three cylindrical reservoirs filled with liquid and three small battery-powered fans above the cylinders. Kaplan and Marshall, *Cult at the End of the World,* p. 235, describe the device in the following way:

> The bacillus was held in solution in vinyl tubes, which were mounted on a small ceramic diaphragm. Powered by dry batteries, this device turned the solution into steam, which was then blown from the brief case by a small electric fan. The whole system was ultrasonic. The vibration of a passing train was enough to trigger the mechanism and release a fine spray of botulinus [sic] toxin.

[150] WuDunn, Miller, and Broad, "How Japan Germ Terror Alerted World," p. A10. See footnote 28 on page 13 for a discussion of the quantities of botulinum toxin required to cause fatalities.

[151] Kaplan and Marshall, *Cult at the End of the World,* p. 232.

[152] This account is based on a longer paper, "A Case Study in Biological Terrorism: The Rajneesh in Oregon, 1984," prepared as part of a project on chemical and biological terrorism sponsored by the Center for Nonproliferation Studies at the Monterey Institute for International Studies. The primary source of information for this account are primary documents obtained in Oregon. Records of the Oregon Attorney General's office relating to the legal proceedings against the cult brought by the state of Oregon are in the Rajneeshpuram case files, 1981-1989, 91A-081, Oregon State Archives (cited as OSA files). In addition, the State of Oregon's Attorney General's office provided copies of certain affidavits, sworn statements, and law enforcement records (cited as AG files). There is additional material related to the court cases, including testimony in several criminal trials, in the records of the U.S. District Court, Portland, Oregon (cited as US District Court files). Among the documentation obtained from these sources are statements by several members of the group who participated in the attacks. Finally, several people provided additional useful material, including the administrator of the Wasco-Sherman County Public Health Department. There remains a significant gap in the accounts of the cult's activities, however, since the key people responsible for the plot never admitted involvement, and never testified or gave statements about what they did. Accordingly, we do not have accounts written from their perspective.

[153] John P. O'Neill, Supervisory Special Agent, Chief, Counterterrorism Section, Federal Bureau of Investigation, p. 238, in Permanent Subcommittee on Investigations, Committee on Governmental Affairs, United States Senate, *Global Proliferation of Weapons of Mass Destruction*, (Washington, D.C.: Government Printing Office, 1996).

[154] Ron Purver, *Chemical and Biological Terrorism: The Threat According to the Open Literature*, Canadian Security Intelligence Service, June 1995, p. 39, summarized the published accounts of the incident. Relying on those versions of what happened,

The Rajneeshee cult was created by an Indian guru who called himself the Bhagwan Shree Rajneesh. Founded in the 1960s, by the early 1970s it began to attract a following among young upper middle class people from Europe and the United States. The Bhagwan was highly charismatic, extremely intelligent, and a master at manipulating people. By the early 1980s, the Bhagwan, called "Enlightened Master" by his followers, had thousands of adherents around the world. Many of his followers were wealthy and donated considerable sums to the group. In addition, the cult made a substantial income from the sale of books and tapes about the Bhagwan's teachings.[155]

Because of the cult's controversial beliefs, it became increasingly notorious in India. By 1980, opposition in Poona, where the cult had its ashram, was growing. For these reasons, the Bhagwan wanted to move the ashram to a new location. Under the influence of one of his followers, Ma Anand Sheela, an Indian who went to college in the United States, in 1981 Rajneesh moved to the United States, where he planned to establish a new ashram. Sheela acquired an Oregon property known as the Big Muddy Ranch, located in Jefferson and Wasco counties. The most important parts of the ranch were in Wasco County, a largely rural area with a population of about 20,000. The county seat of Wasco County was a small town, The Dalles, which in 1985 had a population of about 10,000.

Once the cult settled in Oregon, it proceeded to build a town for its adherents, which they officially named Rajneeshpuram and unofficially called Rancho Rajneesh. Rajneeshpuram was a legally incorporated community. As a mark of the status the group obtained, it created a police force, known as the Peace Force, whose members received training from the state government. For a time, the town even had access to law enforcement computer databases.

The cult was run in a peculiar fashion. All power derived from the Bhagwan's authority, even though he had no direct involvement in the daily operations of the organization. In fact, he was secluded from the other members except for his daily drive through Rajneeshpuram in one of his Rolls Royce's. He relied on Sheela to run the cult, and met with her privately every day to discuss important issues. Sheela controlled the finances and directed the operations of almost all of the organizations created to administer the cult's activities, including the town of Rajneeshpuram. She relied on a small inner circle that directed the operations of Rancho Rajneesh. Almost all of Sheela's trusted aides were women, which led members of the cult to refer to the group's leaders as "moms". The more senior of the "moms" were called the "big moms", although at least one disaffected Rajneeshee derisively called them the "Dowager Duchesses".[156]

Decision-making was a mixture of authoritarian and collegial. Sheela regularly held meetings in her private quarters during which many critical decisions were made. She also made decisions on her own, or after consultation with the Bhagwan, and brooked no opposition. Because she was accountable only to the Bhagwan, members of the cult had to accept her decisions or risk being expelled from Rajneeshpuram. This peculiar decision-making style had a significant impact on the group's move to employ biological agents.[157]

When the cult first moved to Oregon, it hoped to establish good relations with the local inhabitants. Relatively quickly, however, it began to alienate people in the area. Some of the antagonism arose because of

---

Purver inaccurately reports that the Rajneeshees used the pathogen that causes typhoid fever, *Salmonella typhi*. In fact they used another salmonella strain, *Salmonella typhimurium*, which is a common cause of food poisoning.

[155] A considerable amount has been written about the Rajneeshees and their activity in Oregon. Lewis F. Carter, *Charisma and Control in Rajneeshpuram: The role of shared values in the creation of a community* (New York: Cambridge University Press, 1990) provides the best scholarly study of the Rajneeshees in Oregon. Insight into the activities of the cult can be obtained from some of the autobiographies written by former members of the cult, including Satya Bharti Franklin, *The Promise of Paradise: A Woman's Intimate Story of the Perils of Life with Rajneesh* (Barrytown, New York: Station Hill Press, 1992) and Hugh Milne, *Bhagwan: The God That Failed* (New York: St. Martin's Press, 1986). Unfortunately, none of the key individuals involved in the use of biological agents has penned an autobiography. Also useful are accounts written by outsiders who observed the activities of the cult during this period, including Kirk Braun, *Rajneeshpuram: The Unwelcome Society* (West Linn, Oregon, Scout Creek Press, 1984), James S. Gordon, *The Golden Guru: The Strange Journey of Bhagwan Shree Rajneesh* (New York: Viking Press, 1988), Donna Quick, *The Rajneesh Story: A Place Called Antelope* (Ryderwood, Washington: August Press, 1995), and Bert Webber, *Rajneeshpuram: Who Were Its People?* (Medford, Oregon: Webb Research Group, 1990).

[156] Sheela's top lieutenants were Ma Prem Savita, who managed the finances, and Ma Yoga Vidya, who was responsible for personnel matters, deciding where people worked and lived. Under them was a third tier of five women. "The Dowager Duchesses," *Oregonian* (Portland), June 30, 1985, p. A10, and "Charged," *Oregonian* (Portland), December 30, 1985, p. B2.

[157] Sheela's power was not absolute, however, and the presence of potential rivals was a serious threat to her position. The Bhagwan's personal household was a danger because it included the only people with more access to the Bhagwan than Sheela herself. It included the Bhagwan's personal physician, Devaraj, who Sheela believed was an incompetent who undermined the cult by satisfying the guru's drug habit. She also blamed Devaraj for failing to satisfactorily document the supposed health problems that constituted the main justification for the Bhagwan's continued presence in the United States. A second threat to Sheela was the so-called "Hollywood Crowd" composed of wealthy individuals with direct access to the Bhagwan. Ma Prem Hasya, the divorced wife of the man who produced the movie *The Godfather* led this group. By 1984 alliances were developing between these two groups. In 1985 Hasya and Devaraj got married. Hasya became the Bhagwan's chief of staff after Sheela fled the group in September 1985.

the religious beliefs of the group, which offended those with traditional Christian values. The most significant problems, however, emerged because of Oregon's stringent land use laws, which constrained development in rural areas. To get around the land use laws that threatened to limit efforts to expand Rajneeshpuram, the cult exploited Oregon's liberal voter registration laws to seize control of a small town near Rajneeshpuram called Antelope. This was the turning point in relations between the Rajneeshees and the inhabitants of Wasco County, because it offended many people whom otherwise cared little about the group. Faced with growing hostility from the locals, the cult reciprocated with its own aggressive responses, which included such tactics as filing libel suits against people who spoke out against the group.

By early 1984, the cult was under considerable pressure. The U.S. Attorney's office in Portland, Oregon, had taken charge of an immigration investigation that threatened to lead to the deportation of many cult members, possibly including the Bhagwan. In addition, the office of Oregon's Attorney General was conducting an investigation into the legal status of Rajneeshpuram that threatened the continued existence of the community.[158]

Sheela and the other senior Rajneeshees also had come to recognize that the hostility of the Wasco County Court, the name of the county commission, was a problem. The cult had to obtain permits from the county for many of its activities, and the county government was becoming increasingly hostile towards the Rajneeshees. Although the cult could draw on a substantial team of skilled lawyers to contest any unfavorable decisions by the county government, the opposition of Wasco County was a major impediment in the cult's ability to conduct its activities.

Wasco County Court consisted of three elected commissioners. Two commissioners hostile towards the Rajneeshees were up for reelection in November 1984. In early 1984, Sheela and the Bhagwan decided to gain control of the Wasco County Court in the November 1984 election. Initially, Sheela focused on the prospects for large-scale voter, but eventually rejected that approach because investigators would find it too easy to uncover the fraudulent activity.[159] The group tried to find someone sympathetic towards the cult to run against the hostile commissioners. This effort failed when they were unable to get enough signatures to have their preferred candidate placed on the ballot.[160]

Finally, Sheela decided that they would make the voters of Wasco County sick before the election so that they would not be able to vote. According to KD, after the meeting in which she raised this idea, Sheela and Puja started looking at books that described "bacteria and other methods to make people ill."[161] Furthermore, he claimed that Sheela said "she had talked with Bhagwan about the plot to decrease voter turn out in The Dalles by making people sick. Sheela said that Bhagwan commented that it was best not to hurt people, but if a few died not to worry."[162]

Sheela also decided that the group would bring thousands of homeless people to Rajneeshpuram from cities around the country. Oregon had liberal voter registration laws, so that the homeless people would be eligible to vote in the November election. Sheela was sure that these people could be induced to vote for candidates favored by the Rajneeshees. This came to be known as the "Share-A-Home" program, which brought thousands of homeless people to Rajneeshpuram, ostensibly to provide them with a home.[163]

We know a great deal about the plot to employ biological agents, because of information provided by former members of the cult. The most important source was Krishna Diva (the Rajneesh name for David Berry Knapp), familiarly known as KD. He was the mayor of Rajneeshpuram and thus a part of the cult's inner

---

[158] The Immigration and Naturalization Service (INS) had been investigating the cults activities for several years with little result. The INS believed that the group was violating U.S. immigration laws by arranging sham marriages between foreigners and U.S. citizens to ensure that the non-U.S. members could remain at Rajneeshpuram. In addition, the group worried that the INS intended to expel the Bhagwan because of irregularities in his visa application. The application focused on the Bhagwan's need for medical treatment in the United States, which he somehow never bothered to obtain. By 1984, the U.S. Attorney's office had taken charge of the investigation, and it had begun to produce results.

In addition, the cult knew that the Oregon's Attorney General, David Frohnmeyer, was investigating possible violations of church and state separation. He suspected that the town of Rajneeshpuram was run by the cult for the benefit of the cult, which was not permitted under Oregon law. Successful prosecution of this case endangered the legal status of Rajneeshpuram and thus the ability of the cult to operate the town. Without the legal status, the cult; had

[159] David Berry Knapp interrogation, transcribed November 13, 1985, FBI, AG files.

[160] David Berry Knapp interrogation, transcribed November 13, 1985, FBI, AG files.

[161] David Berry Knapp interrogation, transcribed November 13, 1985, FBI, AG files.

[162] Report of Interview, Swami Krishna Deva, AKA David Berry Knapp, November 25, 1985, AG files.

[163] According to KD, it was either Sheela or KD who came up with the original idea to bring in homeless people as voters. See David Berry Knapp interrogation, transcribed November 13, 1985, Federal Bureau of Investigation, AG files.

circle.[164] In addition, at least two other people who participated in the use of biological agents gave accounts of their actions.

About a dozen Rajneeshees were involved in the plots to employ biological agents. At least eleven people appear to have participated in the planning the operation. No more than four appear to have been involved in the laboratory activities, although not all of them necessarily were aware of the nefarious objectives behind the production of the biological agent. At least eight people distributed agent on at least one occasion.[165]

The person most responsible for Rajneeshee activities associated with biological agent acquisition was a woman who went by the Rajneeshee name of Ma Anand Puja. Puja was closely tied to Sheela almost from the time she joined the cult in 1979. Born in the Philippines, Puja was raised in California. She became a family nurse practitioner in 1976 and received a license as a registered nurse the next year. After working in oncology clinics in the Philippines and Indonesia in 1977, she became restless and began to travel. She joined the cult after hearing the Bhagwan speak at the ashram in Poona. In April 1980, she became director of the Shree Rajneesh Ashram Health Center.[166]

Puja was secretary-treasurer of the Rajneesh Medical Corporation, and as such was considered a "big mom".[167] She had total authority over Rajneeshpuram's medical facilities, including both the Pythagoras Clinic and the Pythagoras Pharmacy. Her power also extended beyond the medical realm. For a time, she was a vice president of the Bhagwan's church, Rajneesh Foundation International (RFI). According to the *Oregonian*, "Puja's importance in the ranch hierarchy was greater than outsiders may have guessed from the modest post she held with the medical corporation."[168]

People who encountered Puja found her a sinister figure. She was disliked by members of the commune, who referred to her as "Dr. Mengeles" after the notorious Nazi concentration camp doctor. According to a Rajneeshee who worked under Puja from February 1984 to January 1985, "Puja was feared and disliked by personnel at the RMC. Puja behaved as a tyrant."[169] Another Rajneeshee who clerked at the RMC told authorities that Puja was a "loner" who socialized only with Sheela. She even ate her meals alone at her house.[170] KD recalled that Puja "delighted in death, poisons and the idea of carrying out various plots."[171] Another member of the cult, who joined in 1972 but was not involved in its illegal activities, had the following reaction to Puja:

> There was something about Puja that sent shivers of revulsion up and down my spine the moment I met her. There was nothing I could put my finger on beyond her phony, sickeningly sweet smile; it was years before she became widely-known as the Dr. Mengeles of the sannyas community, the alleged perpetrator of sadistic medical practices that verged on the criminal; my reaction to her seemed irrational. ... Sheela trusted her implicitly.[172]

At least some outsiders shared this impression of Puja.[173]

Some former members suspect that Puja was involved in nefarious activities almost from the time she joined the Rajneeshees. Rumors suggested that she was involved in the June 1980 death of Chinmaya, Sheela's first husband, who was sick with Hodgkin's disease at the time. In addition, some former Rajneeshees believe

---

[164] KD, however, was not in the inner most circles. KD was in the fourth tier of leaders.

[165] Based on a review of all the available documentation.

[166] "Interviews revealed Puja's medical background," *Oregonian*, October 4, 1985, p. D2. The *Oregonian* based its account on a 1984 interview with Puja and a 1983 letter that she sent to the INS. She claimed in the letter that for four years she was director of the Kern County Medical Center outpatient clinic.

[167] "The Dowager Duchesses," *Oregonian*, June 30, 1985, p. A10.

[168] "Profiles: The key Rajneeshees under indictment," *Oregonian*, October 29, 1985, p. D3.

[169] Ava Kay Avalos interrogation, transcribed October 22, 1985, AG files.

[170] Affidavit for Search Warrant, drafted by Lieutenant Dean Renfrow, Oregon State Police, October 1, 1985, OSA files.

[171] From Exhibit E attached to David Berry Knapp interrogation, transcribed November 15, 1985, Federal Bureau of Investigation, AG files.

[172] Franklin, *The Promise of Paradise*, p. 136.

[173] Carla Chamberlain, the administrator of the Wasco-Sherman Public Health Department, met with Puja and Sheela in a futile effort to convince the Rajneeshees to notify the health authorities of cases of reportable diseases. She recalls viewing Puja as a sinister figure, and hence was not surprised at subsequent reports of her involvement in the various poisoning cases. Interview, Carla Chamberlain, Administrator, Wasco-Sherman Public Health Department April 11, 1997.

that others may have been poisoned by Puja.[174] It is known that she was fascinated with poisons. Among the items discovered in her possession after she fled Rajneeshpuram in 1985 were numerous items reflecting an interest in chemical and biological agents, including information on salmonella poisoning.[175]

Puja considered several biological agents for the contamination scheme. The main agent she relied upon was *Salmonella typhimurium*, a strain of salmonella that is a common cause of food poisoning. Puja's interest in salmonella apparently originated in the spring of 1984. Pretending that she needed to identify poisons that could be used against the cult, Puja asked one of the Rajneeshee physicians about difficult to detect poisons that would make people sick without killing them. Salmonella was mentioned as a possible agent.[176]

Puja also considered several other biological agents. One of these was *Salmonella typhi*, the organism that causes typhoid fever. One of the Rajneeshees, Ma Ava, recalled hearing from her friend Parambodhi, who was the laboratory technician at the Rajneesh Medical Clinic, that Puja wanted to culture the organism responsible for typhoid.[177] This was confirmed by KD, whose recollections were recorded by the Oregon law enforcement investigators.

> Sheela and Puja talked about ordering typhoid in the name of the Rajneesh Medical Corporation (R.M.C.) from a lab somewhere in the United States. K.D. objected, pointing out that the typhoid cultures could possibly be traced back to the R.M.C. K.D. states Sheela told him not to be so paranoid and not to worry about the typhoid cultures being traced back to RMC. Puja favored using typhoid because it would cause a couple of weeks of fever. As far as Knapp [K.D.] knows, this plan was never implemented.[178]

There is no information in the available records about why Puja decided not to use *S. typhi*. It is likely, however, that Sheela and Puja heeded KD's advice and decided that causing a typhoid outbreak was too risky.

According to KD, Puja also expressed an interest in hepatitis.[179] There are several forms of hepatitis, and it is unclear which Puja wanted to use.[180] KD also claimed that Puja had some other ideas for spreading infection in The Dalles.

> Other ideas Puja had of making people sick in The Dalles including the putting of dead rodents, especially "beavers" into The Dalles water system. Puja had explained that beavers naturally contained bacteria in their bodies. There was some comment that beavers could not be put into the water tanks in The Dalles because of screens over the tanks. K.D. recalls someone jokingly suggesting that the beavers be put into a blender (and liquefied). Someone suggested rats or mice could be injected with a substance and placed into The Dalles water system. K.D. heard Anugiten talk of trapping mice. K.D. believes some of the traps were set in The Dalles so that the rodents would be indigenous to the area.[181]

The pathogen associated with beavers is *Giardia lamblia*, a protozoan that causes giardiasis, a diarrheal disease.[182] It is commonly called "beaver fever" in the Rocky Mountains area, since most beavers are infected with giardia. Due to the prevalence of giardia-infected animals in the area, it is considered unsafe to drink water in the Rocky Mountains, even from freely flowing streams.[183]

---

[174] Franklin, *The Promise of Paradise*, pp. 136-137. KD claims that in 1985 he was told by Sheela during a trip to India that Sheela had injected Chinmaya with a poison the night of his death. See David Berry Knapp interrogation, transcribed November 15, 1985, Federal Bureau of Investigation, AG files.

[175] Affidavit for Search Warrant, drafted by Lieutenant Dean Renfrow, Oregon State Police, October 1, 1985, OSA files.

[176] Mentioned in the Affidavit for Search Warrant, drafted by Lieutenant Dean Renfrow, Oregon State Police, October 1, 1985, OSA files.

[177] Ava Kay Avalos interrogation, transcribed October 22, 1985, AG files.

[178] Report of Interview, Swami Krishna Deva, AKA David Berry Knapp, Oregon State, November 25, 1985, AG files.

[179] Report of Interview, Swami Krishna Deva, AKA David Berry Knapp, Oregon State, November 25, 1985, AG files.

[180] There are several forms of hepatitis, including types A, B, C, and E. See Abram S. Benenson, editor, *Control of Communicable Diseases Manual*, Sixteenth edition (Washington, DC: American Public Health Association, 1995), pp. 217-233.

[181] Report of Interview, Swami Krishna Deva, AKA David Berry Knapp, Oregon State, November 25, 1985, AG files.

[182] Abram S. Benenson, editor, *Control of Communicable Diseases Manual*, Sixteenth edition (Washington, DC: American Public Health Association, 1995), pp. 202-204.

[183] Stuart Warren and Ted Long Ishikawa, *Oregon Handbook*, third edition (Chico, California: Moon Publications, 1995), pp. 51-52.

According to KD, "Puja was always very excited about the disease AIDS." He noted, "Puja talked about culturing the AIDS virus and she was very secretive concerning her work in that area."[184] According to evidence given law enforcement officials, Puja questioned one of the medical people who worked with her about culturing AIDS. She was told that the Rajneeshees lacked the equipment needed if the laboratory was to grow AIDS. This led to a rush purchase of a "quick-freeze dryer" in September 1984.[185] Unconfirmed reports indicate that she may have deliberately infected at least one individual with HIV to see if it was possible to transmit the disease.[186]

The Rajneeshee obtained their *S. typhimurium* from a commercial supplier. Some time between October 1, 1983 and February 29, 1984, the Rajneeshee Medical Corporation obtained a set of what are known as bactrol disks from VWR Scientific, a medical supply company located in Seattle, Washington. Some of the disks contained *S. typhimurium* of a strain known as ATCC 14028, which is commonly used in medical settings.[187] Puja apparently took samples of the *S. typhimurium* from this set of bactrol disks, which were used by the RMC's state-licensed medical laboratory.[188] The RMC had a legitimate requirement for the *S. typhimurium*. It was one of the control organisms used by licensed clinical laboratories to satisfy quality assurance requirements.[189]

Puja apparently produced *S. typhimurium* in a covert laboratory at a secret location within Rajneeshpuram. The laboratory was dismantled before law enforcement officials could search it, but Ava reported that it contained "a large freeze dryer with tubes and other equipment and an incubator." There was a large, green incubator the size of a "small apartment-type refrigerator" that was filled with petri dishes used to cultivate the *S. typhimurium*. Puja eventually moved the laboratory to a relatively remote location within Rajneeshpuram in what was known as the Alan Watts complex.[190] This complex was located in a canyon northeast of the center of the community, and included about two dozen buildings.[191] According to KD, who saw the Alan Watts laboratory on September 14, 1985, just before Sheela, Puja, and the others fled Rajneeshpuram, it was in a building with boarded up windows.

> When they entered the building, there was cardboard on the floor, and he described a long table on the left, a long table on the right and two other tables in the room. On the left table, Knapp [KD] described a piece of equipment which had a motor on it and rubber tubing coming out of it. Knapp described this piece of equipment as being approximately two and a half feet long, one and a half feet wide, and one foot high. He said that it was on a platform and described the hoses as being firm as opposed to flexible. He said that the machine was gray in color. He asked Anujiten what the machine was, and Anugiten said it was "Puja's salmonella maker." There were also two or three small refrigerators which were empty and unplugged.[192]

After Sheela fled the commune, Rajneeshee officials described it as a "germ warfare" laboratory.[193]

Puja apparently learned how to culture *S. typhimurium* from the RMC's laboratory technician, Parambodhi. Puja apparently asked the laboratory technician to culture salmonella. He initially objected, because he said the organism was dangerous, but eventually obeyed Puja's orders and produced quantities of *S. typhimurium*. One witness remembered receiving two large jars filled with a liquid containing salmonella.[194]

---

[184] David Berry Knapp interrogation, transcribed November 15, 1985, Federal Bureau of Investigation, AG files.

[185] Affidavit for Search Warrant, drafted by Lieutenant Dean Renfrow, Oregon State Police, October 1, 1985, OSA files.

[186] Interview, Lynn Enyart, October 23, 1997.

[187] Government's Statement of Expected Testimony and Evidence, US v. Ma Anand Sheela, et al, CR. 86-53, June 21, 1986, US District Court files. This statement was the presented by the US Attorney's office to the judge in the case and summarizes the evidence that the prosecutors intended to present if the case had gone to trial.

[188] When law enforcement officials searched the clinic laboratory on October 2, 1985 they seized a culture of *S. typhimurium* that proved to be the same strain as on the bactrol disks. See Government's Statement of Expected Testimony and Evidence, US v. Ma Anand Sheela, et al, CR. 86-53, June 21, 1986, US District Court files.

[189] Elmer W. Koneman, et. al., *Color Atlas and Textbook of Diagnostic Microbiology*, 4th edition (Philadelphia: J.B. Lippincott, 1992), pp. 55-58, 118-120. *S. typhimurium* is used to validate growth media used by clinical laboratories to diagnose infectious diseases. Koneman specifically mentions five different growth media that can be tested using *S. typhimurium* as a control organism.

[190] Ava Kay Avalos interrogation, transcribed October 22, 1985, AG files.

[191] James Long and Leslie L. Zaitz, "Lab reputedly used in germ experiments," *Oregonian*, September 28, 1985, p. A1.

[192] David Berry Knapp interrogation, transcribed November 13, 1985, Federal Bureau of Investigation, AG files. See also, Report of Interview, Swami Krishna Deva, AKA David Berry Knapp, November 25, 1985, AG files.

[193] James Long and Leslie L. Zaitz, "Lab reputedly used in germ experiments," *Oregonian*, September 28, 1985, p. A1.

[194] Notes of Interview, Ava Kay Avalos (Ma Ava), October 7, 1985, Oregon Department of Justice, OSA.

The first clearly documented incident in which the Rajneeshees used biological agents occurred on August 29, 1984, during a routine fact-finding visit to Rajneeshpuram by the three Wasco County commissioners. The Rajneeshees gave *S. typhimurium* contaminated water to the two commissioners hostile to the group, Judge William Hulse and Commissioner Ray Matthew. Both became sick; Judge Hulse required hospitalization.[195]

A second incident apparently did not result in any victims, occurred sometime in "late July/August," according to KD's vague recollection. Puja gave KD an eyedropper filled with a "brownish clear liquid" and told him to spread the liquid on doorknobs and urinal handles in the Wasco County Courthouse. KD believed that the liquid contained salmonella, based on Puja's subsequent account of how the material would work. KD spread the liquid as directed, but no one got sick. Consequently, KD told law enforcement officials "Sheela was frustrated and angry that Puja's substance was not working."[196]

On another occasion, also reported to be sometime in July or August, but the recollections were vague, a group of Rajneeshees, including Sheela, Puja, KD, and several other Rajneeshees visited The Dalles to select targets for disruption attacks. During that trip, the Rajneeshees stopped at an Albertson's supermarket in The Dalles. KD gave a graphic description of this episode.

> Sheela said to Puja "Puji lets have some fun". K.D. says that Puja giggled and replied "oh boy" (or words to that effect). K.D. recalls that Sheela, Puja, himself, Jayananda, and probably the others went into the store. Both K.D. and Jayananda were Sheela's bodyguard. While in the store, K.D. recalls observing Sheela in the produce department sprinkling on the lettuce what he assumed to be a similar substance he had been given by Puja to put on door knobs in the courthouse, and salad dressing in the restaurant on an earlier date. K.D. said that Sheela had the container with the substance up her sleeve, at the wrist and palm, to conceal what she was doing. Puja commented to K.D. that she was thinking of injecting the substance into the milk cartons. K.D. objected to her doing that saying it would be obvious that the carton had been tampered with because of the holes in the carton. It was unknown to K.D. if Puja injected the substance into the milk cartons. Comments were made by Sheela that the intent of putting the substance onto the lettuce was to give people in The Dalles "the shits". When they returned to their vehicle Puja was giggling and saying that she had a good time.[197]

Another Rajneeshee, Alma Peralta, was involved in two other attempts to spread salmonella, although her self-described efforts were less than successful.

> I was asked as one of the first projects to drive into The Dalles and visit nursing homes and schools and to see Puja before I left. And Puja gave me a kit -- which then I inspected when I was in the car and by myself.
>
> So I went by myself that time. And because I knew what salmonella is and after I opened it then I realized that's what it was. And I realized that they actually were quite serious about the fact that I needed to drive there alone and try and put that in the food in the nursing homes that I visited and in the schools.
>
> ... I actually got there and went into the nursing homes and went into -- I found two schools, and I believe one or two nursing homes and talked with the people and went through the whole thing ....
>
> What happened is if I didn't put it in because it -- thank god for the fact that those ladies were really watching, you see. So I could at least get in the car and dump the stuff out on the street.
>
> When I got back I lied, I said to them I had done it.[198]

In addition to this abortive attempt, Yogini also participated in one additional operation. At a political meeting in The Dalles, she put some of the salmonella-contaminated liquid on her hands and held hands with an "older gentleman" that she sat with. It is not known exactly when these two incidents took place.[199]

Starting in early September 1984, the Rajneeshees began to pour vials containing *S. typhimurium* into food products at restaurants in The Dalles. According to CDC figures, 751 people became ill after eating at

---

195 Interview, Judge William Hulse, April 1997, and Interview, Ava Avalos, October 22, 1985, AG files.

196 David Berry Knapp interrogation, transcribed November 15, 1985, FBI, AG files.

197 David Berry Knapp interrogation, transcribed November 15, 1985, FBI, AG files.

198 Testimony, Alma Peralta, Grand Jury Testimony, May 21, 1990, US District Court files.

199 Testimony, Alma Peralta, Grand Jury Testimony, May 21, 1990, US District Court files. Ava recalled Yogini talking about spreading salmonella by shaking hands with people. See Ava Kay Avalos interrogation, transcribed October 22, 1985, AG files.

salad bars in ten of restaurants.[200] Our information about these attacks is limited to the accounts of two former Rajneeshees, who apparently were involved in contaminations at only a few of the restaurants. KD admitted to participation in one incident. According to his recollection, Puja gave him a plastic bag containing a test tube filled with a "mostly clear" light brown liquid. He was ordered to spread the contents at a restaurant in The Dalles during a trip to The Dalles. He arrived at a restaurant known as the Portage Inn after lunchtime, and found that the salad bar was closed. Although the salad fixings had been removed, the salad dressing was still there. He poured the contents of the vial into the salad dressing.[201]

Another Rajneesh, Ma Ava, admitted to participating in contaminations at three restaurants. She recalled, "Sheela and Puja told her that they wished to do an experiment in The Dalles which would make people sick so they could not vote." She and another Rajneesh replaced their distinctive Rajneesh clothes with street clothes, took five or six vials containing salmonella, and drove to The Dalles. They put salmonella into the coffee creamers at two restaurants. At a third restaurant, they put the liquid into the bleu cheese salad dressing at the salad bar. Press reports suggest that there were victims at only two of the restaurants.[202]

KD also said that he believed Puja was directly involved in contaminating the salad bar at one restaurant. Another Rajneesh told him, "She described the fact that Puja was being very obvious about pouring a substance in the salad dressing and salads. ... Puja was wearing a wig."[203] Sheela subsequently congratulated Puja on making so many people sick. "Pujy (referring to Puja), you've done a good job making everyone sick. Too bad you didn't make more people sick."[204] Ava also recalled hearing Puja claiming to have put salmonella in "lots of places."[205] Other Rajneeshees also may have been involved in the contamination.[206]

The Rajneeshees also tried to contaminate the water system in The Dalles. Sometime during July or August 1984, efforts were made to obtain maps of the town's water system. Once the maps were obtained, the Rajneeshees decided to contaminate a water tank that supplied the town. A Rajneesh who apparently visited the water system reportedly told Puja that they would need considerably more "salsa" (an apparent reference to salmonella) in order to contaminate the water system. Puja replied that she might not be able to produce sufficient material in time for their return visit to The Dalles.[207]

Two attempts were made to contaminate the water system with "salsa". During one of the trips, a police car showed up while the Rajneeshees were getting reading to contaminate the water tank and "freaked them out."[208] KD described what he had been told about the water poisoning in the following terms.

> Julian described how he and Anugiten climbed up a hill to a water tank that overlooked a nearby school. He recalled something being mentioned about trying to pry open the screen on the water tank and hearing rushing water.[209]

---

200 Thomas J. Török, et al., "A Large Community Outbreak of Salmonellosis Caused by Intentional Contamination of Restaurant Salad Bars," *JAMA*, August 6, 1997, pp. 389-395, reviews the outbreak from the perspective of the federal and state public health officials involved in the investigation.

201 KD told the story both to the FBI and to the Oregon state investigators. See Report of Interview, Swami Krishna Deva, AKA David Berry Knapp, November 25, 1985, AG files., and David Berry Knapp interrogation, transcribed November 13, 1985, Federal Bureau of Investigation, AG files.

This is the only time KD mentions involvement in a restaurant poisoning. He dates it to sometime in August, after the time that he contaminated the Wasco County Courthouse. However, press accounts suggest that he was seen by an employee of the Portage Inn on September 12 near the salad bar. Federal prosecutors eventually came to date this incident to sometime between August 16 and September 12. See Roberta Ulrich, "Indictment of Sheela, Onang applauded," *The Oregonian*, March 20, 1985, p. E6.

202 Roberta Ulrich, "Indictment of Sheela, Onang applauded," *The Oregonian*, March 30, 1985, p. E6.

203 David Berry Knapp interrogation, transcribed November 13, 1985, FBI, AG files. One Rajneeshee saw Puja stop at the Zorba the Buddha restaurant operated by the commune at Rajneesh (formerly Antelope) and change into a disguise during the time of the outbreaks in The Dalles. See Ava Kay Avalos interrogation, transcribed October 22, 1985, AG files.

204 David Berry Knapp interrogation, transcribed November 13, 1985, FBI, AG files.

205 Ava Kay Avalos interrogation, transcribed October 22, 1985, AG files.

206 Ava believed that another Rajneeshee, named Yogini, took part. Specifically, she recalled that Yogini may have placed some salmonella at the "Tapadaro," presumably a reference to the Tapadera Inn and Restaurant Lounge. Ava Kay Avalos interrogation, transcribed October 22, 1985, AG files. The Tapadera was not mentioned in press accounts as one of the restaurants affected by the contamination.

207 David Berry Knapp interrogation, transcribed November 15, 1985, Federal Bureau of Investigation, AG files.

208 David Berry Knapp interrogation, transcribed November 15, 1985, Federal Bureau of Investigation, AG files, and Ava Kay Avalos interrogation, transcribed October 22, 1985, AG files.

It is not altogether clear what was put into the water tank. KD believed that it was salmonella. On the other hand, Ava believed that it might be a mixture of raw sewage taken from Rajneeshpuram and dead rodents. According to her recollections, Puja contacted the woman who was Resource Manager at Rajneeshpuram to obtain raw sewage. She also recalls that there were many empty cages at the Puja's laboratory and thought that Puja might have put dead rats in with the sewage.[210]

Despite the success of the restaurant contamination, no follow-on attacks were made. The Rajneeshee abandoned their efforts to take over Wasco County by early October, when the publicity and legal pressure made it evident that their plot would fail.

***Case 1981-02: "Dark Harvest," October 1981***

On October 10, 1981, a package of soil supposedly removed from Gruinard Island was discovered on the grounds of the Chemical Defence Establishment located at Porton Down, Wiltshire, England. Tests of an anthrax bomb were conducted at Gruinard Island in the Hebrides during 1941, and heavily contaminated soil on the island. According to a press account, the soil was found in a paper package placed inside a bucket. Because the bucket was located on the border of the Porton Down complex, alongside a railway line, police speculated that the soil might have been thrown from a train.[211]

An anonymous statement given to the press indicated that a group calling itself "Dark Harvest" orchestrated the incident. According to the group, they were returning the "seeds of death" to their source. The group claimed that microbiologists from two universities landed on Gruinard Island, and with the assistance of locals had removed 300 pounds of contaminated soil. The group complained that Gruinard Island would remain uninhabitable for 200 to 1,000 years. The statement called for a survey of the island to locate the anthrax-contaminated soil and proposed burying the soil under several feet of concrete. The group threatened to place additional packages at "appropriate places" during the next year.[212]

Subsequent tests indicated that the soil contained anthrax in low concentrations (about 10 organisms per gram of soil). The soil was consistent with other samples taken from Gruinard Island.[213]

A second package was deposited at the site of a Conservative Party meeting on October 14, 1981. In this instance, police received an anonymous tip about the presence of a metal box containing the soil, which was located on the roof of the meeting site. Subsequent analysis indicated that the soil did not contain anthrax.[214]

The Ecology Party condemned the activities of "Dark Harvest". According to the party's general secretary, "Although we agree with the object of the group, which is to bring public attention to the fact that these experiments in germ and chemical warfare leave a deadly legacy for future generations, we cannot condone their action."[215]

The British government subsequently agreed to decontaminate Gruinard Island, although it is not known if the decision to eliminate the contamination resulted from the publicity engendered by "Dark Harvest".

***Case 1978-04: Bulgarian Secret Police (Georgi Markov), September 1978***

The death of the Bulgarian dissident Georgi Markov is one of the most infamous incidents of the Cold War. At the time of his death, Markov was an announcer for Radio Free Europe (RFE), working out of London. He had been a prominent writer in Bulgaria before his 1969 defection. In 1971, he moved to England, where he worked as a commentator first for the BBC's Bulgarian service and then for RFE.[216]

Markov's wife gave the following account of the attack during the inquest.

---

[209] David Berry Knapp interrogation, transcribed November 15, 1985, Federal Bureau of Investigation, AG files. Law enforcement officials confirmed that the metal screens were ripped open on one of the water tanks when they examined it in 1985. Interview, Robert Hamilton, April, 1997.

[210] Ava Kay Avalos interrogation, transcribed October 22, 1985, AG files.

[211] "Anthrax soil claim doubted," *Times* (London), October 13, 1981, p. 2.

[212] David Nicholson-Lord, "Anthrax protest 'puts whole country at risk'," *Times* (London), October 12, 1981, p. 26.

[213] Henry Stanhope, "Anthrax spores found in protest soil sample," *Times* (London), October 14, 1981, p. 2.

[214] David Nicholson-Lord, "Anthrax soil alert near Tory conference," *Times* (London), October 15, 1981, p. 2, and Tony Samstag, "Blackpool 'anthrax' cleared," *Times* (London), October 27, 1981, p. 3.

[215] "Ecologists condemn soil dumpers," *Times* (London), October 16, 1981, p. 6.

[216] Markov's biography appears in his obituary. See "Mr Georgi Markov," *Times* (London), September 16, 1978, p. 14.

> He told me that while waiting for a bus on the south side of Waterloo Bridge he had felt a jab in the back of his right thigh and, looking around, saw a man drop an umbrella. The man said he was sorry and Georgi said that he got the impression that he was trying to cover his face as he rushed off and hailed a taxi.
>
> Georgi told me he thought the man must have been a foreigner because the taxi driver seemed to have some difficulty in understanding him. He showed me some blood on his jeans and a mark like a puncture, about the size of the tip of a ball-point pen on the back of his right thigh.[217]

The next day, she took him to the hospital. Despite the medical care he received, Markov's condition grew progressively worse. He died four days after he was injured, on September 11, 1978.[218] Even before the cause of death was ascertained, Markov's friends suspected that the Bulgarians were involved.[219]

The autopsy located a tiny metallic sphere in the wound. Subsequent analysis found that it was only 1.52 mm in diameter and was 90 per cent platinum and 10 per cent iridium. There were two holes, each 0.35-mm in diameter, drilled all the way through the pellet. The volume of space in the holes was only 0.28 $mm^3$. Given the small quantity of material involved, and Markov's symptoms, British experts were confident that the poison used was ricin.[220]

Revelations continue to emerge about the case, from both Bulgarian and former Soviet sources. Unfortunately, most of the Bulgarian documents relating to the case were destroyed, and it is unlikely that we will ever know the complete story of what happened to Georgi Markov.

Oleg Kalugin, a retired KGB official who was involved in the decision to provide the Bulgarians with the ricin weapon, provided an extended account of the episode from a Soviet perspective.[221] According to Kalugin, the Bulgarians approached the Soviets in early 1978 to obtain assistance in killing Markov. There was some opposition to providing that support. Eventually, it was given with the provision that "there is to be no direct participation on our part." The Soviets proposed three alternative methods for murdering Markov: a jelly-like material containing a poison that would penetrate the skin, poisoning food, and a poison pellet. Kalugin does not mention what poisons were associated with the different methods.

Kalugin claims that several unsuccessful attempts preceded the September assassination. First, the Bulgarians wanted to use the poison jelly, thought about putting it on the door handle of Markov's car. This idea was abandoned when it was realized that someone else might encounter the poison jelly, and thus warn Markov about the plot to kill him. The second scheme emerged when the Bulgarians learned that Markov was visiting an Italian beach resort. The Bulgarians thought that it might be possible for someone to rub the poison jelly on Markov, but the beach was so deserted that their agent had no opportunity to unobtrusively encounter Markov. Finally, the Bulgarians decided to use a food poison, and plotted to use it during a trip that Markov made to West Germany. This attempt also failed.

It was only after the failure of these earlier efforts that the Bulgarians turned to the ricin pellets. Kalugin indicates that when the Bulgarians acquired the pellet weapon, they tested it on a political prisoner. The prisoner survived the attack with no ill effects, apparently because the pellet did not release the ricin. This forced the KGB to make modifications to the weapon so that it would work.

Oleg Gordievsky, a defector from the KGB, provides another account of the Markov murder. First, he claims that the Bulgarians requested assistance in eliminating defectors, not just in killing Markov. Second, he appears to provide a somewhat different version of the unsuccessful attempts on Markov's life. (He indicates that the first victim was "a Bulgarian émigré living in England." It appears from the context that this is meant to apply to Markov, but that is not clear.) According to Gordievsky's account, "While he was on a holiday on the Continent, the DS smeared surfaces in the room where he was staying with a poison that, once absorbed through the skin, would, according to the KGB laboratory, prove fatal and leave no trace. Though the target became seriously ill, however, he survived."[222]

---

[217] Guy Rais, "Markov poison 'stronger than cobra venom'," *Daily Telegraph* (London), p January 3, 1979, p. 1.

[218] Bernard Knight, "Ricin--a potent homicidal poison," *British Medical Journal*, February 3, 1979, p. 350. This account mistakenly claims that Markov died three days after the attack.

[219] Stewart Tendler, "Police inquiry into possible killing of defector in London," *Times* (London), September 12, 1978, p. 4.

[220] Bernard Knight, "Ricin--a potent homicidal poison," *British Medical Journal*, February 3, 1979, pp. 350-351.

[221] Oleg Kalugin, *The First Directorate* (New York: St. Martin's Press, 1994), pp. 178-186.

[222] Christopher Andrew and Oleg Gordievsky, *KGB: The Inside Story of its Foreign Operations from Lenin to Gorbachev* (New York: HarperCollins, 1990), p. 644-645.

Press reports suggest that Bulgarian officials told British police in 1993 that Francesco Guilino, a Danish citizen of Italian extraction, killed Markov. Guilino apparently was warned that he was going to be arrested, and he fled Denmark.[223]

As of 1996, police officials in both Bulgaria and Britain continue to investigate the case. Given the destruction of documents in Bulgaria, however, it is believed that access to KGB material is essential to finally resolving the case.[224]

***Case 1978-03: Bulgarian Secret Police (Vladimir Kostov), August 1978***

On August 26, 1978, the Bulgarian secret police attempted to assassinate Vladimir Kostov, a defector who had served as a Bulgarian news correspondent in France until 1977. He also was a major in the DS (*Darjavna Sigurnost*), Bulgaria's equivalent of the KGB. After Kostov's defection, he broadcast reports beamed to Bulgaria for Deutsche Welle, the West German radio service, and for the BBC's Bulgarian service.[225]

According to Kostov's account of the incident, he was attacked at the Arc de Triomphe Metro station. "I felt a sharp pain in my back and heard a crack like a pistol. The wound started to hurt, and we stopped so my wife could examine my back. My jacket and shirt had been pierced and there was a mark like a bee sting, surrounded by blood." Kostov suffered from a high fever, but never lost consciousness.[226]

Hearing about the death of Georgi Markov, Kostov got in touch with British authorities and had an x-ray that identified a small metal object in his back.[227] The pellet that was subsequently removed from Kostov was identical to the one that killed Markov.[228] Subsequent tests apparently identified the presence of ricin antibodies, which are formed by the body's immune system to counter ricin toxin.[229]

According to Douglass and Livingstone, the pellet "lodged in the subcutaneous fat layer and was surgically removed in time to save his life." They add, "the heat in the fat layer was insufficient to melt the wax before the surgeons were able to remove the pellet."[230] The British doctors who investigated the Georgi Markov case expressed a different view in 1980. Dr. David Gall, a Research Medical Officer at Britain's Chemical Defense Establishment at Porton Down, performed the toxicological studies associated with the investigation. He found that the pellets penetrated about the same distance in both the Markov and Kostov cases, about a half-inch. Gall also noted that these were the first cases ever identified in which ricin was injected. In previous cases, the ricin was ingested. Dr. Rufus Crompton, who performed the autopsy on Markov, provided the following explanation for Kostov's survival:

> I do not think we really have any idea, except that there is a much bandied about phrase these days in toxicology: called the 'LD50', which is a dose that will kill 50 per cent of the population. I can only assume that they were working very closely on that.[231]

***Case 1977-02M: Arnfinn Nesset: May 1977***

Arnfinn Nesset, who ran a nursing home for elderly people in Norway, was convicted in March 1983 of murdering 22 of his patients. He injected them with curacit, which is derived from curare. Some aborigines

---

223 *Agence France Presse*, January 29, 1997.

224 Eve-Ann Prentice, "Moscow 'broke Markov promise'," *Times* (London), March 31, 1994, p. 14, and Roger Boyes, "Bulgarian leader pledges inquiry into Markov case," *Times* (London), November 25, 1996, p. 17.

225 Vladimir Kostov, *The Bulgarian Umbrella: The Soviet Direction and Operations of the Bulgarian Secret Service in Europe* (New York: St. Martin's Press, 1988), and *Times* (London), September 15, 1978, p. 4.

226 *Times* (London), September 15, 1978, p. 4.

227 *Times* (London), September 20, 1978, p. 6.

228 Stewart Tendler, "Bulgarian death case police sent to Paris," *Times* (London), September 27, 1978, p. 1, and Guy Rais, "Markov poison 'stronger than cobra venom'," *Daily Telegraph* (London), p January 3, 1979, p. 1.

229 According to the testimony given by FBI supervisory special agent Drew Campbell Richardson, ricin was identified in a tissue sample from one of the two Bulgarians attacked at the time. He was unable to recall from which of the men the positive sample came. See Richardson's testimony at Dr. Debora Green's preliminary hearing, p. 417, State of Kansas vs. Debora Green – 95CR5387.

230 Douglass and Livingstone, *America the Vulnerable*, p. 84.

231 Dr. Rufus Crompton and Dr. David Gall, "Georgi Markov—Death in a Pellet," *Medic-Legal Journal*, Volume 48 (1980), pp. 51-62.

in South America smear curare on the tips of arrows. The curare paralyzes the victim's respiratory system and cases suffocation.[232]

***Case 1970-01: Eric Kranz, February 1970***

According to press reports, in February 1970 Eric Kranz, a postgraduate student in parasitology at MacDonald College, a small agricultural institute affiliated with McGill University and located near Montreal, Canada, contaminated food eaten by four of his roommates. Kranz was not getting along with his roommates, who asked him to leave the house they shared "because he wasn't paying his share of the rent." [233]

Some days after Kranz finally left the house, four of his five former roommates became seriously ill. According to the *New England Journal of Medicine*, the victims became sick from 10 to 14 days after eating the contaminated food, two of them suffering from acute respiratory failure.[234] Initially, the illness mystified the attended physicians, who later told a reporter that the illness was life threatening. Examination of the victim's sputum, however, revealed the presence of large numbers of worms, which a professor of parasitology at MacDonald College identified as *Ascaris suum,* a parasite found in pigs similar to one (*Ascaris lumbricoides*) that infects people. According to the attending physician, the victims could have died from the disease. [235] They were not released from the hospital until March 5. Following discovery of the parasites, an arrest warrant was issued for Kranz charging him with attempted murder. He surrendered to police on March 10, and was tried on the charges on March 18.[236]

***Case 1964-01: Dr. Mitsuru Suzuki, December 1964-March 1966***

On April 7, 1966, the Japanese police arrested Dr. Mitsuru Suzuki, a physician with training in bacteriology, for infecting four of his colleagues with a sponge cake contaminated with dysentery.[237] Subsequent investigations linked Suzuki to a series of typhoid and dysentery outbreaks between December 1964 and March 1966. Suzuki confessed to the crimes one week after his arrest.[238] Japanese police estimated that 200 people were affected, including four deaths. There is reason to suspect that they exaggerated the number of people who Suzuki infected.[239] A tally of the specific incidents described below suggests that no more than 120 people were affected, including four fatalities.

On December 26, 1964, Suzuki purchased a sponge cake from a store near the Chiba University Hospital. He allegedly laced the cake with dysentery and offered it to four of his colleagues at the hospital that night. All four became ill and needed hospitalization. This came to be described by police as the "sponge cake incident."[240]

The "Calpis case" occurred on August 6, 1965. At the time, Suzuki was working part time at the clinic of the Kawasaki Steel Corporation's Chiba City factory. Suzuki apparently laced bottles of a milk-based Japanese soft drink called "Calpis" with typhoid, and gave the contaminated drinks to 16 of his colleague's at the infirmary. All became sick, although it is unclear if the nature of the illness was diagnosed at the time. Suzuki admitted to police, before his confession, that he was the person who made anonymous phone calls ten days later to three hospitals in Chiba City warning the hospitals to report the typhoid outbreak "because they

---

[232] "Nursing home chief killed 22 patients," *Times* (London), March 12, 1983, p. 5, and Colin Wilson and Donald Seaman, *The Encyclopedia of Modern Murder 1962–1982* (New York: G.P. Putnam's Sons, 1985), pp. 172-173.

[233] "Four treated for parasitic worm as trail of student leads to U.S.," *Globe and Mail* (Toronto), February 27, 1970, p. 1, and Eddie Collister, "Student hunted as would-be 'parasite killer'," *The Gazette* (Montreal), February 26, 1970, p. 2.

[234] James A. Phills, A. John Harrold, Gabriel V. Whiteman, and Lewis Perelmutter, "Pulmonary Infiltrates, Asthma and Eosinophilia due to *Ascaris Suum* Infestation in Man," *New England Journal of Medicine,* May 4, 1972, pp. 965-970, provides a complete clinical review of the case. For additional details on Ascaris, see Abram S. Benenson, editor, *Control of Communicable Diseases Manual*, Sixteenth edition (Washington, DC: American Public Health Association, 1995), pp. 55-57.

[235] Eddie Collister, "Student hunted as would-be 'parasite killer'," *Gazette* (Montreal), February 26, 1970, pp. 1, 2.

[236] Leon Levinson, "Kranz sent to trial in 'bug' murder try," *Gazette* (Montreal), March 19, 1970, p. 3.

[237] "Deliberate spreading of typhoid in Japan," *Science Journal*, Vol. 2 (1966), pp. 2.11-2.76. Dr. Shellie A. Kolavic brought this case and this particular reference to my attention. See also "Doctor accused of spreading germs," *Times* (London), April 30, 1966, p. 8.

[238] "Suzuki Confesses Spreading Typhoid," *Japan Times,* April 14, 1966, pp. 1, 3.

[239] The estimate of 200 infected including four fatalities first appears on April 15, a day after Suzuki's confession was reported. Even after additional cases were reported, the number of victims remained constant, suggesting that 200 was only an estimate.

[240] "Dr. Suzuki Indicted by Prosecutors," *Japan Times*, April 30, 1966, p. 3. An earlier account provides slightly different details. It asserts that Suzuki bought the cake on December 20 "last year," contaminated at 9 p.m. the same night, and then offered it to his colleagues eight days later. See "Dr. Suzuki Says Revenge Led Him to Spread Germs," *Japan Times,* April 16, 1966, p. 4.

are acute and infectious typhoid cases." Police believe that he made the telephone calls to find out the extent of the outbreak.[241]

Suzuki also confessed to injecting dysentery into four of the victims of the "Calpis" contamination under the guise of giving them something "good for curing this kind of disease."[242] Prosecutors charged that he used a duodenal probe to force one of his patients at the Kawasaki Steel plant clinic to drink dysentery-contaminated water.[243]

On September 4, 1965, Suzuki gave a typhoid-contaminated cake to a member of the staff of the First Internal Medicine Department at the Chiba University Hospital. The man shared the cake with two members of his family, and all three became sick with typhoid. That same day, ten nurses and doctors became ill after eating bananas that Suzuki contaminated with typhoid.[244]

On September 5, 1965, Suzuki purchased ten bananas from a shop by the hospital. He took the bananas to his laboratory. He put typhoid on the tip of a platinum probe normally used to clean syringes and jabbed the instrument several times into each of six bananas. Suzuki offered the bananas to the five nurses working on the night shift. All the nurses were infected with typhoid, as were two people related to one of the nurses.[245]

Immediately after Suzuki visited his uncle's family in Gotemba, Shizouka Prefecture, on September 9, 1965, eight of the nine members of his uncle's family came down with typhoid.[246] Suzuki apparently gave them contaminated bananas.[247]

In addition, 13 patients at the Chiba University Hospital became ill from typhoid after eating bananas given them by Suzuki in September.[248] This came to be known as the "banana incident."[249]

On December 27, 1965, he gave typhoid-contaminated bananas to a nurse at the Mishima Hospital in Shizuoka Prefecture. The nurse gave one of the bananas to the hospital's deputy director, Dr. Masahisa Matsuda, who died from typhoid in January 1966.[250]

Suzuki also reportedly confessed that he gave medicines laced with typhoid to patients at the Mishima Hospital, Shizuoka Prefecture. He apparently did this over a several month period starting in December 1965. Reportedly, 42 patients became ill, and three died after taking contaminated medicines.[251]

On January 1, 1966, Lt. Col. Toshikazu Yokoto became ill with typhoid after eating clams given him by Suzuki. Police suspected that Suzuki might have infected the shellfish with typhoid.[252]

On February 28, 1966, Suzuki was accused of putting *S. typhi* organisms into a barium solution given to two outpatient clinics at the Mishima Social Insurance Hospital in Shizuoka. Investigators referred to this as the "barium incident." That same day, Suzuki allegedly used a typhoid-contaminated tongue depressor on a patient.[253]

---

241 "Dr. Suzuki Stays Silent At 2nd Session of Trial," *Japan Times*, August 9, 1966, p. 3. Earlier accounts gave fewer victims. "Suzuki Admits Phoning Hospitals, Police Claim," *Japan Times,* April 12, 1966, p. 4, claimed 13 victims, while "Suzuki Admits Tainting Bananas With Typhoid," *Japan Times,* April 17, 1966, p. 2, says 15 people infected.

242 "Suzuki Admitbs Giving Four 'Dual Treatment'," *Japan Times,* April 20, 1966, p. 2.

243 "Dr. Suzuki Stays Silent At 2nd Session of Trial," *Japan Times*, August 9, 1966, p. 3.

244 "Suzuki Confesses To Another Case," *Japan Times,* April 27, 1966, p. 4.

245 "Suzuki Admits Tainting Bananas With Typhoid," *Japan Times,* April 17, 1966, p. 2, and "Dr. Suzuki facing 2nd Indictment," *Japan Times,* May 3, 1966, p. 3. These two accounts differ somewhat. The first claims only four bananas were infected, while the second says six.

246 "Suspect's Relative Attempts Suicide," *Japan Times*, April 24, 1966, p. 2.

247 "Suzuki Says He Fed Kin With Germs," *Japan Times,* April 21, 1966, p. 3. This story also states that Suzuki gave contaminated bananas to relatives "on several occasions from September last year to January this year," but provides no details of the other incidents.

248 "Police Continuing Suzuki Case Probe," *Japan Times,* April 15, 1966, p. 3.

249 "Suzuki Says He Fed Kin With Germs," *Japan Times,* April 21, 1966, p. 3.

250 "Suzuki May Face Murder Charge," *Japan Times,* May 12, 1966, p. 2.

251 "Police Continuing Suzuki Case Probe," *Japan Times,* April 15, 1966, p. 3. None of the patients who died is named. One is described in this story as a "71-year-old Mishima man," but nothing is said regarding the other two. Another account suggests that the Mishima hospital outbreaks occurred in December and March. See "Suzuki Confesses Spreading Typhoid," *Japan Times,* April 14, 1966, p. 3. This report also places the total number affected at the hospital at 44, including both patients and staff.

252 "Police Arrest Doctor For Germ Spreading," *Japan Times,* April 8, 1966, p. 3, and "Police Continue Quizzing Doctor in Typhoid Case," *Japan Times,* April 9, 1966, p. 3.

253 "Dr. Suzuki Again Refuses To Speak at Arraignment," *Japan Times*, September 27, 1966, p. 3.

On March 15, 1966, three nurses at the hospital became sick after eating mandarin oranges left in the nurses' dressing room. The nurses proved to be carrying the same D2 strain that appeared in other cases infected by Suzuki, and Japanese police believed that he was responsible for that incident as well.[254] Also in March 1966, his brother and sister-in-law, who lived in Koyama, came down with typhoid, as did five of his parent's friends in Koyama.[255]

Originally, Suzuki told police that he gave the dysentery-contaminated cake to his colleagues as an experiment to test a new theory he had developed. He eventually changed his story and said that revenge was what led him to infect people. Suzuki reportedly told the police, "It is true I wanted to see how a mass outbreak of disease would develop from the planted bacilli, but I spread the germs out of my deep antagonism to the seniority system which prevails in [Japanese] medical circles."[256] He added, "I was unpaid and my status was unstable … I thought I was being discriminated against as I am not a graduate of Chiba University."[257] Suzuki also said that he infected his relatives because they refused to provide him with financial support that he needed to conduct research.[258] Prosecutors claimed that Suzuki created the typhoid cases to enable him to complete his dissertation thesis, which involved studies of *S. typhi* organisms recovered from numerous patients.[259]

Subsequent investigations revealed that the hospital discovered Suzuki's activities more than a year before the arrest, but the discovery was suppressed to avoid embarrassment to the university. Only after the Ministry of Health and Welfare received an anonymous tip did an official investigation start.[260]

Suzuki apparently obtained his cultures from several sources. He cultured typhoid taken from a Kawasaki Steel Corporation worker whom he treated on May 8, 1965.[261] In addition, Suzuki told police that he obtained typhoid cultures by stealing them from Japan's National Institute of Health. He worked at the institute in September 1965 as a trainee. According to experts who examined his laboratory, several of the test tubes in his possession clearly came from the National Institute of Health. Forty of the 171 test tubes in his laboratory contained the D2 strain of typhoid.[262] Press accounts do not indicate where he obtained the dysentery organism.

The Chiba District Public Prosecutor's Office ultimately charged Suzuki with 13 separate cases involving 66 infected people. He was charged with no deaths.[263]

***Case 1952-02: Mau Mau, 1952***

British authorities discovered in late 1952 that the Mau Mau, operating in what is now Kenya, poisoned 33 steers at a mission station located in the tribal areas that were reserved for the Kikuyu. British authorities believed that a toxic plant, *Synadenium grantii* Hook, also known as African milk bush, was used in the attack.[264]

The Mau Mau apparently inserted the latex of the plant into incisions cut into the skin of the animals. Eight of the animals died, six of them within five days. It was impossible to determine the cause of the problem, and so the Veterinary Research Laboratory in Kabete, just outside Nairobi, was asked to investigate.

---

[254] "Dr. Suzuki Says Revenge Led Him to Spread Germs," *Japan Times*, April 16, 1966, p. 4.

[255] "Deliberate spreading of typhoid in Japan," *Science Journal*, Vol. 2 (1966), pp. 2.11-2.76. A slightly different account given just after Suzuki made his original confession suggests that police believed that he was responsible for typhoid outbreaks that involved "six members of his family in Oyama-cho, west of Mishima, three members of his brother's family in Odawara and eight relatives in Gotemba, Shizuoka prefecture. All were taken ill after eating fruit given them by Suzuki." See "Police Continuing Suzuki Case Probe," *Japan Times*, April 15, 1966, p. 3.

[256] "Dr. Suzuki Says Revenge Led Him to Spread Germs," *Japan Times*, April 16, 1966, p. 4.

[257] "Deliberate spreading of typhoid in Japan," *Science Journal*, Vol. 2 (1966), pp. 2.11-2.76.

[258] "Suzuki Says He Fed Kin With Germs," *Japan Times*, April 21, 1966, p. 3.

[259] "Dr. Suzuki Again Refuses To Speak at Arraignment," *Japan Times*, September 27, 1966, p. 3.

[260] "Police Continuing Suzuki Case Probe," *Japan Times*, April 15, 1966, p. 3, and "Police Continue Quizzing Doctor in Typhoid Case," *Japan Times*, April 9, 1966, p. 3.

[261] "Suzuki Admits Tainting Bananas With Typhoid," *Japan Times*, April 17, 1966, p. 2.

[262] "Dr. Suzuki Makes New Confession," *Japan Times*, April 28, 1966, p. 3.

[263] According to additional research conducted by Masaaki Sugishima, based on Japanese court documents.

[264] P.W. Thorold, "Suspected Malicious Poisoning," *Journal of the South African Veterinary Medical Association*, Volume 24 (December 1953), pp. 215-217. Thorold was an investigator working at the Veterinary Research Laboratory, which was under the supervision of the Director of Veterinary Services, Kenya Colony.

Identifying the cause of the incident proved difficult. Researchers ruled out a range of potential causes, including infectious disease.[265]

When other possible causes were ruled out, the investigators focused on poisoning as a cause. At first, they considered several common toxic plants, including the seeds of *Abrus precatorius* (also known as jequirity, they contain the toxin abrin), *Ricinis communis* (better known as the castor bean, which contain the ricin toxin), and *Jatropha curcas.*[266] Serologic tests, however, ruled out the involvement of any of these poisons. The investigators then considered African milk bush, which was a plant known to the Kikuyu. They gave subcutaneous injections of the plant material to guinea pigs, which developed symptoms similar to those of the cattle. Based on this research, they concluded that the Mau Mau used latex from either *S. grantii* or another plant in the same family.

In 1951, the Mau Mau, a nationalist liberation movement originating with the Kikuyu tribe, initiated attacks on the British in colonial Kenya. At first, the attacks consisted mainly of sabotage actions directed at British farmers. By October 1952, however, the violence had escalated and the British declared a state of emergency. The revolt was finally suppressed in 1956, by which time an estimated 15,000 people died, almost all people associated with the Mau Mau.[267]

The British believed that the cattle poisonings were one part of a concerted campaign aimed at livestock. In other instances, investigations demonstrated that the animals were killed using arsenic. At the time, arsenic was easily available, because it was then common to routinely dip cattle in arsenic to kill insects on the animals. According to a British investigator, in other suspicious cases it was impossible to discover the cause of death. Researchers apparently suspected that the Mau Mau might have killed the animals using plant-derived toxins.[268]

This episode is not mentioned in histories of the Mau Mau revolt, suggesting that such incidents were rare.[269] While poisoning apparently was uncommon, Mau Mau bands often killed or maimed cattle in their raids. It seems likely that the instances of poisoning were associated with the medicine men who accompanied Mau Mau guerrilla formations. Such men may have had access to traditional medicines and poisons.[270] The African milk bush was common in the area where the Kikuyu lived.[271]

---

[265] Thorold, "Suspected Malicious Poisoning," pp. 215-216. It appears that other accounts of this incident were based on Thorold's article. See Julia F. Morton, "Poisonous and Injurious Higher Plants and Fungi," p. 1504, in C.G. Tedeschi, William G. Eckert, and Luke G. Tedeschi, editors, *Forensic Medicine: A study in trauma and environment, Volume III: Environmental Hazards* (Philadelphia: W. B. Saunders, 1977). Bernard Verdcourt and E.C. Trump, *Common Poisonous Plants of East Africa* (St. James's Place, London: Collins, 1969), p. 62, gives the following account of this incident.

> During the Mau Mau uprising *Synadenium grantii* Hook. F. was suspected of being used maliciously in a case where thirty-three steers were poisoned and eight died. They developed oedematous swellings along the chest, belly and upper part of the limbs; these lesions were assumed to be due to stabbing with a sharp instrument, thus introducing the acute irritant.

Another account of this incident appears in John Mitchell Watt and Maria Gerdina Breyer-Brankwijk, *Medicinal and Poisonous Plants of Southern and Eastern Africa* (London: E. & S. Livingstone, 1962).

> In an outbreak of suspected malicious poisoning of bovines in Tanganyika, in which the affected animals developed large oedematous swellings between the brisket and the near fore leg, extending in some cases to the chest and abdomen, eight steers died, six within five days of the symptoms appearing. Post mortem the swellings showed a gelatinous oedema with numerous petechiae and ecchymoses and the tissues presented a slightly cooked appearance and were oily to the touch. *Synadenium grantii* came under suspicion. Experimentally a similar type of lesion was produced in the guinea-pig by the subcutaneous and intramuscular injection of 0.5 to 1 ml. of the latex, 40 per cent of the animals dying within forty-eight to seventy-two hours of the administration. The survivors developed necrosis and sloughing in the area of the injection.

[266] Descriptions can be found in Morton, "Poisonous and Injurious Higher Plants and Fungi," pp. 1497-8 (*Jatropha curcas* L.), pp. 1501-1503 (*Ricinus communis* L.), and pp. 1504-1508 (*Abrus precatorius* L.). See also Verdcourt, *Common Poisonous Plants of East Africa*, pp. 59-61 and pp. 79-80. British investigations into the mysterious death of Georgi Markov considered the toxin abrin before settling on ricin as the responsible poison.

[267] There appears to be no comprehensive account of the Mau Mau's activities. This discussion is based on Wunyabari O. Maloba, *Mau Mau and Kenya An Analysis of a Peasant Revolt* (Bloomington: Indiana University Press, 1993) and Robert B. Edgerton, *Mau Mau: An African Crucible* (New York: Free Press, 1989).

[268] Thorold, "Suspected Malicious Poisoning," p. 215.

[269] This observation is based on a quick scan of books written about the Mau Mau held by the National Defense University Library.

[270] On the important role of the traditional healers in Mau Mau military strategy and operations, see Maloba, *Mau Mau and Kenya*, pp. 125, 127.

[271 271] Thorold, "Suspected Malicious Poisoning," p. 216.

The Mau Mau were highly decentralized, especially in the early days of the revolt, so the poisonings may not have reflected general policy. According to one account, at least one Mau Mau group produced quantities of a poison for use against the British. Fear that the British might retaliate with chemical weapons led to a decision to refrain from using the poison.[272] There is at least one reported instance in which a Mau Mau fired a poisoned arrow at a policeman. The constable was hit, but the arrow failed to penetrate the skin.[273]

***Case 1939-01: Kikuko Hirose, 1939***

In April 1939, a Japanese physician, Kikuko Hirose, gave pastries contaminated with *Salmonella typhi* and *Salmonella paratyphi* (types A and B) to her former husband, Mikio Kato. Kato shared with food with his brother, Ritsuo, and sister, Fumi. Fumi in turn shared some of the pastries with nine of her colleagues at the Kawaike Elementary School. All twelve of the people who ate the confectionery became sick. Ritsuo died of his infections in May.[274]

Hirose and Kato were married in 1931, but lived separately while Kato conducted research at Kyoto Imperial University. She provided financial assistance. After Kato received his medical degree in 1936, and began working as vice president at the Maiko Hospital in Hyogo Prefecture, he rejected Hirose's request that they begin living together. Ultimately, in March 1938 the two were divorced. Hirose remained angry, however, and in April 1939 she acquired cultures from the Kimura Bacteriological Research Institute, located in Kobe. The method by which she obtained the organisms is not recorded in the available documents, but it appears she did so legitimately.

Authorities determined that Hirose was responsible for the infection through an epidemiological study of the outbreak. The source of the infection was traced to the pastries supplied by the store, which indicated that Hirose had ordered the pastries.

She was convicted of the crime, and sentenced to eight years. The final judgment against Hirose was handed down by the Supreme Court on June 27, 1940.

***Case 1936-01: Tei-Sabro Takahashi, 1936***

The Saitama Prefecture Police Department in Japan arrested Tei-Sabro Takahashi on 8 May 1937 on charges of using food contaminated with *Salmonella typhi* to infect 17 people, including three people who subsequently died. He was convicted on 4 July 1938 and given a death sentence.[275]

According to newspaper reports, Takahashi may have first tried to use S. typhi to inflict harm in March 1935, when he provided some confectioneries laced with the organism to another physician, Tokio Hojo. The physician did not eat the pastry, but someone else in his house allegedly did consume some and become extremely ill. Similarly, Takahashi apparently sent confectioneries to another doctor, Chiyo-Saburo Sato, in October 1936, but Sato did not touch it. It appears that Japanese prosecutors believed that the evidence supporting these allegations was insufficient, and he was never charged with these acts. Takahashi was charged in five other incidents, all involving food contaminated with *S. typhi*.

The first incident involved a competing physician, Kazukichi Tsukada. Takahashi was jealous of Tsukada, and apparently hoped to undermine his practice. On March 7, 1936, Takahashi purchased some cakes, which he proceeded to contaminate with *S. typhi*. That same day, he took the contaminated cakes to Tsukada's office, and gave them to a nurse as a gift to his rival's children. The four children ate the cake, and at least one was diagnosed with typhoid.

The second incident occurred in June 1936, and involved a competing physician, Tadanobu Ono. In order to undermine his rival's practice, Takahashi again contaminated some pastry with *S. typhi*. He brought the contaminated pastries to one of Ono's offices in early June 1936, and offered them to the staff working there. Three people were infected, and one died. In addition, a fourth person became ill with typhoid, probably from contact with one of the infected workers. He was never charged with the fourth victim.

The third incident involved his wife, Sekiko. Takahashi wanted to divorce his wife because she was unable to conceive, and he thought that it would be easier to accomplish this under Japanese law if she were disabled. To accomplish this he contaminated some pastries with *S. typhi*, and left them with her at a spa where

---

[272] Edgerton, *Mau Mau*, p. 130, citing W. Itote, *"Mau Mau" Gener*al (Nairobi: East African Publishing House, 1967), p. 108. Itote was a leading figure in the Mau Mau movement, who commanded 5,000 warriors using the name "General China."

[273] "Three Kikuyu Elders Missing: Murder Feared," *Times* (London), December 11, 1952, p. 6.

[274] This account is derived from an unpublished article by Masaaki Sugishima, Associate Professor at the Asahi University School of Law, supplemented by electronic communications. His account is based on Japanese court documents and press reports.

[275] This account is derived from two unpublished articles by Masaaki Sugishima, Associate Professor at the Asahi University School of Law, who based his account on official court documents and newspaper reports.

he sent her to recover her health before undergoing an operation to correct her inability to conceive. Sekiko ate the pastry, and became ill on October 23. Six days later she was admitted to the hospital. On November 10, Takahashi tried to murder her by using an injection of morphine hydrochloride. This effort failed, largely due to the skill of the hospital staff.

The fourth incident involved yet another physician, Masao Yanagida, who was a competitor and also Sekiko's physician. Takahashi apparently resented Yanagida's prosperity, and also was angry at Yanagida's success in saving Sekiko. On 22 November 1936, he asked a department store to deliver some pastries to Yanagida's house, after having contaminated them with *S. typhi*. Six members of the family became ill, including Yanagida's wife, four of his daughters, and one of his sons. The wife died from the infection on January 3, 1937. One of the daughters died on 4 February 1937, apparently of pneumonia after having recovered from the typhoid infection. It appears that the court considered him response for the second death, perhaps because the typhoid made the victim more susceptible to other diseases.

The final incident occurred on 23 November 1936, and involved several employees of the Do-Ai Hospital, located in Tokyo. Takahashi apparently hoped to infect one of the members of the staff who he disliked, Ei-ichiro Sato. At a party given in honor of one of the physicians at the hospital, Takahashi tried to give Sato some salmon eggs contaminated with *S. typhi*. Sato refused the gift, but three physicians from the hospital ate the eggs. All three became ill, and one died.

Dr. Yanagida was responsible for uncovering Takahashi's activities. Yanagida apparently looked into the foods eaten by his family, and discovered that everyone who became sick had eaten some of Takahashi's confectioneries. He took the remaining pastries to the Hygienic Laboratory operated by the Ministry of Interior, which determined that they were laced with *S. typhi*. The laboratory notified the local authorities. Apparently, the officials became convinced that intentional contamination was responsible for the presence of the *S. typhi*, after an investigation of the confectionery identified no likely source and uncovered no other typhoid cases that could be linked to the producer. This led the police to open an investigation, which began to focus on Takahashi. A local court judge found Takahashi guilty in all five incidents on 4 July 1938, and condemned him to death. The sentence was upheld by an appeals court the following year.

Takahashi reportedly told authorities that he thought his use of *S. typhi* would go unnoticed. He believed that it would be difficult to identify the source of the infection, given that *S. typhi* has a lengthy incubation period and people might forget what they ate at the time of infection. He also thought that other physicians might misdiagnose the disease. Finally, there was considerable typhoid in Japan at that time, so cases of infection would not be considered so unusual.

***Case 1933-01: Benoyendra Chandra Pandey, 1933***

On February 16, 1935, Benoyendra Chandra Pandey and Dr. Taranath Bhatacharya were sentenced to death by hanging for murdering 20-year old Amarendra Pandey, Benoyendra's half-brother.[276] According to the court, the two conspired to infect Amarendra with a lethal dose of the plague (*Yersinia pestis*) organism. The two brothers had feuded over the division of their father's estate.[277] After reviewing the case, an appellate judge asserted that this case was "probably unique in the annals of crime."[278]

Benoyendra, eleven years older than Amarendra, was an unsavory spendthrift who consorted with people of questionable character. The feud appears to have begun once Amarendra became eighteen and began demanding his share of the estate.[279] On November 19, 1933, Amarendra arrived in Calcutta, having been lured there by a telegram written by Benoyendra but falsely sent in the name of their aunt. The two half-brothers again fruitlessly discussed dividing the estate. Finally, on the 26th, Amarendra decided to leave Calcutta. Uncharacteristically, Benoyendra went to the train station to say good-bye. While Amarendra was walking to the train platform, he was bumped by "a black man in khaddar [cotton homespun clothing] who was not a gentleman." At the time, Amarendra felt a prick in his arm, and told his companions, "Someone has pricked me." Although some of Amarendra's relatives were suspicious, and begged him to stay in Calcutta and visit a doctor, Amarendra decided to continue with his trip.

---

[276] The best single source for this case is Dr. D.P. Lambert, "The Pakur Murder," *Medico-legal and Criminological Review*, vol. 5, July 1937, pp. 297-302. Shellie A. Kolavic brought this case to my attention.

[277] According to "Two Indians Sentenced to Death," *Times* (London), February 18, 1935, p. 11. The estate was worth £2,500 per year. In addition, Amarendra was heir to an estate of equivalent value (presumably that of his aunt), but Benoyendra stood to inherit in the event of Amarendra's death.

[278] "Death sentences not confirmed," *Star of India* (Calcutta), January 10, 1936, p. 1.

[279] S.J., "Homicide By Means of Plague Bacilli," *Bulletin of the New York Academy of Medicine*, September 1967, pp. 850-851, Dr. D.P. Lambert, "The Pakur Murder," *Medico-legal and Criminological Review*, vol. 5, July 1937, pp. 297-302, and Hokay El Kay, "Murder by Black Death," n.d. Shellie A. Kolavic provided copies of this material.

Amarendra returned to Calcutta on November 29 to consult with a physician, who noted that the pricked spot looked "something like the mark of a hypodermic needle." The next day, Amarendra became feverish, felt pain in his armpit, and a small weal developed at the site of the prick. A blood sample was taken for testing at that point and sent to the Bacteriology Department of the School of Tropical Medicine. On December 1, Amarendra became sicker, and by December 3, he lost consciousness. Amarendra died on the morning of December 4, just over seven days after he had been pricked. The body was cremated.

A few days after the death, the laboratory identified the presence of *Y. pestis* in the blood sample, and notified the family and the Calcutta Public Health Department. The family attorney made investigations, and discovered that Benoyendra had developed a friendship with Dr. Taranath, a physician with training in bacteriology. The lawyer also found out about the efforts to acquire plague organisms from the Haffkine Institute. Accordingly, the police were notified, a criminal investigation was initiated, and Benoyendra was arrested.

The police discovered that the two conspirators made several attempts to acquire plague cultures. At the time, the only place that kept cultures of *Y. pestis* was the Haffkine Institute, located in Bombay. Dr. Taranath first tried to obtain plague on May 12, 1932. It was not until July 7, 1933, after five previous failures, that Dr. Taranath finally had a viable culture of plague organisms. Dr. Taranath spent the next five days testing the virulence of the culture by infecting white rats.

The defendants appealed their conviction on February 25, 1935 to the Criminal Appellate Side of the High Court. On January 9, 1936, Their Lordships dismissed the appeal, but set aside the death penalty and instead sentenced the defendants to transportation for life. The justices ruled that the Crown had proved beyond a reasonable doubt that the victim was murdered by plague organisms injected into his arm, and that the two defendants were connected to the crime.[280]

The justices gave three reasons for their decision to overturn the death sentence. First, the length of time required to handle the appeal was considered unreasonable, since all of ten months passed between the time of their conviction and the date of the appellate court's ruling. Second, the justices noted that the evidence was entirely circumstantial. Finally, the justices hoped that the defendants might be convinced to give evidence enabling the authorities to apprehend the individuals who actually committed the crime.[281]

***Case 1932-01: Japan, 1932***

According to a 1944 document prepared by Prince Mikasa, younger brother to Japanese Emperor Hirohito, the Japanese military attempted to poison members of the Lytton Commission. The League of Nation's General Assembly established the Lytton Commission in December 1931 to investigate Japan's conquest of Manchuria. Prince Mikasa claimed that a "senior Japanese medical officer in Manchuria" told him that when the commissioners visited Manchuria they were served fruit "laced" with cholera. For unknown reasons none of the commissioners became sick.[282] Press reports indicate that the commission spent about six weeks in Manchuria from April 22 through June 5, 1932.[283]

***Case 1916-01: Arthur Warren Waite, March 1916***

The *New York Times* called Arthur Warren Waite, a dentist, "one of the most remarkable individuals in criminal history."[284] He was convicted on May 27, 1916 of poisoning his wife's parents. He infected both with potentially lethal pathogens, although it appears that he ultimately relied on other means to kill the two. The story received extensive front page coverage in the New York newspapers at the time.

On March 22, 1916, the New York City District Attorney's office was notified that the March 12 death of John E. Peck, a wealthy businessman, was due to arsenic poisoning. Because Peck died in New York City, the case was under the jurisdiction of New York City officials. After the body by returned to Peck's home in Grand Rapids, the authorities in Michigan performed an autopsy based on a mysterious telegram claiming that Peck's death was suspicious. The autopsy identified the presence of a lethal dose of arsenic, which led the

---

[280] "Death sentences not confirmed," *Star of India* (Calcutta), January 10, 1936, p. 1.

[281] "Death sentences not confirmed," *Star of India* (Calcutta), January 10, 1936, p. 1.

[282] Gwen Robinson, "Hirohito's brother tells of war crimes by army," *Times* (London), July 7, 1994, p. 15.

[283] *Times* (London), April 23, 1932, p. 11, reports the arrival of the commission in Mukden, while "Lytton Commission in Peking," *Times* (London), June 6, 1932, p. 11, reports its return to Beijing.

[284] "Dr. Waite, Calm, Goes to his Death," *New York Times*, May 25, 1917, pp. 1, 20. I am indebted to Jason Pate, Center for Nonproliferation Studies, Monterey Institute for International Studies, for bringing this case to my attention.

Michigan authorities to alert officials in New York City. A team was sent to Grand Rapids, including the Coroner's Physician, who performed a second autopsy and confirmed the results of the first.[285]

Peck died while staying at the 435 Riverside Drive apartment of his daughter and son-in-law following the death of his wife. He was in good health, until he became ill on the night of March 11, 1916. He died at 3 a.m. the next morning.

According to Schindler, "Waite always said 'he' or 'the other fellow' in talking about the murders of Mrs. Peck and Mr. Peck." Schindler reported that Waite made the following statement while reviewing his confession.

> The other fellow killed Mr. Peck, but I don't believe he really was responsible for the death of Mrs. Peck, although he tried to kill her. He gave her germs, first one kind and then another, but they didn't seem to have much effect. She was already sick, but the germs didn't seem to make her any sicker. Finally he got impatient, and one night he gave a lot of cocaine. She did soon after that, but I believe she died from her disease, and not from the germs or cocaine which he gave her.[286]

Investigators subsequently discovered that Waite made serious efforts to learn about pathogens. He began his studies in September 1915 under the tutelage of a Dr. Louis Heitzman, a pathologist at the Flower Hospital in New York City. Subsequently, he worked with Dr, P. L. De Nyse, an associate pathologist at the hospital. Dr. De Nyse turned over "a large quantity of virulent disease germs" that Waite had left at the Flower Hospital to the District Attorney's office. According to the District Attorney's office, Dr. De Nyse reported that Waite was always trying to obtain the most virulent organisms possible. After complaining that the organisms available to him were not "live enough," Dr. De Nyse directed Waite to obtain more virulent organisms from a commercial suppler, the Parke Davis & Company, then a Detroit corporation.[287]

Sometime in November, Waite also began studying under Dr. David Nye Barrowes, a physician on the staff of Cornell Medical School. Barrowes told investigators that Waite was especially interested in the symptoms produced by the organisms responsible for typhoid. To learn more about the disease, Waite infected himself and experienced a mild case.[288]

The private detectives hired by the family discovered further evidence of Waite's interest in biological agents in his apartment. Hidden in a closet and elsewhere, they found about 180 glass slides containing samples of different microorganisms. There were slides labeled tetanus (lockjaw), Asiatic cholera, pneumonia, tuberculosis, typhoid, typhus, and anthrax. In addition, the detectives apparently found approximately 100 test tubes. There is no indication of what was in the test tubes.[289]

During his trial, Waite admitted that he murdered both his in-laws, and that he tried to murder his father-in-law's sister. He also provided some details of his murder plots. According to his courtroom testimony, his murder attempts involved pathogens, arsenic, chloroform, powdered glass, chlorine gas, burned flypaper, colomel, and varinol. According to his testimony, he infected his in-laws with several pathogens, including typhoid, influenza, diphtheria, pneumonia, tuberculosis, streptococcus, "and some others."[290]

He had considerable success against his mother-in-law. She came to New York to stay with Waite and his wife. The first time she ate at their house, he put pathogens into her food. She was dead within a week. It is unclear which pathogen he used or in what quantities. He initially tried to repeat this process with his father-in-law, because the pathogens left no implicating evidence. Unfortunately for Waite, his father-in-law failed to become sick. Waite then tried an experiment. Press reports about the fighting in France indicated that soldiers exposed to chlorine gas became more susceptible to pathogens. To test this, he opened bottles of chlorine gas in his father-in-law's bedroom, and then put dosed his food with pathogens in the next day. For several weeks, he contaminated his father-in-law's food with a test tube of pathogens daily. Waite finally gave up on the pathogens, and purchased a large quantity of arsenic, which he put into Mr. Peck's food.[291]

Waite also admitted that he made several attempts before his marriage to murder his future father-in-law's sister. He expected that his wife would inherit substantial amounts of money. On one occasion, he tried to extract the arsenic from flypaper by burning the paper and collecting the residue. The substance had no effect. He also tried other ways to kill her. He put powered glass in her food, arsenic, and experimented with

---

[285] "Arsenic in Body of John E. Peck, Autopsy Shows," *New York Times*, March 23, 1916, p. 1.

[286] "Waite in New Story Names Another Aid," *New York Times*, March 30, 1916, p. 8.

[287] "New Waite Letter Uses Kane's Name," *New York Times*, April 7, 1916, p. 7.

[288] "Waite Once Victim of His Germ Study," *New York Times*, April 8, 1916, p. 22.

[289] "Dig Up the Money Waite Gave Kane," *New York Times*, April 1, 1916, p. 20.

[290] "Murdered Two, Tried for a Third, Waite Tells Jury," *New York Times*, May 26, 1917, p. 1.

[291] "Murdered Two, Tried for a Third, Waite Tells Jury," *New York Times*, May 26, 1917, p. 1.

several pathogens, including anthrax, tuberculosis, typhoid, and some others never named. It was his apparent lack of success with the pathogens that led Waite to try to obtain more virulent organisms.[292] Waite also admitted that he planned to murder his wife, according to his attorney.[293]

Waite was sentenced to death. He unsuccessfully appealed the conviction. Waite was electrocuted at Sing Sing prison on May 24, 1917.[294]

***Case 1915-01: German Secret Service, 1915-1917***

The Germans mounted a covert biological warfare campaign in the United States during the early part of World War I, while the United States was still neutral. The target of the effort were draft animals, horses and mules, that the Allies purchased in the United States for use by their military forces in Europe. The Germans devised a plan to infect the animals with glanders and anthrax organisms. Glanders, caused by *Burkholderia mallei* (once known as *Pseudomonas mallei*), is a highly contagious disease that affects horses, mules, and donkeys. It rarely affects humans, except those who work closely with the animals.[295]

The first effort to implement this plot involved a German naval officer, Captain Erich von Steinmetz, who illegally entered the United States dressed as a woman. He brought with him a vial containing glanders cultures. Attempts to use the pathogen failed, and von Steinmetz discovered his organisms were dead when he took the risk of bringing the culture to a laboratory for analysis.[296]

The effort was resumed in late 1915. A German agent, also involved in other sabotage activities, organized operations to infect horses being kept in pens in Van Courtland Park in New York City. Long after the war, he described these operations to U.S. officials.

> The germs were given to me by Captain Hinsch in glass bottles about an inch and a half or two inches long, and three-quarters of an inch in diameter, with a cork stopper. The bottles were usually contained in a round wooden box with a lid that screwed on the top. There was cotton in the top and bottom to protect the bottles from breaking. A piece of steel in the form of a needle with a sharp point was stuck in the underside of the cork, and the steel needle extended down in the liquid where the germs were. We used rubber gloves and would put the germs in the horses by pulling out the stopper and jabbing the horses with the sharp point of the needle that had been down among the germs. We did a good bit of work by walking along the fences that enclosed the horses and jabbing them when they would come up along the fence or lean where we could get at them. We also spread the germs sometimes on their food and in the water that they were drinking.
>
> Captain Hinsch gave me the instructions as to where I would find the horses and also gave me bottles of germs and the money [to pay his associates]. I used a good many of the same men on this work that I did in starting the fires. I had about ten or twelve men working on these matters with me. We would work at it sometimes at night and sometimes in the daytime. A good many of the men were also doing other work and they made this extra money on the side. Captain Hinsch was accustomed to giving me brown paper bags filled with these tubes and with the fire things.... Captain Hinsch spoke often when I met him of different fires that had occurred and of outbreaks of disease among horses and would make remarks about how well things were going.[297]

The operation was expanded in 1916 with the creation of a laboratory in Chevy Chase, Maryland, a town just outside Washington, D.C. Dr. Anton Dilger was put in charge of the new lab, which was given the name "Tony's Lab." Dilger joined the German army in 1914 at the start of the war. He was sent to the United States, ostensibly to recuperate from a nervous breakdown brought on by a bombing raid on a hospital that killed a considerable number of children. On the trip to the United States, he carried with him "E and B cultures," codenames for anthrax and glanders cultures. Working with his brother Carl, Dr. Dilger produced cultures of the organisms for Hinsch, who then distributed them to the men actually involved in the inoculation

---

292 "Murdered Two, Tried for a Third, Waite Tells Jury," *New York Times*, May 26, 1917, p. 3.

293 "Waite Now Admits Intent to Kill Wife," *New York Times*, April 3, 1916, p. 1.

294 "Dr. Waite, Calm, Goes to his Death," *New York Times*, May 25, 1917, p. 1.

295 Abram S. Benenson, editor, *Control of Communicable Diseases Manual*, Sixteenth edition (Washington, DC: American Public Health Association, 1995), p. 301.

296 Jules Witcover, *Sabotage at Black Tom: Imperial Germany's Secret War in America, 1914-1917* (Chapel Hill, North Carolina: Algonquin Books of Chapel Hill, 1989), p. 92. Witcover's account is based on archival material and on memoirs written by participants.

297 Witcover, *Sabotage at Black Tom*, pp. 126-127.

of the draft animals. The Germans explored setting up a second laboratory in St. Louis, but decided that the cultures would die in the cold Midwestern winters.[298]

The Germans conducted similar operations elsewhere, which the British discovered through reading decoded German cables.[299] According to various reports, the Germans tried to introduce plague cultures into St. Petersburg in 1915, sent anthrax and glanders cultures to Romania in August 1916 to infect sheep being shipped to Russia, tried to infect Norwegian reindeer with glanders organisms in January 1917, infected 4,500 mules used by British forces in Mesopotamia during 1917 with glanders organisms, infected sheep, cattle, and horses being shipped from Argentina to Britain and to the Indian Army with glanders and anthrax during 1917 and 1918, and tried to infect advancing Allied forces with glanders and cholera organisms during the German retreat in October 1918.[300] The Germans also infected horses being shipped from Argentina to France and Italy. They believed the operation was so successful that it ended all such shipments.[301] Another report suggests that the Germans attempted to introduce cholera organisms into Russia.[302]

In addition, decoded German cables suggest that the Germans undertook other operations using biological agents. First, German operatives tried to spread a wheat fungus. One cable sent by the German General Staff to Germany's Military Attaché in Madrid, ordered that "work against grain is to be suppressed as it promises little success." Second, the Germans apparently attempted to contaminate food produced at "meat factories." The British intercepted one message, directing that such operations were to be "held in abeyance," apparently because the operations were considered too risky.[303]

---

[298] Witcover, *Sabotage at Black Tom*, pp. 136-137.

[299] W. Reginald Hall and Amos J. Peaslee, *Three Wars with Germany* (New York: G.P. Putnam's Sons, 1944), pp. 85-88. Then Captain Hall was the Royal Navy's Director of Naval Intelligence. In this capacity he directed OB40, Britain's code breaking organization at that time.

[300] Martin Hugh-Jones, "Wickham Steed and German Biological Warfare Research," *Intelligence and National Security*, Vol. 7, No. 4 (1992), pp. 379-402, and LCDR Andrew G. Robertson, RAN, "From Asps to Allegations: Biological Warfare in History," *Military Medicine*, August 1995, pp. 370-371. Hall and Peaslee, *Three Wars with Germany*, p. 85, claims that 5,400 mules being shipped to Mesopotamia from Argentina were "thoroughly treated." A recent detail concerning the Norwegian operations became known in June 1997, when a vial of viable anthrax was discovered in the Norwegian Police Museum in Trondheim. The vial was taken from a German, Baron Otto Karl von Rosen, in January 1917. The baron was in Karasjok, apparently attempting to infect reindeer that the Germans thought were being used to transport supplies from through Norway to Russia. See Doug Mellgren, "Potent anthrax capsule found," *Associated Press*, June 30, 1997, 2:03 p.m. feed.

According to R.V. Jones, *Reflections on Intelligence* (London: Mandarin Paperbacks, 1990), p. 181, British intelligence discovered many of these plots during the war. R.V. Jones was director of scientific intelligence for the Royal Air Force during World War II.

> Berlin did decline to a proposal to infect the rivers of Portugal with cholera to cause human casualties and thus seal the Spanish frontier; but it did approve a proposal to employ anthrax against reindeer sledging British arms through north Norway to the Russians, against Romanian sheep being supplied to Russia, and Argentinean sheep, cattle and mules being supplied to Britain and the Indian Army. Most of these moves were uncovered by the cryptographic efforts of Room OB40, and confirmed by on-the-spot investigations by agents both from Britain and from neutral countries being attacked. Thanks to their surveillance, the only German success appears to have been 200 mules that were being shipped from the Argentine. The means of infection were ampoules inside sugar cubes, taken to Buenos Aires by U-Boat.

[301] Hall and Peaslee, *Three Wars with Germany*, p. 85.

[302] Dr. G. Woker, "Chemical and Bacteriological Warfare," pp. 388-389, in Inter-Parliamentary Union, Geneva, *What Would Be the Character of a New War* (London: Victor Gollancz, 1933). He made the following remarks about this incident:

> [I]t was only the collapse of one of the great Powers and the merest chance which prevented that Power from attempting to spread infection among the civilian population of an enemy state. Anarchist elements in the latter State had already been hired to carry bacteria cultures, such as cholera bacteria, from the neutral state in which the discovery was made to the intended victim State, where they would have distributed them. The collapse came before this diabolical crime could be accomplished. The consul-general in whose office the cultures were stored, fearing discovery, instructed a porter to throw the incriminating evidence into the river. Fortunately the porter was suspicious and informed the police. Such was the origin of the notorious Zurich bomb and baccilli case, the documents of which, along with the instructions of the Ministerial Department in question, must contain valuable information as to the possible application and effects of bacteriological warfare at the end of the Great War. A study of the relevant documents should also show whether the alleged attempt to send cholera cultures to Russia in fountain pens was ever actually made, and if so with what success.

[303] Hall and Peaslee, *Three Wars with Germany*, pp. 86-88. Hall suspected that certain disease outbreaks on troop ships carrying U.S. soldiers to Europe in 1918 might have resulted from contaminated meat, but no investigation was conducted at the time.

***Case 1913-01: Karl Hopf, 1913***

In January 1914, a German court tried Karl Hopf on charges that he murdered his father, two of his children, and his first wife. He also was accused of attempting to poison his second and third wives and his mother. Arsenic was used in all of the poisonings. In addition, he admitted that in 1913 he infected his third wife with cholera and typhus organisms, "because he wanted to see how they worked." He was convicted of poisoning his two children and his first wife, and of attempting to poison his second and third wives, and was sentenced to death.[304]

It appears that Hopf benefited financially from many of these deaths, although it is unclear whether or not that was the only motivation for his actions. He had some training in handling drugs. From 1884 to 1888 or 1889, he worked in a chemist's shop in London. Among the poisons found in Hopf's house were "morphia", opium, and arsenic, and he apparently had other pathogens besides typhus and cholera. The cultures were acquired from a supply house in Vienna. According to press reports of the trial, he complained to the supplier about the quality of the cultures. This led him to order cholera obtained from the battlefields in Bulgaria.[305]

According to *Frankfurter Zeitung*, this was the first known case in Germany in which someone used bacteria for murder.[306]

***Case 1912-01: Henri Girard, 1909-1918***

On April 21, 1921, Henri Girard was committed for trial by the French examining magistrate charged with investigating suspicions that Girard had poisoned several people using *Salmonella typhi*, the organism that causes typhoid fever, and poisonous mushrooms. He was arrested in August, 1918, but the magistrate needed 32 months to investigate the case.[307] Girard died in June before the start of his scheduled July 1921 trial.[308] Girard reportedly confessed to his crimes before dying.[309] Police also seized a diary that recorded his activities, including his acquisitions of *S. typhi* cultures, poisonous mushrooms, the purchase of laboratory equipment, and scientific and medical literature. On one occasion, Girard reportedly recorded in his diary, "Poisons; prepare bottle, tubes, rubber gloves; buy microbe books."[310]

Girard eventually enlisted four people into his activities, including his wife, his mistress Jeanne Douétèau, a chauffeur named Bragnier and a wine merchant named Rieu. All four were subsequently convicted for roles in his crimes. His wife received a life sentence with hard labor, his mistress was sentenced to 20 years, and the other two were given sentences of two years.[311]

Girard was an Alsatian born into what was called a "good family." He was trained as a druggist, but abandoned that field for work as an insurance broker.[312] According to one newspaper account, "he liked good

---

[304] "The Hopf Poisoning Case," *Times* (London), January 19, 1914, p. 7. The author first came across a reference to this case in Georges Claretie, "L'affaire des poisons: II," *Le Figaro*, October 24, 1921, p. 2. The full account reads, "En 1914, à Berlin, un boucher nomme Hoff, avait déjà donne sa femme la fièvre typhoïde au moyen de bacilles mêlés aux aliments." A search of the London *Times* index indicated that it had four stories on the case. The *Frankfurter Zeitung* appears to have published more than a dozen stories on the trial in January 1914, but the author is awaiting an English translation of the text.

[305] "German Poisoning Case: Administration of bacilli," *Times* (London), January 13, 1914, p. 8. For additional coverage, see "The German Poisoning Case," *Times* (London), January 16, 1914, p. 49, and "The German Poisoning Case," *Times* (London), January 17, 1914, p. 7.

[306] "The Hopf Poisoning Case," *Times* (London), January 19, 1914, p. 7.

[307] There is no really satisfactory English-language account of this case. The accounts disagree on certain key facts, and none of them provides a complete version of the case. There is a short account in C.J.S. Thompson, *Poisons and Poisoners: With Historical Accounts of Some Famous Mysteries in Ancient and Modern Times* (London: Harold Shaylor, 1940), pp. 369-371. English-language newspaper stories appeared in the *Times* (London), the *New York Times*, and the *New York Herald* (European Edition–Paris). The story was extensively reported in the French papers, including *Le Figaro,* which published a four part account of the case by Georges Claretie, "L'affaire des poisons," on October 22, 1921, p. 2, October 24, 1921, p. 2, October 25, 1921, p. 2, and October 27, 1921, p. 3. On Girard's arrest, see "Le courtier empoisonneur," *Le Figaro*, April 21, 1921, p. 2, "Life Insurance Crimes Charged Against Girard," *New York Herald* (European Edition—Paris), April 22, 1921, p. 3, "Insures his friends, then poisons them," *New York Times*, April 22, 1921, p. 17, and "Fatal luncheon parties," *Times* (London), April 22, 1921, p. 10.

[308] "Gentleman Girard Dead: Paris Deprived of Sensation," *Times* (London), June 14, 1921, p. 9. He died of tuberculosis, according to "La Mort de l'empoisonneur," *Le Figaro*, June 14, 1921, p. 1.

[309] Thompson, *Poisons and Poisoners,* p. 371.

[310] Thompson, *Poisons and Poisoners,* p. 369.

[311] "Girard poisoning case," *Times* (London), November 2, 1921, p. 9.

[312] "La Mort de l'empoisonneur," *Le Figaro*, June 14, 1921, p. 1.

living without working too hard for it." He was convicted in 1914 of a fraud connected with the lottery, and served time in 1917 for theft.[313]

The investigation of this case was lengthy and difficult. The investigators employed a number of bacteriologists, and several autopsies were performed on suspected victims. Police investigations determined that Girard was studying bacteriology at the time of his first suspected murder. The prosecution was aided by Girard's diary, which referred to at least some of his activities. In addition, a search of Girard's apartment revealed a considerable number of medical texts, cultures of *S. typhi*, the organism responsible for typhoid, and, according to one account, other "toxic organisms and toxins." He is known to have purchased cultures of *S. typhi*, reportedly from wholesale drug suppliers. In addition, he created a laboratory in a house where his mistress, Mlle. Douétèau, lived.[314]

Girard's first victim is believed to have been a man by the name of Pernotte. The two met in 1910. Girard quickly became extremely friendly with Pernotte and convinced him to purchase two life insurance policies from separate companies, and to make Girard a beneficiary of the policies. Some time after purchasing the policies, Pernotte, his wife, and two children contracted typhoid. Fortunately, all recovered from the illness. After recovering from the immediate effects of the illness, the entire family left for a vacation. Pernotte apparently was still suffering from his exposure to typhoid. Girard reportedly convinced Pernotte to take an injection of a medicine that Girard possessed. Soon after that injection, Pernotte died. On November 3, 1912, Girard recorded in his diary, "Pernotte innocu...," apparently a reference to the fatal injection.[315]

In April, 1913, Girard became acquainted with M. Godel. He agreed to purchase insurance policies worth 200,000 francs to be paid to the survivor. Sometime after the policy was purchased, Godel had lunch with Girard. Soon thereafter, he contracted typhoid. He recovered from the disease, but became suspicious of Girard and completely severed his connections with him.[316]

During the First World War, Girard served in the Paris ambulance service. In 1915, he met and became friendly with Delmas, a French soldier. Girard apparently obtained copies of Delmas' papers and used them to purchase insurance with a death benefit of 40,000 francs. From the beginning of March, 1915, Delmas began to feel sick. By early April, he was diagnosed with typhoid. Just before he had to pay the second premium on the policy, Girard invited Delmas for dinner at his mistress' house. During that meal, Girard infected Delmas using a *S. typhi* culture that he had recently purchased. Delmas subsequently contracted typhoid, and was hospitalized. Accounts of the event report that he was sick with "abnormal typhid fever, criminal contamination." The basis for that judgment is unclear from the press accounts. Having survived his illness, Delmas became suspicious of Girard and broke off the relationship.[317]

It appears that at about this time, Girard began to focus on poisonous mushrooms. Girard purchased several large life insurance policies worth 40,000 francs in the name of Michel Duroux, a postal employee. Duroux knew nothing of policies, which designated as beneficiary a man named Emile Ramon, which was one of Girard's known aliases. Girard apparently gave Duroux aperitifs contaminated with typhoid, but Duroux never got sick. Girard then tried to kill Duroux at a dinner by putting poison mushrooms in one of the dishes, a possibility suggested by some comments recorded in his diary on three occasions in May, 1917. Duroux survived the episode with no ill effects. On two occasions during December 1917, Duroux became ill after eating with Girard at a café. Although he had not eaten any mushrooms, the doctors who treated him diagnosed mushroom poisoning. Duroux was advised to break off the relationship with Girard.[318]

Girard's last reported victim was a widow, Madame Monin, who worked at the Ministry of Pensions. She supplemented her income by making hats. Jeanne Drouhin met Mme. Monin at a small restaurant, and apparently told Girard about her. It appears that at the beginning of April 1918, Girard paid a visit to Mme.

---

[313] "Fatal luncheon parties," *Times* (London), April 22, 1921, p. 10.

[314] "Insures his friends, then poisons them," *New York Times*, April 22, 1921, p. 17, and Thompson, *Poisons and Poisoners*, p. 370-371. Jeanne Douétèau destroyed some papers of his before police were able to seize them.

[315] "Four accomplices of dead poisoner in court today," *New York Herald* (European Edition–Paris), October 28, 1921, p. 6, and "Gentleman Girard," *Times* (London), October 29, 1921, p. 7. Thompson, *Poisons and Poisoners*, p. 369, claims that £8,400 was involved. Two accounts date the events to 1912, not 1909. See are "Insures his friends, then poisons them," *New York Times*, April 22, 1921, p. 17, and "Girard poisoning case," *Times* (London), November 2, 1921, p. 9. The accounts vary on when this episode took place. Some claim that the two met in 1909, while another states 1910. There is also some dispute about the date of the events.

[316] "Four accomplices of dead poisoner in court today," *New York Herald* (European Edition–Paris), October 28, 1921, p. 6, and Thompson, *Poisons and Poisoners*, p. 370.

[317] "Four accomplices of dead poisoner in court today," *New York Herald* (European Edition–Paris), October 28, 1921, p. 6, and Thompson, *Poisons and Poisoners*, p. 370.

[318] "Four accomplices of dead poisoner in court today," *New York Herald* (European Edition–Paris), October 28, 1921, p. 6, "Insures his friends, then poisons them," *New York Times*, April 22, 1921, p. 17, and Thompson, *Poisons and Poisoners*, p. 370.

Monin, posing as a genealogist, and, claiming that there was an inheritance at stake, obtained personal information from her. On April 8 and 9, 1918, Girard visited four life insurance companies accompanied by a woman who identified herself as Mme. Monin. Three of the policies, each worth 20,000 francs, named Drouhin as the beneficiary, and the fourth, also worth 20,000 francs, named Girard. The two made the initial payments on the policies; the next installments were owed July 9 to 11. To ensure that the bills were not sent to Mme. Monin, they either had to pay them in person at the company offices or make sure that she was dead before July.

Sometime in April, Drouhin gave Monin a hat to repair. Monin was asked to deliver it to the residence that Drouhin shared with Girard. During this visit, Girard offered Monin an apéritif containing a mushroom poison. Soon after Monin left to return home, she became so ill that some policeman had to help her get home. Within three hours, she was dead.

Eight days after Mme. Monin's death, Girard claimed the death benefit from the policy for which he was the beneficiary. Similarly, Mlle. Drouhin was paid by one the companies that held policies naming her a beneficiary. However, when she attempted to claim money from the third company, it refused to pay and accused the pair of fraud. This led to a criminal investigation that culminated in Girard's arrest in August. Worried that they might be prosecuted, the two married in July.

An autopsy was not performed for six months. The expert who performed the autopsy was unable to find any traces of poisoning. At the same time, he was also unable to identify a cause of death. Based on the symptoms Mme. Monin reportedly suffered, he concluded that she had been poisoned.[319]

It appears that Girard was responsible for killing two people, M. Pernotte and Mlle. Monin. Six other people recovered after Girard infected or poisoned them, including Pernotte's family, Godel, Delmas, and Duroux.

***Case 1910-01: Patrick O'Brien de Lacy and Vladimir Pantchenko, May 1910***

On February 16, 1911, Patrick O'Brien de Lacy, and his accomplice, Vladimir Pantchenko, were convicted by a Russian court in St. Petersburg, Russia, of murdering Captain Vassilli Buturlin, de Lacy's brother-in-law. A third defendant, Yekaterina Muravieff, was acquitted. According to evidence offered at their trial, Pantchenko, a physician, injected Captain Buturlin with diphtheria toxin at the instigation of de Lacy, De Lacy was sentenced to life imprisonment and Pantchenko was given fifteen years.[320]

De Lacy was a Polish nobleman who claimed to be a descendent of Irish kings. In 1906, de Lacy, then in his second marriage, met Ludmilla, the married daughter of General Dmitry Buturlin. Despite the General's objections, Ludmilla divorced her husband and married the now divorced de Lacy in December 1908. According to one newspaper account, he was "said to have been a ne'er-do-well" who wasted the fortune of his first wife.[321]

De Lacy apparently lost his fortune in the shipbuilding industry. He reportedly owned a shipyard in Poland and built a shipyard in Finland that built two ships for the Russian fleet. He once had sufficient wealth to donate two ships to the Russian fleet that fought Japan. The failure of these businesses left him financially ruined. Even a wedding gift from General Buturlin of two estates and mill was insufficient to cover his debts. Nor was an allowance of 500 rubles a month sufficient for a man of his ambitions.[322]

Ludmilla's parents were extremely wealthy. General Buturlin was worth 1,400,000 rubles (apparently about $700,000). His two children were the heirs to this fortune. His son, Captain Buturlin, was to receive 1,000,000 rubles ($500,000), while Ludmilla was to get 400,000 rubles ($200,000). De Lacy reportedly resented this distribution, believing that his wife was not to receive her fair share of the estate. In addition, Ludmilla's mother, the former Countess Bobrinsky, had a fortune of 1,000,000 ($500,000), which she intended

---

[319] The best account is "L'affaire des poisons IV," *Le Figaro,* October 27, 1921, pp. 3-4. See also "Four accomplices of dead poisoner in court today," *New York Herald* (European Edition–Paris), October 28, 1921, p. 6, "Insures his friends, then poisons them," *New York Times*, April 22, 1921, p. 17, and Thompson, *Poisons and Poisoners,* p. 370-371.

[320] "Russian Poisoners Are Found Guilty," *New York Times*, February 17, 1911, p. 4. The most complete accounts of this case are Herman Bernstein, "The Doctor Who Killed His Patients With Germs," *New York Times*, February 19, 1911, section five, p. 1, and "Criminal Poisoning with Bacteria: The Remarkable Case of O'Brien de Lacy and Panchenko," pp. 213-219, in C.J.S. Thompson, *Poisons and Poisoners: With Historical Accounts of Some Famous Mysteries in Ancient and Modern Times* (London: Harold Shaylor, 1940). Bernstein appears to have attended the trial, while Thompson provides no indication of his sources of information. The spelling of names follows those used in the *Times* (London).

[321] "A Russian Murder Trial," *Times* (London), January 11, 1911, p. 7.

[322] Bernstein, "The Doctor Who Killed His Patients With Germs," *New York Times*, February 19, 1911, section five, p. 1. De Lacy apparently depended on receiving orders to supply ships to the Russian Navy, and it was a decision of the Marine Ministry to cancel orders from his shipyard that led to his financial troubles. See "Experts in Clash at Russian Trial," *New York Times*, February 7, 1911, p. 4.

to give to her two children. (She had divorced the General some twenty years earlier, and in 1910 lived in Paris married to a man called Lizardi.)[323]

De Lacy decided that he could solve his financial problems by murdering his in-laws. He apparently did not want to wait for his in-laws to die natural deaths, and wanted his wife to inherit the bulk of their estates. There is some evidence that he embarked on this plan even before his marriage to Ludmilla.

To accomplish his objectives, de Lacy recruited the services of Pantchenko, an indigent physician with a dubious reputation.[324] Pantchenko was a purveyor of quack medicines. While living in Paris in 1895, he reportedly sold poison used in a suicide. He also was implicated in other dubious activities, including faking death certificates and producing pornography. In early 1911 one of his patients died due to Pantchenko's use of dirty needles.[325]

Pantchenko first encountered Captain Buturlin in the fall of 1908, when his future victim inquired about an anti-cholera injection that Pantchenko peddled. The two met periodically after that. In February 1910, Pantchenko convinced Captain Buturlin of the beneficial effects of a compound known as spermin, and began to give him regular injections.[326]

According to one account, de Lacy approached Pantchenko in the fall of 1908, even before his marriage to Ludmilla. In their first meeting, de Lacy offered Pantchenko 1,500 rubles to perform an abortion. A few days later, de Lacy told Pantchenko what he really wanted: the murder of his in-laws through use of biological agents. He offered Pantchenko 10,000 rubles for the death of Captain Buturlin, 50,000 rubles to kill General Buturlin, and 500,000 rubles to go to Paris to dispose of the mother.[327]

De Lacy told Pantchenko that he wanted his brother-in-law killed by infecting him with cholera. The disease was endemic in St. Petersburg at the time, and de Lacy hoped that people would believe that his victims had died of natural causes.

> Now that cholera is raging, it would seem the safest way of removing him. When he dies, as a victim of the epidemic, he will be buried immediately. And even if he should be exhumed, they will find that he died of cholera.[328]

Pantchenko, however, was doubtful about relying on cholera, and instead suggested diphtheria toxin, which he obtained from two different research laboratories. Ultimately, Pantchenko found an opportunity to inject Captain Buturlin with the diphtheria toxin, which killed him.

There were questions about Captain Buturlin's death almost immediately. General Buturlin was suspicious and demanded a post-mortem, a request seconded by the dead man's wife. At the same time, a man approached the police with a story suggesting that Buturlin had been murdered. Apparently, the man rented a room from Mme. Muravieff, who was Pantchenko's lover. This sparked a police investigation. Pantchenko and de Lacy initially denied any complicity in the death, but the two were arrested, as was Mme. Muravieff.[329]

Following his arrest, Dr. Pantchenko confessed to his involvement in the crime. (According to one account, "the Russian legal procedure for worming avowals out of prisoners resembles the so-called American 'third degree'."[330] Although he retracted the confession during his trial, the jury found it credible in their deliberations.[331] This is a unique document, since it describes one man's account of his involvement with the use of biological agents.

> Patients were brought to me occasionally by a friend named Raffoff, who acted as a tout, receiving a share of the profits. One day he introduced me to O'Brien de Lacy. We adjourned to a private room in a restaurant, where, in Raffoff's presence, he asked me if I would perform a certain illegal operation [an abortion] for 1,700 rubles. I assented. O'Brien de Lacy seemed pleased and gave me

323 Bernstein, "The Doctor Who Killed His Patients With Germs," *New York Times*, February 19, 1911, section five, p. 1.

324 "Pantchenko's Many Crimes," *New York Times*, February 8, 1911, p. 4.

325 "Poison Trial Drags On," *New York Times*, February 12, 1911, Section 3, p. 4.

326 Bernstein, "The Doctor Who Killed His Patients With Germs," *New York Times*, February 19, 1911, section five, p. 1.

327 Bernstein, "The Doctor Who Killed His Patients With Germs," *New York Times*, February 19, 1911, section five, p. 1.

328 Bernstein, "The Doctor Who Killed His Patients With Germs," *New York Times*, February 19, 1911, section five, p. 1.

329 Thompson, *Poisons and Poisoners*, pp. 214-215.

330 "Doctors Gave Fatal Germs to Poisoner," *New York Times*, February 4, 1911, p. 1.

331 He told the court, "When I gave evidence to the examining magistrate and denounced de Lacy I was simply investing a tale of the Arabian Nights. Had I really been guilty I could easily have fled before my arrest." See "The Russian Murder Trial," *Times* (London), February 10, 1911, p. 5.

100 rubles. I asked him to visit me in my own study. I was a physician of the Petrograd district of the North Railway.

Subsequently O'Brien intimated that he would prefer to talk with me without a witness. I acquiesced. He told me he had just become a bridegroom, and the operation he really wanted was to have his future brother-in-law made away with. For this service he would pay 10,000 rubles. After that it would be necessary to remove the father-in-law. For that riddance I would be paid 50,000 rubles, and lastly, the old man's divorced wife must be launched into eternity. For this job he would not grudge 500,000 rubles. He impressed upon me the necessity of extreme circumspection, and advised me to begin with young Buturlin, to whom he proposed I should administer cholera germs on bread, buttered and covered with caviar. Death by cholera, he explained, would evoke no surprise at a moment when that epidemic was making havoc in Petrograd. Therefore he had much to say in favor of cholera germs, and informed me that young Buturlin was using anti-cholera subcutaneous injections.

By this time I had extracted 2,000 rubles from O'Brien de Lacy. At last he introduced me to Buturlin, on the ground that were interested in founding a sanatorium, but I was to whet his curiosity about a certain drug and get him as a patient. Then, instead of the drug, I was to inject some poison or other, and having done the job, to abstain sedulously from writing or telegraphing, as a kinsman of his, Count Roniker, who had been charged with murder in Warsaw, had been tripped up by a telegram. The plan was successful; I treated young Buturlin, substituting diphtheria toxin for the other drug.

I received the germs from a chemist, who believed my story that it was required for experiments on rabbits. I injected two large doses into the victim's thigh. Later, I learned he was very ill, and, being conscience smitten, I wired for O'Brien de Lacy, who was furious that the telegram should have been sent. He exclaimed: 'You may as well give yourself up now.' I visited young Buturlin after this, and learned from his own lips that he had had high fever and sharp pains, but was now much better. The other physician who was called in did not diagnose the malady. Then I read of Buturlin's death in the papers. It occurred exactly as had been calculated, seven days after the injection. When I read that the day of the burial would be announced later, I knew it boded evil.

Meanwhile, General Buturlin arrived ad demanded a post-mortem. O'Brien de Lacy supported the demand, convinced that the examination would be fruitless. I, too, was of the same opinion, because throats are never analyzed during such investigation, and few symptoms of diphtheria infection would be visible in the throat.[332]

Pantchenko subsequently made the following statement about the injections given to Captain Buturlin.

On May 16th [1910] I visited Buturlin, and injected a pure drug [of anti-cholera serum] from a phial. I repeated the injection on the following day. Before my evening visit to Buturlin on the same day, I broke the necks of the two drug-phials in my own lodging that nobody should notice it. Having emptied the contents, I filled the phials with diphtheria poison by means of a paper funnel., plugging them with wadding, and putting them into my waistcoat-pocket, set out for Buturlin's. Before starting I gulped down vodka for courage.

I got to Buturlin's about eight or nine in the evening, with trembling in my legs and throbbing waves of darkness filling my eyes and fitfully blotting out my sight. I had been wont to break off the necks of the phials in Buturlin's presence, first putting them in a handkerchief to avoid cutting my fingers. That is why he could not notice that this time the necks were already snapped off. I made two incisions in Buturlin's body, injecting each time the contents of one phial of the diphtheria poison. Each vessel held about two cubic centimeters, but as the effects of the diphtheria poison had not been tested on human beings, I injected two phials full in order to be quite sure of a deadly issue, and I quivered in every limb. I was in dread that Buturlin might discern my state. Pulling myself together, and mastering my failing voice, I asked him whether it hurt. He answered, 'not at all.' I then left for home and threw the phials into the street. The livelong night I could not close an eye. Conscience-ache racked me ruthlessly.[333]

Court testimony revealed that Pantchenko obtained both diphtheria toxin and cholera endotoxin. Dr. Heinrich, assistant director of a medical laboratory, testified that Pantchenko requested cholera endotoxin and was provided with two tubes containing the substance. He returned several months later, and asked for more, since he said that he had used the first batch experimenting on guinea pigs. He was provided with additional

---

[332] Thompson, *Poisons and Poisoners,* pp. 215-216.

[333] Thompson, *Poisons and Poisoners,* pp. 217. Thompson appears to imply that this statement was given at the time of the trial.

toxin.[334] Pantchenko admitted to acquiring the cholera endotoxin, but claimed that he sold it to O'Brien de Lacy for 25 rubles. The material was apparently to be used to kill General Buturlin.[335]

Pantchenko subsequently approached Professor Zabolotny, a microbiologist, who gave the physician a small quantity of diphtheria toxin for what Pantchenko claimed was research into its effects on the nervous system. Zabolotny testified that he subsequently learned that his toxin was not virulent, although he never informed Pantchenko.[336] After supplying Pantchenko, Zabolotny suggested that he approach the Institute of Experimental Medicine to obtain additional quantities of the toxin. Professor Zdrjekoffski, a chemist at the Institute of Experimental Medicine, testified during the trial that, "I gave him, I forget whether one or two phials of diphtheria toxin, each containing thirty or forty cubic centimeters. I explained to Dr. Pantchenko the action of this toxin and the minimum dose that would cause death." A prisoner who shared a jail cell with Pantchenko subsequently claimed that the physician told him about experiments with a guinea pig to test the toxin.[337]

## Probable or Possible Use

In these cases, the perpetrators may have used a biological agent, but there is no authoritative confirmation. It also includes some cases in which a biological agent was used, but there is no information to indicate whether the perpetrator knowingly caused the infection. The probability of intentional contamination for these cases ranges from highly likely to highly unlikely.

### *Case 1994-03M: Orville Lynn Majors, January 1994*

Orville Lynn Majors was arrested on December 29, 1997 on charges that he poisoned at least six people at the Vermillion County Hospital from 1993-1995. In addition to use of potassium chloride, a chemical, Majors is alleged to have used epinephrine, also known as adrenaline. He was suspected of involvement in as many as 100 deaths, and police investigators performed autopsies on 15 people.[338] In November 1998, a seventh murder charge was filed against Majors, although it is unclear whether the substance involved was a chemical or biological poison.[339]

### *Case 1993-04: Animal Liberation Front, December 1994*

A spokesman for the Animal Liberation Front (ALF) claimed that several bombs placed by ALF activists at several Boots pharmacies in the United Kingdom were contaminated with HIV. Authorities discounted the claim, but also suggested that even if true the HIV was unlikely to pose a hazard.[340]

### *Case 1992-06: Marilyn Tan, June 1992*

Authorities in Alberta, Canada, alleged that Marilyn Tan deliberately injected Con Boland with HIV-contaminated blood during a sexual encounter. Prosecutors claimed that Tan got the idea from an episode of the television series *Murder, She Wrote*. She allegedly obtained the HIV from her sister, a nurse who lived in the United States. Although Tan allegedly admitted the plot to a friend, the presiding judge found that witness' testimony less than credible. In addition, the judge noted that the prosecution could provide no convincing evidence that Boland acquired his HIV through injection. The judge believed that Boland's promiscuous lifestyle opened the possibility that he was infected in other ways. For this reason, the judge acquitted Tan.[341]

---

[334] "The Russian Murder Trial," *Times* (London), February 4, 1911, p. 7, and Thompson, *Poisons and Poisoners*, pp. 215-216.

[335] "The Russian Murder Trial: History of the Case," *Times* (London), February 17, 1911, p. 5, and Thompson, *Poisons and Poisoners*, p. 218.

[336] "Doctors Tell of Autopsy," *New York Times*, February 4, 1911, p. 2.

[337] Thompson, *Poisons and Poisoners*, p. 218, and "The Russian Murder Trial," *Times* (London), February 4, 1911, p. 7.

[338] See Charles Hoskinson, "Indiana Nurse Pleads Not Guilty in Hospital Deaths," *Washington Post*, December 31, 1997, p. A6, Charles Hoskinson, "Former Nurse Charged in Six Deaths," *Washington Post*, December 30, 1997, p. A7, and Dirk Johnson, "Nurse Held in Six Killings," *New York Times*, December 31, 1997, p. A10.

[339] Amy Cahill, "Seventh murder charge filed in Majors case," *Brazil Times* (Indiana), November 3, 1998, as found at the newspaper's World Wide Web site, *http://braziltimes.com*.

[340] Chris Court, "Police Seek Woman in Firebomb Inquiry," *Press Association*, January 4, 1994. I am indebted to Jason Pate of the Monterey Institute for International Studies for bring this reference to my attention.

[341] "Model accused of injecting lover with AIDS virus," *Agence France Presse*, May 17, 1995, 13:11 Eastern Time, "HIV Trial Told of Strange Thigh Bruise", *Toronto Globe and Mail*, May 4, 1995, p. A11, and Alanna Mitchell, "Tan Not Guilty of Injecting Lover," *Toronto Globe and Mail*, May 24, 1995, p. A4.

***Case 1990-05X: Suicide using HIV-infected blood (1990?)***

In early 1991, several French physicians reported on a case in which a 41-year-old woman tried to commit suicide by injecting herself with two to three milliliters of HIV-contaminated blood taken from a friend who had AIDS. Two hours after the event, she went to a hospital emergency room, where she was treated with zidovudine. Despite the treatment, three months after the injection laboratory tests indicated that she was infected with HIV.[342]

***Case 1990-02: Giardia in Scotland, June 1990***

According to a report that appeared in *The Lancet*, a British medical journal, during June 1990 nine people living in an apartment building in Edinburgh, Scotland, became sick with a diarrheal disease caused by *Giardia lamblia*. Investigators discovered that the one of the tanks that supplied water to the building had been broken into and deliberately contaminated with *Giardia*-containing fecal material.[343]

The identity of the perpetrator was not reported, and the motivation for the contamination is not known. It is not known if the perpetrator knowingly intended to cause giardiasis, or was even aware that the feces were contaminated with *Giardia*.

***Case 1989-04M: Efren Saldivar***

In March 1998, a respiratory therapist named Efren Saldivar confessed to having murdered between 40 and 50 patients at the Glendale Adventist Medical Center in Los Angeles. According to the confession, he killed the patients over a nine year period starting in 1989 by smothering them or by injecting them with lethal substances. He claimed to have used morphine, Pavulon, or succinylcholine chloride. Pavulon and succinylcholine chloride are both muscle relaxants. He subsequently retracted the confession, claiming that he was suicidal at the time of his confession but lacked the will to kill himself.[344]

The case is currently under investigation. Press reports suggest that law enforcement officials believe that at least one patient was murdered, but lack the evidence needed to make an arrest.[345] As of March 1999, the case was still under investigation.[346]

***Case 1989-03: South Africa, August 1989***

In May 1990, a South African newspaper, *Vrye Weekblad*, reported that a South African government covert operations unit, known as the Civilian Cooperation Bureau (CCB), employed biological agents against SWAPO, the South West African People's Organization. The CCB had nearly 300 people working for it, and reportedly consumed about 0.28 per cent of the entire South African defense budget. The group had authority to operate inside South Africa and in neighboring countries. It was apparently disbanded around April 1991.[347]

The claim that South Africa used biological agents is based on the statements of Petrus Jacobus Botes, who claimed to have directed operations by CCB in Mozambique and Swaziland. According to his account, in May 1989, he was ordered to contaminate the water supply at Dobra, a refugee camp located in Namibia, with cholera and yellow fever organisms provided him by a South African army doctor. The attempt to contaminate the water supply was made in late August, but apparently failed to have any effect because of the high chlorine content of the treated water at the camp.[348] A Namibian health official subsequently confirmed that the water

---

[342] Eric Durand, Claire Le Jeunne, and François-Claude Hugues, "Failure of prophylactic zidovudine after suicidal self-inoculation of HIV-infected blood" [letter], *New England Journal of Medicine*, Vol. 324 (April 11, 1991), p. 1062.

[343] C.N. Ramsey and J. Marsh, "Giardiasis due to deliberate contamination of water supply," *Lancet*, Vol. 336 (October 6, 1990), pp. 880-881. This incident was brought to my attention by Robert S. Root-Bernstein, "Infectious Terrorism," *Atlantic*, May 1991, p. 48.

[344] Buck Wargo, Donna Huffaker, and Julie Marquis, "Hospital Worker Says He Killed Up to 50," *Los Angeles Times*, March 28, 1998, p. A1.

[345] T. Christian Miller, "Possible Victims of Alleged Mercy Killer Identified," *Los Angeles Times*, May 6, 1998, Valley Edition, Metro section, p. 1.

[346] Scott Glover, "Critics Lament Slow Pace of 'Angel of Death' Investigation," Los Angeles Times, March 28, 1999, as found at *http://www.latimes.com*.

[347] For a short discussion of the role of CCB, see Jacques Pauw, *In the Heart of the Whore: The story of apartheid's death squads* (Halfway House, South Africa: Southern Book Publishers, 1991), pp. 150-155. Pauw is a South African journalist who investigated efforts by the apartheid regime to forcibly suppress dissent. Bruce Hoffman and *The RAND-St. Andrews Terrorism Chronology* brought this incident to my attention.

[348] Pauw, *In the Heart of the Whore*, pp. 187-188. See also "Dirty Tricks and Dirtier Germs," *CovertAction Quarterly*, Winter 1998, p. 29, citing Jacques Pauw, *Into the Heart of Darkness: Confessions of Apartheid's Assassins* (Johannesburg: Jonathan Ball Publishers, 1997).

supply was treated, and that the camp's water was monitored during that period. No evidence of cholera was ever found.[349]

Sketchy details of South Africa's biological weapons program emerged following the arrest of Wouter Basson in January 1997. Basson, a physician, was the project leader for Project Coast, the codename for South Africa's covert biological and chemical weapons program. In that capacity, he is thought to have had comprehensive knowledge of South Africa's entire biological weapons program. Four trunks full of material related to Project Coast were seized by law enforcement officials at the time of his arrest, providing the first real insight into the full dimensions of the program. Only a limited amount of information was made public, however, because of four separate investigations into Project Coast: South Africa's Commission on Truth and Reconciliation; the Office of Economic Offences; the Gauteng Attorney-General's Special Investigation Team; and, the National Intelligence Agency (NIA).[350]

Additional details of the program were provided in the course of hearings held before the Commission's Human Rights Violations Committee during June and July 1998. Scientists involved in the biological weapons program provided details of their activities to the committee. According to the researchers, pathogens and toxins were developed for use against opponents of the apartheid regime. One operation associated with the program was the Roodeplaat Research Laboratories (RRL). Schalk van Rensburg, formerly a director of the facility, told the Committee, "I would say that 95 percent of what went on was covert work. Over the five year offensive period at RRL, some 500 products were issued, many in small quantities capable of killing just a few people."[351] Significantly, the company reportedly produced 32 bottles containing cholera cultures. In addition, the laboratory produced chocolates and cigarettes laced with anthrax, beer contaminated with botulinum toxin, and sugar containing an unidentified salmonella species.[352] Another person who testified before the Commission, Dr. Schalk van Rensburg, claimed that the South Africans infected three Russians advising the African National Congress with anthrax, and that one died.[353]

No evidence was presented to the Commission confirming allegations of use of cholera against SWAPO.

***Case 1988-01: Poisoner of Colonel Jean-Claude Paul, November 1988***

On November 6, 1988, Colonel Jean-Claude Paul, the recently retired commander of Haiti's elite Dessalines Battalion, died after eating a bowl of pumpkin soup for lunch. Paul was a leader of the notorious Tontons Macoutes, essentially the terror squad created by the Duvalier regime to maintain its power. Even after the President Jean-Claude "Baby Doc" Duvalier was forced from power in 1986, the Tontons Macoutes remained a power in the country. Until he was retired from the military following a September 1988 coup, Paul was considered one of the most powerful figures in Haiti. At the time of his death, the United States government was attempting to extradite Paul for his alleged involvement in smuggling drugs from South America to the United States.[354]

Following Paul's death, the Haitian police arrested Paul's wife, Mireille Deinois, and two of their servants, based on suspicions that they might have poisoned him. They were subsequently released.[355] Some accounts suggest that Paul's wife was arrested to protect her from vengeful members of his family.[356]

---

[349] "South African paper reports cholera plot," *San Jose Mercury News*, May 11, 1990, p. 21A, and *San Jose Mercury News*, May 12, 1990, p. 7F.

[350] These details are from Commission on Truth and Reconciliation, *Final Report*, Volume 2, Chapter 6, as found (at the time) at the Commission's World Wide Web site, *http://www.truth.org.za*.

[351] Jeremy Lovell, "S. African panel told of secret murder factory," *Reuters*, June 9, 1998, 05:18 p.m. EST feed.

[352] Suzanne Daley, "In Support of Apartheid: Poison Whisky and Sterilization," *New York Times*, June 11, 1998, p. A3.

[353] David Beresford, "Mandela on apartheid's poison list," *Age* (Melbourne, Australia), June 11, 1998, taken from the paper's World Wide Web site, *http://www.theage.com.au/*.

[354] Alan Tomlinson, "Poison suspicion after Haiti colonel on drug charges dies," *Times* (London) November 8, 1988, p. 7, "Haitian Officer Charged by U.S. Is Reported Dead," *New York Times*, November 7, 1988, p. A11, and "Possibility of Poisoning Is Raised In the Death of a Haitian Colonel," *New York Times*, November 8, 1988, p. A14. See also Christine Toomey, "Tontons' terror lives on as boss dies from poison," *Sunday Times* (London), November 13, 1988, p. A24. Bruce Hoffman and *The RAND-St. Andrews Terrorism Chronology* brought this incident to my attention.

[355] "Haiti police seize wife, two servants in Colonel's death," *Miami Herald*, November 8, 1988, p. 3A, and "Haiti colonel poisoned," *Sunday Times* (London), December 4, 1988, p. A20.

[356] "Indicted Haitian Colonel dies," *Miami Herald*, November 7, 1988, p. A1.

Initial press reports indicated that Paul died of a heart attack. It was generally assumed, however, that he was poisoned, and the press soon indicated that "poisoning is suspected."[357] The Haitian press noted that his lips were suspiciously dark. According to one newspaper, it had information that his table salt was contaminated with cyanide. A sample of the pumpkin soup that he was eating just before his death was sent to a laboratory in Miami, Florida.[358] Tests of the soup did not identify any poisons. According to press accounts, however, the autopsy suggested that he had been poisoned. It is not known if the poison was ever identified.[359] The Port-au-Prince police chief, Colonel Georges Valcin, asserted that Paul died after "absorbing a toxic substance," but he never identified the substance involved.[360]

It is possible that Paul was poisoned using any one of several toxins known to Haitian practitioners of voodoo. For example, they employ tetrodotoxin in the preparations supposedly used in the process of zombification. Similarly, it appears that the plant-derived drug datura, another powerful toxin, is used to counter the effects of the tetrodotoxin. It appears that Haitians are also familiar with other toxins derived from plants and animals.[361]

There is some evidence suggesting that some of the compounds used by traditional Haitians in their rituals have made their way to the United States. In February 1986, a fireman in Delray Beach, Florida, was hospitalized after entering a burning house where it is believed certain of these preparations were stored.[362]

***Case 1987-01: Dr. David Acer, December 1987-1990***

According to the Centers for Defence Control and Prevention (CDC), a Florida dentist infected with HIV, Dr. David Acer, transmitted the disease to six of his patients. It is not known how the patients became infected. For several reasons, the Acer case has been the focus of intense controversy. CDC was concerned due to fears that health care providers might transmit the disease to their patients. In fact, this was the first known instance in which a health care provider appeared to have transmitted HIV to a patient.[363]

Both the infected patients who sued Acer's estate and his malpractice insurance company, and the insurance companies, have had an interest in determining whether Acer transmitted the disease to his patients, and, if he did, how it happened. Because of the controversy, CDC has spent more than $1 million on the Acer investigation. More than two dozen CDC personnel have been involved.[364]

A senior CDC official, Harold Jaffe, has offered three alternative explanations of how Acer transmitted the disease. First, Acer could have contaminated his own dental instruments and then failed to sterilize them before using them on his patients. Second, Acer might have cut himself in some fashion and his blood could have infected the patients when he performed dental work on them. Third, Acer might have intentionally infected the patients. According to Jaffe, "There is no direct evidence for any of these three theories."[365]

The first of Acer's victims became known on July 27, 1990, when the CDC reported the case in its *Morbidity and Mortality Weekly Report.* According to CDC, the victim had no obvious risk factor for AIDS,

---

[357] "Haiti police seize wife, two servants in Colonel's death," *Miami Herald*, November 8, 1988, p. 3A.

[358] Christine Toomey, "Tontons' terror lives on as boss dies from poison," *Sunday Times* (London), November 13, 1988, p. A24.

[359] "Haiti colonel poisoned," *Sunday Times* (London), December 4, 1988, p. A20.

[360] *Miami Herald*, December 3, 1988, p. 25A.

[361] Wade Davis, *The Serpent and the Rainbow: A Harvard Scientist's Astonishing Journey into the Secret Societies of Haitian Voodoo, Zombis, and Magic* (New York: A Touchstone Book published by Simon and Shuster, 1997). On the role of tetrodotoxin in Haitian rituals, see pp. 116ff and 165ff. On datura, see pp. 35ff and 164-165. Among the other toxins that the Haitians appear to employ are bufogenin and bufotoxin (see p. 114 in Davis), derived from the *Bufo marinus* toad, and saponin extracted from the plant *Albizzia lebbeck* (p. 111).

[362] "Haiti poisons pose problem in a new land," *Orlando Sentinel*, July 19, 1987.

[363] There is a considerable literature on this case. It has received enormous press coverage, and there have been numerous scientific articles reviewing aspects of the case. In addition, it has been the subject of several books, including Mark Carol Rom, *Fatal Extraction: The Story Behind the Florida Dentist Accused of Infecting His Patients with HIV and Poisoning Public Health* (San Francisco: Jossey-Bass Publishers, 1997). For a shorter review of the case, see "CDC Closes the Case of The Florida Dentist," *Science*, May 22, 1992, p. 1130.

[364] Dennis L. Breo, "The dental AIDS cases—Murder or an unsolvable mystery," *JAMA*, December 8, 1993, p. 2732.

[365] Breo, "The dental AIDS cases," p. 2732.

and had a strain of HIV genetically identical to Acer's.[366] The young woman involved, Kimberly Bergalis, subsequently sued Acer's estate, and mounted a public campaign to force mandatory HIV testing of medical workers. Over time, five additional cases surfaced. The last of the victims was identified in May 1993.

Almost from the beginning, there have been attacks on the CDC research. Some critics have argued that the victims had risk factors not identified by CDC, and that the methodology used by CDC to compare the HIV strains was flawed. These arguments were publicly aired in a segment broadcast by *60 Minutes*, the CBS television program.[367] Most scientific experts, however, appear to agree with CDC that Acer somehow infected his patients.[368] Most of the controversy centers on whether or not Acer infected them deliberately.[369]

Edward Parsons, a friend of Acer's, came to suspect that the dentist might have deliberately infected his patients. Parsons recalled in 1992 comments that he heard Acer make in 1988, "When it starts affecting grandmothers and younger people, then you'll see something done." For Parsons, this seemed to convincingly suggest Acer's guilt, given that two of the first victims were Bergalis, a young woman, and Barbara Webb, a grandmother.[370] According to Jaffe, however, Parsons gave a different account in his sworn testimony, which casts doubt on his subsequent statements.[371]

Many of those who have looked into the case believe that Acer deliberately infected his patients. According to one expert, "Whether it's scientifically valid or not, it is definitely the most prevalent theory today—at least in the dental community."[372] For example, one scientist who looked into the case claims, "It was murder ... simply because we've eliminated everything else."[373]

Other investigators have taken CDC to task for failing to properly investigate the case. They argue that CDC focused too much on the victims, and insufficiently on the activities and character of Dr. Acer. For example, CDC spent three months investigating the first known victim, Bergalis, before looking into Acer's activities. One critic argues that strong similarities can be identified between Dr. Acer's behavioral patterns and those of known sexual criminals. This critic contends that CDC's investigation of the case was flawed from the beginning, and consistently overlooked evidence supporting the intentional contamination theory.[374]

Experts at the CDC, however, do not believe that there is compelling evidence to support the deliberate contamination theory. Similarly, an investigator in the Florida Department of Health and Rehabilitative Services told a reporter, "The only evidence we have to support the theory of criminal intent is the lack of evidence supporting any of the other theories. We will probably never know the answer."[375]

***Case 1985-02: Unknown, 1985***

According to an official of the U.S. Department of Agriculture, Mexican contract workers involved in a screwworm eradication program may have deliberately spread that pathogen among livestock. Although the perpetrators were never charged, the workers apparently spread the screwworm because they were seeking to protect their jobs, which would have disappeared once the parasites were eliminated. The releases apparently took place in an area of Mexico about 50 miles south of the border with the United States.[376]

---

[366] "Possible Transmission of Human Immunodeficiency Virus to a Patient during an Invasive Dental Procedure," *Morbidity and Mortality Weekly Report*, July 27, 1990, p. 489-493. Dr. Shellie A. Kolavic provided me with copies of this and other articles on the Acer case.

[367] "AIDS From Dentist Disputed: 60 Minutes Raises Doubts in '80s Cases," *Miami Herald*, June 18, 1994, p. 5B. The arguments advanced in the 60 Minutes segments are reviewed and generally dismissed in Stephen Barr, "The 1990 Florida Dental Investigation: Is the Case Really Closed?," *Annals of Internal Medicine*, January 15, 1996, pp. 250-254.

[368] David Brown, "The 1990 Florida Dental Investigation: Theory and Fact," *Annals of Internal Medicine*, January 15, 1996, pp. 255-256.

[369] David Kidwell, "AIDS dentists lethal weapon? Accidental transmission unlikely in latest case, experts say," *Miami Herald*, June 6, 1993, p. 1A.

[370] "Friend dentist may have spread AIDS on purpose," *Miami Herald*, June 11, 1992, p. 2B. See also Hal Boedeker, "AIDS dentist will be focus of 20/20 segment on Friday," *Miami Herald*, September 30, 1993, p. 5B.

[371] Breo, "The dental AIDS cases," p. 2733. According to Jaffe, "He said under oath only that Acer was angry about his AIDS infection, and he specifically said that Acer did *not* tell him that he was going to intentionally infect patients."

[372] David Kidwell, "AIDS dentists lethal weapon? Accidental transmission unlikely in latest case, experts say," *Miami Herald*, June 6, 1993, p. 1A.

[373] Hal Boedeker, "AIDS dentist will be focus of 20/20 segment on Friday," *Miami Herald*, September 30, 1993, p. 5B.

[374] Leonard G. Horowitz, "Murder and cover-up could explain the Florida dental AIDS mystery," *British Medical Journal*, December 1994, p. 423-427.

[375] Hal Boedeker, "AIDS dentist will be focus of 20/20 segment on Friday," *Miami Herald*, September 30, 1993, p. 5B.

[376] Judith Miller, "U.S. to Use Lab for More Study Of Bioterrorism," *New York Times*, September 22, 1999, p. A25.

***Case 1981-01: Unknown (Boris Korczak), September 1981***

We have two distinctly different versions of what happened to Boris Korczak in September 1981. These two accounts are totally inconsistent, and while one appears to originate with U.S. intelligence agencies, it is the other version that appears more credible.

The first version was initially reported by Joseph D. Douglass, Jr., and Neil C. Livingstone in their 1987 book *America the Vulnerable: The Threat of Chemical/Biological Warfare.* According to Douglass and Livingstone, Korczak was killed using a technique similar to that used on Georgi Markov and Vladimir Kostov in 1978.

> Intelligence sources in the West say that a similar pellet-firing weapon has been responsible for at least six assassinations in recent years, including a CIA double agent, Boris Korczak, who was hit at Tyson's Corner, Virginia. Korczak was rushed to Fairfax hospital, where a major fight developed between the CIA and the Soviets over custody of the body. The CIA held off the Soviets until the cause of Korczak's death was fixed, which turned out to be a small platinum-iridium pellet, which presumably contained ricin. The CIA got the pellet; the Soviets got the body, which they immediately shipped to Russia on an Aeroflot plane from which all passengers were excluded.[377]

Dr. Benjamin C. Garrett, a scientist specializing in chemical and biological agents working at EAI Corporation, wrote a similar version of this story, which he attributed to the Central Intelligence Agency.[378]

A totally different account emerges from other sources, including a review of press articles published in 1981 and 1996 and interviews with the alleged victim. According to newspaper accounts, in October 1981 Boris Korczak, a Lithuanian-Pole who had acted as a double agent for the Central Intelligence Agency in the 1970s, claimed that the KGB attempted to assassinate him with ricin pellets. Korczak had lived in Denmark while working for the CIA, but came to the United States in 1979 when he came to believe that the KGB had discovered his CIA connections. According to the newspaper report, the Senate Intelligence Committee confirmed that Korczak had worked for the agency.[379]

Korczak claims that in mid-September 1981 he was attacked while shopping at the Tyson's Corner shopping mall. He told a reporter, "My friends say they saw a blond man, wearing British clothes, who seemed to be following us around the shopping center. I believe he shot the pellet at me." At that time, he felt "something like a mosquito bite" on his back near his kidneys. A few hours later, his temperature climbed to 106° F, and he became delirious. He recovered after three days. He claims that several days later he excreted a metal ball about one-five hundredth of an inch in size. "That ball has a niche that was filled with some deadly poison which got into my kidneys when the ball lodged there." Korczak made his allegations public because he believed that the CIA had refused to protect him, despite his previous work for the agency.[380]

According to a February 1996 *Associated Press* report, Korczak had just filed a lawsuit against the CIA in the U.S. Court of Federal Claims. In that suit, he claimed that he was owed $725,000 by the CIA, and asked for a $25,000 annuity. At that time, he told journalists that in 1981 he was struck with a poisoned pellet while grocery shopping. According to this account, he provided reporters with copies of his medical records describing a "tiny … pellet" removed from the wound.[381]

It is impossible to ascertain the truth of the Korczak's story, given that there has never been an official investigation into his allegations. Moreover, it is clear that Korczak had a strong motivation to invent the story, given his dispute with the CIA. At the same time, however, the medical records that he has shown researchers indicate that he did become quite ill at the time of the alleged incident, and he did show a small pellet to reporters soon after the incident. In addition, his account of what happened has remained consistent over the years, although he has given various explanations for why he was attacked.

The most unusual feature of this case is the discrepancy in the two accounts of what happened. The story attributed to the Central Intelligence Agency is clearly specious. If Korczak had been murdered, there is no question but that U.S. law enforcement officials could have performed an autopsy and taken any other steps necessary to prosecute an investigation. The fact that certain people within the intelligence community allegedly have spread what is clearly a specious story is in itself high suspicious. It is possible that the conflict

---

[377] Douglass and Livingstone, *America the Vulnerable*, pp. 84-85. In another place (p. 185), the authors date the assassination to 1980, and describe the incident as follows: "Assassination of CIA agent Boris Korczak in McLean, Virginia (Tyson's Corner), using ricin weapon, possibly in umbrella configuration."

[378] Benjamin C. Garrett, "Ricin: A Case Study for the Treaty," *ASA Newsletter*, No. 92-2, April 3, 1992, pp. 1, 10.

[379] Joseph Volz, "Ex-Agent Says KGB Trying to Kill Him, CIA Refuses Help," *Washington Post*, October 4, 1981, p. A14.

[380] Joseph Volz, "Ex-Agent Says KGB Trying to Kill Him, CIA Refuses Help," *Washington Post*, October 4, 1981, p. A14.

[381] See "Double Agent for the CIA sues 'the big bully'," *Philadelphia Inquirer*, February 25, 1996.

between Korczak and his CIA handlers may have motivated the false account, but, in the absence of additional information, any such conclusion is at best speculative.

***Case 1970-04: Additional East Bloc bioassassinations, 1970s-1980s?***

According to Douglass and Livingstone, intelligence officials believe that at least six other people were victims of "a similar pellet-firing weapon," besides Markov and Kostov. They mention Boris Korczak, as well as the Algerian leader Houari Boumedienne. They claim that Boumedienne was killed using a pellet gun identical to the type used against the Bulgarians.[382]

According to press accounts, Boumedienne was diagnosed as suffering from a rare disorder known as Waldenstrom's macroglobulinemia, a blood disease characterized by an enlarged spleen and liver. He became ill in the period September 19-24, 1978, during an Arab summit in Damascus, Syria. At the time, he was suffering from fever, chills, malaise, anemia, and blood in his urine.[383] Around October 4 or 5, he was flown to Moscow for treatment of what was by then thought to be a kidney infection.[384] The Soviets continued to treat him until mid-November.[385] After Boumedienne returned to Algiers, the Algerians brought in additional specialists, and he was diagnosed with Waldenstrom's macroglobulinemia. During this period, Boumedienne was attended by a medical team that at one point included 62 physicians drawn from 14 countries. Among those attending were 14 doctors from the United States. The Algerians also brought in Dr. Jan Waldenstrom, the Swedish doctor who first characterized the disease.[386] These accounts cast doubt on the theory that Boumedienne was assassinated.

Another source claims, "U.S. intelligence figures privately indicated there had been other suspicious attacks and at least two deaths involving other exiles, including a Bulgarian and a Croat."[387] British authorities might have looked into other such attacks during their Markov investigation. For example, *The Times* (London) reported in November 1978 that British police had already traveled to West Germany on three occasions to talk with Bulgarian dissidents, and that the police were interviewing a doctor in Munich. However, the subject of the conversations was not specified, so it is only speculation that it may have involved other attacks on dissidents.[388]

During a March 13, 1980 discussion, Dr. Rufus Compton, the pathologist who performed the autopsy on Georgi Markov, recounted the story of Mrs. Angela Hoppett, who traveled to the Soviet Union with her father, apparently soon after the Markov murder. She reported that the Russians attempted to incriminate her father by tricking him into reading anti-Soviet material. Crompton describes what happened next in the following way:

> ... she felt a sting or a blow at the back of her neck, and noticed a small puncture mark there. She described symptoms, a number of which were similar to those of the Markov and Kostov cases. She developed a fever and backache with severe headache and malaise which lasted for a long time. However, with all due respect, you really have to take her story with a certain pinch of salt, coming after the Markov/Kostov affair.[389]

Despite his skepticism about Mrs. Hoppett's story, Crompton noted, "I believe that it probably is the case that this instrument has been used not on numerous occasions but certainly on a number of occasions, other than on these two men." He added, that these other cases had "not been detected."[390] During the same presentation, Dr. Robin Keeley of the London Metropolitan Police Laboratory stated that the pellet's platinum-iridium alloy is biologically inert, so that it could remain inside the body without causing inflammation.[391] This would reduce chances of the pellet being detected.

---

382 Douglass and Livingstone, *America the Vulnerable*, pp. 84-85.

383 Lawrence K. Altman, "Huge Medical Team Treated Algerian," *New York Times*, December 28, 1978, p. A11.

384 Jim Hoagland, "Algerian Leader Ill, Treated in Moscow," *Washington Post*, October 21, 1978, p. A13, and Ronald Koven, "Algerian Deathwatch," *Washington Post*, December 13, 1978, p. A30.

385 "Algerians Told Boumediene Is Sick and Unable to Work," *New York Times*, November 20, 1978, p. A6.

386 Lawrence K. Altman, "Huge Medical Team Treated Algerian," *New York Times*, December 28, 1978, p. A11.

387 Carl Sifakis, *Encyclopedia of Assassination* (New York: Facts On File, 1991), p. 122.

388 Stewart Tendler, "Police see Mr Markov's brother for clues in killing," *Times* (London), November 28, 1978, p. 2.

389 Dr. Rufus Crompton and Dr. David Gall, "Georgi Markov--Death in a Pellet," *Medico-Legal Journal*, Volume 48 (1980), p. 60.

390 Crompton and Gall, "Georgi Markov--Death in a Pellet," pp. 60-61.

391 Crompton and Gall, "Georgi Markov--Death in a Pellet," p. 61.

Following the reports of Markov's death in September 1978, another Bulgarian dissident, Stefan Bankov, also claimed to have experienced a mysterious attack of a similar nature. Bankov told a French newspaper, *L'Aurore*, that the incident took place during a 1974 airplane flight between Seattle, Washington, and London. During the flight, someone violently bumped into Bankov. He told reporters, "He [the assailant] didn't apologize for bumping into me and I immediately experienced a terrible feeling of cold, beginning of paralysis and difficulties in breathing." He says that he was hospitalized after the trip and was ill for several days.[392]

***Case 1979-02: Zimbabwe guerrillas, November 1979***

The *RAND-St. Andrews Terrorism Chronology* attributes the following incident to November 1979.

> Rhodesian officials publicly accused nationalist guerrillas of responsibility for the spread of anthrax in 12 districts. Twenty people reportedly died from the disease, which also affected cattle. The incident has not been confirmed and may in fact have been Rhodesian propaganda.[393]

***Case 1976-02: Rhodesian Central Intelligence Organization, 1976-1980***

There is some evidence suggesting that the Rhodesian government used biological agents against black civilians in Rhodesia and Mozambique. According to these accounts, the operation was organized by the Central Intelligence Organization, the intelligence agency of the Apartheid government of Ian Smith.[394]

The CIO drew on the services of Robert Symington, a professor of anatomy at the University of Rhodesia. He recruited other members of the faculty and some students into his program to develop chemical and biological agents. In 1975, the researchers tested their new agents on detainees.

The dissemination of the agent was the responsibility of Inspector Dave Anderton, chief of the "Terrorist Desk." He used members of the Selous Scouts, an antiterrorist group made up mostly of captured members of the black nationalist guerrilla armies. According to a researcher who interviewed former members of the CIO, they were responsible for the following operations:

> **"bacteriological agents"** as yet unidentified which were used to contaminate boreholes, rivers, and other water sources. There are several cases of deaths attributed to drinking water and Henrik Ellert [a former CIO official] recounts one incident in which the Ruya River was infected with an unidentified biological agent in 1976. This incident corresponds to a cholera epidemic along the Ruya River in Mozambique in which fatalities were reported. In Mozambique, the water supply of the town of Cochemane was poisoned by Selous Scouts. The CIO later reported 200 deaths in Cochemane attributed again to cholera.
>
> **anthrax bacterium** which was introduced into rural areas of Western Zimbabwe, resulting in several hundred human deaths.[395]

In 1979 and 1980, there were 10,738 documented cases of human anthrax in Rhodesia, resulting in 182 deaths. In contrast, during the previous 29 years there were only 334 cases.[396] Most researchers believe that the anthrax epidemic was a natural outbreak. The extent of the outbreak resulted from the collapse of public health and veterinary medicine programs due to the civil war.[397]

---

[392] "Other Bulgarians claim poison umbrella attacks," *Tucson Citizen*, September 15, 1978, p. 10A, and "2 more report being stabbed with umbrellas," *Arizona Republic*, September 16, 1978, p. A26 (city edition). The original report is Jacques Chambaz, "Les Parapluies de Sofia," ["The Umbrellas of Sofia"], *L'Aurore*, September 15, 1978, p. 16a.

[393] *The RAND-St. Andrews Terrorism Chronology*.

[394] Meryl Nass, "Anthrax Epizootic in Zimbabwe, 1978-1980: Due to Deliberate Spread?," *PSR Quarterly*, December 1992, pp. 198-209, Meryl Nass, "Zimbabwe's Anthrax Epizootic," *CovertAction*, Number 43, Winter 1992-93, pp. 12-18+, and Brickhill, "Zimbabwe's Poisoned Legacy," *CovertAction*, Number 43, Winter 1992-93, pp. 4-11+.

[395] Brickhill, "Zimbabwe's Poisoned Legacy," p. 8. The following account appears in H. Ellert, *The Rhodesian Front War: Counter-insurgency and guerrilla war in Rhodesia 1962-1980* (Gweru, Zimbabwe: Mambo Press, 1989), p. 113:

> During 1976 a group of [Selous] Scouts moved into the Ruya wild-life area near the Mozambique border. At several points along the Ruya river they introduced measured quantities of bacteriological cultures into the water. Whether any fatalities resulted from these experiments is not known but it did correspond with a reported epidemic of deaths among people living on the banks of the Ruya river in Mozambique. The deaths were officially attributed to cholera.

[396] Nass, "Anthrax Epizootic in Zimbabwe, 1978-1980, pp. 199 and 202, and Nass, "Zimbabwe's Anthrax Epizootic," p. 13.

[397] See James C. Pile, John D. Malone, Edward M. Eitzen, and Arthur M. Friedlander, "Anthrax as a Potential Biological Warfare Agent," *Archives of Internal Medicine*, March 9, 1998, as taken from *http://www.ama-assn.org*. The Rhodesian medical

A December 10, 1998 article that appeared in the Harare *Financial Gazette*, the Zimbabwe government has opened an investigation into the claims, according to a statement by the country's Health Minister, Dr. Timothy Stamp. Stamp told the newspaper, "It is true that we are researching into the activities of Rhodesian security agents during the liberation struggle and that they may have used bacteriological warfare." The newspaper also indicated that a former Rhodesian army office. Colonel Lionel Dyck said, "Poison was used on clothes, but other forms of germ warfare, no. The war was not fought honorably and techniques used by both sides were not honorable. Cholera was also used, mostly in Mozambique."[398]

***Case 1971-01: KGB (Alexander Solzhenitsyn), August 1971***

In 1992, a Russian newspaper, *Sovershenno Sekretno* (Top Secret) published a story claiming that the KGB attempted to kill Alexander Solzhenitsyn as the noted author was standing at a department store candy counter in Novocherkassk on August 8, 1971. KGB Lt. Col. Boris Ivanov, a member of the team allegedly involved in the plot, recalled, "The whole operation lasted two or three minutes. The man left the shop and our boss started to smile. Outside, he said, quickly but firmly, 'It's all over. He won't live much longer.'"[399]

Solzhenitsyn told the Russian journalists that he was feeling well, and that he and a friend "visited the cathedral and the shops." He then gave the following account of subsequent events

> I don't remember any injection, I certainly didn't feel it, but by mid-morning the skin on my left side suddenly started to hurt a great deal. Towards evening (we had stopped to see people we knew), I continued to deteriorate and had a very large burn. The following morning I was reduced to a terrible state: my left hip, left side, stomach and back were covered with blisters, the largest of which were 15 centimeters in diameter.[400]

Solzhenitsyn's wife told a Western reporter that he had "a strange, inexplicable disease" and that it took him months to recover. For long periods, he was barely able to get out of bed or write. Doctors who examined Solzhenitsyn could not figure out what had happened to him, although some surmised that he had suffered from a severe allergic reaction. According to the Russian article, after consulting with a respected Russian toxicologist, it was determined the substance used was probably ricin. [401]

Oleg Kalugin confirms the reports that an attack was made against Solzhenitsyn. He states that the KGB's Operational and Technical Directorate "had a laboratory that invented new ways of killing people, from poisons that could be slipped into drinks to jellies that could be rubbed on a person to induce a heart attack. A KGB agent rubbed such a substance on Alexander Solzhenitsyn in a store in Russia in the early 1970s, making him violently ill but not killing him."[402] Kalugin does not indicate what poison was used in the jelly.

***Case 1969-01: John R. Hill, March 1969***

On March 19, 1969, Joan Robinson Hill died in a small suburban hospital in the Houston area. Within days of the death, Ash Robinson, father of the dead woman, became convinced that her husband, Dr. John R. Hill, a plastic surgeon, had murdered her. Dr. Hill's relations with his wife were strained due to his on-going affair with Ann Kurth, which he had previously promised to terminate. It appears that Joan Hill was contemplating a divorce at the time of her death. Dr. Hill married Ann Kurth about three months after Joan Hill's death, but the two were in divorce court within four months.[403]

Without Ash Robinson's tenacity, wealth, and political resources it is highly unlikely this case would have been investigated, much less prosecuted. Robinson made a fortune as an independent oilman, and was one of Houston's leading citizens. Therefore, his influence kept the case alive, even when the prosecutors doubted that any evidence existed to warrant a criminal investigation.

---

community, despite the war, extensively studied the outbreak. See, for example, See J.C.A. Davies, "A Major Epidemic of Anthrax in Zimbabwe, part I," *Central African Journal of Medicine*, December 1982, pp. 292-298, and J.C.A. Davies, "A Major Epidemic of Anthrax in Zimbabwe, part II," *Central African Journal of Medicine*, January 1983, pp. 8-12.

[398] "Zimbabwe probing warfare gem use by colonial govt," *Reuters*, December 10, 1998, 7:41 a.m. Eastern.

[399] David Remnick, "KGB Plot to Assassinate Solzhenitsyn Reported," *Washington Post*, April 21, 1992, p. D2.

[400] Remnick, "KGB Plot to Assassinate Solzhenitsyn Reported," p. D1.

[401] Remnick, "KGB Plot to Assassinate Solzhenitsyn Reported," p. D1.

[402] Oleg Kalugin, *The First Directorate* (New York: St. Martin's Press, 1994), p. 180.

[403] This account of the Hill case is based largely on Thomas Thompson, *Blood and Money* (Garden City, New York: Doubleday and Company, 1976).

The evidence to support a charge of murder was tenuous at best. Three autopsies failed to clarify the cause of Joan Hill's death. Since she had died within 24 hours of her admission to the hospital, state law required an autopsy. For reasons that were never clarified, Joan Hill's body was embalmed within a few hours of her death before an autopsy could be performed. The initial autopsy by the hospital pathologist identified the cause of death as pancreatitis, a conclusion which was clearly flawed and that the pathologist revised within days of his finding.[404]

The coroner, who stated that the cause of death was hepatitis, performed a second autopsy soon thereafter. The coroner discounted septicemia as the cause of death, since blood tests performed at the time of Joan Hill's hospital admission did not detect any infection. Unfortunately, the specimens were discarded after her death, and no attempt was made to culture the blood. The coroner apparently was unaware that it was not uncommon to get negative results from such tests even when patients were septicemic.[405] After the third autopsy, he changed his official opinion and attributed her death to a "fulminating infectious process."[406]

Considerably later, a grand jury ordered a third autopsy. Dr. Milton Helpern, who was the chief medical examiner for New York City, performed the last autopsy. Dr. Helpern concluded that Joan Hill died from a widespread infection, identifying massive damage to organs throughout the body characteristic of overwhelming septicemia. However, Dr. Helpern also concluded that it would be impossible to determine the actual cause of death, since the embalming process killed any organisms that might have been present.[407]

Ann Kurth also made some spectacular charges against Dr. Hill. During the trial, she testified that Dr. Hill spent time in her apartment before his wife's death. In the week before Joan Hill's death, Ann Kurth discovered something peculiar in her apartment.

> ... I went into the bathroom. And the door had been closed. There was a gooseneck light over the side of the basin, and there were three petri dishes there with red something in them and little dots of something in that ...
>
> I really didn't get much of a look, because Dr. Hill came up behind me and said, 'Oh, I am doing an experiment and this room is supposed to stay warm.' He had this little gooseneck light over them. He backed me out of there and closed the door, and I really didn't think about it.[408]

According to Ann Kurth, she also found some pastries in her refrigerator, which apparently were the same ones that Dr. Hill subsequently gave to his wife. Ann Kurth also claimed that Dr. Hill told her that he deliberately infected his dead wife. She recalled the statement as follows.

> I really didn't want it to be this way. It didn't really have to be this way, but Joan would never have given me a divorce. Ash was going to see to that. So I took every kind of human excretion I could find. I saved feces, urine from patients, pus from a boil off somebody's neck, and I mixed them all together and I grew cultures in those petri dishes ... And I first gave her the pastries and that did not do anything. Then I gave her some ipecac, and she threw up everything but her toenails .... And she was so sweet about it, She was begging me to do something for her .... So I gave her a shot. I gave her some broad-spectrum antibiotic, and I mixed in some of this culture in liquid suspension ... and that did it ....[409]

Hill was never officially charged with the alleged murder. Rather, the state charged him with murder by omission, which essentially held that he was acting as his wife's physician and had failed to take appropriate steps to treat her. The trial against Dr. Hill was brought to an abrupt end when the judge ordered a mistrial over statements made by Ann Kurth. Under Texas law, wives (even former wives) were not able to testify against their husbands. The Judge allowed Kurth to testify on certain specific issues, but she made statements that went beyond those limits, and so the judge felt compelled to end the trial.

Dr. Hill was never retried. In 1972, a man allegedly hired by Joan Robinson Hill's father, Ash Robinson, murdered him. Robinson was never formally charged with the crime, apparently because of his age and ill health.

The scanty evidence supporting a murder charge in this case is evident. It might be possible to clarify the cause of death using modern analytic tools, such as PCR, which could identify DNA present in tissues

---

[404] Thompson, *Blood and Money*, pp. 119, 124.

[405] Thompson, *Blood and Money*, p. 124, 133.

[406] Thompson, *Blood and Money*, p. 169.

[407] On Dr. Helpern's role in the case, see Thompson, *Blood and Money*, pp. 152-165, 182-188.

[408] Thompson, *Blood and Money*, p. 232.

[409] Thompson, *Blood and Money*, p. 235.

removed during the autopsies left by any dead pathogens. Presumably, if such tests identified multiple pathogens, it would suggest deliberate infection along the lines alleged by Ann Kurth.

***Case 1966-01M: Mario Jascalevich, 1966***

Mario Jascalevich, a surgeon, allegedly poisoned five patients at Riverdell Hospital in Bergenfield, New Jersey, during 1966. Prosecutors claimed that he injected the patients with tubocurarine, a form of curare. Jascalevich was suspected of poisoning patients of a surgeon who was new to the hospital; he allegedly viewed the new doctor as a threat to an extremely lucrative practice. An initial investigation by local law enforcement officials was inconclusive, but following a series of *New York Times* reports of the case, the investigation was reopened more than ten years later. In 1978, a New Jersey jury acquitted Jascalevich of the crimes. Jascalevich subsequently lost his New Jersey medical license for unrelated acts, and returned to Argentina.[410]

***Case 1961-01: "J.L.", October 1961***

According to an outbreak investigation reported in *the New England Journal of Medicine*, 23 U.S. Navy personnel (22 officers and one enlisted man) were stricken with Hepatitis A, possibly as a result of a deliberate contamination of food served at an officer's mess. Following a careful study of the outbreak, the CDC concluded that one of the food handlers contaminated potato salad that he prepared on October 26, 1961. This individual, who had a history of psychological problems, apparently was ill with Hepatitis A at the time of the contamination. The investigators believed that he contaminated the salad at the time he was preparing it.[411] At the time, the investigators apparently believed that "J.L." might have deliberately contaminated the food by urinating into it. Contemporary authorities tend to discount this mode of transmission, since the current belief is that Hepatitis A is extremely difficult to transmit through urine.[412]

Because Hepatitis A has a lengthy incubation period, the first case was not reported until November 18. The bulk of the cases emerged between November 25 and 30. It was not until December 5 that the CDC investigation was initiated. The careful records kept by the military aided the investigation. It was possible to identify the officers who ate at each meal. There were even records of when jars of salad dressing were taken from storage, making it possible to determine when new batches of the potato salad were prepared. It would have been considerably more difficult to conduct a similar investigation in a setting in which less accurate records were available.

The outbreak occurred at Cecil Field, a naval air station located near Jacksonville, Florida. Subsequent investigation determined that the suspect, identified only as "J.L." in the journal article, had a history of psychiatric problems. Prior to the outbreak, he had been diagnosed as schizophrenic with a recommendation that he be discharged from the Navy.[413]

While there is reasonable evidence to support the belief that "J.L." did urinate into the dressing, it is not evident that he understood that doing so would transmit disease. Indeed, it is not even clear that he knew that he had a communicable disease. In addition, even if "J.L." knowingly contaminated the food with the intention of transmitting his hepatitis A, it is uncertain that the route used could transmit the disease. It remains possible that the food was actually contaminated by accident because of poor hygiene.

For these reasons, it appears doubtful that this case meets the definition of a biological agent incident.

***Case 1957-01: Brazilian Indian Protection Service (SPI), 1957-1965***

Brazil's Indian Protection Service, known by its Portuguese initials as SPI, reportedly used biological agents as part of a campaign of genocide against Brazilian aborigines.[414] The allegations were contained in a report issued by Brazil's Attorney General in March 1968, the so-called Figueiredo Report. Consisting of twenty volumes and 5,115 pages, the report "found evidence of widespread corruption and sadism, ranging

---

[410] For a discussion of this case, see Matthew Lifflander, *Final Treatment: The File on Dr. X* (New York: W.W. Norton, 1979) and Myron Farber, *Somebody Is Lying: the Story of Dr. X* (Garden City, N.Y.: Doubleday, 1982).

[411] Joseph, P.R., Millar, J.D., and Henderson, D.A., "An Outbreak of Hepatitis Traced to food contamination," *New England Journal of Medicine*, July 22, 1965, pp. 188-194.

[412] Electronic communications, Dr. Thomas Török, August 1, 1997, and Dr. Shellie A. Kolavic, July 15, 1997. Telephone interview, Dr. J.R. Joseph, August 19, 1997. According to Dr. Joseph, Alexander Langmuir, director of the Epidemic Intelligence Service, cautioned the CDC investigators about drawing any firm conclusions about the mode of transmission.

[413] Telephone interview, Dr. Carter S. Bagley, M.D., July 16, 1997.

[414] Catherine Caufield, *In the Rainforest* (New York: Alfred A. Knopf, 1985), p. 12. According to Caufield, "The SPI was disbanded in 1967, after a government investigation revealed that Indian agents had practiced genocide by deliberately introducing smallpox, influenza, tuberculosis, and measles into Indian groups and had joined with speculators and landowners in systematic murder and robbery of their charges." Paula DeSutter brought this case to my attention after finding a mention of it on the Internet.

from the massacre of whole tribes by dynamite, machine guns and sugar laced with arsenic to the removal of an 11-year-old girl from school to serve as a slave to an official of the Service."[415]

Smallpox, influenza, tuberculosis and measles allegedly were spread in the Mato Grosso area from 1957 to 1963. Moreover, it appears that tuberculosis was spread in the northern part of the Amazon Basin in 1964 and 1965. According to one investigator, diseases "were deliberately brought into Indian territories by landowners and speculators utilizing a metizo previously infected."[416] The commission was unable to confirm reports that two tribes of Pataxo Indians, located in Bahia State, were injected with smallpox.[417]

Although strong evidence supports the contention that biological agents were deliberately spread among the aborigines, the mode of transmission appears not to fit the case definition used in this study. Only if strong evidence existed that some of the victims were deliberately injected would the case definition be satisfied.

***Case 1949-01: Toshima Hospital Outbreak, November 1949***

The Toshima Metropolitan Hospital, located in Tokyo, experienced a substantial outbreak of typhoid in November 1949. The outbreak was traced to food served at the hospital. In all, 20 people became ill from consuming the contaminated food, including both hospital employees and members of their families. In addition, another 20 people contracted the disease from those originally infected. Police reportedly believed that a hospital intern was responsible for the outbreak, but lacked the evidence needed to mount a prosecution.[418]

***Case 1947-01: "Zionist" terrorists, 1947-1948***

On July 22, 1948, the Palestinian Arab Higher Committee submitted a thirteen-page report to the United Nations accusing Palestinian Jews of using biological agents against Egypt and Syria. According to the document, "For several years the Zionists have planned and prepared for the use of bacterial warfare. To that end, they set up laboratories in Palestine. The Jews plan to use this inhuman weapon against the Arabs in the Middle East in their war of extermination." The report contended that there was "some" evidence to link Palestinian Jews to cholera outbreaks in Egypt in November, 1947, and in Syria "about February, 1948."[419]

In addition, the report noted that on May 28, 1948, the Egyptian Ministry of Defense issued a communiqué claiming that the Egyptian military had captured four "Zionists" who were attempting to contaminate wells around Gaza with "a liquid which was discovered to contain the germs of dysentery and typhoid." The Palestinian Arab Higher Committee Report claimed that one of the perpetrators confessed to the plot, which the Egyptian government planned to communicate to the International Red Cross.[420] According to another source, two Israeli soldiers were involved in the plot: David Horeen and David Mizrachi. Both were caught by Egyptian forces in May 1948, and were hanged three months later. This account indicates that to Rachel Katzman, Horeen's sister, said, "I met one of his commanders in a lecture in Jerusalem. I asked him whether my brother had really attempted to poison wells. 'These were the weapons we had,' he said, 'and that's that." This account also claims that the Israelis poisoned the water supply of the Arab town of Acre, causing a major outbreak, and other Arab villages, to prevent the villagers from returning, citing military historian Uri Milstein as a source.[421]

The cholera outbreaks in Syria and Egypt received extensive attention in the international press. The first reports of the Egyptian outbreak date appeared on September 25, 1947.[422] By the time the final cases appeared in January 1948, 10,262 people died, about half of those contracting the disease. At the time,

---

[415] Paul L. Montgomery, "Killing of Indians Charged in Brazil," *New York Times*, March 21, 1968, p. 1.

[416] "Germ Warfare Against Indians is Charged in Brazil," *Medical Tribune and Medical News*, December 8, 1969, as quoted in Shelton H. Davis, *Victims of the Miracle: Development and the Indians of Brazil* (New York: Cambridge University Press, 1977), pp. 10-11.

[417] Paul L. Montgomery, "Killing of Indians Charged in Brazil," *New York Times*, March 21, 1968,p. 8.

[418] This account is derived from an unpublished article by Masaaki Sugishima, Associate Professor at the Asahi University School of Law, who based his account on press reports.

[419] Thomas J. Hamilton, "Arab Assails Idea of Minority Shifts," *New York Times*, July 24, 1948, p. 3.

[420] Thomas J. Hamilton, "Arab Assails Idea of Minority Shifts," *New York Times*, July 24, 1948, p. 3.

[421] Wendy Barnaby, *The Plague Makers: The Secret World of Biological Warfare* (London: VISION Paperbacks, 1997), pp. 114-116.

[422] "Cholera outbreak near Cairo," *Times* (London), September 26, 1947, p. 4.

Egyptian health officials told the World Health Organization that the disease reached Egypt from India, which had suffered a massive outbreak the previous summer.[423]

There were at least two additional allegations that the outbreak resulted from human intervention. In October 1947, a "well-known radio commentator," accused the Soviet Union of responsibility for the outbreak. Theodor Rosebury and Elvin A. Kabat flatly rejected this allegation in a letter to the *New York Times*. The two were involved with the U.S. biological warfare program during the Second World War.[424] In addition, at about the same time Egypt's Muslim Brotherhood was accusing the British of causing the outbreak in order to distract the Egyptian people from the upcoming withdrawal of British forces from Egypt. It is unclear whether the Muslim Brotherhood believed that the British deliberately introduced the disease, or if they thought the response to the outbreak was deliberately inadequate.[425]

The outbreak in Syria was much smaller, apparently limited to two towns about 60 kilometers south of Damascus. The first report of the outbreak appeared on December 21.[426] The Syrian army formed a *cordon sanitaire* around the villages: only health care providers, food convoys, and a water train were allowed into the villages. Ultimately, the outbreak was contained, and there were only 44 cases, including 18 deaths.[427]

There was an allegation that the outbreak resulted from intentional contamination. According to a report that appeared in a French-language newspaper published in Beirut, *Orient*, the Damascus police arrested several Zionist Jews who employed cholera to disrupt the mobilization of the "People's Army" being created to intervene in Palestine. The *New York Times* account, however, states that "official quarters" did not confirm the allegation.[428]

### *Case 1942-02: Polish resistance, December 1942*

Himmler told Hitler in a December 4, 1942 report that the Germans had just discovered a laboratory in a safe house used by the Polish underground. He added that they found "three flasks of typhus baccilli, seventeen sealed rubber tubes presumably containing bacteria, and one fountain pen with instructions for use for spreading bacteria."[429] In September 1943, a Polish Liaison Officer informed the Combined Chiefs of Staff that Polish forces had killed "a few hundred" Germans using "typhoid fever microbes and typhoid fever lice."[430]

Another source, a member of the Polish underground during the Second World War, claims that the State Institute of Hygiene, apparently located in Warsaw, Poland, was used by the Polish resistance, then known as the Union for Armed Resistance (ZWZ). According to this account, the German Gestapo received anonymous letters denouncing people for various purposes. In many cases, the letters were written to settle grudges, but the fake charges were sufficient to get the victims arrested by the Germans. To put a halt to this practice, the staff of the Institute of Hygiene prepared anthrax cultures, and infected fake anonymous letters that were sent to the Gestapo. When Gestapo agents began to suffer from the symptoms of cutaneous anthrax, they started throwing away anonymous letters without opening them. The source gives no date for the incident.[431]

---

[423] *New York Times*, January 27, 1948, p. 7.

[424] *New York Times*, October 19, 1947, section 4, p. 10.

[425] "Cairo sprayed against Cholera," *Times* (London), October 7, 1947, p. 3, and "Cholera in Egypt unabated: Anti-British accusations," *Times* (London), October 8, 1947, p. 3. Egypt's Under-Secretary for Health was dismissed from the government for claiming that the British caused the outbreak due to a failure to implement a quarantine. The Muslim Brotherhood also claimed that the British sent cholera vaccine that had passed the expiration date to poison the Egyptian people.

[426] "Cholera reported in Syria," *New York Times*, December 22, 1947, p. 5.

[427] "Syria moves quickly to stamp out cholera," *New York Times*, December 24, 1947, p. 7, "U.S. Group in Syrian Cholera Aid," *New York Times*, January 3, 1948, p. 28.

[428] Dana Adams Schmidt, "Cholera spreads to Syria, Lebanon," *New York Times*, December 23, 1947, p. 13.

[429] From a report that Himmler gave to Hitler, according to David Irving, *Hitler's War* (New York: Viking Press, 1977), p. 463. Irving claims that the Gestapo also discovered from captured documents that the laboratory had handled 20 pounds of arsenic. In addition, he cites a Gestapo report to Hitler that the Soviet NKVD had given instructions for use of arsenic against Germans in occupied Soviet territory. The reference to this source came from Robert Harris and Jeremy Paxman, *A Higher Form of Killing: The Secret Story of Chemical and Biological Warfare* (New York: Hill and Wang, 1982), p. 89.

[430] From a document in the records of the Combined Chiefs of Staff, as quoted in Harris and Paxman, *A Higher Form of Killing*, p. 89. Typhoid cannot be transmitted by lice, suggesting that the source meant louseborne typhus. See Benenson, pp. 502-510.

[431] Jan Nowak, *Courier from Warsaw* (Detroit: Wayne State University Press, 1982), pp. 62-63. Milton Leitenberg brought this reference to my attention.

***Case 1942-01: British SOE (against Reinhard Heydrich), May 27, 1942***

According to Robert Harris and Jeremy Paxman, Czech agents used British-supplied hand grenades filled botulinum toxin to assassinate Reinhard Heydrich. The basis of this claim is an alleged assertion by Paul Fildes, the British scientist who was responsible for work on botulinum toxin at Porton Down, Britain's biological warfare research center. Long after the event, Fildes reportedly told several scientists that he "had a hand" in the killing of Heydrich. In particular, he told one scientist that the Heydrich killing "was the first notch on my pistol."[432]

In October 1941, the British Special Operations Executive (SOE) initiated a plot to assassinate Heydrich, who had just been named *Reichsprotektor* of Bohemia and Moravia. Working with the Czech government in exile, the British put together a team of agents who were flown into Bohemia on December 29, 1941. They brought with them two specially-modified versions of a standard British hand grenade, which Harris and Paxman believe were adapted to carry botulinum toxin.

It was not until May 27 that the assassination team had an opportunity to kill Heydrich. On that day, the Czech team—armed with submachine guns and the modified grenades—ambushed Heydrich's car as he was driving near Prague. One of the grenades was thrown at the car after the submachine gun jammed, and at least some fragments from it injured Heydrich.[433] Harris and Paxman believe that fragments were contaminated with botulinum toxin and that he died on June 4, 1942 from the effects of botulinum poisoning.

Some experts have cast doubt on this account. The historian M.R.D. Foot, who wrote the official history of SOE operations in France, and probably knew as much about SOE as anyone, doubted that a poison was used. "Rumour has it that the grenade was poisoned. There is no need to believe this; Prague's wartime suburban gutters were not clean. And the grenade fragments carried filth enough to kill him once embedded in his insides."[434] Callum MacDonald, who wrote a comprehensive history of the plot to kill Heydrich, discounted the Harris and Paxman claims for two reasons. First, he argued that fragments from the grenade that hit Heydrich also wounded one of the assassins, yet the attacker survived the attack. Second, he believed the toxin could not have survived during the six months that the assassins were in Czechoslovakia before they used the grenade.[435]

G.B. Carter, who worked at Porton Down in the 1980s and researched the Harris and Paxman allegations, rejected MacDonald's arguments. According to Carter, experience suggests that an explosion can destroy the toxin on some fragments but not others. Hence, it was perfectly possible that poisoned fragments hit Heydrich, while poison-free fragments hit his attacker. In addition, he contended that there is no reason to doubt that the toxin could have survived. Nevertheless, his investigations revealed no evidence to support the story. He determined that Fildes undertook no pertinent research on botulinum toxin until after the assassination. Since he argues that the symptoms of botulinum poisoning can mimic those of other diseases that might infect wounds, he draws no conclusions from the symptoms that Heydrich suffered. Others have noted that the grenade fragments passed through the door of Heydrich's car and that dirt and other debris contaminated his wounds. Finally, Erhard Geissler, who has undertaken an extensive review of the German sources, also found little evidence to support the idea that the assassins used botulinum. Accordingly, as Carter notes, "Until further evidence emerges, the matter remains obscure."[436]

***Case 1940-01X: Egyptian "gangster", 1940s?***

In October 1947, an Egyptian newspaper reported that "a few years ago" an Egyptian gangster used typhoid culture stolen from "the Government chemical laboratories" as part of a plot to murder insured victims. The test tube was taken with the assistance of a laboratory technician.[437]

---

[432] Robert Harris and Jeremy Paxman, *A Higher Form of Killing: The Secret Story of Chemical and Biological Warfare* (New York: Hill and Wang, 1982), pp. 88-94.

[433] For a comprehensive history of the entire plot to kill Heydrich, see Callum MacDonald, *The Killing of SS Obergruppenführer Reinhard Heydrich* (New York: Collier Books, Macmillan Publishing Company, 1989).

[434] M.R.D. Foot, *SOE: An outline history of the Special Operations Executive, 1949-1946* (Frederick, Maryland: University Publications of America, 1986), p. 200.

[435] Callum MacDonald, *The Killing of SS Obergruppenführer Reinhard Heydrich*, p. 227.

[436] See the stories that appeared in 1996 issues of *ASA Newsletter*: Dr. Benjamin Garrett, "The CW Almanac: April 1996," 14 June 1996, issue 96-3, p. 9, G.B. Carter, "The Legend of Fildes and the Heydrich Assassination," 16 August 1996, issue 96-4, p. 8, Jiri Matousek, "A BTX-bomb for Reinhard Heydrich? Doubts and Questions Still Remain," 11 October 1996, issue 96-5, p. 8, Erhard Geissler, "More about Heydrich Assassination," 5 December 1996, issue 96-6, p. 10. Richard Price kindly supplied me with copies of these articles.

[437] "Epidemic due to lost flask?" *Egyptian Gazette*, October 3, 1947, p. 3, citing a story that appeared in the *Wafd*-controlled newspaper, *Sowt El Umma*.

***Case 1930-02X: German doctor, about 1930***

A German-language medical journal published in1930 reported on the case of a physician who attempted to commit suicide by injecting himself with tetanus toxin. He recovered when he was given tetanus antitoxin after his symptoms were identified.[438]

***Case 1930-01X: Hungarian Artist, about 1930***

Writing in 1940, Charles Thompson described an incident case that "occurred about ten years ago."

> A Hungarian artist was tried for attempting to murder his wife by means of typhoid and cholera germs. The cholera medium in his possession was found to have lost all activity through having been kept too long, while the typhoid culture, though quite a virulent one, failed to kill the victim. The discovery of the crime was made through his attempts to obtain cultures from a private laboratory and demanding virulent strains.[439]

Thompson gave no additional details and provided no source.

***Case 1917-01: German sympathizers, July 1917***

In July 1917, it was discovered that certain brands of courtplaster being sold in the United States were contaminated with tetanus. Courtplaster is an adhesive plaster that was used to cover small wounds, something like a Band-Aid. Itinerant peddlers in several states were found to be selling tetanus-contaminated courtplaster.[440] On July 28, 1917, the Department of Justice issued an official statement about the case.

> The Department of Justice, without sharing in any sensational view as to the manner in which sticking plaster or courtplaster became infected, states that some of the samples submitted and analyzed have been thereby shown to contain tetanus germs. The public is consequently cautioned against purchasing this remedy except from approved sources, the warning being particularly directed against purchases in small packages from street peddlers and venders.[441]

It was suspected at the time that German-Americans sympathetic towards Germany in the war were responsible for the contaminated material. The New York State Department of Health's issued a statement through the State Defense Council that specifically referred to the allegation.

> This warning comes close on the heels of the circulation of stories that Germans have sent agents throughout the United States to spread such diseases as tetanus and typhoid by means of poisoned courtplaster.[442]

There is no indication that any such connection was ever established or that any prosecutions resulted.

***Case 1910-02X: Pancho Villa, 1910s?***

According to a description that appears in the autobiography of the novelist William Burroughs, supporters of Pancho Villa used botulinum toxin against the Mexican federal troops. He describes the events as follows:

> Fill a water canteen to the top with freshly cooked and drained green beans. Close it and put aside for several days. A few slivers of rotting pork are then added, and the canteen sealed tightly. Ten incubators are buried underground. After seven days most will be swollen, indicating a thriving botulism culture.
>
> Can be smeared on any fruit, meats, or vegetables, dabbed on thornbushes and fragments of glass. Guerrilla children sniped sentries with pottery shards or with obsidian chips dipped in botulism. A little ingenuity. There are many ways and it takes such a little to do the Big Job.[443]

---

[438] Reported in Thomas A. Gonzales, Morgan Vance, and Milton Helpern, *Legal Medicine and Toxicology* (New York: D. Appleton-Century Company, 1940), p. 611.

[439] C.J.S. Thompson, *Poisons and Poisoners: With Historical Accounts of Some Famous Mysteries in Ancient and Modern Times* (London: Harold Shaylor, 1940). The first edition of this study was published in 1930, so the episode could have occurred any time during the 1920s or 1930s.

[440] According to a statement by the U.S. District Attorney for Kansas City, Fred D. Robertson, at least one brand of courtplaster being sold by peddlers was found to be contaminated. He indicated that tests of the courtplaster using guinea pigs suggested that the material was sufficiently contaminated to cause harm to humans but not to kill someone. See "Tetanus Germs Found in Sticking Plaster," *New York Times*, July 29, 1917, p. I, 1. A subsequent report from Freeport, Illinois, indicated that courtplaster being sold by a peddler there was found to be contaminated. "Tetanus Germs in Plaster," *New York Times*, July 31, 1917, p. 5.

[441] Quoted in "Tetanus Germs Found in Sticking Plaster," *New York Times*, July 29, 1917, p. I, 1.

[442] Quoted in "Tetanus Germs Found in Sticking Plaster," *New York Times*, July 29, 1917, p. I, 1.

***Case 1909-01: Bennett Clark Hyde, November 1909***

On February 9, 1910, Bennett Clark Hyde, a surgeon living in Kansas City, Missouri, was indicted for the alleged murder of Colonel Thomas H. Swope, one of Kansas City's founding fathers. Thus began what one writer called "one of the most amazing and puzzling poison cases to be found in history".[444] The Hyde case is also probably the most famous criminal case in Kansas City's history. In 1996, the *Kansas City Star* called the case "Kansas City's litigation of the century".[445] Its notoriety arose from the prominence of the victims, Hyde's close relations to the alleged victims (he was married to one of Swope's nieces), and the bitter legal fight that led to one civil trial and three criminal trials. Ultimately, however, Hyde was never convicted.[446]

Colonel Swope is best remembered today for donating the 1,300 acres that became Kansas City's Swope Park, the second largest urban park in the United States. (When he died, the park was valued in excess of $2 million.)[447] Even after such acts of philanthropy, Swope died with a fortune of just under $2 million.[448]

In 1909, Colonel Swope, then 82-years old, lived in Independence, Missouri, about 20 miles outside Kansas City, along with his brother's widow, Mrs. Logan Swope, and her children. Swope's will divided the bulk estate among his ten surviving heirs, meaning his sister-in-law and her children were named in the will. The will stipulated that if any of them were to die, the assets designated for that person were to be redistributed among the remaining heirs. James Moss Hunton, a cousin, was named as the trustee and administrator of the will.

Among the beneficiaries of the will was Frances Hyde, one of Logan Swope' daughters. Frances married Hyde in 1907 over the strong objection her mother. Despite Mrs. Swope's views, Colonel Swope liked Hyde, and helped the newly weds buy and furnish a house in Kansas City, where Hyde had a profitable practice.

In September 1909, Hunton became ill, and Hyde was asked to look after him. According to Hyde, Hunton was suffering from apoplexy, and determined that it was necessary to bleed him to reduce his blood pressure. During the bleeding, Hyde took six pints of blood. On October 1, 1909, Hunton died. Subsequently, the state claimed that Hyde essentially allowed Hunton to bleed to death.

Only two days later, on October 3, Colonel Swope became ill. Hyde was called in to look after the old man. According to the testimony of a nurse, Hyde gave Colonel Swope a capsule. Twenty minutes later, Colonel Swope turned blue and suffered convulsions. He died soon thereafter. The state alleged that he was given a mixture of strychnine sulfate and potassium cyanide, relying on the different effects of the two poisons to prevent a diagnosis of the cause of death.

Some weeks later, a typhoid epidemic broke out in Colonel Swope's house. The first to become ill was Mrs. Logan Swope. On December 2, one of the nieces also showed signs of typhoid. Around December 3, one of Colonel Swope's nephews, Chrisman Swope, became ill with typhoid. On December 4, three servants in the household became sick. The next day, a visitor to the household, Mildred Fox, was stricken. Another niece, Sarah Swope, became ill on December 9, followed by one of her sisters, Stella, on December 11. The last member of the household to become ill was Lucy Lee Swope, who was traveling abroad and only returned home four days before she became ill. All recovered, except one of Colonel Swope' nephews, Chrisman. Although the young man appeared to be getting better, he was suddenly seized with convulsions and died on December 6, 1909.[449]

After the death of Chrisman, one the attending nurses became suspicious, and threatened to quit because "people are being murdered in this house." This led Mrs. Swope to give a Dr. G. T. Twyman charge of the case. Twyman investigated and could find no obvious cause for the typhoid outbreak. Consequently, Mrs. Swope brought her concerns to the attention of the trustee for her brother-in-law's estate. He launched a series of investigations. A bacteriologist was employed to review conditions in the house. He also could find no

---

[443] Quoted in Benjamin Weissman, "Dream Control," *Los Angeles Times*, Book Review, p. 15. The alleged use of botulism toxin by Pancho Villa's followers is mentioned in passing in Uncle Fester, *Silent Death*, Revised and Expanded 2nd Edition (Port Townsend, Washington: Loompanics Unlimited, 1997), p. 93.

[444] Edward H. Smith, *Famous Poison Mysteries* (New York: The Dial Press, 1927), pp. 176. I am indebted to Jason Pate, Center for Nonproliferation Studies, Monterey Institute for International Studies, for bringing this case to my attention.

[445] Brian Burnes, "Turning back the clock on justice UMKC law school re-creates trial in death of philanthropist Thomas Swope," *Kansas City Star*, January 13, 1996, as found at the newspaper's World Wide Web site, *http://www.kcstar.com*.

[446] Smith, *Famous Poison Mysteries*, p. 176.

[447] "Thomas H. Swope," *New York Times*, October 4, 1909, p. 9.

[448] "$118,000 for Mrs. Hyde," *New York Times*, November 8, 1912, p. 22.

[449] "Two Rich Men Dead, Murder is Charged," *New York Times*, January 14, 1910, p. 2.

obvious reason for the outbreak. The water used in the house was not infected. This led the bacteriologist to suspect that the disease was being brought into the house.

Especially suspicious were the circumstances under which Lucy Lee Swope became ill. She became ill only four days after returning from a trip abroad, although it was thought that the incubation time was ten days. As it happened, Hyde had traveled to meet here on the East coast to bring her back to Independence. Later, she recalled being given a foul tasting drink of water by Hyde during the trip home.

By this time, the family was firmly convinced that something was wrong. An exhumation order was granted, and autopsies were performed on the dead men. Toxicological tests were conducted, which demonstrated that strychnine was present in the remains.

Hyde had access to typhoid organisms, according to testimony given to the grand jury that indicted Hyde. In September 1909, Hyde had lunch with Edward L. Stewart, a pathologist and bacteriologist. Hyde asked for Stewart's assistance in working on bacteria. Stewart agreed, and on November 10 prepared six cultures for Hyde:

- No. 1: Bacillus anthrax
- No. 2: Bacillus pyocyanous
- No. 3: Bacillus prodigissis
- No. 4: Bacillus staphycoceus albus
- No. 5: Bacillus typhoid
- No. 6: Diphtheria (later proved not to be diphtheria)

Stewart delivered the cultures to Hyde on November 11 or 12. After the outbreak of typhoid in the Swope family, Stewart became suspicious. Stewart went to Hyde's office on December 14, and discovered that the entire top surface of the culture tube for the typhoid organisms had been "swept clean". According to Stewart, "there were enough germs taken out to inoculate the whole of Kansas City." He removed the tube and locked it up. The next day he replaced it with a similar tube so that Hyde would not get suspicious. Stewart subsequently went to meet with Hyde at the latter's office on December 27, and noted that this time there was a stroke through the culture in the tube containing the diphtheria. Because the bottom of the tube was cracked, Stewart took that tube away with him. At that time, Hyde told Stewart that he had "just fooled around a bit" with the cultures.[450]

Hyde's trial lasted for a month. The lead attorneys were highly respected figures in the Missouri legal community. The Swope family hired the prosecutor, while Frances Hyde used her money to pay for an extremely expensive defense. According to one newspaper account, the legal bills for the defense totaled more than $75,000 by late 1911. Ultimately, the prosecution prevailed, and the jury voted to convict the defendant, although the first ballot was eight to four in favor of acquittal.

On April 11, 1911, the Missouri Supreme Court issued a ruling overturning the conviction. According to the court, the evidence that Hyde was involved in the typhoid epidemic was inconclusive. Moreover, the court held that the evidence for the presence of poison in the case of Colonel Swope was marginal, and that the old man could have died of "senile debility" or "uraemic" poisoning.[451] Recently, legal experts who have looked into the case appear to agree that the autopsies and subsequent analyses were seriously mishandled.[452]

A second trial began in November 1911, but a mistrial was declared when the one of the sequestered jurors escaped from the hotel where he was being lodged by climbing through a transom and jumping 15 feet from a fire escape. When he returned to the court four days later, the presiding judge declared that the juror was insane and declared a mistrial.[453]

A third trial held in 1912 ended in a hung jury. The County Prosecutor intended to bring the trial to court yet again. The trial was again delayed. In January 1917, a judge decided that enough was enough and

---

[450] "The Grand Jury Testimony," *Kansas City Star*, April 24, 1910, p. 4A. Generally, grand jury information is permanently secret. In this case, a transcript of the testimony became public because one of the prosecutors lost a copy, which found its way into the hands of the defense.

[451] "Swope Poison Case Must Be Retried," *New York Times*, April 12, 1911, p. 7.

[452] Burnes, "Turning back the clock on justice," *Kansas City Star*, January 13, 1996.

[453] "Hyde Juror Flees," *New York Times*, December 12, 1911, p. 4, and "Hyde Juror Back; Is Insane," *New York Times*, December 15, 1911, p. 10.

dismissed the case.[454] Thus, Hyde was never convicted or acquitted of the alleged murders. The state never legally established that he was responsible for the typhoid outbreak in the Swope household.[455]

***Case 1900-01X: Deaths in Malawi, unknown dates***

Some have asserted that castor beans, which contain the toxin ricin, have been involved in numerous murders. It has been possible to identify only one claim that appears based on substantive data. According to a comprehensive survey of poisonous plants located in East Africa, "There have been many cases in Malawi of unwanted offspring having been murdered by the inclusion of the seed in food." One of the co-authors of this study was at one time the Botanist in Charge, East African Herbarium, Nairobi, Kenya, and he drew on those records in writing his account. Unfortunately, he gives no other details of the alleged incidents.[456]

[454] "To Try Hyde a Fourth Time," *New York Times*, December 19, 1913, p. 3, and "To Drop Case Against Hyde," *New York Times*, January 3, 1917, p. 4.

[455] Smith, *Famous Poison Mysteries*, p. 187.

[456] Bernard Verdcourt and E.C. Trump, *Common Poisonous Plants of East Africa* (St. James's Place, London: Collins, 1969), p. 60.

# Chapter 6:
# Threatened Use

## Threatened Use (Probable or Known Possession)

This category includes cases in which the perpetrators threatened to use biological agents, and subsequent investigations confirmed that they possessed or probably possessed biological agents. This category includes cases in which the perpetrators never implemented planned attempts to use biological agents. It also includes cases in which the perpetrator's intentions were kept secret.

### *Case 1998-06: Iraqi terrorism in UK, March 1998*

On March 18, 1998, the Home Office circulated an "all-ports warning" that Iraq might attempt to smuggle chemical or biological weapons into the United Kingdom. The confidential memorandum was sent to Customs and Excise, the Special Branch, the Foreign Office, and the Ministry of Defence. According to press reports, the alert contained the following language.

> Iraq may launch a chemical and biological attack using materials disguised as harmless fluids. Could officers therefore be alert for any items which may contain harmful substances. Particular attention should be given to containers of any size holding liquids with specific characteristics.[457]

Press reports suggest that British authorities were worried that the suspect materials might be smuggled into the country inside bottles disguised as liquor bottles, perfume sprayers, or cigarette lighters. The report apparently was based on intelligence information, originally obtained prior to Christmas in 1997.[458] According to the report that made the alert public, a March 24 story in a British tabloid, *The Sun*, the threat was directed at the United States, Britain, and other NATO countries that might support military operations against Iraq.[459]

The press reports led the Blair government to issue several clarifying comments. The Home Secretary, Jack Straw, made the following statement to the parliament.

> It is right to take sensible measures. But it is unnecessary to be alarmist. But our information is that there is no specific threat to the UK. There is no evidence to indicate that any attempt has actually been made to smuggle anthrax into this country. There is also no evidence that such an attempt at smuggling might be in prospect.[460]

The Iraqi government claimed that the whole story was "silly and baseless."[461]

### *Case 1997-01: Thomas Leahy, January 1997*

Thomas Leahy, a resident of Janesville, Wisconsin, was arrested on April 28, 1997 and charged with possession of ricin as a weapon in violation of federal law. He was indicted on May 15, 1997 by a federal grand jury. A superceding indictment, containing three counts, was issued on September 17, 1997. Count 1 was identical to the May 15 charge. Count 2 charged Leahy with possession of nicotine as a weapon. Count 3

---

457 As quoted in Philip Webster, Richard Ford, Michael Evans, and Stewart Tendler, "Anthrax alert on duty-free spirits," *Times* (London), March 24, 1998, as it appeared on the newspapers web site, *http://www.sunday-times.co.uk*.

458 Webster, et al., "Anthrax alert on duty-free spirits," *Times* (London), March 24, 1998.

459 "World must be constantly wary of Baghdad–Blair," *Reuters*, March 24, 1998, 12:42 p.m.

460 John Morrison, "UK plays down Iraq anthrax scare," *Reuters*, March 24, 1998, 11:47 a.m.

461 Hassan Hafidh, "Iraq Denies Smuggle Anthrax to Britain," *Reuters*, March 24, 1998, 04:33 p.m.

charged him with possession of a delivery system in the form of the mixture of nicotine and DMSO in a spray bottle.[462]

On October 28, 1997, Leahy entered a guilty plea to the first count, admitting that he possessed the ricin, that he knew it was a weapon, and intended to use it as a weapon.[463] On January 7, 1998, the U.S. District Court in Madison, Wisconsin sentenced Leahy, to 151 months in prison with no possibility of parole. In giving this sentence, the judge stated that he believed Leahy was dangerous. The judge increased the length of the sentence beyond that specified in the federal sentencing guidelines because of the lethality of the poisons that Leahy possessed and the judge's belief that Leahy essentially possessed a weapon of mass destruction.[464] Leahy has appealed the length of the sentence, arguing that the judge abused his discretion when he increased sentence beyond the limits specified by the sentencing guidelines.[465] The U.S. Court of Appeals agreed with the defendant's lawyers that the original sentence was excessive, and ordered the trial judge to reconsider his sentence.[466]

The origins of the case date to November 23, 1996, when Leahy was arrested for allegedly shooting his 13-year-old stepson in the face. At the time, Leahy's wife, Debora Ann Leahy, informed police that he talked about poisoning using bacteria and poisons. She indicated that Leahy had "many books and manuals in reference to poison," that he had threatened to poison family members, and that he claimed to have substances that could "kill without a trace."[467] On December 3, 1996, she gave the Janesville police several plastic bags which contained bottles of poisons and other chemicals, some books, a number of items that appears to indicate an interest in biological agents. Specifically, the police inventory indicates that Leahy had biological growth media, petri dishes, a book called *Procedures for the cure and handling of bacteria and fungi*, and a collection of biologicals. Among the agents in Leahy's possession were several vaccines and toxoids (including for *Clostridium perfringens*). This material posed a problem for the police. According to a Janesville Police Department Incident Report, "If there is any chance these substances are hazardous there is no safe place for their keeping and they will be destroyed."[468]

On January 9, 1997, Leahy's wife again approached the Janesville Police Department concerning Leahy's activities. According to the FBI, she told the police that Leahy "had many books and manuals referring to poison and creating bacterial strains to make poison." She also told the police that Leahy was growing materials on petri dishes, which he claimed to her "are capable of killing people without a trace." On January 13, 1997, a detective from the Janesville Police Department contacted the FBI, and informed them of Leahy's activities.[469] Press reports suggest that the police initiative resulted from the continued complaints of Leahy's wife.[470] She was sufficiently concerned about the contents of their former apartment that she had convinced their landlord to let her move into another apartment.[471]

---

[462] Letter from John W. Vaudreuil, Assistant U.S. Attorney, Office of Peggy A. Lautenschlager, U.S. Attorney, Western District of Wisconsin, August 18, 1998.

[463] Press Releases, Office of Peggy A. Lautenschlager, U.S. Attorney, Western District of Wisconsin, April 28, 1997, May 15, 1997 and October 28, 1997. I am grateful to Myra Longfield in the U.S. Attorney's office for providing copies of the first two press releases.

[464] Press Release, Office of Peggy A. Lautenschlager, U.S. Attorney, Western District of Wisconsin, January 8, 1997.

[465] Letter from John W. Vaudreuil, Assistant U.S. Attorney, Office of Peggy A. Lautenschlager, U.S. Attorney, Western District of Wisconsin, August 18, 1998.

[466] Kevin Murphy, "Sentence to be reduced in toxin case," *Journal Sentinel* (Milwaukee, Wisconsin), February 23, 1999, as found on the newspaper's World Wide Web site at *http://www.jsonline.com.*

[467] Kathleen Ostrander, "Janesville man charged with possession of toxin," *Milwaukee Journal Sentinel*, April 29, 1997, at *http://www.onwisconsin.com.* Leahy entered a guilty plea on October 14, 1997 to charges associated with the shooting of his stepson. See Kathleen Ostrander, *Milwaukee Journal Sentinel*, October 15, 1997.

[468] As attached to the indictment against Thomas Leahy, April 26, 1997, provided by the Office of Peggy A. Lautenschlager, U.S. Attorney, Western District of Wisconsin.

[469] Complaint against Thomas Leahy, April 26, 1997, provided by the Office of Peggy A. Lautenschlager, U.S. Attorney, Western District of Wisconsin.

[470] Kathleen Ostrander, "Janesville man charged with possession of toxin," *Milwaukee Journal Sentinel*, April 29, 1997, and Kevin Murphy, "Judge orders man held for toxin," *Milwaukee Journal Sentinel*, May 2, 1997. Additional coverage of the case appears in the reporting of the *Beloit Daily News*, available from its web site at *http://www.beloitdailynews.com.*

[471] Complaint against Thomas Leahy, April 26, 1997, provided by the Office of Peggy A. Lautenschlager, U.S. Attorney, Western District of Wisconsin.

On January 17, 1997, the FBI, the Janesville police, and the hazardous materials team of the Madison Fire Department searched Leahy's apartment and a garage storage area.[472] Leahy's wife, who had keys to the apartment and the garage, let them into the sites.[473] According to statements made by Assistant U.S. Attorney John Vaudreuil, a massive amount of material was seized. "The volume of evidence in various searches is more than anything I can recall in my time here. Boxes of equipment, poisons and unknown substances would fill the jury box in this (court) room."[474]

Among other items found in Leahy's possession were three six-ounce bags and five and one-half 7-ounce bags of caster beans.[475] The search also turned up two pickle jars with "rotted vegetable in clear liquid solution" and two pickle jars with an "unknown clear liquid/residue on bottom." These might have been an effort to produce botulinum toxin. In addition, the agents found a 400-milligram bag with Foxglove digitalis seeds, a book *Bacterial Infections of Humans*, and a guidebook to venomous animals and poisonous plants.[476] This material was shipped to the Wisconsin State Crime Laboratory, located in Milwaukee, Wisconsin.[477]

Following these discoveries, the FBI interviewed Deborah Leahy and learned that her husband claimed that he could "never have too many poisons." In addition, she said that Leahy had claimed "that he could make poisons that were organic in nature and which would break down in the human body so that the cause of death could not be determined and these poisons would not show up in the victim's blood."[478]

Another informant told the FBI that Leahy claimed to possess bacteria "to be utilized to kill his enemies via the United States Postal Service." Leahy told the informant that he had airborne bacteria "that he would mail to his enemies, so that when they opened the envelopes the bacteria would become airborne and infect the victims." He also allegedly asserted that he could to put "killer viruses" on razor blades that he intended to attach to envelopes mailed to his enemies. He hoped that when his enemies opened their mail, they would cut themselves on the razor and become infected.[479]

Authorities also interviewed Leahy's stepson, Dillon Leahy. According to Dillon, during the summer of 1996 he first discovered his stepfather wearing a gas mask and a white plastic gown. Leahy also talked to his stepson about weapons, and showed him his stocks of chemicals and biologicals. At one point, Leahy showed him a poison mixed with DMSO, which he used to kill a mouse. Finally, Dillon told authorities that Leahy threatened his own mother, and that he claimed to have "killed people before."[480]

For reasons that are unclear, the evidence in the case was not analyzed during the following three months. Immediately following the April 23, 1997, B'nai B'rith incident (see page 110 for a discussion of that incident), for reasons that are not clear, the FBI began to take a closer look at Leahy's activities. As a result, the Hazardous Materials Response Unit at the FBI's Laboratory tested items found in the January 17 search. They discovered ricin in a small bottle and a "pulverizer/mixer."[481] Subsequent reports indicate that the vial proved to contain 0.7 grams of 4 per cent pure ricin. The pestle apparently had been used to grind the castor

---

[472] Kevin Murphy, "Judge orders man held for toxin," *Milwaukee Journal Sentinel*, May 2, 1997.

[473] Complaint against Thomas Leahy, April 26, 1997, provided by the Office of Peggy A. Lautenschlager, U.S. Attorney, Western District of Wisconsin.

[474] "Man faces second charge in toxin possession case," *Star Tribune* (Minneapolis-St. Paul), September 10, 1997, at *http://www.startribune.com*.

[475] Exhibit 2 of Complaint against Thomas Leahy, April 26, 1997, provided by the Office of Peggy A. Lautenschlager, U.S. Attorney, Western District of Wisconsin.

[476] Exhibit 2, Complaint against Thomas Leahy, April 26, 1997, provided by the Office of Peggy A. Lautenschlager, U.S. Attorney, Western District of Wisconsin.

[477] Complaint against Thomas Leahy, April 26, 1997, provided by the Office of Peggy A. Lautenschlager, U.S. Attorney, Western District of Wisconsin.

[478] Complaint against Thomas Leahy, April 26, 1997, provided by the Office of Peggy A. Lautenschlager, U.S. Attorney, Western District of Wisconsin.

[479] Complaint against Thomas Leahy, April 26, 1997, provided by the Office of Peggy A. Lautenschlager, U.S. Attorney, Western District of Wisconsin.

[480] Brief of Plaintiff-Appellee, United States of America, Plaintiff-Appellee, v. Thomas C. Leahy, Defendant-Appellant, No. 98-1176, in the United States Court of Appeals for the Seventh Circuit, May 26, 1998. These details were drawn from the presentence report prepared after Leahy's conviction.

[481] Complaint against Thomas Leahy, April 26, 1997, provided by the Office of Peggy A. Lautenschlager, U.S. Attorney, Western District of Wisconsin.

beans that are the source of ricin. According to law enforcement officials, that was enough ricin to kill 125 people.[482]

On April 26, 1997, the FBI raided a storage locker rented by Leahy and made additional discoveries. Among the items found were 13 plastic petri dishes with "unknown cultures" and 9 glass jelly jars with "unknown substances." On that same day, the FBI searched Leahy's apartment and found a number of books demonstrating an interest in poisons.[483] Finally, they obtained laboratory equipment and supplies from the apartment where Leahy's wife was living. Among the more interesting items were an incubator, pipettes, instructions for rehydrating biological cultures, growth media for bacteria, and plastic tissue culture dishes. There was a box labeled "Intro to Natural Genetic Engineering." He apparently also had some biological cultures, including *E. coli*.[484] Tests were made of 27 samples taken from the petri dishes and jelly jars and sent to the IIT Research Institute in Chicago, Illinois. The only organism detected in the samples was an avirulent strain of *C. botulinum*.[485] The laboratory analyst believed that Leahy was probably trying to produce the toxic form of the organism.[486]

Based on this evidence, Leahy was arrested April 28, 1997 and was charged with possession of a toxin for use as a weapon. At that time, federal officials alleged that Leahy had claimed that he intended to produce lethal airborne bacteria that he could use to kill people by mailing packages to them. A federal magistrate determined that there was sufficient basis to support the allegations against Leahy, and ordered that he be held without bail.[487] A federal grand jury indicted Leahy on May 15 on a single count of possessing a toxin for use as a weapon.

Additional laboratory tests reportedly indicate that Leahy possessed other poisons as well. On September 9, 1997, Vaudreuil told reporters that Leahy would soon be indicted on a second charge for possession of a toxin. According to Vaudreuil, police discovered three spray bottles containing a mixture of nicotine and DMSO (dimethyl sulfoxide). Vaudreuil asserted that three sprays of the mixture would kill someone.[488]

According to Leahy's lawyer, he takes medicines to treat schizophrenia and has "perceived enemies, real or unreal." Leahy's sisters reportedly told police that he was dangerous and they feared he might try to kill them. Accordingly, they refused to allow their addresses to appear on police reports. Similarly, Leahy's mother was frightened of him, and initially refused to testify in court from fear that he would harm her.[489]

***Case 1996-04: Michael Just, May 1996***

In May 1995, Michael Just initiated a product contamination blackmail scheme by acquiring a pathogen, *Yersinia enterocolitica*, from a catalogue supply house.[490] Just was heavily in debt from failed

---

[482] Kevin Murphy, "Judge orders man held for toxin," *Milwaukee Journal Sentinel*, May 2, 1997, and "Man faces second charge in toxin possession case," *Star Tribune* (Minneapolis-St. Paul), September 10, 1997. These press reports put the ricin purity at 5 percent, and says that there was enough ricin to kill 100 people. The purity is given as 4 percent in subsequent statements by prosecutors, who also changed the estimate of the number of lethal does to 125. See Press Release, Office of Peggy A. Lautenschlager, U.S. Attorney for the Western District of Wisconsin, October 28, 1997.

[483] Exhibit 4, Complaint against Thomas Leahy, April 26, 1997, provided by the Office of Peggy A. Lautenschlager, U.S. Attorney, Western District of Wisconsin.

[484] Exhibit 3, Complaint against Thomas Leahy, April 26, 1997, provided by the Office of Peggy A. Lautenschlager, U.S. Attorney, Western District of Wisconsin. For some reason, Leahy also had animal vaccines and toxoids.

[485] John Vaudreuil, electronic communication, December 30, 1997.

[486] Brief of Plaintiff-Appellee, United States of America, Plaintiff-Appellee, v. Thomas C. Leahy, Defendant-Appellant, No. 98-1176, in the United States Court of Appeals for the Seventh Circuit, May 26, 1998. This view was drawn from the presentence report prepared after Leahy's conviction.

[487] Kevin Murphy, "Judge orders man held for toxin," *Milwaukee Journal Sentinel*, May 2, 1997.

[488] "Man faces second charge in toxin possession case," *Star Tribune* (Minneapolis-St. Paul), September 10, 1997. For sources on DMSO, see footnote 496 on 99. The inventory of items seized on January 17 from Leahy's apartment and garage includes "1 plastic container—unknown reddish colored liquid (mixture of nicotine sulfate and DMSO?)."

[489] Kevin Murphy, "Judge orders man held for toxin," *Milwaukee Journal Sentinel*, May 2, 1997.

[490] *Y. enterocolitica* causes diarrhea. Contaminated chocolate milk, tofu, and undercooked pork have transmitted it. Significantly, it can grow even when refrigerated in storage containers with little free oxygen. There are more than 50 strains of the organism, many not pathogenic. See Abram S. Benenson, editor, *Control of Communicable Diseases Manual*, Sixteenth edition (Washington, DC: American Public Health Association, 1995), pp. 524-527. According to a 1999 CDC calculation, Y. enterocolitica was responsible for an estimated 96,368 cases of infection a year in the United States, about 90 percent through foodborne transmission. Most of the cases resulted from consumption of contaminated pork. About half a percent of those infected died from the disease. See Paul S. Mead, et al., "Food-Related Illness and Death in the United States," *Emerging Infectious Diseases*, September-October 1999, pp. 607-625.

business ventures, and attempted to extort £250,000 from five British dairies by threatening to contaminate their milk with the *Y. enterocolitica*. He had a degree in microbiology and virology from Nottingham University. He sent threatening letters to the companies on several occasions. In one letter, he sent a milk carton to a company that was contaminated with a dye to demonstrate that he could inject substances into cartons without the tampering being evident. In a subsequent package, he sent test tubes containing *Y. enterocolitica* cultures.

In response to Just's demands, the companies deposited money in an anonymous Austrian bank account. When Just attempted to withdraw money from the account, however, Austrian police arrested him. He was tried in Austrian courts and sentenced to three years in prison on a charge of serious blackmail.[491] Just's wife, Nora Just, was arrested and sentenced to three years in prison for her part in the plot.[492]

***Case 1993-05: Dwayne Kuehl, March or May 1993***

An Escanaba, Michigan businessman, Dwayne Kuehl, was tried in December 1999 on charges of plotting to use ricin to murder a building inspector. Kuehl admitted that he planned to murder the official, Jim O'Toole, and that he considered using ricin to poison the building inspector. O'Toole was closing buildings that Kuehl owned and thus depriving him of rent revenues. According to Kuehl's account, "I was in the process of making the poison. I was almost done." He planned to smear the ricin on the doorknob of a rental property that O'Toole was scheduled to inspect. In courtroom testimony, Kuehl claimed, " I didn't end up putting any poison there." According to other accounts, however, he actually went through with the attempt. A former girlfriend and a former employee told the court that Kuehl told them that he had gone through with the attempt. Other testimony suggested that he actually told people that he had gone through with the attempt. Prosecutors claimed that the attempt was made in March 1993, while Kuehl claimed that it occurred in May 1993. The discrepancy in the date was significant, because the statute of limitations in Wisconsin for attempted murder is only six years and police arrested Kuehl in April 1999.[493]

The jury acquitted Kuehl. However, federal authorities charged him with possession of ricin. He pled innocent to the federal charges.[494] On March 27, 2000, he pleaded guilty to charges of possessing ricin. He was sentenced to three years and 10 months of prison time and fined $10,000.[495]

***Case 1992-03: Minnesota Patriots Council, May 1992***

In May 1992, Collete Baker informed the Swift County Sheriff's office that her husband, Douglas Allen Baker, possessed a substance "that would kill a person on contact." At that time, she also filed a complaint against him for threatening to kill her with a shotgun. She later brought a coffee can to the authorities to support her story. Inside the can were a baby food jar and a canister containing the solvent dimethyl sulfoxide, commonly known as DMSO.[496] FBI testing determined that the baby food jar contained ricin.[497] Also in the coffee can was a note with the following text:

---

[491] Sarah Boseley, "Man held over threats to poison food," *Guardian* (London), July 9, 1996, p. 4, Lin Jenkins, "Blackmailer threatened to poison dairy foods," *Times* (London), August 28, 1996, p. 4, and Steward Tendler, "Coded Times messages used to trap blackmailer," *Times* (London), July 9, 1996, p. 1.

[492] Adrian Lee, "Wife who connived in plot to blackmail food firms is jailed," *Times* (London), January 29, 1997, p. 8.

[493] "Businessman denies trying to poison Escanaba's housing inspector," *Associated Press State and Local Wire,* December 11, 1999, AM cycle. See also "Jury selection begins for trial in Delta County," October 25, 1999, a report found at *http://www.msnbc.com* and attributed to WLUC, an NBC affiliate in Marquette, Michigan.

[494] *Associated Press State and Local Wire*, December 13, 1999, BC cycle, and *Associated Press State and Local Wire,* December 17, 1999, BC cycle.

[495] "Businessman admits to making poison", *Detroit News*, March 31, 2000, and "Pub owner gets 3 years in prison," *Detroit News*, August 2, 2000, both articles found at *http://detnews.com*.

[496] See Jonathan B. Tucker and Jason Pate, "The Minnesota Patriots Council (1991)," pp. 159-183, in Jonathan B. Tucker, editor, *Toxic Terror: Assessing Terrorist Use of Chemical and Biological Agents* (Cambridge, Massachusetts: MIT Press, 2000). Wayne Wangstad, "Trial begins for men accused of possessing deadly poison," *St. Paul Pioneer Press*, February 22, 1995, p. 1D. A discussion of how a terrorist might use DMSO in this fashion appears in Neil C. Livingstone, *The War Against Terrorism* (Lexington, Massachusetts: Lexington Books, 1982), p. 112. For a scientific discussion of DMSO, see "Dimethyl Sulfoxide," pp. 1429-1431, in Matthew J. Ellenhorn, et al., editors, *Ellenhorn's Medical Toxicology: Diagnosis and Treatment of Human Poisoning*, 2nd Edition (Baltimore: Williams & Wilkins, A Waverly Company, 1997). According to Ellenhorn, DMSO has been used to enhance the absorption of a large number of drugs, including insulin, antibacterial agents, and local anesthetics.

[497] Wayne Wangstad, "2 Minnesota men first to be convicted under Biological Weapons Act," *St. Paul Pioneer Press*, March 1, 1995, p. 3B.

> Doug, Be extremely careful! After you mix the powder with the gel, the slightest contact will kill you! If you breathe the powder or get it in your [sic] eyes, your [sic] a dead man. Dispose all instruments used. Always wear rubber gloves and destroy them also. Good hunting!! P.S. Destroy this note."[498]

The fingerprints of a second man, Leroy Charles Wheeler, also were found on the coffee can.[499]

This provided law enforcement officials with the evidence needed to conclude an investigation that actually began a year previously. In May 1991, Scott Loverink, informed the Douglas County Sheriff's office that Henderson belonged to a tax-protest group known as the "Patriots Council" and that they were talking about bombing a federal office building and murdering a sheriff's deputy using the ricin. According to information that Loverink provided at the trial, Henderson called the ricin "Maynard," and intended to mix the ricin with DMSO and Aloe Vera to enable it to penetrate the skin.[500] The name refers to Maynard Campbell, who sold them the book of directions and the castor beans that were the source of the ricin.[501]

During the investigation, the FBI set up a wiretap, which caught one of Wheeler's sons telling someone that his father kept stocks of beans and ammunition buried in his yard. In addition, an informant told Deputy U.S. Marshall William Ott that Douglas Baker put out a "contract" on Ott. Apparently, Ott was responsible for serving the court papers in a judgment against a friend of Baker's.[502]

The two were indicted and arrested in August 1994 for violating the Biological Weapons Antiterrorism Act of 1989. No explanation was provided for the time required to bring the case before a grand jury.[503] Baker and Wheeler were convicted after a jury trial.[504] They both received 33 month sentences.[505]

In September 1996, a federal appeals court ruled two to one that Baker deserved a new trial, accepting his lawyer's contention that his conviction was tainted by the inclusion of evidence that only implicated Wheeler.[506]

Two other conspirators, Dennis Bret Henderson and Richard Oelrich, were indicted by a federal grand jury in August 1995. They were accused of violating the Biological Weapons and Antiterrorism Act of 1989. Specifically, Henderson and Oelrich were accused of purchasing in April 1991 castor beans and the ricin-making instructions from a man in Ashland, Oregon.[507] In addition, Oelrich was accused of talking about murdering a deputy U.S. Marshall using the ricin. Oelrich and Henderson were co-owners of a carpet cleaning business.[508] Henderson and Oelrich were convicted at their trial.[509] Henderson received a sentence of four years in prison followed by three on probation.[510]

***Case 1990-03: Iraqi terrorism, 1990-1991***

William Burrows and Robert Windrem claim that inspectors for the United Nations (presumably working for the United Nations Special Commission, or UNSCOM) discovered evidence that Iraq developed

---

498 Wayne Wangstad, "Trial begins for men accused of possessing deadly poison," *St. Paul Pioneer Press*, February 22, 1995, p. 1D.

499 Wayne Wangstad, "Trial begins for men accused of possessing deadly poison," *St. Paul Pioneer Press*, February 22, 1995, p. 1D.

500 Wayne Wangstad, "2 Minnesota men first to be convicted under Biological Weapons Act," *St. Paul Pioneer Press*, March 1, 1995, p. 3B.

501 According to the Southern Poverty Law Center (SPLC), Maynard Campbell, who lived in Ashland, Oregon, wrote two books, *Catalogue of Silent Tools of Justice* and *Kingdoms At War*. In 1994, he was given a ten-year federal jail sentence for resisting arrest in 1992. He was murdered in prison in 1997. SPLC reported that Campbell was a tax protester, had anti-Semitic beliefs, and was involved in *Posse Comitatus*, an anti-government movement that flourished in the late 1970s and 1980s. See the entry on Campbell at the SPLC web site, *http://www.splcenter.org*.

502 "Tax protesters charged with plot to blow up building, poison officials," *Grand Forks Herald*, February 17, 1995, p. 6A.

503 "Tax protesters charged with plot to blow up building, poison officials," *Grand Forks Herald*, February 17, 1995, p. 6A.

504 "Jury convicts two of intending harm," *Grand Forks Herald*, March 1, 1995, p. 7A.

505 "Man gets three years for poison possession," *St. Paul Pioneer Press*, June 2, 1995, p. 2B.

506 Molly Guthrey, "New trial ordered for man convicted of terrorism," *St. Paul Pioneer Press*, September 28, 1996.

507 "Two face charges in poison case," *Grand Forks Herald*, August 6, 1995, p. 5C.

508 Wayne Wangstad, "2 Minnesota men first to be convicted under Biological Weapons Act," *St. Paul Pioneer Press*, March 1, 1995, p. 3B.

509 "Men convicted of producing deadly poison," *Grand Forks Herald*, October 26, 1995, p. 4B.

510 "Man sentenced for having toxin," *Grand Forks Herald*, January 21, 1996, p. 4A.

plans to use its biological agents for "terrorist activities."[511] They provide no details of the alleged plans, and do not identify the source of their information.

A Russian press report, written by a "special correspondent," appeared in *Komsomolskaya Pravda* on January 25, 1991, and claimed that Iraq had a "network of secret agents in Europe prepared to use chemical and bacteriological bombs." The article cites as its source a report appearing in the Egyptian newspaper *Al-Ahbar*. The intended targets allegedly were airports and airline offices, factories, schools, railroads, oil refineries, and hospitals treating wounded soldiers. Specifically, the story claimed that the Iraqis had targeted a refinery in Rotterdam described as the world's largest refinery and media targets, especially the BBC.[512]

***Case 1984-03: Kevin T. Birch and James B. Cahoon, November 1984***

On November 21, 1984, the FBI arrested two Canadians at the Buffalo, New York, Federal Express office when they picked up a shipment of what they thought was *Clostridium botulinum*. In fact, the FBI had substituted an "inert substance" for the *C. botulinum* culture before it was shipped by the American Type Culture Collection because it had reason for suspicions concerning the order. At the time of the arrest, FBI Special Agent John Thurston said that the shipment could have been used to produce enough *C. botulinum* "to wipe out a whole city."[513]

The case developed on September 24, 1984, when someone claiming to be Thomas Plaxton, a vice president at ICM Sciences, placed an order for 500-grams of freeze-dried *Clostridium tetani*. The material was delivered to a Federal Express office in Cheektowaga, New York, a suburb of Buffalo, where someone identifying himself as B. Bones picked it up.[514]

The illicit purchase became known when a copy of the shipping invoice was sent to ICM Science by Federal Express. ICM Science Ltd. was a small Canadian supplier of biological cultures located in Mississauga, Ontario. The company's president and owner, Serge Julien, contacted the American Type Culture Collection, which provided him with the letter ordering the culture. It had a fake ICM Sciences letterhead, and Julien contacted the police. In addition, the FBI was alerted of the illicit purchase.

Approximately a month after the first order was placed, Thomas Plaxton ordered more material, including both *C. tetanii* and *C. botulinum*. The same fake ICM Sciences letterhead was used. As previously noted, a harmless substance was substituted for the pathogen. The FBI then arrested the two men who came to pick up the order on November 21, 1984.

Further investigation determined that the two suspects were Kevin Birch, a Bell Canada employee who worked as a marketing supervisor, and James Cahoon, who was a senior consultant responsible for assessing loan applications with the Ontario Development Corporation. Cahoon reportedly analyzed a loan application from ICM Sciences.

According to an FBI statement, the two men acquired the material "for personal gain" and were not involved in a terrorist plot.[515] One press report suggests that the two "intended to kill a racehorse in an insurance fraud scheme."[516] Another account implies that they intended to kill a harness race horse that failed to perform well.[517]

The two were indicted by a federal grand jury on April 18, 1985 on charges that they committed telephone fraud and that they conspired to commit telephone fraud.[518] The two were accused of obtaining the

---

511 William E. Burrows and Robert Windrem, *Critical Mass: The Dangerous Race for Superweapons in a Fragmenting World* (New York: Simon and Shuster, 1994), p. 49.

512 A. Shumilin, "Husayn's Secret Weapon," *Komsomolskaya Pravda*, January 25, 1991, p. 3, as translated in Foreign Broadcast Information Service, *Foreign Report: Soviet Union*, January 25, 1991, FBIS-SOV-91-017, p. 16.

513 Margaret Hammersley, "Canadians Held In Purchase of Deadly Bacteria," *Buffalo News*, November 23, 1984, p. A1, and "FBI still searching for motive in botulism smuggling case," *Sun* (Vancouver), November 26, 1984, p. A10.

514 "2 Canadians held in U.S. over bacteria," *Sun* (Vancouver), November 24, 1984, p. A7.

515 "Bacteria terrorism ruled out," *Sun* (Vancouver), November 30, 1984, p. A14, and Zuhair Kashmeri, "Quick reaction by Mississauga lab foiled botulism scheme, police say," *Globe and Mail* (Toronto), November 30, 1984, pp. M1, M3.

516 Karl Vick, "Man gets hands on bubonic plague germ, but that's no crime," *Washington Post*, December 30, 1995, p. D1.

517 Margaret Hammersley, "Two Canadians Are Indicted in Bacteria Case," *Buffalo News*, April 18, 1985, p. B5, and *Associated Press*, December 2, 1985, PM cycle. This was confirmed by Assistant U.S. Attorney Joseph M. Guerra, III, in a telephone interview, February 26, 1998.

518 Margaret Hammersley, "Two Canadians Are Indicted in Bacteria Case," *Buffalo News*, April 18, 1985, p. B5, and *Associated Press*, April 18, 1985, AM cycle.

biological cultures under false pretenses. They negotiated a plea bargain agreement, and pled guilty to the charges. On December 2, 1985, each was fined $1,000.[519]

***Case 1972-01: R.I.S.E., January 1972***

On January 18, 1972, the Chicago police arrested two teenagers who were reportedly plotting to infect the Chicago municipal water system with *Salmonella typhi*, the organism that causes typhoid fever. The two men charged in the plot were Steven Pera, 18, and Allen C. Schwander, 19. Pera and Schwander were students at Chicago City College. Police believed that the two were "within a few days" of contaminating the Chicago water system.[520]

The Chicago police had arrested Schwander in September 1971 for theft and possession of stolen property, in November 1971 for sexual delinquency, and for burglary on January 13, 1972. Pera was a C student who had dropped all his courses, except biology, which gave him access to a laboratory at Chicago City College's Amundsen-Mayfair campus. Pera also had volunteered to work at a laboratory at Rush-Presbyterian-St. Luke's Medical Center "to gain additional knowledge of biology," but he had been ejected from it after his activities alarmed officials at the hospital. According to the hospital's account, "it became evident that he had been growing cultures in the laboratory that were not part of the research activities, and these cultures were destroyed."[521]

Illinois State's Attorney Edward V. Hanrahan said that Pera and Schwander had created a white racist organization called "R.I.S.E." In a public statement, Hanrahan indicated that "Members of 'RISE' were allegedly to be inoculated and immunized, enabling them to survive ... and to form the basis of a new master race. Water filtration plants in the Midwest were allegedly to be infected with typhoid and their deadly bacteria."[522] Chicago police believed that Pera and Schwander had only begun to recruit members to their organization, and had seven or eight members. Two of these new recruits, apparently alarmed at what Pera and Schwander planned to do, informed police of their activities on January 16, 1972. At that time law, enforcement authorities mounted a heavy guard over the city's two main water treatment facilities. In addition, a hunt was initiated for Pera and Schwander, and the two were arrested at Schwander's home two days later. The two informants told police that they had each received two injections to protect them against typhoid, and were supposed to receive a third at the time that they decided to report the plot.

Subsequent analyses apparently confirmed that the two had possession of quantities of *S. typhi* at the college laboratory and at Schwander's apartment. There were initial concerns that the two also had botulinum toxin.[523] Another account also suggests that the two had diphtheria cultures as well.[524] Subsequent tests, however, indicated that the two did not have any botulinum toxin.[525]

Bail for the two was initially $250,000, but that was subsequently lowered to $50,000 for Pera and $40,000 for Schwander. Pera and Schwander subsequently skipped bail and fled to Cuba. According to an FBI statement, the two hired a small plane to take them from Jamaica to Cuba in early May 1972.[526] The Cubans later arrested Schwander and sentenced him to six years in prison for "counterrevolutionary activities."[527]

Pera returned to the United States in late 1974, and voluntary surrendered. After initially pleading not guilty, he negotiated a plea agreement with the Cook County District Attorney's office. On June 20, 1975, Pera was sentenced to five years probation. On January 7, 1977, Pera's attorney filed a motion requesting that the probation be terminated, which apparently happened in a court hearing on February 4, 1977.[528]

---

519 *Associated Press*, December 2, 1985, PM cycle, and Karl Vick, "Man gets hands on bubonic plague germ, but that's no crime," *Washington Post*, December 30, 1995, p. D1.

520 Ronald Koziol, "Tighten Water Plant Guard After Poison Scare Arrests," *Chicago Tribune*, January 19, 1972, pp. 1, 6, Andrew H. Malcolm, "2 Youths Charged With Plot to Poison Water of Chicago," *New York Times*, January 19, 1972, p. 18, and Gene Bludeau, "Two in Chicago Accused of Plot to Poison Water," *Washington Post*, January 19, 1972, p. A3.

521 Ronald Koziol, "Tighten Water Plant Guard After Poison Scare Arrests," *Chicago Tribune*, January 19, 1972, p. 6.

522 Ronald Koziol, "Tighten Water Plant Guard After Poison Scare Arrests," *Chicago Tribune*, January 19, 1972, p. 1.

523 Jerry Crimmins, "Bond Cut Denied in Poison Plot, *Chicago Tribune*, January 26, 1972, section 1A, p. 16.

524 "Diphtheria cultures found in plot case," *Los Angeles Times*, January 27, 1972, p. 20.

525 Jerry Crimmins, "Two in Germ Plot Sought in 3 States," *Chicago Tribune*, March 31, 1972, section 1A, p. 1.

526 "2 Sought in Plot to Poison Water," *Washington Post*, May 23, 1972, p. A7.

527 "Cuba jails Chicago water plotter," *Chicago Tribune*, p. 3, and Jerry Crimmins, "Cuba will free me: water plot suspect," *Chicago Tribune*, July 11, 1973, p. 1B.

528 This information comes from the archives of the Office of the Circuit Court Clerk of Cook County, Chicago, Illinois, People vs. Pera et al., case 72-475 seq.

It is not known what happened to Schwander. The outstanding warrant was quashed on March 22, 1983, apparently due to the statute of limitations.

***Case 1960-02: CIA (against Lumumba), September 1960***

In 1960, the U.S. government was concerned that Patrice Lumumba might exploit the political instability in the former Belgian Congo to gain political power there. Assassination was one method explored to eliminate this perceived political threat. Among the assassination tools considered were poisons supplied to the CIA Station Officer. According to the Station Officer, on September 26, 1960 he was supplied with "rubber gloves, a mask, and a syringe" along with the unnamed biological poison. The object was to place the poison on something that Lumumba would put into his mouth, "whether it was food or a toothbrush." The poison was never used. It appears that by early October the poison was reaching its expiration date, the point where it would lose its potency. According to one account, the material was dumped into the Congo River by October 5, 1960.[529]

***Case 1960-01: CIA (against Castro), 1960-1961***

Congressional investigators identified at least two plots to assassinate Castro that involved use of biological substances.[530] In the first instance, on August 16, 1960 cigars contaminated with botulinum toxin were given to a CIA official by the organization's Office of Medical Services. According to the congressional account, "The cigars were contaminated with a botulinum toxin so potent that a person would die after putting one in his mouth." There is no evidence to indicate whether an attempt was made to give the cigars to Castro.

A second attempt took place in March-April 1961, and involved a batch of botulinum toxin pills designed to dissolve in water. The plot involved organized crime figures working with the CIA to assassinate Castro. Castro was known to frequent a particular restaurant, and a Cuban in the pay of the mobsters worked there. The CIA produced an initial batch of pills, but since they did not dissolve in water, a second batch had to be prepared. This batch dissolved as needed, and testing with monkeys determined that the pills "did the job expected of them." According to one of the mobsters involved in the plot, "As far as I remember, they [the pills] couldn't be used in boiling soups and things like that, but they could be used in water or otherwise, but they couldn't last forever.... It had to be done as quickly as possible." The plot was never executed, for reasons that are not altogether clear. One source claimed that Castro stopped visiting the targeted restaurant, while another said that the Cubans needed authorization to use the poison and it was never given.

A third plot involved a CIA agent known by the codename "AM/LASH." According to the congressional investigations, the agent approached his contacts at the CIA and requested assistance in assassinating Castro. To satisfy this request, a poison pen device was produced. The device contained a hypodermic needle so small that the victim would not feel the penetration. The CIA, however, did not supply a poison, and the agent was advised to use Blackleaf-40, described by the congressional account as "a deadly poison which is commercially available."[531]

***Case 1952-01: MGB (against Tito), late 1952***

In 1993, General Dimitrii Volkogonov, a military historian and then an advisor to Russia's President Boris Yeltsin, reported that documents in Soviet archives proved that the Soviet Union considered assassinating Joseph Broz Tito. Marshall Tito, the wartime leader of Yugoslavia's communist resistance forces, broke with Stalin and the Soviet Union in 1948. According to the accounts uncovered by Volkogonov, Stalin became increasingly angered by Tito's policies, and criticized the head of the MGB (predecessor of the KGB), the notorious Lavrenti Beria, for failing to remove Tito from power. In late 1952, Beria ordered his subordinates to explore options for killing Tito.[532]

---

[529] Select Committee to Study Governmental Operations, U.S. Senate, *Alleged Assassination Plots Involving Foreign Leaders*, (Washington, D.C.: U.S. Government Printing Office, 1975), pp. 24-25, 29-30. Warren Hinckle and William Turner, *Deadly Secrets: The CIA-Mafia War Against Castro and the Assassination of J.F.K.* (New York: Thunder's Mouth Press, 1992), pp. 28-29, claim that the agent was a disease "indigenous to that area," without citing any sources.

[530] Select Committee to Study Governmental Operations, U.S. Senate, *Alleged Assassination Plots Involving Foreign Leaders*, (Washington, D.C.: U.S. Government Printing Office, 1975), pp. 73, 79-82, 88-89.

[531] Blackleaf-40 is a solution of 40% nicotine extracted from tobacco leaves.

[532] Anne McElvoy, "Archives prove Stalin wanted Tito killed," *Times* (London), June 12, 1993, p. 15, and "Soviet Plan to Assassinate Tito Told," *Los Angeles Times*, June 12, 1993, p. A12. I first came across this story in Wendy Barnaby, *The Plague Makers: The Secret World of Biological Warfare* (London: VISION Paperbacks, 1997), p. 37.

To execute the murder, Beria recruited an agent, I.R. Grigulevich, known by the code name Max. At the time, Max had managed to insinuate himself as a special plenipotentiary of Costa Rica in Italy and Yugoslavia. He was a seasoned operative: he had participated in the 1940 murder of Leon Trotsky in Mexico. Beria's minions developed several alternative schemes by which Max could murder Tito. One option called for Max to obtain a private meeting with Tito, during which Max would activate a mechanism secreted in his clothes that would release enough plague to kill everyone present. To protect Max, he was to be treated with "an anti-plague serum in advance." Other options did not involve biological agents. The remaining options relied on other techniques. A second option relied on use of an unspecified poison gas, which was to be released upon opening of a jewel box. Finally, consideration was given to providing Max with "a silent mechanism concealed as a personal item" that fired a bullet."[533]

The plan was forwarded to Stalin. It is not known if Stalin formally approved the document, but apparently some preliminary preparations were made to implement the proposal, since Max was directed to write a "farewell letter" to his wife in the event of his capture. In any case, the operation never proceeded after Stalin's death in March 1953.[534]

***Case 1944-01: British SOE (against Hitler), June 1944***

According to documents released by the Public Record Office, the British considered assassinating Adolph Hitler during the Second World War. The plot originated with Special Operations Executive (SOE). SOE was the organization created by the British to conduct covert operations against the Germans. The plans were never implemented.[535]

The primary focus of the British plans appears to have involved use of a sniper to kill Hitler at Berchtesgaden, his retreat in the Bavarian mountains. The British also considered using a bomb to destroy Hitler's train. Alternative plans involved putting an unidentified poison into either Hitler's food or the water supply of his railroad car. Someone also suggested that a poisoned dart fired from a specially modified fountain pen could be used. These methods were rejected for practical reasons. Someone might eat the poisoned food before Hitler. Similarly, Hitler probably would drink bottled water, not water taken from a railroad car tap. Finally, the use of a poison dart was considered too risky for the operative responsible for operating the device.[536]

Some consideration was given to use of a biological agent. One of the ideas discussed involved contaminating Hitler's clothes with anthrax. The anthrax was to be smuggled into Germany inside a fountain pen, eyeglasses, or false teeth. The available evidence suggests that these ideas were rejected at a relatively early stage. They were not incorporated into the final report that outlined the alternative approaches recommended for use in an assassination.[537]

## Threatened Use (No Known Possession)

This category includes cases in which the perpetrators threatened to use biological agents, but subsequent investigations determined that they did not possess biological agents. This category also includes cases in which it seems unlikely that the perpetrators possessed biological agents although no definitive

---

533 This account is based on a translation of the original document describing the proposed operation. It originally appeared in the Russian newspaper *Izvestiia*, June 11, 1993, and was translated by Natasha Shur and published in "Stalin's Plan to Assassinate Tito," *Cold War International History Project Bulletin*, Number 10, March 1998, p. 137. I am indebted to Professor Joshua Lederberg for bring this document to my attention. Ken Alibek, *Biohazard* (New York: Random House, 1999), p. 173, describes a conversation about this incident with a KGB liaison officer. According to Alibek's source, a dry powdered form of plague was produced in the late 1940s for use in assassinations.

534 Based on the editor's note accompanying "Stalin's Plan to Assassinate Tito," *Cold War International History Project Bulletin*, Number 10, March 1998, p. 137.

535 A copy of the report prepared by SOE outlining the plans given serious consideration is reproduced in *Operation Foxley: The British Plan to Kill Hitler* (London: PRO Press, 1998). For press coverage of the reports, see "Britain Planned to Kill Hitler," *Associated Press*, July 23, 1998, 6:27 a.m. EDT, and "British agents plotted to kill Hitler in 1944,' *Reuters*, July 22, 1998, 1:39 p.m. Eastern time.

536 Michael Evans, "Britain's secret plot to assassinate Hitler revealed," *Times* (London), July 23, 1998, as found at *http://www.sunday-times.co.uk.*

537 Michael Smith, "Britain planned to kill Hitler with anthrax," *Daily Telegraph* (London), July 23, 1998, as found at *http://www.telegraph.co.uk.* Significantly, anthrax does not appear in the final assassination plan reproduced in *Operation Foxley: The British Plan to Kill Hitler*, suggesting that the mission planners rejected use of biological agents at an earlier stage. Mark Seaman, who wrote an introduction to Public Records Office publication of the plan, also does not mention anthrax.

determination was ever made. It also includes some cases in which the perpetrator's allegedly planned to employ biological agents but never made any public threats. Anthrax hoaxes that occur in the United States, which have become extremely common since 1998, are found in the next section.

***Case 2000-08: Biological threat (against potteries), June 2000***

Two potteries in East Liverpool, Ohio, were sent letters that contained a green, moldy substance. The targets were Pioneer Pottery, which makes apothecary jars, coffee mugs, and other items using traditional patterns, serving ware, and W.C. Bunting, which decorates quality pottery produced in the East Liverpool area, including items produced by Pioneer. An employee of Bunting took the letter that they received back to the post office. Postal employees apparently were concerned that it might be an anthrax threat, leading them to notify the local fire department. The post office was evacuated, and three people were decontaminated. One of the owners of Bunting apparently believed that he knew who was responsible for sending the letters, but it is unclear anyone was charged for the incident. Press reports do not indicate whether a note giving an explicit threat was included in the envelope. Authorities indicate that the envelopes did not contain anthrax, but suspect that it may have contained talcum powder or cornstarch.[538]

***Case 2000-07: Klingerman Virus, May 2000***

According to e-mail messages widely circulated on the Internet, an organization known as the Klingerman Foundation was mailing blue envelopes containing sponges contaminated with a pathogen known as the Klingerman virus. According to the e-mail alert, 23 people have been infected by the virus, including seven who died.[539] According to the Centers for Disease Control and Prevention, the Internet warning is a hoax.[540]

Even though the Klingerman virus is a hoax, it has caused a number of emergency responses by people fearful that they have been exposed to it. For example, Geraldine Emanuel received an envelope that she feared might contain the Klingerman virus on May 20, 2000. Two days later, she called authorities. The Palm Beach County Sheriff's office, precipitating a response that also involved the local bomb squad, hazardous materials, and the U.S. Postal Service inspectors.[541]

This case is included as a threat, and not as a hoax, because of the extent to which people apparently believed in the reality of the danger and because it caused actual response operations.

***Case 1999-66: Ricin threat (against federal judge, September 1999***

James Kenneth Gluck was arrested in Tampa, Florida, on November 5, 1999 for allegedly threatening two Colorado state judges with ricin. In September 1999, Gluck reportedly sent a threatening, eight-page letter to Colorado Court of Appeals Judge Daniel Taubmann. In that letter, Gluck apparently claimed that he had the ability to kill 10,000 people using ricin, and implied that he could use ricin to kill everyone in the Jefferson County Administration and Courts Facility. The letter also reportedly claimed that ricin was "a quintessential American weapon for 'making a killing' (literally) without any responsibility because it cannot be determined who used it and it cannot be determined where it came from."[542]

Press accounts suggest that Gluck was angry about two clashes with Jefferson County officials.[543] In 1997, a Jefferson County judge ruled against Gluck on a zoning dispute related scrap materials stored on some property he owned. In 1989, he was fined for illegal possession of a dead barn owl.[544] An FBI hazardous materials team searched the Tampa house where he was living. Gluck had a makeshift laboratory. The FBI told

---

[538] "FBI Enters Case of Two Suspicious Mailings," *Dayton Daily News*, June 14, 2000, p. 4B, and "Anthrax ruled out in suspicious mailings," *Associated Press State and Local Wire*, June 14, 2000, BC cycle.

[539] "E-Mail Warning About Virus Is Hoax, Health Officials Say," *New York Times*, December 23, 2000. p. B8.

[540] Centers for Disease Control and Prevention, "False E-Mail Report about 'Klingerman Virus'," May 17, 2000, as found at *http://www.cdc.gov*. See also U.S. Postal Service, "False 'Klingerman Virus' E-Mail Rumor," May 25, 2000, as found at *http://www.new.usps.com*.

[541] "Internet hoax spurs woman to call bomb squad about mailed envelope," *Associated Press State and Local Wire*, May 23, 2000, BC cycle.

[542] Ace Atkins, "Man denies threatening with poison," *Tampa Tribune*, November 9, 1999, Florida/Metro section, p. 1

[543] Peggy Lowe, "Toxin suspect denied monitor," *Denver Post*, November 9, 1999, p. B-2, Peggy Lowe, "Ex-Boulder man arrested for toxin threat," *Denver Post*, November 8, 1999, p. B5, Pat Leisner, "No bond in case of alleged terrorist threat,' *Miami Herald*, November 9, 1999, as found at *http://www.herald.com*.

[544] Jose Patin O Girona and Janet Leiser, "Toxin threat leads FBI to search, arrest," *Tampa Tribune*, November 7, 1999, Florida/Metro section, p. 1, and "New hearing ordered in 'junk' fight," *Rocky Mountain News*, August 8, 1997, p. 43A.

a U.S. Magistrate that he had simple laboratory equipment, unspecified books on toxicology, and the *Anarchist's Cookbook.* According to FBI Agent Francis Gallagher, "there is no evidence that any refined ricin existed within the residence."[545]

***Case 1999-77: Diazien Hossencofft, September 1999***

On October 6, 1999, a federal grand jury indicted Diazien Hossencofft on a charge of threatening to give the government of China the code for a virus that "would kill the entire population except for a few people." Hossencofft apparently believed that his son, who had been given up for adoption, was being subjected to experiments by the government.[546] At the time, Hossencofft was a suspect in the disappearance of his estranged wife. Subsequently he was charged with murdering her.[547]

Hossencofft had a long record of telling bizarre stories about his activities. Reportedly, he told a friend that he worked for the CIA and developed for them a virus that the government plans to put into the world's water supply in 2007 to kill two-thirds of the world's population.[548]

***Case 1999-76: Robberies with HIV threats in Vancouver, August 1999***

The Vancouver, British Columbia, Canada, police reported that a man attempted to rob three people at automatic teller machines on 22 and 23 August 1999. Reportedly, a 25-year-old white male approached the victims while brandishing a syringe filled with a red colored liquid. The robber claimed that the syringe contained HIV contaminated blood. In one case, the assailant told a victim, "Excuse me sir. I really hate to do this, but I have AIDS and this a syringe with AIDS-tainted blood." One of the incidents occurred on August 23, while the other two took place on the previous day.[549]

According to a report by the *Vancouver Sun*, such incidents are relatively common. Writing in early 1998, the newspaper quoted a Vancouver police officer who indicated that the city had suffer a spate of such attacks in the past two months, including two on February 8, 1998. In many cases, the robbers did not even bother to fill the syringe with a red liquid, because people understood that even a used needle might be contaminated with HIV.[550]

***Case 1999-64: World Islamic Front for Fighting Jews and Crusaders, April 1999***

Ahmed Salama Mabruk, the military operations chief of Egyptian Islamic Jihad, told the Arabic newspaper *Al-Hayah* that the World Islamic Front for Fighting Jews and Crusaders "has biological and chemical weapons which it intends to use in operations against US and Israeli targets."[551] In a follow-on story, the newspaper reported, "a prominent fundamentalist residing outside Egypt has revealed that these weapons have been purchased from Eastern European countries and the former Soviet Union over the past two years." This unnamed individual also reportedly said, "Plans had been developed to distribute quantities of these weapons to elements belonging to the front in several states for use when necessary against US and Israeli targets in case of the failure to carry out operations against these targets through the use of explosives and conventional weapons."[552]

---

[545] Many Gonzales, "Agents find nerve gas materials," *Rocky Mountain News*, November 7, 1999, p. 14A.

[546] Guillermo Contreras, "Man Accused of Telephone Threats," *Albuquerque Journal*, October 6, 1999, p. B2, "Lawyer says client wanted assurance of son's safety," *Santa Fe New Mexican*, September 25, 1999, p. B-3, and Guillermo Contreras, "Woman Missing 2 Weeks," *Albuquerque Journal*, September 24, 1999, p. B1. This case was brought to my attention by Gavin Cameron, Jason Pate, Diana McCauley, & Lindsay DeFazio, "1999 WMD Terrorism Chronology: Incidents Involving Sub-National Actors and Chemical, Biological, Radiological, and Nuclear Materials," *The Nonproliferation Review*, Summer 2000, p. 172.

[547] Joline Gutierrez Krueger, "Missing wife's husband charged with murder," *Albuquerque Tribune*, November 18, 1999, p. A1.

[548] Rick Maese, "Hossencofft's life story reads like a sci-fi tale," *Albuquerque Tribune*, October 5, 2000, p. A1.

[549] Kim Bolan, "Police seek thief who threatened bank customers with syringe," *Vancouver Sun*, August 24, 1999, p. B5. This episode was brought to my attention by Gavin Cameron, Jason Pate, Diana McCauley, & Lindsay DeFazio, "1999 WMD Terrorism Chronology: Incidents Involving Sub-National Actors and Chemical, Biological, Radiological, and Nuclear Materials," *The Nonproliferation Review*, Summer 2000, p.171.

[550] "Police Warn of Bandits Armed with Syringes," *Vancouver Sun*, February 10, 1998, p. B1.

[551] Mohammad Salah, "Al-Zawahiri Aide Tells Al-Hayah: We Have Biological Weapons," *Al-Hayah* (London), April 19, 1999, p. 1, as translated by Foreign Broadcast Information Service.

[552] Mohammad Salah, "Fundamentalist Source: Bin-Laden Front Purchased Chemical Weapons from Eastern Europe," *Al-Hayah* (London), April 20, 1999, p. 1, as translated by Foreign Broadcast Information Service. See also "Jihad obtained bio-chemical weapons from ex-Soviet bloc," *Agence France Press*, April 20, 1999, 07:59 GMT,

***Case 1999-71: Chechen interest in biological weapons, February 1999***

According to Russian newspapers, in February 1999 a Chechen separatist military leader, Salman Raduyev, threatened to forcibly acquire biological weapons from Russian laboratories involved in the Soviet biological weapons program unless the Russian government released two women sentenced for participation in a terrorist attack. The Chechen also claimed that they would use radiological weapons against the Russians. The Russian government reportedly increased security at certain biological laboratories in reaction to the threat.[553]

Subsequently, Russian press reports suggested growing concerns regarding Chechen interest in biological weapons. The Russian Interior Minister, Vladimir Rushaylo, claimed that instructions for use of biological weapons had been discovered on Chechens captured in Dagestan. He told reporters, "Abstracts from instructions on the use of bacteriological weapons were found on killed Chechen bandits who took part in the attack on Dagestan last August and September."[554]

Other reports also appeared suggesting that the Chechens may possess biological agents. According to *Izvestia*, Valery Manilov, Senior Deputy Chief of the Russian General Staff, claimed that a disease outbreak among Chechen forces was caused by mishandling of biological weapons.[555] Subsequently, Chechen officials claimed that epidemics among their forces resulted from Russian use of biological agents.[556] Insufficient information is available to evaluate the veracity of any of these claims.[557]

***Case 1999-70: Theft using "HIV-contaminated" syringe, January 1999***

According to a story that originated with the Croatian news agency HINA, a currency exchange in Zadar, Croatia was robbed of 500 German marks by a man who threatened a clerk with a syringe that the robber claimed was filled with HIV. Police indicated that they had no way to confirm if the perpetrator might have possessed an HIV contaminated fluid.[558]

***Case 1999-68: Threat against milk producer, March 1999***

According to a report issued by the U.S. General Accounting Office, someone found or received a note claiming that milk, apparently produced by a specific plant, was contaminated with a biological agent. The allegation was reported to the state agriculture department, which initiated an investigation that also involved state and local law enforcement and public health organizations. In addition, the FBI opened a criminal investigation. The allegedly contaminated milk was sequestered, and the producer voluntarily halted production. Within 12 hours, investigators determined that there was no contamination. As of October 1999, no one had been charged in the case.[559]

***Case 1999-75: Christian Millenarian Groups, Throughout 1999***

According to a compilation of chemical and biological terrorism incidents, the U.S. government reportedly warned the Israeli government that certain Christian groups might use biological weapons. The full account reads as follows:

> US security forces allegedly warned their Israeli counterparts that Christian millenarian groups could use biological weapons for an attack in Israel during 2000. Such groups have supposedly

[553] Valentina Lezvina, Andrey Bagrov, and Sergey Gorbatov, "Moscow Preparing for Biological War with Chechnya," *Kommersant* [Moscow], February 17, 1999, p. 1, both translated from the Russian by Foreign Broadcast Information Service.

[554] Andrei Chitov, "Russia Rushailo ends visit to USA over terrorism, crime," *TASS*, October 29, 1999, and British Broadcasting System, "Biological warfare instructions found on Chechen rebels—interior minister," *BBC Summary of World Broadcasts*, November 1, 1999.

[555] Dmitry Koptev, "Federal Forces all but admit presence of Biological Weapons in Chechnya," *Izvestia*, August 12, 2000, p. 3, as reported in Agency WPS, August 16, 2000.

[556] "Chechen commander denies plans to disrupt election, condemns Russia's dirty war," Kavkaz-Tsentr News Agency, 16 August 2000, as found on the Internet and translated by the Foreign Broadcast Information Service, August 16, 2000.

[557] The Chechen threats and the Russian claims of Chechen interest in biological weapons, were brought to my attention by Gavin Cameron, Jason Pate, Diana McCauley, & Lindsay DeFazio, "1999 WMD Terrorism Chronology: Incidents Involving Sub-National Actors and Chemical, Biological, Radiological, and Nuclear Materials," *The Nonproliferation Review*, Summer 2000, pp. 163, 172.

[558] "Man robbed exchange office threatening with AIDS syringe," Associated Press, January 6, 1999, 07:46 Eastern Time. This incident was brought to my attention by Gavin Cameron, Jason Pate, Diana McCauley, & Lindsay DeFazio, "1999 WMD Terrorism Chronology: Incidents Involving Sub-National Actors and Chemical, Biological, Radiological, and Nuclear Materials," *The Nonproliferation Review*, Summer 2000, p. 162.

[559] General Accounting Office, *Food Safety: Agencies Should Further Test Plans for Responding to Deliberate Contamination*, GAO/RCED-00-3, p. 5.

been purchasing poisons and bacteria from a variety of sources and have been seeking scientists and engineers to help in the development of "a doomsday weapon."[560]

***Case 1998-31: HIV threat (against Emmpak Foods), December 1998***

According to press reports, a Milwaukee meat products company, Emmpak Foods, was the target of a threat to contaminate its products with HIV.[561] The incident began when a local law enforcement agency received a telephone call telling it where to find a threat note. The letter, found on December 8, 1998, apparently indicated that a terrorist group had contaminated meat products with HIV. A substantial response was mounted involving local, state, and federal agencies. According to an account of the incident provided by the U.S. General Accounting Office (GAO), the FBI and the U.S. Department of Agriculture's Office of Inspector General searched the plant.[562] The local police department assisted the criminal investigation. More than 800 people were interviewed during the investigation. In addition, a risk assessment was conducted by Agriculture's Food Safety and Inspection Service (FSIS), supported by the Centers for Disease Control and Prevention (CDC) and the Occupational Health and Safety Administration (OSHA), to determine the extent of the potential danger to the public. Press accounts suggest that the Food and Drug Administration (FDA) became involved in the investigation, although it is unclear in what capacity. The Wisconsin Department of Health and Family Services and other state and local agencies were a part of the investigation.

After a three-day investigation, a U.S. Department of Agriculture spokesman declared, "At this point, we have no reason to express to you any concerns that public health has been compromised." The Wisconsin Department of Health and Family Services reported that, "We did not feel that there was a viable threat." Consequently, Emmpak Foods was allowed to resume shipments of food. The GAO reports that as of October 1999, no perpetrator had been identified and the case remained open.

***Case 1998-10: Republic of Texas, June 1998***

On July 1, 1998, law enforcement officials arrested three men in Olmito, Texas, on charges of threatening to use biological agents against federal officials. Johnnie Wise, 72, Jack Abbott Grebe, Jr., 43, and Oliver Dean Emigh, 63, were arrested at mobile home by a team comprised of agents from the FBI, the Texas Department of Public Safety, the U.S. Secret Service, the Internal Revenue Service, the McAllen police, and the Cameron County Sheriff's Department. According to an FBI official, the men "had sent threatening documentation to several federal agencies regarding the use of these weapons of mass destruction." FBI spokesman refused to comment on the motivation of the suspects.[563] The Brownsville Herald reported that the three men were members of the Republic of Texas, a militant group that believes that Texas should be an independent nation.[564]

According to the arrest affidavit, only unsealed by a federal magistrate judge on July 13, 1998, the investigators were hunting for biological agents when they searched the homes of the three perpetrators. According to the search warrant, among the items sought were containers thought to contain HIV-infected blood, rabies virus, and anthrax spores. In addition, federal agents were looking for instruction manuals, written threats, and production equipment. Authorities reportedly seized a syringe and a container marked

---

[560] Gavin Cameron, Jason Pate, Diana McCauley, & Lindsay DeFazio, "1999 WMD Terrorism Chronology: Incidents Involving Sub-National Actors and Chemical, Biological, Radiological, and Nuclear Materials," *The Nonproliferation Review*, Summer 2000, p. 161.

[561] Jesse Garza, "Threat made on products at Emmpak Foods," *Journal Sentinel* (Milwaukee), December 11, 1998, as found at the newspaper's World Wide Web site, *http://www.jsonline.com*, "Threat of mean contamination unsubstantiated, authorities say," *Associated Press*, December 11, 1998, as found at the *Journal Sentinel's* World Wide Web site. Additional details of this incident are provided in General Accounting Office, *Food Safety: Agencies Should Further Test Plans for Responding to Deliberate Contamination*, GAO/RCED-00-3, p. 4. Although the GAO report does not identify the target of the threat or the agent involved, the details provided clearly indicate that it is describing this case.

[562] It is unclear why the search for contaminated product did not appear to involve the Department of Agriculture's Food Safety Inspection Service, the federal agency responsible for monitoring food safety. As such, it had both legal authorities to prevent distribution of potentially contaminated meat products, as well as personnel with considerable experience in conducting such investigations when no intentional contamination is suspected.

[563] Dane Schiller, "Valley threats land 3 in jail: Use of biological weapons feared," *San Antonio Express*, July 1, 1998. All references to this paper are from its World Wide Web site, *http://www.expressnews.com*. See also, Madeline Baro, "FBI mum on biological weapons arrests," *Associated Press*, July 2, 1998, 10:05 a.m. EDT.

[564] Karisa King, "Alleged plot involved anthrax, HIV and rabies," *Brownsville Herald*, July 14, 1998. All references to this newspaper are from its World Wide Web site, *http://www.brownsvilleherald.com*.

"DMSO".[565] Subsequent reports, however, indicate that investigators discovered nothing that could be used to prepare biological agents, and found no indications that the trio had attempted to acquire such agents.[566]

Press reports indicate that Emigh wrote a letter, "Declaration of War," which promised to "bring utmost grievous harm to federal agents and their families." The affidavit also recounted the text of a message allegedly sent by Wise an Grebe to FBI Director Louis Freeh:

> Your FBI employees and their families have been targeted for destruction by revenge. We, the people are extremely mad and will not accept the inequities any longer. Non-traceable, personal delivery systems have been developed to inject bacteria and/or viruses for the purpose of killing, maiming and causing great suffering. Warn all concerned so that they may protect themselves and be made aware of this threat to themselves and their families. Good Luck.[567]

Other officials who received threatening messages included local, state, and federal officials. Cameron County Judge Migdalia Lopez, who apparently was the first intended victim. State officials reportedly included Texas Attorney General Dan Morales and the Director of the Texas Department of Public Safety. Federal officials targeted included U.S. Attorney General Janet Reno, the Director of the Central Intelligence Agency, the Director of the U.S. Secret Service, the Commissioner of the Internal Revenue Service, the Director of the Bureau of Alcohol, Tobacco, and Firearms (ATF), and the Director of the U.S. Drug Enforcement Agency. President Bill Clinton's family also was threatened.[568]

The case was tried in October 1998. Wise and Grebe were convicted by a jury of sending two threatening e-mail messages, one to the IRS and the other to the DEA. The two men were acquitted of all other charges. Emigh was acquitted of all the charges.[569] The two men were given a sentence of more than 24 years in prison followed by 60 months of supervised release.[570]

***Case 1998-34: HIV Hoax, April 1998***

An unidentified perpetrator spread rumors that the meat at a Pittsfield, Maine grocery store, Bud's Shop 'n Save, had been deliberately contaminated with HIV. An investigation by state and federal agencies was conducted involving the federal Department of Agriculture, the Maine State Police, and the state Attorney General's Office. According to a State Police official, the investigation determined that "there is no factual basis to the allegations." According to the store's owner, "Our biggest concern was our customers. Even when it's not true, a rumor like this can raise havoc with a business. There's nothing worse than losing the consumer's confidence."[571]

***Case 1998-08: Palestine Islamic Jihad, April 1998***

On April 8, 1998, a Jordanian newspaper, *Al-Bilad*, reported that Asad Bayud At-Tamimi, a leading figure in "Islamic Jihad-Jerusalem," talked about the possibility of using biological warfare at a memorial service for Muhyuddin Ash-Sharif, the bomb maker who was reportedly murdered by a competing group within Hamas. According to the newspaper report, "Tamimi elaborated that the Islamic movements had finally learned the secret that would allow them to defeat their enemies by using weapons of mass destruction." The account also noted, "Tamimi stressed how easy and simple it is to get such weapons. He clearly mentioned the furor created earlier by the British government regarding Iraq's capability of spreading germ warfare all over the world by means of cosmetics."[572]

---

565 Dane Schiller, "Anthrax, HIV are suspected in Valley plot," *San Antonio Express*, July 13, 1998, and "Three accused in biological weapons plot appear in court," *Associated Press*, July 14, 1998, 00:52 CDT.

566 Karisa King, "Defense team seeks evidence being used in killer cactus case," *Brownsville Herald*, October 14, 1998.

567 Karisa King, "Alleged plot involved anthrax, HIV and rabies," *Brownsville Herald*, July 14, 1998.

568 Karisa King, "Alleged plot involved anthrax, HIV and rabies," *Brownsville Herald*, July 14, 1998.

569 Madeline Baro, "Two men convicted in biological weapons case," *Associated Press*, October 30, 1998, 0114 EST.

570 Madeline Baro, "Men sentenced to more than 24 years each in biological weapons case," *Associated Press*, February 5, 1998, 1544EST.

571 Brenda Seekins, "Meat contamination at Pittsfield untrue," *Bangor Daily News* (Bangor, Maine), April 13, 1998.

572 *Israel's Business Arena*, Apr 13, 1998, as found in *http://www.globes.com.il*, citing a report that appeared in the Jordanian newspaper, *Al-Bilad*. A copy of the original article and a translation was provided by David Schenker, then a Senior Researcher at the Investigative Project. See Mahmud Khalil, "At-Tamimi alludes to the use of germ warfare, and Netanyahu on the top of the hit," *Al-Bilad*, April 8, 1998.

***Case 1998-50: Lawrence A. Maltz, April 1998***

According to the FBI's annual terrorism report for 1998, the bureau arrested Lawrence A. Maltz on April 8, 1998 on charges of threatening to use a weapon of mass destruction. According to this account of the incident, Maltz made "implied threats involving biological, chemical, and nuclear devices over a twenty year period." Among the recipients of the threat were the President, members of Congress, the Director of the FBI, the Department of State, and the Internal Revenue Service. Maltz was a manic depressive trained as a physicist. The FBI apparently discounted the threats because of his mental health. Over time, however, his threats became more specific. Because of concerns that Maltz was increasingly likely to resort to violence, and because of evidence that he was probably capable of producing sarin nerve agent, the Bureau opened an intensive investigation into his activities. In September 1998, Maltz was sentenced to 16 months in federal prison and three years of supervised probation after pleading guilty to a charge of mailing threatening communications. He also paid a $3,000 fine.[573]

The nature of his biological threats is unclear from the available account. Nor is it evident when they were made.

***Case 1997-11: Ricin threat against "Retail Store Chain", December 1997***

A Federal Bureau of Investigation report on terrorism contains the following comments on a ricin threat:

> In December 1997, a retail store chain in Oklahoma was notified that ricin (a biological toxin) had been placed in and on items in a number of stores. The perpetrators requested $75,000 in exchange for information on which items were contaminated. However, investigation revealed no evidence of ricin in the stores.[574]

No additional information has been located concerning this incident.

***Case 1997-04: PKK, August 1997***

In September 1997, the British newspaper *Guardian* published a story that purported to be the results of an interview with a man who claimed to have been a bomb-maker for the PKK, a Kurdish terrorist group. Their source, Seydo Hazar, a 31-year-old Kurd, gave details of the activities of the PKK, claiming that they were receiving assistance from the Greek government, and that they were considering use of chemical and biological agents. Hazar specifically asserted that PKK could culture *E. coli* and *C. botulinum*, and considered contaminating beaches with *E. coli*. The newspaper claimed that his reports were confirmed by Western intelligence sources.[575]

***Case 1997-05: Counter Holocaust Lobbyists of Hillel, April 1997***

A package was delivered in the Wednesday, April 23, 1997, mail to the international headquarters of the B'nai B'rith, a Jewish organization located in Washington, D.C. Although B'nai B'rith was closed for Passover, a mail clerk was working to sort through the incoming mail. The clerk put aside this package because the postmark was impossible to read, an indication of a potentially suspicious package, and because the address did not identify a specific recipient. When the clerk examined the package the next morning, there was a red liquid seeping out of it with an "ammonia-type" smell. At that point, the clerk alerted the organization's security chief. Together, they put the envelope into a trashcan, which they moved to a grassy area in front of the building. At that point, around 10:30 a.m., the security chief called 911.[576]

The result was a massive response. The District police department's bomb squad examined the envelope, and concluded that it was not an explosive device. Upon opening the package, the police discovered

---

[573] Federal Bureau of Investigation, National Security Division, Counterterrorism Threat Assessment and Warning Unit, *Terrorism in the United States 1998*, no date, p. 6. There appears to have been no press coverage of this incident, but it is possible to identify letters to the editor that Maltz sent to newspapers in New Jersey.

[574] Federal Bureau of Investigation, *Terrorism in the United States 1997*, no date, as found at the FBI's web site, *http://www.fbi.gov*.

[575] Shyam Bhatia, "Bomber on the run has no place to hide," *Observer*, September 28, 1997, p. 14. See also Shyam Bhatia Naxos and Leonard Doyle, "Poison bomber offers secrets for Sanctuary," *Observer*, September 28, 1997, p. 1, and "PKK member says splinter group planning chemical attacks, *Agence France Presse*, September 28, 1997, 27:23 GMT. All sources are from the *Lexis-Nexis* database. The author is indebted to Jason Pate, Center for Nonproliferation Studies, Monterey Institute of International Studies, for bringing this case to his attention and providing the references.

[576] Sara Horwitz, "FBI Sends Alert to Jewish Groups, Package in D.C. Incident Called Threatening but Not Toxic," *Washington Post*, April 26, 1997, p. C1.

that it contained a broken petri dish swathed in plastic bubble wrap. The petri dish had a label with the word "anthracis" written on it. Included in the package was a business envelope containing a two page, typed, unsigned letter attributed to an unknown group calling itself the Counter Holocaust Lobbyists of Hillel. The letter reportedly described the included material as a "chemical weapon".

While trying to determine what was in the package, District authorities blocked off a two-block area in the heart of the downtown area for nearly nine hours. By 5:00 p.m., officials had determined that the substance did not contain anthrax, but it was not until 8:00 p.m. that people were allowed to leave. Traffic was snarled in downtown. The people working in the building were prevented from leaving, and nearby roads were cordoned off. Initial tests were made at the site, apparently using rapid identification kits developed by the U.S. Navy's Naval Medical Research Institute (NMRI).[577] These tests proved negative for a set of commonly accepted biological warfare agents (probably including anthrax, botulinum toxin, plague, ricin, and SEB). The package was taken from the B'nai B'rith headquarters to the laboratories of the Naval Medical Research Institute (NMRI), located in Bethesda, Maryland, at the Naval Medical Research Center.

According to press reports, laboratory investigation confirmed that the material in the package was agar, a common laboratory growth media. Routine culture techniques revealed only *Bacillus cereus*, a common household organism that is known to be pathogenic only under limited conditions involving poorly prepared foods, such as recooked rice.[578]

*B. cereus* is closely related to *B. anthracis*. According to one microbiology account, studies of the DNA of the two organisms shows that they are so similar "that they should be considered to belong to a single species." This opens the possibility that the perpetrator may have believed that the organism present was *B. anthracis*.[579]

***Case 1997-12: Neil Francis Roberts, March 1997***

On June 25, 1997, Neil Francis Roberts, an accountant at a Coca-Cola distribution plant in Akron, Ohio, pled guilty to a charge of tampering with consumer products. Roberts apparently approached plant's human resources director in March 1997 and claimed to have placed an unspecified substance in a batch of soft drink. He had worked for the company for ten years when he made the threat. Roberts reportedly played a videotape that showed him contaminating the product, and threatened to send a copy of the tape to the press unless he was paid an unspecified amount of money over a six-year period.[580]

The threat was investigated by the FBI and the Food and Drug Administration's Office of Criminal Investigations. Within a week, they determined that there was no evidence of contamination.[581] Testing subsequently determined that 14 bottles and 5 bags of product were adulterated with sugar water. The contamination took place sometime between 1994 and December 31, 1996.[582]

Roberts was indicted for extortion and product tampering on May 8, 1997 by a federal grand jury. On June 25, he pled guilty to a charge of product tampering and in return the U.S. Attorney's office dropped the extortion charge. He was sentenced to one year and one day in prison.[583]

The General Accounting Office categorizes this case as an instance of bioterrorism, and claim that Roberts suggested that he put a biological substance into the product.[584] Press reports, however, suggest that he never identified the nature of the contaminant, so the basis for the GAO's classification is unclear.

---

[577] Michael Powell and Allan Lengel, "Chemical Alert Traps Workers in Buildings, Discovery of Leaking Package at B'nai B'rith Turns Into Nine-Hour Ordeal in D.C.," *Washington Post*, April 25, 1997, p. A1.

[578] Sara Horwitz, "B'nai B'rith Package Contained Common Bacteria, Involved Tests Were Needed to Identify Substance; 'It Was Nothing Harmful,' FBI Says," *Washington Post*, April 29, 1997, p. B2. *B. cereus* infections are rarely fatal, and usually last for only 24 hours. See Abram S. Benenson, editor, *Control of Communicable Diseases Manual*, Sixteenth edition (Washington, DC: American Public Health Association, 1995), pp. 188-189.

[579] *Bergey's Manual of Determinitive Bacteriology*, p. 1112. See also, *CRC Handbook of Microbiology*, p. 321. Dr. Dave Huxsoll drew my attention to this literature and pointed out its implications in this case.

[580] Debra Dennis, "Employee Admits Tampering with Coke," *Plain Dealer*, June 27, 1997, p. 1B, and Debra Dennis, "Coke Worker Indicted by U.S.; Charges include Extortion, Tampering," *Plain Dealer*, May 9, 1997, p. 1B.

[581] General Accounting Office, *Food Safety: Agencies Should Further Test Plans for Responding to Deliberate Contamination*, GAO/RCED-00-3, p. 4.

[582] Debra Dennis, "Employee Admits Tampering with Coke," *Plain Dealer*, June 27, 1997, p. 1B.

[583] "Coca-Cola Tampering," *Plain Dealer*, September 5, 1997, p. 4B, and "Former Coca-Cola Official Sentenced," *Associated Press*, September 4, 1997, 11:12 Eastern Time.

[584] General Accounting Office, *Food Safety: Agencies Should Further Test Plans for Responding to Deliberate Contamination*, GAO/RCED-00-3, p. 4.

***Case 1996-03: Tokiyuki Asaoka, August 1996***

On September 4, 1996, the Japanese police arrested Tokiyuki Asaoka on suspicion of attempting to extort ¥60 million (estimated at the time to equal US$550,000) from the Yamazaki Bakery. He allegedly threatened to contaminate their product by injecting them with body fluids infected with *E. coli* bacteria.[585]

According to press reports, he sent a threatening letter to the company on August 26. He ordered the company to display a cellular telephone number in the window of a company store. The number was put out on September 3. When he called the number, police were able to trace the connection, and identify the caller. After his arrest, Asaoka confessed to the extortion.[586]

***Case 1996-07: Hiroaki Chiku, August 1996***

On August 18, 1996, someone called a Seven-Eleven Umeshima 2-chome store located in Tokyo and warned that he had placed poisoned bread in the store. A search revealed a package with a message that said, "Beware, O-157. Eat it and you'll die." It was signed "Shin Kitsuneme no Otoko" (meaning the new fox-eyed man). Subsequent analysis failed to identify the presence of any pathogens. The next day, the Seven-Eleven Japan Company received a letter threatening to place food poisoned with E. coli O-157 H7 on the shelves of its store unless the company paid an extortion of ¥120 million. The letter reportedly said, "O-158 would be the most appropriate poison today." On the 22nd and 23rd someone made 21 telephone calls to the company demanding payment. At the request of police, the company agreed to make the payment. A suspect was arrested on the 24th while attempting to collect the extortion payment. The alleged perpetrator was a 51 year-old "corporate executive" who was attempting to pay off a ¥30 million debt.[587]

***Case 1996-08: Justice Department, March 1996***

An animal rights group calling itself the Justice Department sent envelopes allegedly containing razor blades covered with HIV-infected blood to fur retailers in Canada. The envelopes included a letter and a second, sealed envelope that supposedly contained the contaminated razor blades. The letter contained the following message.[588]

> Fur is dead. And hopefully so are you. We placed these razor blades (coated with AIS infected blood, by the way) in the hopes of eliminating scum like yourself from the earth. There is no excuse for the fur trade. This is war and in war, people die. Enough animals have been killed, now it's your turn.
>
> You have been marked.
>
> You have six months to shut down your business. After that you will start receiving [sic] explosive devices which WILL kill you.
>
> This is not a joke.

According to the letter, similar packages were sent to 87 retailers. Authorities identified only a few of the stores that allegedly received the packages. Several Canadian media outlets also were recipients.

It was unclear if the razor blades were contaminated with HIV-infected blood, but, even if that were the case, experts believed that the HIV could not have survived. Accordingly, the letters posed no threat.

***Case 1996-01: German blackmailers, January 1996***

A German prosecutor in Essen reported in April 1996 that unidentified blackmailers had threatened to contaminate food with venom taken from cobras, mambas, and other poisonous snakes unless they were paid DM 400 million (about US$ 264 million) in diamonds. The threats were first made in January. Reportedly, the

---

585 "Blackmail food scare," *Guardian* (London), September 5, 1996, p. 13, and "Police Arrest Man They Say Threatened to Spread Deadly Bacteria," *Associated Press*, September 4, 1996. The *Guardian* story is based on AP reporting, so the two stories are essentially drawn from the same source.

586 "Police Arrest Man They Say Threatened to Spread Deadly Bacteria," *Associated Press*, September 4, 1996.

587 "Executive arrested in O-157 extortion attempt," *Mainichi Daily News*, August 25, 1996, "Man Suspected of Trying to Use Food Poison Scare in Extortion Scam," *Associated Press*, August 24, 1996, 06:18 Eastern time, and *Kyodo News Service, Japan Economic News Wire*, August 24, 1996. All sources are from the Lexis-Nexis database. The author is indebted to Jason Pate, Center for Nonproliferation Studies, Monterey Institute of International Studies, for bringing this case to his attention and providing the references.

588 Pete McMartin, "Anti-fur group sends death threat," *Vancouver Sun*, March 9, 1996, p. A17, Larry Pynn, "Police warn fur retailers about mail-terror threat," *Vancouver Sun*, March 8, 1996, p. B3, and "Police warn fur dealers to watch for letters with bloody razor blades," *Edmonton Journal*, March 8, 1996, p. A4,

demands were sent to food manufacturers on computer disks. According to the German newspaper *Bild Zeitung*, the threats were kept secret until April when the prosecutor held a meeting with the senior managers of sixty European companies to discuss the threat.[589]

***Case 1995-06: Biological weapons threats against Latin American cities, April 1995***

Paraguay's president, Juan Carlos Wasmosy, told reporters that several embassies in Washington, D.C., received letters that threatened to launch biological weapons attacks against several cities in Latin America. The letters, which were sent from California, were not attributed. According to Wasmosy, the letter provided a list of cities being targeted, and mentioned several biological agents, cholera, typhoid, malaria, and yellow fever.[590]

***Case 1995-04: Barry Dixon, November 1995***

Barry Dixon, a onetime warehouse worker, attempted to extort £100,000 from Sainsbury's, a UK supermarket chain, by threatening to contaminate food with HIV-infected blood. Dixon reportedly sent a letter to Sainsbury's headquarters in November 1995 making the threat. In the letter, Dixon wrote, "Don't tell the police. If this goes to the papers it would read 'Aids and HIV--everyone's favorite ingredient.'" He also sent two syringes filled with blood, which proved to come from a pig. In the letter, he told the company that HIV-contaminated blood would be placed in the stores. The letter added, "Imagine the horror on your customers' faces when they see this Aids blood next to fresh meat, bread and cheese." He was sentenced to four years in prison for the crime. A second man implicated in the plot was acquitted.[591]

***Case 1995-05: Frank Riolfo, October 1995***

In October 1995, Frank Riolfo, a former member of the Royal Army Medical Corps, was sentenced to eight years in jail for attempting to blackmail the Tesco supermarket chain. Riolfo told the company that he had AIDS, and threatened to contaminate food at its stores unless the chain agreed to give him a bank debit card allowing him to withdraw sums of money. The company supplied Riolfo with such a card. He was arrested after withdrawing £7,000 using the card.[592]

***Case 1994-02: Michael Norman and Alexander Taylor, January 1994***

In January 1994, two men attempted to extort £12 million from three British supermarket chains, Safeway, Sainsbury's, and Tesco.[593] The two co-conspirators, Michael Norman and Alexander Taylor, sent letters demanding payment of a "tax" to aid small businesses. Unless paid the money, the two threatened to contaminate foods that were purchased and eaten by customers without further cooking.

According to a letter sent to one of the chains, "There are a small number of our members who are tested HIV positive. We can have the supply of infected fluid whenever and we can deliver this to the produce in your store." The letter claimed to be from a group that called itself Action in the Community. Other letters apparently threatened to contaminate food products with bacteria and chemicals.

After the stores contacted police about the threats, policemen posing as supermarket executives negotiated payment of a ransom with the two men. Eventually, they were given £475,000, and then were arrested for extortion. Taylor pled guilty to the charges and was sentenced to five years in prison. Norman was convicted and received eight years.

After his arrest, Norman claimed to the police that a mystery novel, *The Banker*, written by Dick Francis, was the inspiration for the plot.[594]

---

[589] "Blackmailers threaten to spike food with snake venom," *Guardian* (London), April 16, 1996, p. 11, and "World Briefly: Blackmailers threaten to poison food supply," *Orange County Register*, April 17, 1996, p. A13.

[590] "Paraguay: Chemical Warfare Planned by Terrorists, President Warns," *Inter Press Service*, April 28, 1995. I am grateful to Jason Pate, Monterey Institute for International Studies, for drawing my attention to this material.

[591] "Blackmail pair 'made Aids threat to store'," *Times* (London) September 18, 1996, p. 6, "Man cleared," *Times* (London), September 21, 1996, p. 9, Adrian Lee, "Store blackmailer sent Aids threat," *Times* (London), December 17, 1996, p. 4, "Store blackmailer jailed," *Times*, December 18, 1996, p. 2.

[592] "Ex-soldier jailed for Tesco food blackmail," *Times* (London), October 14, 1995, p. 3, and "Blackmailer jailed for 8 years," *Financial Times*, October 14, 1995, p. 7.

[593] Catherine Milton, "Aids plot denied by man on blackmail charge," *Times* (London), November 2, 1994, p. 3, "Blackmail plot," *Times* (London), December 3, 1996, p. 2, "Police foiled plot to poison foods," *Independent*, December 3, 1994, p. 4.

[594] "Store blackmail pair sent to jail," *Financial Times*, December 3, 1994, p. 4.

***Case 1994-01: Animal Liberation Front, January 1994***

Ron Purver reports, without providing attribution, that in January 1994 a group calling itself the Animal Liberation Front (ALF) mailed "a number of postal devices containing fragments of hypodermic needles, which it claimed had been infected with the HIV virus." His account does not say in what country the needles were mailed.[595] This incident does not appear on the list of Animal Liberation Front activities maintained by the Animal Liberation Frontline Information Service.[596]

***Case 1992-04: "The Terminator", September 1992***

An unknown extortionist, who signed his letters as "The Terminator", threatened that he would contaminate products at the Budgens supermarket chain with HIV unless he was paid £300,000.[597] In the third letter that he mailed, which was sent to the *Daily Mirror*, the blackmailer claimed that he had placed HIV-contaminated products in nine of the chains 100 stores.

As far as is known, the perpetrator was never identified.

***Case 1992-01: Animal Aid Association, January 1992***

Ron Purver indicates that on January 15, 1992, British Columbia News received a report that "the Animal Aid Association (AAA) had injected 'Cold Buster' bars with the AIDS virus to protest the use of animals in research and the diversion of funds from AIDS research."[598]

An Internet listing of Animal Liberation Front activities, maintained by Animal Liberation Frontline Information Service, contains the following passage:

> 1/1/92-AB; Animal Rights Militia claims to have poisoned 87 Canadian Cold Buster Chocolate bars in Edmonton and Calgary because of the University of Alberta vivisector Larry Wang's 16 years of experiments on rats that led to the invention of the bar. Production halted and bars pulled from store shelves across Canada, $250,000 damage. -A.R.M.[599]

A newsletter produced by the Canadian Intelligence Service states that this incident involved oven cleaner, not a biological agent.[600] The Animal Liberation Frontline Information Service listing includes no incident similar to the one reported by Purver.

***Case 1991-02: Threatening the Kelowna, BC, water supply, January 1991***

Ron Purver reports that on January 25, 1991 Canadian authorities received a letter that contained a threat to pollute the water supply of the town of Kelowna, British Columbia, with "biological contaminates." According to Purver, the incident was "associated with the Gulf War." He reports that security at the water system was enhanced due to the threat, but law enforcement agencies never identified who made the threat.[601]

***Case 1989-01: Robin Smith, May 1989***

In September 1989, Robin Smith was sentenced to five years in prison by a Scottish court for an extortion scheme involving more than £600,000. Starting in May 1989, Smith sent letters to a number of companies threatening to contaminate their products with HIV-infected blood. At least some of the extortion letters were signed "the Bogyman". In all, he threatened five companies, including two food chains, Safeway and Littlewoods, and several consumer products companies, including Proctor and Gamble and Vidal Sassoon. Police traced a telephone call that he made to one of the companies, and arrested him.[602]

---

[595] Purver, *Chemical and Biological Terrorism*, p. 38. For a discussion of ALF, see Rachel Monaghan, "Animal Rights and Violent Protest," *Terrorism and Political Violence*, Vol. 9, No. 4 (Winter 1997), pp. 106-116.

[596] Taken from *http://www.envirolink.org/ALF/doa/nadoa94.html.*

[597] Nicholas Watt, "Blackmail letters warn of HIV plot," *Times* (London), October 6, 1992, p. 3, David Connett, "Supermarket threatened by HIV blackmailer," *Independent* (London), October 6, 1992, p. 3.

[598] Purver, *Chemical and Biological Terrorism*, p. 34.

[599] Taken from *http://www.envirolink.org/ALF/doa/nadoa92.html.*

[600] G.D. Smith, "Militant Activism and the Issue of Animal Rights," Commentary Number 21, Canadian Security Intelligence Service, April 1992, found at *http://www.csis-scrs.gc.ca/eng/comment/com21e.html.*

[601] Purver, *Chemical and Biological Terrorism*, p. 34.

[602] Kerry Gill, "Shop blackmailer gets five years for food poison threat," *Times* (London), September 29, 1989, p. 3, "'Bogeyman' jailed for extortion attempts," *Guardian* (London), September 29, 1989, p.5, and "Poison food blackmailer gets 5 years, *Daily Telegraph*, September 29, 1989, p. 3.

***Case 1984-01: Peter Vivian Wardrop, January 1984***

On January 16, 1984, the Queensland's State Premier, Joh Bjelke-Peterson received a letter threatening to spread foot-and-mouth disease unless prison reforms were implemented within twelve weeks. Specifically, the anonymous letter said that wild pigs would be infected with the disease, which would then spread to cattle and sheep.[603] In response, the State Premier offered an A$45,000 reward and the Cattleman's Union in Queensland offered an A$450,000 reward for evidence leading to the arrest of the extortionist.[604] The State Premier later increased the reward to A$75,000.[605] The perpetrator turned out to be a 37-year old murderer serving a life sentence in Townsville's Stuart Jail, Peter Vivian Wardrop.[606]

In December 1984, Queensland's premier said that he had received a similar letter, also threatening to spread foot-and-mouth disease unless prison reforms were instituted within three months.[607]

***Case 1983-01: Montgomery Todd Meeks, October 1983***

On January 30, 1985, a jury in Orange County, Florida, convicted Montgomery Todd Meeks, a 19-year old high school senior, of attempted murder and solicitation to murder in connection with a plot to kill his father using ricin toxin. On March 7, 1985, Orange County Circuit Court Judge Lawrence Kirkwood sentenced him to three years in prison, 50 years probation, and 200 hours of community service during every year of probation, for plotting to murder his father using ricin. In addition, the judge specified that Meeks was to obtain psychiatric treatment, and ordered him to pay the costs of the trial (estimated at about $10,000). Meeks was eligible for parole in 18 months, but if he violated the terms of parole the Judge indicated that Meeks could face 17 to 22 years in prison.[608]

Meeks was extremely intelligent. According to Judge Kirkwood, he had an IQ of 147. However, he had failed a course in his senior year in high school, and never graduated. His father, Prentice Meeks, owned a mobile home dealership in Orange County.[609]

According to testimony at his trial, Meeks openly discussed murdering his father during the spring of 1983. After conducting research on poisons at the University of Central Florida's library, he settled on ricin as his agent of choice. Meeks purchased the ricin from a company in Louisville, Kentucky, known as Aardvark Enterprises. The company apparently produced ricin for commercial uses. On October 21, 1983, one of Meek's classmates, Robert Peterson, flew to Louisville to pick up the ricin, paying $200 for it. Peterson, however, was convinced by friends who knew of the plot not to give the ricin to Meeks, and, upon returning to the Orlando International Airport, emptied the vial of ricin into a toilet at the airport and refilled it with water. The county sheriff's office was informed of the plot at that time.[610]

On October 24, Peterson gave the vial supposedly containing the ricin to Meeks. The next day, Meeks told Peterson that he had poured the substance into a glass of water that his father was about to drink. That same day, the sheriff's office informed the elder Meeks about the plot. Prentice Meeks and his wife moved out of the house that day, telling their son that they were going on a trip. On November 2, 1985, Meeks was arrested on a charge of solicitation to murder.[611]

At his trial, Meeks admitted to pouring the contents of the vial into a glass of water and a water pitcher being served to his father. He claimed, however, that he gave up the plot and poured out the poison

---

603 Tony Duboudin, "Australian livestock threatened," *Times* (London), January 21, 1984, p. 5, and *Reuters*, January 20, 1984, PM cycle.

604 *Reuters*, January 22, 1984, BC cycle.

605 *Reuters North European Service*, January 24, 1984.

606 Tony Duboudin, "Murderer in court over virus threat," *Times* (London), February 22, 1984, p. 5.

607 *Reuters*, December 5, 1984, PM cycle.

608 Louis Trager, "Meeks gets 3-year term for trying to poison father," *Orlando Sentinel*, March 8, 1985, p. D-1, and *Associated Press*, March 7, 1985, AM cycle. According to Judge Kirkwood, the sentencing guidelines called for a 12 to 17 year term, but he gave a lower sentence in response to the requests for a shorter sentence by Meeks' father, the prosecutors, the jury, and the probation office investigating officer.

609 Trager, "Meeks gets 3-year term," *Orlando Sentinel*, March 8, 1985, p. D-11.

610 Elaine Bennett and Jonathan Susskind, "Police charge teen with attempting to kill father," *Orlando Sentinel*, November 3, 1984, p. C1.

611 Bennett and Susskind, "Police charge teen," *Orlando Sentinel*, November 3, 1984, pp. C1, C11.

before his father drank any of the water. The prosecution argued that Meeks intended to carry out his murder plot. The jury clearly rejected the defense position.[612]

According to the prosecutor, Buck Blankner, Meeks stood to gain substantially from the death of his father. He stood to earn several hundred thousand dollars as a beneficiary of a life insurance policy and would have inherited his father's mobile home business.[613] The defense argued that Meeks' father abused his first wife and that the memory of his actions led to the murder plot.[614]

***Case 1982-01: William Chanslor, April 1982***

On August 3, 1982, a jury in Houston, Texas, convicted William Chanslor, a Texas attorney, of plotting to murder his wife, Sue Chanslor. Chanslor was accused of planning to poison her with ricin toxin. Sue Chanslor was paralyzed from the waist down due to a stroke she suffered in 1979.[615] Chanslor was a past president of the Houston Trial Lawyers Association and played on the University of Texas football team.[616]

In 1981, Chanslor placed advertisements under the alias John G. Thomas, in paramilitary journals, including *Soldier of Fortune* and *Gung-Ho*, for an "expert in poisons & chemical agents with access to same." In those magazines he saw an advertisement for the *How to Kill* volumes written by John Minnery, a Canadian living in Ontario. Chanslor purchased the volumes, and then got into touch with Minnery. Between October 1981 and April 1982, the two had about six telephone conversations. Initially, Chanslor apparently evidenced an interest in using poisons to kill animals. He asked Minnery for advice on cyanide and questioned him about the availability of shellfish toxins. Eventually, however, he told Minnery that he intended to murder a 42-year old partially paralyzed woman, and asked for help in obtaining poison. He apparently told Minnery that the medical examiner in his small town would never detect use of an unusual poison.[617]

Minnery, alarmed by Chanslor's request, informed the Ontario Provincial Police of the request. According to his testimony, he also was aware of the ads placed by Chanslor. The Ontario police recorded at least one of the telephone calls. The two finally met on April 8, 1982 at a lounge in the Toronto airport. Joining the two was Keith Symons, an Ontario policeman who posed as someone who could supply poisons. During the hour-long conversation, which Symons taped, Minnery and Chanslor discussed possible poisons that could be used. Most were rejected because they would leave identifiable traces. Eventually they settled on ricin.[618]

At that time, the Canadian authorities were unaware of Chanslor's identity. Based on wiretaps, they apparently were aware that Chanslor was calling from Texas, but they had no other information about him. The Canadian authorities took Chanslor's fingerprints off a glass he drank from. This information enabled the authorities to identify Chanslor.[619]

About two weeks later, Symons flew to Houston and met with Chanslor in a hotel at the airport. During the meeting, which was videotaped by the Houston police, Symons gave Chanslor two "Ricin" tablets (which actually contained vitamin C), a surgical mask and gloves, and tweezers to handle the "poison". Chanslor paid $2,500 for the poison. Chanslor also asked Symons to obtain poison for use in another murder. After Chanslor left the hotel, the police arrested him.[620]

During the trial, Chanslor claimed that his wife was despondent and wanted to die to get out of her misery. This assertion was supported by dramatic testimony given by his wife. Prosecutors cast some doubt on the accuracy of her testimony. According to police witnesses, on the day of Chanslor's arrest she denied asking

---

[612] Bennett and Susskind, "Police charge teen," *Orlando Sentinel*, November 3, 1984, pp. C1, C11, and "Teen on trial in attempt on dad's life," *Miami Herald*, January 24, 1985, p. 2B.

[613] Trager, "Meeks gets 3-year term," *Orlando Sentinel*, March 8, 1985, p. D11, and *Associated Press*, March 7, 1985, AM cycle.

[614] Trager, "Meeks gets 3-year term," *Orlando Sentinel*, March 8, 1985, p. D11, and *United Press International*, January 30, 1985, AM cycle.

[615] This account is based largely on "Case of the Willing Victim," *Newsweek*, August 16, 1982, p. 27, and "Poison Plot: A kaleidoscope of deception," *Time*, August 16, 1982, p. 43. In addition, *Houston Post* coverage of the trial was reviewed. Jim E. Lavine, who prosecuted the case for the Harris County District Attorney's office, clarified some of the details in a telephone interview on February 27, 1998.

[616] *Associated Press*, August 3, 1982, PM cycle.

[617] Minnery's role is described in *United Press International*, April 23, 1982, PM cycle. For his testimony at the trial, see Mary Flood, "Lawyer sought advice on poison method, expert testifies," *Houston Post*, July 28, 1982, p. 2A.

[618] The testimony of Judson and Minnery at Chanslor's trial is recounted in *United Press International*, July 28, 1982, AM cycle.

[619] Mary Flood, "2nd poisoning allegedly planned," *Houston Post*, July 29, 1982, p. 22A.

[620] Flood, "2nd poisoning allegedly planned," *Houston Post*, July 29, 1982, p. 22A.

for help in committing suicide, and Chanslor was captured on tape telling Minnery that his wife was not willing to commit suicide.[621]

In the end, it took the jury only three hours to reach a guilty verdict. Prosecutors asked for a 16-20 year sentence. Possibly swayed by the pleas of Sue Chanslor during the sentencing hearing to treat her husband leniently, the jury gave Chanslor to a three-year jail sentence and a $5,000 fine. A state judge rejected a request for a new trial.[622]

The conviction was overturned on appeal, based on a conclusion by the appellate court that the trial judge erred in his instructions to the jury. In a 9-0 decision, the Texas Court of Criminal Appeals ruled that the trial judge should have instructed the jury to consider a lesser offense of aiding a suicide. According to the appellate court, "The jury could have reasonably believed that that if (Chanslor) was guilty at all he was guilty only of aiding a suicide." At the time, the district attorney's office indicated that it intended to retry the case.[623] Before he could be brought to trial again, Chanslor pled guilty and was given probation.[624]

***Case 1980-02X: Tamil "militants": 1983-1987?***

According to an account of the ethnic strife in Sri Lanka, a Tamil militant group issued a communiqué threatening to wage biological warfare against the Sinhalese-dominated government of Sri Lanka. The text of the message, as reported by this source is as follows.

> The Ceylon Government has announced that it will get the help of the devil to fight the terrorists—that is to subjugate the Tamil race. It is now quite apparent to the whole world that the Government is doing exactly that by its diabolical acts against innocent Tamils. Hence it is quite fit and proper for the Tamils to counter the Government in a similar manner, and with this object in view, we have formed an operation squad to wage total war against the Government in all parts of Ceylon. One strategy is to wage a biological war which we believe will cripple Ceylon in a few years. Doctors and scientists have got over their scruples and now working on methods to implement the following:
>
> 1. Sending qualified volunteers to bring infected material, cultures and infected water snails to spread Bilbariasis (River Blindness) in the canals and reservoirs of the Mahaweli at several points. It may take some time before infected people come to the hospitals, but by that time the damage will have been achieved.
>
> 2. Similarly, bring infected material and mosquitoes to spread Yellow Fever in the South, where the carrier mosquito is already found.
>
> 3. A Tamil in South America has already volunteered to supply infected material for rubber trees (Leaf Curl) not presently found in Ceylon. It is hoped to wipe out the rubber plantations by spreading the infection at widely separated points.
>
> 4. Arrangements are being made to send competent volunteers to collect infected tea to propagate diseases not presently found in Ceylon tea plantations. Diseases not found in Ceylon tea bushes are prevalent in Assam.
>
> Other activities such as poisoning water supplies of the army in the North and East, continuing the overseas propaganda to halt tourism and investment in Ceylon, will continue on an intensified scale. We have little doubt that unborn Sinhalese generation will curse the folly and wickedness of the government which will make Ceylon a cursed land shunned by the world. History will record the just demands of the Tamils and diabolical actions and policy of the Ceylon Government. Actions speak louder than words.[625]

Which Tamil secessionist organizations made the threat is not specified. There were five main Tamil groups, the most famous being the Liberation Tigers of Tamil Eelam (LTTE), usually known as the Tamil

---

[621] Mary Flood, Chanslor found guilty of plotting to poison his wife," *Houston Post*, August 4, 1982, p. 1A.

[622] Mary Flood, "Jury gives Chanslor 3 years in jail, fine, " *Houston Post*, August 5, 1982, p. 1A, and *United Press International*, January 18, 1983, AM cycle.

[623] Jane Elliott, "Poison plot conviction reversed," *Houston Post*, July 11, 1985, p. A1.

[624] Telephone interview, Jim E. Lavine, February 27, 1998.

[625] Rohan Gunaratna, *War and Peace in Sri Lanka* (Sri Lanka: Institute of Fundamental Studies, 1987), pp. 51-52. I am indebted to Milton Leitenberg, *Biological Weapons Arms Control*, Project on Rethinking Arms Control, Center for International and Security Studies at Maryland School of Public Affairs, University of Maryland at College Park, PRAC Paper No. 16, May 1996, pp. 53-54, for bringing this reference to my attention.

Tigers. In addition, there were numerous smaller groups, most with only a transitory existence. One such group, the Tamil Eelam Army, claimed in early 1986 that it contaminated Sri Lankan tea with potassium cyanide in an apparently successful attempt to disrupt exports of this commodity.[626]

Most of the major Tamil groups received substantial assistance from the government of India. The available histories of the conflict suggest that officials of the Research and Analysis Wing (RAW), India's CIA-equivalent, provided funding, training, and weapons to the Tamil groups. In addition, the groups were allowed to operate relatively freely in Tamil Nadu, the Indian state across the water from Sri Lanka with a predominantly Tamil population. It is likely that the involvement of the Indian government would have had an impact on the tactics pursued by any of the Tamil groups, even those that the Indians did not support. On at least one occasion, the Indians allowed the LTTE to suppress a rival group because it paid insufficient attention to New Delhi's wishes.[627]

The communiqué does not necessarily reflect a highly refined knowledge of biological agents. Schistosomiasis, also known as bilharziasis or snail fever, is caused by one of several species of *Schistosoma* worms that infect the blood and livers. The disease is spread when people are exposed to *Schistosoma* larvae that have contaminated water. The larvae grow in snails, which are essential to the natural life cycle of the disease. The disease is found in Africa, the Middle East, South America, and Southeast Asia. It has been eradicated from Japan.[628]

The authors of the communiqué may have confused bilharziasis with another disease, Onchocerciasis, also known as river blindness, which is caused by a different species of parasitic worms, *Onchocerca volvulus*, which create nodules under the skin or near bones. The female worms produce offspring, known as microfilaria. Blindness results when the microfilariae invade the eyes. The worms are found in areas of Mexico, Central America, and parts of South America, as well as a large part of sub-Saharan Africa. The worms are spread by the bites of one of several species of blackflies of the genus *Simulium*. Control measures concentrate on eliminating the blackflies.[629]

Yellow fever is a viral disease of the genus *Flavivirus* spread by one of several mosquito species of the *Aedes* genus. The most common species believed involved in yellow fever transmission is *Aedes aegypti*, which is found in tropical regions of sub-Saharan Africa and Latin America. Yellow fever has never been identified in Asia. Between 1986 and 1991 there was an outbreak in Nigeria that resulted in 20,000 cases, including 4,000 deaths.[630]

***Case 1970-05X: Red Army Faction, 1970s***

There are numerous allegations that members of the Red Army Faction received training in biological warfare or were interested in using it. According to a story that appeared in *Defense & Foreign Affairs Daily*, "Several press agencies report that West German terrorists—the remnants of the Baader-Meinhof group (Red Army Faction)—are preparing to use bacteriological weapons. At least 13 terrorists are being trained in a camp south of Beirut, which is run by FPLP [probably PFLP], the most radical Palestinian terror organization." The account claims that "Western security agencies treat this information with skepticism."[631] Jeffrey Simon also reports, "A few years earlier, the Baader-Meinhof gang had threatened to poison water in 20 West German towns if three radical lawyers were not allowed to defend a comrade who was on trial." He does not cite any sources for this allegation, but the report was contained in the "RAND Chronology of International Terrorism".[632]

---

[626] "Sri Lanka Denies Report Of Tainted Tea Exports," *New York Times*, January 5, 1986, p. I-5, and "U.S. Holds Up Sri Lankan Tea After Rebels Warn of Cyanide," *New York Times*, January 7, 1986, p. A4.

[627] There is a substantial literature on the Sri Lankan troubles, and on the role of the Indians in supporting the Tamil groups. The author consulted three: Dagmar Hellmann-Rajanayagam, *The Tamil Tigers: Armed Struggle for Identity* (Stuttgart: Franz Steiner Verlag, 1994), Edgar O'Ballance, *The Cyanide War: Tamil Insurrection in Sri Lanka 1973-88* (Washington: Brassey's (UK), 1989), and M.R. Narayan Swamy, *Tigers of Lanka, from boys to guerrillas* (Delhi: Konark Publishers, 1994). The Tamil Tigers gave their soldiers cyanide capsules to take if captured. O'Ballance (pp. vii, 126) estimates that 300 killed themselves in this way.

[628] Abram S. Benenson, editor, *Control of Communicable Diseases Manual*, Sixteenth edition (Washington, DC: American Public Health Association, 1995), pp. 417-421.

[629] Benenson, editor, *Control of Communicable Diseases Manual*, pp. 336-339.

[630] Benenson, editor, *Control of Communicable Diseases Manual*, pp. 519-524.

[631] "Lebanon: Bacteriological Warfare Training By Terrorists?" *Defense & Foreign Affairs Daily*, May 18, 1979, p. 1. Bruce Hoffman provided a copy of this article from the archives of the *RAND-St. Andrews Terrorism Chronology*.

[632] Jeffrey D. Simon, *Terrorists and the Potential Use of Biological Weapons: A Discussion of Possibilities*, RAND Corporation, December 1989, p. 8, and Jeffrey Simon, electronic communication, August 24, 1998.

Another source claims that "an unconfirmed report denied by authorities" alleges that "domestic terrorist elements, possibly hard-core RAF members, were planning to attack the Federal Research Institute for Animal Virus Diseases in Tuebingen [Germany] in order to steal highly infectious viruses." The story claims that "the targeted facility was secretly photographed by unidentified persons planning the attack." The source of the allegations is never identified in the account.[633]

Finally, there is a claim that during some unspecified period the Baader-Meinhof gang threatened to send anthrax through the mails. The account does not specify the intended targets, nor does is clarify whether the terrorists intended to mail some kind of dissemination device or if they only intended to send contaminated letters.[634]

***Case 1979-01: Aliens of America, July 1979***

According to the *RAND-St. Andrews Terrorism Chronology*, in July 1979 "An individual claiming membership in Aliens of America threatened to contaminate the U.S. consulate in Munich with Legionnaires Disease bacteria."[635]

***Case 1978-02: Tucson Extortionist, September 1978***

Early in September 1978, the mayor of Tucson, Arizona received two letters threatening to "spread a plague" in that city unless certain conditions were met.[636] Press accounts suggest that he intended to use fleas to spread the disease, although those reports do not clarify whether it was clear from the letters that *Yersinia pestis*, the organism that causes bubonic and pneumonic plague, was mentioned.

The extortionist reportedly wanted a payment of $500,000, demanded that the city provide free food for poor people, and insisted that the Kino Community Hospital resumed providing free abortions for indigent patients.[637] An unsuccessful attempt was made to pay the money. Following directions given by the extortionist, on September 14, a police officer went to a phone booth in the North Side of Tucson. He received the first of several telephone calls that directed him to different pay phones. The perpetrator, however, never appeared, so no payment was made.[638]

The mayor, Lewis C. Murphy, believed that the letters were the work of a "crank." He told reporters, "We're paying absolutely no attention to it, as far as I know ... The police may have a slightly different reaction because they get nervous so easily." According to Murphy and police officials, the letters were poorly typed with numerous misspelled words. For this reason, one law enforcement official told a reporter, "It's a prank. I wouldn't get too excited about it. The possibility of pulling this thing off is very, very remote." Nevertheless, law enforcement officials took the threat sufficiently seriously to mobilize a task force consisting of about 25 people drawn from the Tucson Police Department, the Pima County Sheriff's Department, the Narcotics Task Force, and the FBI.[639]

Press reports differed on whether the plague threats were linked to the threat earlier in the year to spread typhoid.[640] The letters were typed using a different typewriter than used in the April extortion attempt.[641]

---

[633] *Risk Assessment Weekly*, May 19, 1989, p. 3. Bruce Hoffman provided a copy of this article from the archives of the *RAND-St. Andrews Terrorism Chronology*.

[634] Richard Charles Clark, *Technological Terrorism* (Old Greenwich, Connecticut: Devin-Adair, 1980), p. 137. The complete reference is the following: "We recall also the threat made by the Baader-Meinhof gang to spread anthrax through the mails of West Germany."

[635] *The RAND-St. Andrews Terrorism Chronology*.

[636] The dates on which the letters were written do not appear in press accounts. According to "New extortion try threatens Tucson with bubonic plague," *Arizona Daily Star*, September 15, 1978, p. 1B, however, they were sent "in the past two weeks," citing police and city officials.

[637] "Tucson police discount plague plot," *Arizona Republic*, September 16, 1978, p. B2.

[638] Mark Kimble, "Mayor calls plague threat 'crank'," *Tucson Citizen*, September 15, 1978, p. 1C.

[639] Mark Kimble, "Mayor calls plague threat 'crank'," *Tucson Citizen*, September 15, 1978, p. 1C.

[640] The *Tucson Citizen* says "Police officials and Murphy say they don't think the letters were written by the same persons," in Mark Kimble, "Mayor calls plague threat 'crank'," *Tucson Citizen*, September 15, 1978, p. 1C. In contrast, the *Arizona Daily Star* is equally definitive that the threats were the work of the same people. See "New extortion try threatens Tucson with bubonic plague," *Arizona Daily Star*, September 15, 1978, p. 1B.

[641] "New extortion try threatens Tucson with bubonic plague," *Arizona Daily Star*, September 15, 1978, p. 1B.

***Case 1978-01: Tucson Extortionist, April 1978***

In early April 1978, the mayor of Tucson, Arizona received an anonymous letter threatening to contaminate the city's water system with typhoid. The letters demanded a payment of $750,000.[642] Mayor Lewis C. Murphy told reporters that the letter specifically mentioned the city's water fountains, while an FBI source claimed that the letter threatened the water system itself.[643]

The city government immediately brought the FBI into the case. The FBI had jurisdiction because of the use of U.S. mails to send the letter. A task force with more than 200 people was put together in response to the threat, drawing from the Tucson Police Department, the Pima County Sheriff's Office, the Pima County Attorney's Office, and the FBI.[644]

The letter ordered the city to insert a classified advertisement with the following language into the city's two major newspapers: "Wanted to buy—any car manufactured before 1900. We pay top dollar." The ad was run from April 8 through April 14.[645] A second letter was then received, which ordered the city to send a female police officer to a phone booth to await a telephone call with further instructions. On April 17, 1978, the city attempted to comply with these directions. A police officer went to the specified telephone, and awaited further instructions. She received a series of telephone calls, which directed her to move from one pay telephone to another. Eventually, she arrived as instructed at a particular telephone but received no additional messages.

Another attempt was made to comply with the demands on April 21. The police went through the same routine, moving from one pay telephone to the next. Finally, a package of money was left at the spot demanded by the perpetrator, although not the $750,000 demanded. The site was monitored to see if anyone would claim the money, but nobody showed up. Approximately 100 law enforcement officials participated in the operation. In addition, the police requested the telephone company to attempt to trace the telephone calls.

Tucson did not normally need to add chlorine to its water at that time.[646] Although city officials doubted that the perpetrators could contaminate the city's water system, Tucson's Department of Water and Sewers developed contingency plans, apparently including reserve stocks of chlorine and other chemicals.[647] The water was entirely drawn from wells. The system was spread out over 1,200 square miles, stretching from Catalina, which was 15 miles north of Tucson, to Corona de Tucson, which was 15 miles southeast. There were 2,400 miles of underground pipe, 300 wells, 101 pumping stations, and 83 storage facilities. The six largest storage tanks stored 99 million gallons of water.[648]

It appears that the perpetrators were never identified.

***Case 1977-01: Unknown, March 1977***

According to the *RAND-St. Andrews Terrorism Chronology*, in March 1977 "A U.S. advertising firm received a letter alleging the discovery of a lethal bacterium capable of contaminating the fresh water of nuclear-armed nations."[649]

***Case 1977-03: Unnamed extortionists, 1977***

According to the *RAND-St. Andrews Terrorism Chronology*, "Extortionists threatened to put botulism toxin in Miami's water supply" sometime in 1977.[650]

---

[642] Accounts of this case appear in John Rawlinson and Tom Beal, "Letter demands $750,000 for water safety," *Arizona Daily Star*, April 22, 1978, p. 1A, and Mark Kimble, "Extortionist threatens city's water supply," *Tucson Citizen*, April 22, 1978, p. 2A. The two newspapers differ on some of the details. According to the *Arizona Daily Star*, the letter was delivered on April 7. The *Tucson Citizen* dates it to April 9.

[643] John Rawlinson and Tom Beal, "Letter demands $750,000 for water safety," *Arizona Daily Star*, April 22, 1978, p. 1A

[644] Mark Kimble, "Extortionist threatens city's water supply," *Tucson Citizen*, April 22, 1978, p. 2A.

[645] Mark Kimble, "Extortionist threatens city's water supply," *Tucson Citizen*, April 22, 1978, p. 2A.

[646] John Rawlinson and Tom Beal, "Letter demands $750,000 for water safety," *Arizona Daily Star*, April 22, 1978, p. 1A.

[647] Mark Kimble, "Extortionist threatens city's water supply," *Tucson Citizen*, April 22, 1978, p. 2A.

[648] Mark Kimble, "Extortionist threatens city's water supply," *Tucson Citizen*, April 22, 1978, p. 2A.

[649] *The RAND-St. Andrews Terrorism Chronology.*

[650] *The RAND-St. Andrews Terrorism Chronology.*

***Case 1976-01: Stephen Grant Morton, June 1976***

From October 13, 1975 through January 1, 1977, extortion letters were sent to approximately 250 companies around the United States demanding that substantial payments be made to a bank in Matamoros, Mexico. The letters were attributed to "B.A. Fox" and "J. Foxworth." However, FBI investigations determined that the accounts identified in the letters did not exist.[651] In June 1976, letter bombs were sent to at least 18 of the threatened companies. Several people were injured when some of the devices exploded.[652]

In addition, at least four letters were mailed containing ticks.[653] One letter was sent to the Combined Insurance Company of America, located in Colorado. It was accompanied by a letter making the following statement: "The secret is that B.A. Fox has a fine bacteria lab, well stocked with various types of bacteria, viruses, germs--ranging from simple staph type infections up to and including rabies."[654] Another tick letter was sent to Mobile Chemical Company's plastic division.[655] One was sent to FBI Director Clarence M. Kelley. According to the Tulsa, Oklahoma postmaster, "three or four" letters carrying ticks were sent to recipients in that area. He indicated, however, "They were just mashed. By the time they got through the canceling machines and equipment they were dead."[656]

Federal authorities believed that it was highly unlikely that the ticks could transmit disease. According to an FBI statement, "Laboratory examinations of some of these ticks have been conducted to determine if they constitute a health hazard. Preliminary results of these tests indicate that the chances of these ticks transmitting any infectious diseases to humans are extremely remote."[657] It was determined that the ticks were not infected.[658]

On July 14, 1977, Stephen Grant Morton was indicted in Denver, Colorado, by a federal grand jury on extortion charges. According to the indictment, Morton mailed more than 250 threatening letters, including four containing ticks. Morton also was charged with poisoning drugs at grocery stores in Colorado Springs and with contaminating foods at grocery stores in Houston.[659]

The case against Morton was dismissed at the request of the government.[660]

***Case 1975-01: Polisario, February 1975***

According to the *RAND-St. Andrews Terrorism Chronology*, sometime in February 1975 "Polisario reportedly contacted the ETA (a Spanish Basque nationalist group) to plan the poisoning of water supplies of Paris, Madrid, Rabat, and Nouakchott with cholera viruses. This action would be in retaliation for the policies of France, Spain, Morocco, and Mauritania regarding Western Sahara."[661]

***Case 1974-03: "Middle East firm", 1974***

According to the *RAND-St. Andrews Terrorism Chronology*, sometime in 1974 "a Middle East firm was reported to be engaged in the development of means of poisoning the Jordan River sources by bacteria."[662]

---

[651] Whit Sibley, "Indictment Charges Letter-Bomb Threats," *Denver Post*, July 15, 1977, p. 2, "Bombs Mailed to Firms; One Injures Four Workers," *Washington Post*, June 15, 1976, p. C9, Edward C. Burke, "Extortion Note Preceded Letter Bombs," *New York Times*, June 17, 1976, p. 24, and John M. Goshko, "Letter Bombs Tied to Extortion Ring," *Washington Post*, June 16, 1976, p. A1.

After briefly describing this incident, one source also claims, "There had been earlier reports of a "germ letter" written on paper impregnated with deadly bacteria that would infect the recipient." It is unclear whether the source intended to link this allegation with the sender of the tick-infested letters, or if this was a totally different case. Brian M. Jenkins and Alfred P. Rubin, "New Vulnerabilities and the Acquisition of New Weapons by Nongovernment Groups," p. 228, in Alona E. Evans and John F. Murphy, editors, *Legal Aspects of International Terrorism* (Lexington, Massachusetts: Lexington Books, D.C. Heath and Company, 1978).

[652] "Terrorism by Mail," *New York Times*, June 20, 1976, p. IV-3.

[653] Sibley, "Indictment Charges Letter-Bomb Threats," p. 2.

[654] Edward C. Burke, "Extortion Note Preceded Letter Bombs," *New York Times*, June 17, 1976, p. 24

[655] "2nd Mailing of Ticks Reported," *New York Times*, June 17, 1976, p. 24.

[656] "Postal Ticks Discounted by FBI As Health Peril, Kelley Gets One," *Washington Post*, June 19, 1976, p. A16.

[657] "Postal Ticks Discounted by FBI As Health Peril, Kelley Gets One," *Washington Post*, June 19, 1976, p. A16.

[658] "Terrorism by Mail," *New York Times*, June 20, 1976, p. IV-3.

[659] Sibley, "Indictment Charges Letter-Bomb Threats," p. 2, "Extortion Suspect Freed on Bond," *Denver Post*, July 16, 1977, p. 3, "Denver Man Accused of Mail Threats Involving Bomb and Live Ticks," *New York Times*, July 16, 1977, p. 6.

[660] According to information provided by the Office of the Court Clerk, U.S. District Court, Denver, Colorado, March 10, 1998.

[661] *The RAND-St. Andrews Terrorism Chronology* for identifying this incident.

[662] *The RAND-St. Andrews Terrorism Chronology*.

***Case 1974-02: Legion of Nabbil Kadduri Usur, 1974***

According to the *RAND-St. Andrews Terrorism Chronology*, sometime in 1974 "The 'Legion of Nabbil Kadduri Usur' (of which nothing else is known) distributed leaflets in Germany demanding money and threatening to release bacteria if their demands were not met."[663]

***Case 1973-01: The German "mad scientist", November 1973***

In November 1973, German press reports indicated that a "mad scientist" had threatened to use anthrax and botulinum toxin against targets in Germany. According to press accounts, on November 8, 1973 an unidentified biologist sent an English-language extortion letter to the office of Chancellor Willy Brandt, and perhaps to other senior government officials. The extortionist threatened to contaminate the water supplies of German cities, to place "biological bombs" in synagogues and in stores and hotels owned by Jews, and to mail letters infected with pathogens to politicians. He demanded a payment of DM 22 million (about $8.5 million) in "atonement money" for the killing of five Palestinian terrorists during the 1972 Munich Olympics. Some of the letters were signed "The Commander in Chief of the Legion."[664]

Press reports indicate that the German government took the threats extremely seriously. Police guards were placed around water reservoirs and regular water samples were taken. In addition, press accounts suggested that the Germans mounted a massive manhunt to track down the perpetrators. The German public reacted by buying large quantities of bottled water.

German press accounts also indicated that the police were hunting for an unnamed biology professor who lived in Hamburg, who, it was claimed, was trying to flee to Denmark with his female laboratory assistant. German and Danish border police, however, denied that they were looking for any such person.

It is not known if the alleged "mad scientist" was ever identified and arrested, or if the whole incident was a hoax.

***Case 1970-06X: Poisoner of Los Angeles water supply, no date***

Neil C. Livingstone alleged in a 1982 book that the FBI and Los Angeles police arrested someone "who was preparing to poison the city's water supply with a biological poison." No date or other particulars are provided.[665] No such episode is listed in the chronology that Douglass and Livingstone prepared for their 1987 book.[666]

## Threatened Use (Anthrax Hoaxes)

This section includes all incidents that involved threats involving anthrax that suggest no likely possession of the agent by the perpetrator. All these cases occurred in the United States. Anthrax hoaxes in other countries are described in the previous category.

***Case 2000-10: Anthrax threat (against Florida industrial park), November 2000***

The Cape Coral Industrial Park received a letter that claimed to contain anthrax. A white powder was found in the envelope, but tests conducted by the Centers for Disease Control and Prevention indicated that it contained nothing harmful. Fourteen people were exposed to the envelope and sent to the Cape Coral Hospital for treatment. The Cape Coral Fire and Rescue hazardous materials team responded to the report, as did the Cape Coral Police and the FBI.[667]

---

[663] *The RAND-St. Andrews Terrorism Chronology.*

[664] "Bonn silent on postal germs story," *Times* (London), November 22, 1973, p. 1, "Scientist held in germ blackmail case," *Times* (London), November 23, 1973, p. 6, "Hunt for 'mad scientist' concentrates on Hamburg," *Times* (London), November 24, 1973, p. 5, John M. Goshko, "'Mad Scientist' Threatens Germans," *Washington Post*, November 25, 1973, p. A14.

[665] Neil C. Livingstone, *The War Against Terrorism* (Lexington, Massachusetts: Lexington Books, 1982), p. 112, states "the Los Angeles police, acting in conjunction with FBI agents, arrested a man who was preparing to poison the city's water supply with a biological poison."

[666] Douglass and Livingstone, *America the Vulnerable*, pp. 184-187.

[667] "Lab tests show 'anthrax' powder in letter is hoax," *St. Petersburg Times*, November 28, 2000, p. 5B.

***Case 2000-09: Anthrax hoax (misidentified item), September 2000***

Police investigating a pipe bomb in Palm Bay, Florida, discovered a plastic container labeled "anthrax". The 19-year-old occupant told authorities that the jar was filled with a muscle enhancer that he was trying to keep friends from using.[668]

***Case 2000-06: Anthrax threat (against University of Pennsylvania Jewish group), April 2000***

The director of the University of Pennsylvania Hillel Foundation received an anthrax threat letter on April 20, 2000. The envelope contained a powder and a threat letter. The letter, which contained an anti-Semitic diatribe, asserted that the powder was anthrax. After the director made contact with the powder, he contacted authorities. A response was mounted by the University of Pennsylvania Police, the Philadelphia Fire Department, the FBI, the University's Office of Environmental Health, and members of a federal counter-terrorism task force. The powder was not anthrax or a chemical hazard.[669]

***Case 2000-05:Anthrax hoax (US Post Office mailbox), March 2000***

On March 30, 2000, a postal worker discovered a package in a Lincoln, Nebraska mailbox labeled "anthrax". The postal employee took the package back to his post office, and law enforcement and public health officials were notified. A jar filled with a white powder was found inside the package. Preliminary tests suggested that the material was not anthrax, but it was sent to the Nebraska State Public Health Laboratory, located in Omaha.[670]

***Case 2000-04:Possible biological threat (against IRS service center), March 2000***

On March 23, 2000, the Ogden IRS Service Center received an envelope that proved to contain an unidentified blue powder. Three employees exposed to the powder appeared to break out in a rash, possibly because of the exposure. Ultimately, 10 people were sent to a hospital for treatment. The powder was sent to a laboratory at the Dugway Proving Grounds, which is located in Utah. The envelope reportedly also contained a threatening letter, but no details were made public. Tests determined that the substance was not a known pathogen or poison.[671]

***Case 2000-03: Anthrax threat (against Fredonia High School), March 2000***

A 15-year-old student was arrested on March 6, 2000 on charges of making bomb and anthrax threats against Fredonia High School, located in the town of the same name in the Buffalo, New York area. According to the press account of the incident, the threats were made on March 2 and March 3, but it is unclear which threats were made on which day. There is no information on how the threats were transmitted.[672]

***Case 2000-02: Anthrax threats (in Milwaukee area), January 2000***

On January 14, 2000, the FBI arrested Micky A. Sauer on charges of mailing threatening communications. Authorities believe that he sent 17 threats, including 16 involving threats of anthrax use. The letters, which were delivered January 5-18, 2000, were received by two schools, a grocery store, two women's clinics, and other locations. He was sentenced to 21 months in prison on September 26, 2000.

***Case 2000-01: Anthrax threats (against abortion clinics), January 2000***

On January 3, 2000, abortion clinics located across the United States began receiving anthrax threat letters. It appears that the clinics all received the same threat letter. The white envelopes were post-marked December 30, 1999 in Cincinnati, Ohio, and had a return address that corresponded to an abortion clinic in Indianapolis, Indiana. The letters apparently all contained the same typewritten text.

> You will die in less than 24 hours from exposure to the anthrax on this letter. There is simply no other way to get rid of you., we're sorry.

---

[668] Mike Strobe, "Bay area agencies train against biological terror," *The Tampa Tribune*, September 17, 2000, p. 1.

[669] Jonathan Margulies, "U. Penn Hillel receives death threat in hate mail," *Daily Pennsylvanian*, April 25, 2000, and Jonathan Margulies, "Students feel safer as crime decreases," *Daily Pennsylvanian*, June 1, 2000, as found at *http://www.dailypennsylvanian.com*.

[670] Tanya Eiserer, "Lincoln Officials Await Results On Package Labeled 'Anthrax'," *Omaha World Herald*, March 30, 2000, p. 16, and "'Anthrax' Jar Was a Hoax, Officials Say," *Omaha World-Herald*, April 1, 2000, p. 14.

[671] Matthew Ott, "Letter Powder Seen As an IRS Threat," *Associated Press*, March 23, 2000, 1:04 PM, and "IRS Powder Harmless," *Salt Lake Tribune*, March 25, 2000, as found at *http://www.sltrib.com*.

[672] "Teen Arrested on Threat Charges," *Buffalo News*, March 7, 2000, p. B5.

In addition, it appears that the letters were addressed to the "Security Director" at the clinics. According to one source, the threatening letters were sent to abortion clinics in 21 states, including Alabama, Connecticut, Delaware, Florida, Georgia, Illinois, Indiana, Kentucky, Maine, Michigan, North Carolina, New Jersey, New York, Ohio, Pennsylvania, Rhode Island, South Carolina, Tennessee, Vermont, Virginia, and Wisconsin, as well as the District of Columbia.[673]

It appears that several of the letters were misdirected. One letter was delivered to a Pinkerton Security Services office in Knoxville, Kentucky. There was a Planned Parenthood office below the Pinkerton office.[674] Similarly, it appears that a Social Security Administration office in the Bronx received one of the letters. A Planned Parenthood office was in the same building.[675] A social services agency in Richmond, Virginia, The Daily Planet, also got one of the letters. Planned Parenthood previously ran an abortion clinic at the same location.[676]

***Case 1999-59: Anthrax threat (against high school), December 1999***

The Bedford North Lawrence High School was closed on Monday, December 13, 1999, after an unidentified man called the school at 7:25 a.m. and claimed to have contaminated it with anthrax. The school district decided to cancel classes for the day after consulting with local, state, and federal authorities. Classes resumed the next day.[677]

***Case 1999-62: Anthrax threat (against high school), November 1999***

On November 20, 1999, a note was found in the Fredonia High School claiming that the school was contaminated with anthrax., Police arrested an unidentified juvenile the next day.[678]

***Case 1999-55: Anthrax threat (against Department of Energy site), November 1999***

On November 8, 1999, an employee at the administrative offices of a one-time uranium processing plant in Fernald, Ohio, found a note attached to a coffee cup, "Anthrax sample. Do not touch." The people in the building were evacuated, and other employees were not allowed in the building. The analysis was conducted by an Environmental Protection Agency laboratory, which determined that afternoon that no anthrax was present in the cup. The investigation was turned over to the FBI.[679]

***Case 1999-78: Anthrax threat (against Providian Bancorp Services), October 1999***

On October 29, 1999, an employee working in the mailroom of the Providian Bancorp Services office in Concord, New Hampshire noticed that an envelope sent through the automated mail opener released a cloud of particles. The office processes credit card payments. Further examination revealed that it contained a small package the size of a sugar packet containing with Spanish printing on it. The packet was sealed in a plastic bag and put aside. Subsequently, the employee put his finger in his mouth and got a bitter taste. Worried that the packet may have contained something harmful, he notified authorities.

The Concord Fire Department activated its hazardous materials response unit. The team decontaminated five employees who were exposed to the envelope, and turned the envelope over to the state laboratory for further analysis. Reportedly, the envelope was taken by the came out of an envelope when put off a An envelope On 29 October, an employee at a bank in Concord, New Hampshire, opened an envelope containing an unidentified white powder.[680]

---

673 "Clinics Begin Year with Spate of Anthrax Hoaxes," *Anti-Abortion Violence Watch*, January 19, 2000, Number 22, p. 2. This source claims that the letters were post-marked December 29, but some news reports put the date at December 30.

674 Don Jacobs and Scott Barker, "Anthrax Scare: Pinkerton manager being treated after getting letter apparently meant for Planned Parenthood," *Knoxville News-Sentinel*, January 4, 2000, p. A4.

675 Philip Messing, "Anthrax Scare at SS Office," *New York Post*, January 4, 2000, p. 26.

676 Mark Bowes, "Testing fins letters claiming to contain anthrax were hoaxes," *Richmond Times Dispatch*, January 12, 2000, p. B-6.

677 "Students Sent Home," *Associated Press State and Local Wire*, December 13, 1999, AM cycle.

678 "Juvenile Arrested in Anthrax Scare," *Buffalo News*, November 20, 1999, p. 5B.

679 "Building evacuated because of anthrax scare," *Associated Press*, November 8, 1999, 5:54 PM EST.

680 "Authorities investigate possible anthrax scare," *Associated Press State and Local Wire*, October 29, 1999, AM cycle, "Probe continues," *New Hampshire Sunday News*, October 31, 1999, p. A3, and "Anthrax scare," *The Union Leader*, October 30, 1999, p. A5. This incident was brought to my attention by Gavin Cameron, Jason Pate, Diana McCauley, & Lindsay DeFazio, "1999 WMD

***Case 1999-53: Anthrax threat (against Kentucky Educational Television), October 1999***

On October 12, 1999, a package containing an unidentified organic substance was opened in the mailroom of the offices of Kentucky Educational Television in Lexington, Kentucky. According to an accompanying letter, the substance was anthrax. The employees in the building were isolated in the building from 10:30 a.m. until 2:00 p.m. The material in the package tested negative for anthrax.[681]

***Case 1999-52: Anthrax threat (against U.S. Post Office administrative office), September 1999***

An envelope containing an anthrax threat was opened on September 13, 1999 at a U.S. Post Office administrative office in Robinson, Pennsylvania. Nine people working in the office were decontaminated, and then transported to Ohio Valley General Hospital. No evidence of anthrax was detected.[682]

***Case 1999-54: Anthrax threat against Truman Library, August 1999***

The Truman Library in Independence, Missouri received an anthrax hoax letter on August 16, 1999. The note, described by an FBI agent as "a rambling letter; it didn't make a lot of sense," was written in three languages, German, Swedish, and Greek. After opening the letter, and attempting to translate it, the staff of the library concluded that it contained an anthrax hoax. Local authorities were notified at about 3:20 p.m. The building was quarantined, and 70 people were kept in the building until authorities concluded that it posed no threat. The people were allowed to leave at 5:00 p.m.[683]

***Case 1999-60: Anthrax threat (against internet service provider), August 1999***

An Internet service provider located in downtown Seattle received an envelope containing a white powder. Tests by the Seattle Fire Department gave "inconclusive results," according to an unnamed government official. Subsequent tests by the Washington state Department of Health determined that the substance was not anthrax. Based on the appearance of the material, however, authorities were convinced that the threat was a hoax. Three people were exposed to the package, but none were treated. The FBI was investigating the case.[684]

***Case 1999-57: Anthrax threat (against Proctor and Gamble), August 1999***

An anthrax hoax letter was mailed from Seattle to a Cincinnati, Ohio, office of Proctor and Gamble. A powdery substance was found in the envelope. The letter said that the company would receive more packages if it continued to use animals for testing.[685]

***Case 1999-56: Anthrax threat (against Aldi's grocery store), July 1999***

On the morning of July 28, 1999, employees at a Kansas City grocery store found a duffel bag containing a note that was thought to be an anthrax threat. Authorities were notified, and at least four employees were decontaminated. The store was reopened that afternoon.[686]

***Case 1999-58: Anthrax threat (against Planned Parenthood), July 1999***

The Planned Parenthood Association of Northwest/Northeast Indiana received an anthrax threat letter on July 2, 1999. After opening it, a staff member called the Merrillville police. The Merrillville police and FBI

---

Terrorism Chronology: Incidents Involving Sub-National Actors and Chemical, Biological, Radiological, and Nuclear Materials," *The Nonproliferation Review*, Summer 2000, p. 172.

[681] Patricia Lynch Kimbro, "KET building quarantined for anthrax scare in mail," Herald-Leader (Lexington), October 13, 1999, and Patricia Lynch Kimbro, "Anthrax scar is lesson for Lexington," Herald-Leader (Lexington), October 14, 1999, as found at the newspaper's Web site, *http://www.kentuckyconnect.com/heraldleader/.*

[682] "Postal workers treated after anthrax threat," *Associated Press*, September 14, 1999, AM cycle, and "Anthrax threat investigated," *Pittsburgh Post-Gazette*, September 16, 1999, p. B-4.

[683] Trisha L. Howard, "Anthrax scare closes Truman Library," *Kansas City Star*, August 17, 1999, p. B3, and Trisha L. Howard, "False alarm on anthrax," *Kansas City Star*, August 17, 1999, p. B1.

[684] Rebecca Cook, "FBI Investigates mysterious white powder mailed to Seattle Internet Business," *Associated Press State and Local Wire*, August 13, 1999, PM cycle.

[685] "Anthrax Hoax Postmarked in Seattle," August 12, 1999, as found at *http://dailynews.yahoo.com.*

[686] Kevin Hoffman, "Officials respond to anthrax threat at store," *Kansas City Star*, July 29, 1999, p. B2, and "Abandoned duffel bag at store contained letter with 'threats of anthrax'," *Associated Press, State and Local Wire*, July 28, 1999, BC cycle.

agents went to the scene to investigate the threat, which appeared to have been mailed locally. Hazardous materials and fire teams were put on alert, but not activated.[687]

***Case 1999-42: Anthrax threats (against Nassau County, New York, courthouses), June 1999***

Letters claiming that the recipients had been exposed to anthrax were delivered on June 15, 1999 to two courthouses in Nassau County, New York: the 1st District Court (Hempstead) and the County Court Building (Mineola). According to authorities, the letters contained a message, written using letters cut from newspapers and magazines, that indicated, "Congratulations. You've been infected with anthrax." The envelopes were addressed using a computer printer.[688]

The letter in the Hempstead courthouse was discovered about 1:00 p.m., and the other was found about an hour later. The buildings were sealed off for several hours after the letters were discovered. During that time, the air conditioning systems were turned off to ensure that the anthrax would not spread if any were present. Officials from the local police and fire departments and the FBI reacted to the threats. Tests on the spot indicated that no anthrax was present, and people were allowed to leave the buildings about three hours after the letters were found.

***Case 1999-45: Anthrax threat (against Planned Parenthood clinics, Cincinnati, Ohio, June 1999***

Two clinics in Cincinnati, Ohio, received anthrax threats on June 2, 1999. The clinics, operated by Planned Parenthood of Southwest Ohio and Northern Kentucky, received letters claiming to have been contaminated with anthrax. The letters were turned over to the FBI for examination. Both letters were sent from Columbus, Ohio.[689]

***Case 1999-51: Anthrax threats (against Catholic college and high school), May 1999***

The alumni office at LeMoyne College, a Jesuit-run college located in Syracuse, New York, received an anthrax threat letter on May 17, 1999. On the same day a similar letter was delivered to Bishop Sudden High School, also in Syracuse. The FBI is investigating the case.[690]

***Case 1999-41: Anthrax threat (against Mentor, Ohio, high school), May 1999?***

The Mentor High School, in Mentor, Ohio, reportedly received an anthrax threat letter during the last few weeks of the school year. According to a press report, a secretary opened a letter that contained a message claiming that it had been contaminated with anthrax. The FBI and the local police, fire, and public health departments responded to the incident. In addition, the CDC provided advice on how to respond to the incident. Five employees and two students were isolated for several hours.[691]

***Case 1999-38: Anthrax threat (against Madison, Tennessee, library), May 1999***

On May 15, 1999, library employees discovered an envelope in a book returned to the night repository at the Madison Public Library, in Madison, Tennessee, containing a note claiming that the envelope was tainted with anthrax. The employees contacted the city fire department, which sent its hazardous materials unit to the library. In addition, health department officials responded to the event.

On May 19, Joseph M. Calvert, Jr., confessed to police that he was responsible for the incident. Five days later, May 24, after further investigation, the man was arrested and charged with making a threat to use a weapon of mass destruction. The man lived with his grandmother, who claimed that he had confessed to the crime because he could not afford a place to live and wanted to get sent to prison. According to a spokesman for the FBI's Nashville office, "The FBI doesn't take confessions on their face value. There has to be supporting evidence."[692]

---

[687] *Associated Press State and Local Wire*, July 5, 1999, PM cycle.

[688] Al Baker and Chau Lam, "A Scare at Two Nassau Courts," *Newsday*, June 16, 1999, p. A4, and Robert Gearty, "Anthrax threats Heeded," *Daily News (*New York), June 16, 1999, p. 9.

[689] "Planned parenthood gets anthrax threat," *Beacon Journal* (Akron, Ohio), June 3, 1999, as found at the newspaper's World Wide Web site, *http://www.ohio.com/*, and Al Andry, "FBI helps probe threats at Planned Parenthood," *Cincinnati Post*, June 3, 1999, as found at the paper's web site, *http://www.cincypost.com*.

[690] Sue Weibezahl, "Letter Hoax a Real Ordeal for Opener," *Post-Standard* (Syracuse, New York), May 21, 1999, p. A1. I am indebted to Leonard Cole for bringing this case to my attention.

[691] Andrea Simakis, "Administration Relieved School is Out," *Plain Dealer* (Cleveland), June 13, 1999, p. 1B.

[692] Beth Warren, "Police Arrest Madison Man in Library Anthrax Scare," *Tennessean* (Nashville), May 25, 1999, p. 2B.

***Case 1999-37: Anthrax hoax (Brooklyn, New York), May 1999***

On May 13, 1999, emergency medical technicians entered an apartment in Brooklyn, New York, and discovered an unidentified dead man, possibly killed by a drug overdose. They also found a package of drain cleaner marked "radioactive", an empty oxygen tank labeled "anthrax", and three red tubes with "TNT" written on them. The next day, a team of police and fire officials returned to the building, and evacuated everyone in the building where these items were discovered, as well as the three buildings that surrounded it. A fire department hazardous materials unit recovered the items from the apartment. All were discovered to be harmless.[693]

***Case 1999-40: Anthrax threat (against Sharonville, Ohio, anti-pornography group), April 1999***

On April 30, 1999, a letter containing a white powder was delivered to the offices of the Citizens for Community Values (CCV), a Sharonville, Ohio, anti-pornography organization. When the envelope was opened, about a teaspoon of the powder spilled from the envelope. There was a letter in the envelope, but its contents were not reported in press accounts of the incident. Two officers on the first floor of the building where CCV had its offices were evacuated, and the Greater Cincinnati Hazardous Materials Unit decontaminated three CCV employees. Subsequent analysis determined that the powder was baking soda.[694]

***Case 1999-61: Anthrax threat (against Blackfeet tribal offices), April 1999***

The offices of the Blackfeet tribal council received an anthrax threat on April 19, 1999. The threat was sent in an envelope with a greeting card and the message, "You have been exposed to anthrax, die, die, die." Unidentified granules also were in the envelope. The substance tested negative for anthrax, but was sent to "a laboratory in Maryland" for further testing.[695]

***Case 1999-36: Anthrax hoax (Lake Worth, Florida, law office), April 1999***

A letter containing an unidentified white powder was opened in the offices of a Lake Worth, Florida, law office, on April 14, 1999. Also in the envelope was a folded, blank piece of paper. Initially, authorities thought that it might be cocaine. When it proved negative for that drug. The Sheriff's deputy who responded to the event reported feeling a "tingling" sensation on his tongue, and the law firm's employee's began to feel itchy. At that point, the hazardous materials team was sent to the scene, and the Sheriff's deputy and six law firm employees were decontaminated and sent to the JFK Medical Center for treatment. They were given antibiotics and released.[696]

***Case 1999-35: Anthrax threat (against Intel Corporation), April 1999***

A letter sent to an Intel Corporation office in Rio Rancho, New Mexico, contained a note claiming that whoever opened the envelope would be infected with anthrax. There was no powder in the envelope. Local, state, and federal officials were notified of the letter.[697]

***Case 1999-27: Anthrax threat (Dunkirk High School, Chautauqua County, New York), April 1999***

On May 7, 1999, police arrested Jessica Lane, a 17-year-old student on a charge of third-degree false reporting of a threat. The arrest was made in connection with an anthrax threat letter delivered to a faculty member of Dunkirk High School in Chautauqua County, New York, on April 16, 1999. According to the letter, it was contaminated with anthrax. The high school was locked down for 2 _ hours. Because a teacher from the high school visited the middle school, the middle school also was affected. The letter and people who came into contact with the letter were tested for the presence of anthrax. All the tests were negative. Authorities suggested that others in addition to Jessica Lane might be arrested.[698]

---

[693] Sean Gardiner, "Toxic Scare Evacuation in B'klyn," *Newsday*, May 15, 1999, p. A34.

[694] Lew Moores and Earnest Winston, "Mysterious powder empties office," *Cincinnati Enquirer*, May 1, 1999, p. B2, "Office Evacuated," *Cincinnati Post*, May 3, 1999, p. 11A, and "Powder Harmless," *Cincinnati Post*, May 28, 1999, p. 19A.

[695] "Lab tests show substance wasn't anthrax," *Associated Press State and Local Wire*, April 22, 1999, BC cycle.

[696] Lillian Weis, "7 Taken to Hospital After Powder Scare," *Palm Beach Post*, April 15, 1999, p. 6B.

[697] "Virus Letter Didn't Deliver on Threat," *Albuquerque Journal*, April 15, 1999, p. 1.

[698] "Dunkirk School Gets Anthrax Scare," *Buffalo News*, April 17, 1999, p. 4B, "No Anthrax Found at Dunkirk School," *Buffalo News*, April 22, 1999, p. 4C, and "Teen Held in Anthrax Scare," *Buffalo News*, May 8, 1999, p. 5C.

***Case 1999-34: Anthrax hoax (against Logan, Utah, grocery store), April 1999?***

Two men reportedly marked a load of milk at a grocery store in Logan, Utah, with the word "anthrax" as a practical joke. Several gallons of milk were destroyed as a result. An Assistant U.S. Attorney for Utah indicated that the men did not have the criminal intent to justify a prosecution, and so they were not charged.[699]

***Case 1999-33: Anthrax threat (against Grand Rapids, Michigan abortion clinic), April 1999***

The employees at a Planned Parenthood office in downtown Grand Rapids, Michigan turned over a suspicious package that appeared to contain a powdery substance to authorities on April 13, 1999. The package was turned over to the FBI after it had been X-rayed by local police to ensure that it was not an explosive device.[700]

***Case 1999-49: Suspected biological agent threat (against IRS Service Center), April 1999***

Suspicions that two letters with dark stains on them might be contaminated with some hazardous substance led officials to quarantine the Internal Revenue Service's Kansas City Service Center the facility for three hours on April 21, 1999. Employees reportedly detected a smelly, slimy substance on the letters, leading them to implement emergency procedures. The air handling system in the building was shut down, and local emergency response organizations were contacted. No hazardous materials were detected on the letters, but the Kansas City hazardous materials response team decontaminated 38 employees. Approximately 2,000 IRS employees were in the building while it was quarantined. Authorities apparently treated the incident as a possible hazardous materials threat, including potential involvement of a biological agent such as anthrax.[701]

***Case 1999-48: Anthrax threat (against county courthouse, Biloxi, Mississippi), April 1999***

On April 19, 1999, the Harrison County Sheriff's Department discovered a note "threatening the deployment of anthrax" while investigating a bomb threat against the Harrison County Courthouse in Biloxi, Mississippi. The threat was classified as a hoax.[702]

***Case 1999-47: Anthrax threat (against individual in Lewisville, Texas), March 1999***

On the morning of March 6, 1999, the occupant of a house in Lewisville, Texas, opened a letter addressed to a former resident and discovered an anthrax threat. After being called about the threat, the Lewisville Police Department notified the FBI, which activated the North Texas Joint Terrorism Task Force. The task force concluded that the threat was a hoax. The motive for the threat was not known.[703]

***Case 1999-65: Anthrax threat (against high school), March 1999***

On March 12, 1999, an anthrax threat was discovered written on a note found in a classroom at Hamburg Senior High School. The school was located in Hamburg, New York, a town outside of Buffalo. According to an FBI official, "It didn't even rise to the level of a hoax." The school remained open. At the end of the day, students were sent home with a letter that told parents that the threat was assessed as "extremely minimal." It advised parents that the students should shower, that their clothes should be washed, and that they should be alert for signs of illness.[704]

***Case 1999-32: Anthrax and Ebola hoax (at Pittsburgh International Airport), March 1999***

Jason Anthony Chippich was detained at the Pittsburgh International Airport on March 26, 1999, when he placed two vials on a U.S. Airways ticket counter labeled "anthrax" and "Ebola". According to a county official, "It was a practical joke." According to authorities, the perpetrator was an intern at Children's Institute of Pittsburgh, where Chippich also worked. The culprit "said it was her last day of work at the institute, and she decided to play a joke on Chippich. She put ground-up cereal in one of the vials, ground-up

---

[699] "Anthrax Suspects Will Not Be Charged," *States News Service*, April 14, 1999, 6:20 AM ET.

[700] "Grand Rapids clinic wary of mail package," *Associated Press*, April 15, 1999, as found at *http://www.detnews.com.*

[701] Matt Campbell, "Suspicious mail disrupts IRS center," *Kansas City Star*, April 22, 1999, p. B1. I am indebted to Leonard Cole for bringing this case to my attention.

[702] "Anthrax report treated as a hoax," *Associated Press* (State and Local Wire), April 21, 1999, BC cycle. I am indebted to Leonard Cole for bringing this case to my attention.

[703] "Anthrax letter in Lewisville a hoax, FBI reports," *Dallas Morning News*, March 7, 1999, p. 34A. I am indebted to Leonard Cole for bringing this case to my attention.

[704] "Anthrax Threat Said to be a Hoax," *Buffalo News*, March 13, 1999, p. 5C.

antacids in the other, labeled them anthrax and Ebola and slipped them into his coat pocket." County police and FBI detained Chippich and his sister, who was accompanying him, at the airport for five hours.[705]

***Case 1999-31: Anthrax threat (against Southern Baptist Convention), March 1999***

An anthrax threat letter was opened at the offices of the Southern Baptist Convention in Nashville, Tennessee, on March 5, 1999. A secretary, who found a note claiming that it was contaminated with anthrax spores, opened the letter. A Nashville fire fighter who responded to the report, and who handled the letter, and four employees were decontaminated and given antibiotics. The FBI took the letter for further analysis.[706]

***Case 1999-30: Anthrax threat (against Lumberton, North Carolina, dialysis clinic), March 1999***

An unidentified individual placed a telephone call to the Lumberton Dialysis Clinic in Lumberton, North Carolina, claiming that anthrax was present in the clinic. The call, placed at 10:00 a.m. on March 4, 1999, led authorities to quarantine the 50 people then in the clinic for 3 _ hours. Local authorities responded to the call, and the hazardous materials teams of the Lumberton Fire Department decontaminated the room with a bleach solution. The people in the clinic were not decontaminated, but were advised by local health officials to go home and take showers to clean off any possible contamination. The FBI took samples from the clinic for further testing, but assessed the incident as a probable hoax.[707]

***Case 1999-28: Anthrax threat (against offices of Latter-Day Saints, Salt Lake City, Utah), March 1999***

An anthrax threat letter was discovered on March 3, 1999 in the Church Office Building of the Church of Jesus Christ of Latter-Day Saints in Salt Lake City, Utah. The envelope was opened at about 9:57 a.m. in the mailroom, and was found to contain a letter claiming, "Congratulations, You've been exposed to anthrax." Three employees were decontaminated at the scene, and taken to University Hospital for medical treatment. The letter was taken to the University of Utah for testing. Officials declared the letter a hoax.[708]

***Case 1999-26: Possible anthrax threat (Planned Parenthood clinic, Chicago, Illinois), March 1999***

A suspicious package received in the mail by a Planned Parenthood clinic in Chicago, Illinois, was found to contain a vial of liquid when bomb squad technicians X-rayed it. The incident apparently was treated as a bomb threat, but was considered a possible biological threat after the initial examination.[709]

***Case 1999-29: Anthrax threats (against Blanca, Colorado, town officials), February 1999***

In mid-February several anthrax threat letters were sent to the elected town officials in Blanca, a small town of 125 families in southern Colorado. The letters were tested in a "military laboratory," which determined that no anthrax was present. The FBI is investigating the threats. According to press reports, this small town has been wracked by a bitter political dispute, suggesting that the enemies of the town officials sent the letters.[710]

***Case 1999-25: Anthrax threat (Honolulu, Hawaii), February 1999***

The Honolulu, Hawaii, office of the state Department of Motor Vehicles was closed on February 24, 1999, due to an anthrax threat letter. An administrator at the facility opened the letter. He notified authorities some time later, about 11:00 a.m., after hearing about the incident at the Ala Moana Center the previous day

---

[705] Lawrence Walsh, "Airport police grab vials, detain 2," *Post-Gazette* (Pittsburgh), March 27, 1999, and Lawrence Welch, "Airport officials weren't amused," *Post-Gazette* (Pittsburgh), March 28, 1999, as found at the newspaper's web site, http://www.post-gazette.com.

[706] Leon M. Tucker, "Southern Baptist office receives anthrax scare in letter," *Tennessean*, March 6, 1999, as taken from the newspaper's World Wide Web site, *http://www.tennessean.com*.

[707] Jennifer Fuller, "Clinic receives anthrax threat," Fayetteville Observer-Times (North Carolina), March 5, 1999, as found at the paper's web site, *http://www.fayettevillenc.com*.

[708] "Latest Anthrax Scare Called Hoax," *Salt Lake Tribune*, March 4, 1999, as found at the newspaper's web site at *http://www.sltrib.com*, and Lois M. Collins and Jennifer Dobner, "An anthrax threat at LDS offices," *Deseret News*, March 3, 1999, as found at the newspaper's World Wide Web site, *http://www.desnews.com*.

[709] "Planned Parenthood clinic receives suspicious package," *Associated Press*, March 16, 1999, 4:39AM EST.

[710] Kit Miniclier, "Blanca: Town weathers stormy politics," *Denver Post*, June 12, 1999, p. B4.

(see page 133). The office was closed from 11:45 a.m. through 1:30 p.m., until local police and fire officials, along with the FBI, determined that there was no threat.[711]

***Case 1999-24: Chemical and biological threats (U.S. Capitol), February 1999***

According to a Capitol Police spokesman, "Several Congressional offices had received threats contained in them indicating that the recipient had been exposed to a biological hazard."[712] The spokesman also indicated, "We have received one letter which is exactly like those which have been received elsewhere in the United States, claiming exposure of the recipient to anthrax. In addition, another individual has sent several members of Congress letters which indicate the recipient has been exposed to a chemical or biological agent."[713]

***Case 1999-23: Anthrax threat (man in Gwinnett County, Georgia), February 1999***

At 3:30 a.m. on February 10, 1999, a man in Gwinnett County, Georgia, received a phone call from someone who said that an anthrax bomb had been placed in his mailbox. Nothing was found in the mailbox.[714]

***Case 1999-22: Anthrax hoax (Spring Hill, Florida, car wash), February 1999***

On February 24, 1999, a milk bottle with the word "anthrax" written on it was found at a car wash in Spring Hill, Florida. The plastic bottle was filled with a clear liquid. According to a press report, a customer discovered the container in a trashcan. A sheriff's deputy who responded to the call reportedly poured some of the liquid onto the ground. The car wash was closed off, and traffic was routed around the adjoining street for a period of time. Based on conversations with the CDC and FBI, local authorities determined that the substance was unlikely to be anthrax. Subsequent analysis determined that the container was filled with water and urine.[715]

A similar incident occurred on March 20, 1999, when another milk jug was discovered with the word "anthrax" written on it. The container was discovered by a Spring Hill man, who picked it up while cleaning up debris near his apartment. He only noticed the writing after picking it up the jug. He put it in the back of his pick-up truck, and called the offices of the Fernando Sheriff. The man was directed to drive to an open field, where deputies packaged it. The container was turned over to the FBI for further investigation.

A third incident, apparently related, took place on March 25, 1999, in a deserted area of Spring Hill. A milk jug marked with the word anthrax was discovered by a jogger at about 10:00 a.m. Three additional containers were found about 200 feet away with references to Jim Morrison and the Doors written on them with what appeared to be the same marker and handwriting. The FBI removed it around 12:40 p.m.

On July 4, 1999 an elderly man who had found one of the earlier containers found a fourth jug. It had "anthrax:" written on it, along with additional references to the Doors. The jug was empty, but as precaution the area where it was found was decontaminated with bleach.

***Case 1999-21: Suspected anthrax threat (Atlanta Federal Courthouse), February 1999***

On February 18, 1999, a suspicious package, reportedly filled with an unidentified powder, was found at the loading dock of the U.S. Court of Appeals in Atlanta, Georgia. The address was, United FBI Lab, World Court of Appeals.[716]

---

711 Crystal Lau and Mary Adamski, "Second 'anthrax' letter arrives in Honolulu," *Honolulu Star Bulletin*, February 24, 1999, Rod Ohira, "Islanders get crash course on anthrax", *Honolulu Star Bulletin*, February 24, 1999, Terence Lee, "Terrorism controls found lacking, *Honolulu Star Bulletin*, March 2, 1999, as found at the paper's Web site, *http://www.starbulletin.com*.

712 Amy Keller, "Livengood Warns House Offices About Anthrax Threat," *Roll Call*, February 18, 1999.

713 Laura Dunphy, "Capitol Police probe anthrax threats," *The Hill*, February 10, 1999, p. 1.

714 Scott Marshall, "Law and Order: No evacuation needed after anthrax threat," *Atlanta Constitution*, February 13, 1999, p. 7JJ (Gwinnett County extra).

715 Graham Brink, "Anthrax scare closes car wash," *St. Petersburg Times*, February 25, 1999, p. 1, Graham Brink, "Anthrax scare exposes lack of training," *St. Petersburg Times*, February 28, 1999, p. 1, Robert King, "Hernando County has another anthrax scare," ," *St. Petersburg Times*, March 21, 1999, p. 3B, Graham Brink, "County, FBI officials investigate anthrax false alarm in Spring Hill," *St. Petersburg Times*, March 26, 1999, p. 1, and Graham Brink, "'Anthrax' hoax grows with another bottle found in Spring Hill," *St. Petersburg Times*, July 7, 1999, p. 2.

716 "Mystery parcel to U.S. Court sent to FBI lab," *Atlanta Constitution*, February 19, 1999, p. 5C.

***Case 1999-20: Anthrax threats against abortion clinics, February 1999***

In late February 1999, more than 30 anthrax threat letters were sent abortion clinics in all parts of the United States. A few of the letters went to other targets, either because of support for abortion or due to mistakes in the addresses. It appears that most, if not all, of the letters were postmarked in Lexington, Kentucky.[717] Laboratory tests showed that none of the letters contained anthrax.

On February 18, it appears that anthrax letters were received in Asheville, North Carolina, Charleston, West Virginia, Cincinnati, Ohio, Manchester, Vermont, Milwaukee, Wisconsin, Portland, Oregon, Rapid City, South Dakota, and Sioux Falls, South Dakota, and Washington, D.C.

Femcare, a woman's clinic in Asheville, North Carolina, received a box containing an anthrax threat on February 18. After the package was opened, and the threatening note was discovered, it was put into a sealed plastic bag.[718] An abortion clinic in the Charleston, West Virginia, area, Kaneohe Surgicenter, received a letter with the message, "Anthrax. Have a nice death." The letter was sent from Lexington, Kentucky.[719] A woman's health clinic, Cincinnati Woman's Services, located in Walnut Hills, discovered an anthrax threat letter at 11:00 a.m. on February 18. Four employees in the facility were decontaminated and given antibiotics. Preliminary tests indicated that no anthrax was present.[720]

A Planned Parenthood clinic in Manchester, Vermont, received an anthrax threat letter on February 18. The letter was opened at 11:45 a.m. by an employee, and was found to contain a white powder and a threatening note. The powder tested negative for anthrax.[721]

The Summit Health Clinic, a Milwaukee, Wisconsin, abortion clinic also received an anthrax threat letter on February 18. Fire fighters using so-called "Smart Tickets" to test for the presence of anthrax received a positive indication for the presence of anthrax. A test on a second ticket, using a control solution, also indicated a positive result, suggesting possible problems with the first test. It took 12 hours to confirm that no anthrax was present, relying on tests made at a laboratory in Maryland.[722]

A Planned Parenthood clinic in Portland, Oregon, received an anthrax threat letter, but did not open it. After recognizing that the letter was similar to anthrax threat letters sent to other clinics, employees notified the FBI of the letter.[723] Clinics in two cities in South Dakota, Rapid City and Sioux Falls, also received letters on February 18.[724]

In Washington, D.C., the Washington Surgical Center received a package on February 18 with a label claiming that it contained anthrax. The Washington, D.C. fire department recovered the package and placed it in container for transport. It was then taken to the Naval Medical Research Institute for examination.[725]

On February 19, threat letters were received in Birmingham, Alabama, Des Moines, Iowa, Minneapolis, Minnesota, Portland, Maine, St. Johnsbury, Vermont, and St. Paul, Minnesota. In addition, a Nashville, Tennessee, clinic received a letter that was mistakenly identified as a threat.[726]

A Birmingham, Alabama, clinic, New Woman All Woman Healthcare, turned over to the FBI an unopened letter that was similar to those delivered elsewhere. According to an FBI spokesman, "We really

---

[717] Angela Galloway and Adrienne Lu, "Del. Clinic receives anthrax hoax letter," *Philadelphia Inquirer*, February 23, 1999, as found at the newspaper's World Wide Web site, *http://www.phillynews.com*.

[718] "Clinic in Asheville received anthrax threat," *Winston-Salem Journal*, February 20, 1999, as found at *http://www.journalnow.com/*, Valerie Honeycutt, "Threats postmarked Lexington," *Herald-Leader* (Lexington, Kentucky), February 20, 1999, as found at the newspaper's World Wide Web site, *http://www.kentuckyconnect.com*, and "Official: Clinic Threats from Ky.," *Associated Press*, February 20, 1999, 6:41 AM ET.

[719] Malia Rulon, "Charleston abortion clinic receives letter with anthrax threat," *Associated Press*, February 24, 1999. Reports that a Charleston, South Carolina, clinic was involved appears to be a mistake.

[720] Tanya Bricking and Tim Bonfield, "Anthrax threat mailed to local clinic," *Cincinnati Enquirer*, February 19, 1999, as found at the newspaper's World Wide Web site, *http://enquirer.com*.

[721] Mark Hayward and Denis Paiste, "Planned Parenthood gets anthrax scare," *Union Leader* (Manchester, New Hampshire), February 19, 1999, "Anthrax hoax exposed, clinic set to reopen, *Union Leader* (Manchester, New Hampshire), February 22, 1999, as found at the paper's Web site, *http://www.theunionleader.com*.

[722] "Abortion clinic gets anthrax threat," *Journal Sentinel* (Milwaukee), February 19, 1999, and Jessica McBride, "Field test didn't rule out anthrax," *Journal Sentinel* (Milwaukee), March 2, 1999, both from the paper's Web site, *http://www.jsonline.com*.

[723] "Portland clinic gets fake anthrax threat," *Oregonian*, February 25, 1999, as found at the paper's Web site, *http://www.oregonlive.com*.

[724] "Official: Clinic Threats From Ky," *Associated Press*, February 20, 1999, 6:40 a.m. EST.

[725] "Abortion Clinic Gets Threatening Package," *Washington Post*, February 19, 1999, p. B2.

[726] Kathy Carlson, "Letter no threat to abortion clinic," *Tennessean*, February 27, 19999, as posted on the newspaper's Web site, *http://www.tennessean.com*.

don't know [if the letter is one of those threatening anthrax], but we think it probably is." The letter was recovered by a hazardous materials team and sent to a Virginia laboratory for testing.[727] A Des Moines, Iowa, Planned Parenthood clinic received an anthrax threat letter on February 19. The letter arrived that morning, and caused the clinic to shut down for two hours. An estimated 10 people were evacuated from the facility, including some patients.[728]

A Minneapolis, Minnesota, Planned Parenthood clinic received an anthrax threat on February 19. The letter was turned over to the FBI, and the Minnesota Department of Health determined that no anthrax was present.[729]

A Planned Parenthood clinic in Portland, Maine, received an anthrax threat letter. The letter was not opened, because clinic employees were suspicious of the return address, which named a laboratory not used by the clinic, and had a Lexington, Kentucky postmark. Aware that other abortion clinics had received anthrax threat letters, the envelope was turned over authorities. Laboratory tests demonstrated that no anthrax was present.[730] A Planned Parenthood clinic in St. Johnsbury, Vermont, received an anthrax threat letter, apparently similar to the one sent to the clinic in Portland, Maine.[731] A St. Paul, Minnesota, Planned Parenthood clinic also received an anthrax threat letter. When tested by the Minnesota Health Department, no anthrax was identified.[732]

On February 22, anthrax threat letters appeared at clinics in Atlanta, Georgia, Billings, Montana, Charleston, West Virginia, Cranston, Rhode Island, Kansas City, Missouri, Minneapolis, Minnesota, Salt Lake City, Newark, Delaware, Utah, and Spokane, Washington. A clinic in Albany, New York, may have received a letter on that date, but threw it away.[733] An anthrax threat letter was delivered to a National Organization for Women chapter in New York City.[734] Similarly, the National Abortion Rights Action League in Washington, D.C., also reportedly received an anthrax threat.[735]

At 10:30 a.m. on February 22, Compassionate Services, the administrative arm of Atlanta Northside Family Planning Services, received a package with a return address marked "PAACO Surgical Instruments." This return address was associated with at least a dozen previous anthrax threat packages. Aware of the connection, employees at the facility, located in Sandy Springs, left the envelope unopened and turned it over to authorities. The office building was evacuated for three hours.[736] A Planned Parenthood clinic in Billings, Montana, reportedly received an anthrax letter on February 22.[737] A Planned Parenthood center in Wood County, near Charleston, West Virginia, received an anthrax threat on February 22.[738] The Women's Medical Center in Cranston, Rhode Island, received an envelope similar to those sent to abortion clinics around the

---

[727] "Birmingham clinic among those receiving anthrax letters, " *Associated Press*, February 20, 1999, 12:36 Eastern.

[728] Valerie Honeycutt, "Threats postmarked Lexington," *Herald-Leader* (Lexington, Kentucky), February 20, 1999, as found at the newspaper's World Wide Web site, *http://www.kentuckyconnect.com*, and "Anthrax scare forces clinic evacuation," report issued by KTIV-4, a television station in Sioux City, Iowa, and found at *http://www.msnbc.com.*

[729] Wayne Wangstad, "Germ threat to Planned Parenthood ruled hoax," St. *Paul Pioneer Press*, February 20, 1999, as found at the newspaper's Web site, *http://www.pioneerplanet.com,/* and "Twin Cities Women's Clinics Receive Threats," *WCCO*, posted February 19, 1999, 5:45 p.m., as found at *http://www.wcco.com.*

[730] "Suspect letter to Portland clinic part of hoax," *Press Herald* (Portland, Maine), March 4, 1999, as found at the paper's Web site, *http://www.portland.com*, Dale Vincent, "Vermont, Maine clinics get anthrax threat letters," *Union Leader* (Manchester, New Hampshire), February 20, 1999, from the newspaper's World Wide Web site, *http://www.theunionleader.com*, and "Anthrax hoaxes hit Maine," *Bangor Daily News*, March 3, 1999, from the newspaper's Web site, http://www.bangornews.com.

[731] Dale Vincent, "Vermont, Maine clinics get anthrax threat letters," *Union Leader* (Manchester, New Hampshire), February 20, 1999, from the newspaper's World Wide Web site, *http://www.theunionleader.com.*

[732] Wayne Wangstad, "Germ threat to Planned Parenthood ruled hoax," St. *Paul Pioneer Press*, February 20, 1999, as found at the newspaper's Web site, *http://www.pioneerplanet.com,/* and "Twin Cities Women's Clinics Receive Threats," *WCCO*, posted February 19, 1999, 5:45 p.m., as found at *http://www.wcco.com.*

[733] "Anthrax Letter Scare," *States News Service*, February 24, 1999, as found at *http://dailynews.yahoo.com.*

[734] Beth Gardiner, "Anthrax threats at women's clinic, NOW office," *Associated Press*, February 23, 1999, 10:12 PM.

[735] Ruth E. Igoe and Mark Morris, "Kansas City is not alone in dealing with anthrax hoax, *Kansas City Star*, February 23, 1999, as found at the newspaper's World Wide Web site, *http://www.kcstar.com.*

[736] Brad Schrade, "Anthrax scare empties offices hit by '97 bomb," *Atlanta Journal-Constitution*, February 23, 1999, as found at *http://www.accessatlanta.com.*

[737] Bill Morlin, "FBI Investigates valley anthrax threat," *Spokesman-Review*, February 23, 1999, as found at *http://www.spokane.net/*, includes this city in a list of Planned Parenthood clinics targeted with anthrax threat letters on February 22.

[738] Malia Rulon, "Abortion clinic receives letter with anthrax threat," *Associated Press*, February 24, 1999.

country. It was turned over to authorities without being opened. Preliminary tests did not identify any anthrax.[739] A Planned Parenthood clinic in Kansas City, Missouri, received an anthrax threat letter on February 22. The letter had a Kentucky postmark. Twenty-seven people were decontaminated, including seven firefighters. Two people were treated at hospitals, one because of an adverse reaction to the bleach used in the decontamination. The response to the incident involved about 100 people and took five hours.[740]

In Newark, Delaware, a Planned Parenthood clinic was the recipient of an anthrax threat letter. The letter was contained in a manila envelope, and had a West Virginia return address for a nonexistent surgical supply company. As with other letters, it contained the words, "Have a nice death." No one was quarantined, decontaminated, or treated at the clinic, although the person who opened the letter immediately washed her hands. The clinic was closed until the next day.[741]

Another Planned Parenthood clinic in Salt Lake City, Utah, was the target of an anthrax threat. One person was given antibiotics as a precaution, but tests indicated that anthrax was not present.[742]

On February 22, a Christmas card was delivered to a dentist's office in Spokane County, Washington. The envelope was addressed to the "Director of Medical Operations, South 20 Pines," which was the building that contained a Planned Parenthood clinic. The envelope was almost certainly meant for the clinic, but it received all its mail through a post office box. According to initial press reports, the envelope contained a powder, but subsequently authorities said that there was no powder and no threats were made.[743]

On February 23, 1999, anthrax threats were delivered to clinics in Honolulu, Hawaii, New York, New York, and Pittsburgh, Pennsylvania. The Queen's Medical Center, located in the Ala Moana Building in Honolulu, Hawaii, was the target of an anthrax threat letter on February 23. Five people in the clinic were treated at a hospital, and three floors of the building were evacuated. The letter was taken to the state's Public Health Laboratory, located in Pearl City, and tested negative.[744] That same day, the Eastern Women's Center in New York, New York, received a letter claiming to have been contaminated with anthrax.[745] Women's Health Services, an abortion clinic in Pittsburgh, Pennsylvania also received an anthrax threat letter on February 23. Three people were decontaminated.[746]

A Planned Parenthood clinic in Boise, Idaho, received an anthrax threat letter on February 25. There was powder in the envelope, and three people were exposed to it. No anthrax was present.[747]

***Case 1999-19: Anthrax threat (Yemen), February 1999***

An otherwise unknown group, identifying itself as the "Army of Suicidals, Group No. 66, Bin Laden Militant Wing," issued a statement threatening to kill American and British citizens in Yemen unless they left within 12 days. According to the letter, "If you stay, then you've chosen death .... We'll make you pay for every drop of Arab and Muslim blood you shed since the Crusades." The letter apparently stated that all those

---

739 Richard Salit, "Anthrax threats are keeping clinics on heightened alert," *Journal* (Providence, Rhode Island), February 28, 1999, as found at the paper's Web site, *http://www.projo.com*.

740 Oscar Avila and Cristine Vendel, "Planned Parenthood is first KC target of anthrax threats," *Kansas City Star*, February 22, 1999, as found at *http://www.kcstar.com*,

741 Angela Galloway and Adrienne Lu, "Del. Clinic receives anthrax hoax letter," *Philadelphia Inquirer*, February 23, 1999, as found at the newspaper's World Wide Web site, *http://www.phillynews.com*.

742 Jennifer Dobner, "Anthrax scare at S.L. clinic," *Deseret News*, February 23, 1999, and "Brown stuff on letter to S.L. clinic isn't anthrax," *Deseret News*, February 24, 1999, as taken from the newspaper's Web site, *http://www.desnews.com*.

743 Bill Morlin, "FBI Investigates valley anthrax threat," *Spokesman-Review*, February 23, 1999, and Bill Morlin, "No anthrax found in card sent to clinic," *Spokesman-Review*, February 26, 1999, as found at *http://www.spokane.net/*.

744 "Building evacuated after doctor's office receives anthrax threat," *Associated Press*, February 23, 1999, 10:13 PM, Crystal Kua and Mary Adamski, "Second 'anthrax' letter arrives in Honolulu," *Star-Bulletin* (Honolulu), February 24, 1999, and Rod Ohira, "Islanders get a crash course on anthrax," *Star-Bulletin* (Honolulu), February 24, 1999, as found at the paper's Web site, *http://starbulletin.com*.

745 Beth Gardiner, "Anthrax threats at women's clinic, NOW office," *Associated Press*, February 23, 1999, 10:12 PM.

746 Kim Burger, "Abortion clinic target of deadly anthrax threat," *Tribune-Review* (Pittsburgh), February 24, 1999, and Torsten Ove, "Scare tactics: Harmless envelope similar to those sent to clinics in 30 cities," *Tribune-Review* (Pittsburgh), February 24, 1999, as found in the paper's Web site, *http://www.triblive.com*, and "A new anthrax threat letter found to be a hoax," *Associated Press*, February 24, 1999.

747 "Anthrax Hoax Letter Writer Sought," *States News Service*, March 1, 1999, as found at *http://dailynews.yahoo.com*.

remaining in Yemen after the deadline would be attacked with anthrax. The letter reportedly was delivered to a Yemeni newspaper by fax from London.[748]

***Case 1999-18: Anthrax threat (Los Angeles Times Offices, Los Angeles), February 1999***

Several square blocks of downtown Los Angeles were shut down on February 12, 1999, when the main offices of the Los Angeles Times received a letter that claimed contain anthrax. Included in the envelope was a small quantity of a gray powder.[749]

***Case 1999-17: Anthrax threat (against State Department, Washington, D.C.), February 1999***

An envelope containing what were claimed to be anthrax pellets was delivered to the State Department building in Washington, D.C. The letter was opened on the seventh floor of the building, the same floor that contains the offices of the Secretary of State. According to the State Department spokesman, "At 11 a.m. ... a letter was received in which pellets fell out of the letter an there was a note saying by opening this letter the openers were being hit by anthrax." The FBI, the D.C. Joint Terrorism Task Force, and the D.C. police responded.[750]

***Case 1999-16: Anthrax threats (against offices in multiple cities), February 1999***

Several apparently related anthrax threats were made on February 5, 1999. In all the incidents it appears that letters were found claiming that plastic bags found in the envelopes contained anthrax. According to one account, the letter was "rambling" and the unknown substance was in double plastic bags. One of the letters was sent to the offices of the Washington Post in Washington, D.C. Another was delivered to the Old Executive Office Building next to the White House. A third letter was sent to the NBC News bureau in Atlanta, Georgia, and a fourth was found at the U.S. Post Office in Columbus, Georgia.[751] Two additional envelopes, apparently similar, arrived the next day at the Old Executive Office Building and the U.S. Court of appeals.[752]

In addition, it appears that an anthrax threat letter was received on February 8 by "an unnamed federal agency," according to a press report. In addition, a spokesman for the Capitol Police reported, "We have received one letter which is exactly like those which have been received elsewhere in the United States, claiming exposure of the recipient to anthrax." The delivery date for the last threat was not specified.[753]

***Case 1999-15: Anthrax threat (against East Aurora, New York, school), February 1999***

The Main Street School in East Aurora, New York, was closed on February 5, 1999, after a note was found on the front door of the school at 5 a.m. The building was searched to determine if the threat was real. A seventh-grade student was arrested for making the threat.[754]

***Case 1999-14: Anthrax threat (against Lackawanna, New York, school), February 1999***

On February 2, 1999, the Lackawanna, New York, police arrested two students for making an anthrax threat in a phone call to 911. The call was made at 3:07 p.m., and claimed that the Lackawanna High School

---

[748] "Yemen Steps Up Security After West Threatened With Attack," *Agence France Press* (Northern European Service), English, February 20, 1999, 1201 GMT, and "Unknown group warns Americans, Britons to leave Yemen," *Associated Press*, February 16, 1999, 1119 ET.

[749] "Anthrax Hoax at Times Building Disrupts Traffic," *Los Angeles Times*, February 13, 1999, as found at the newspaper's World Wide Web site, *http://www.latimes.com*, and "Los Angeles Times sealed off because of anthrax scare," *Associated Press*, February 12, 1999, 6:14 PST.

[750] Toni Marshall, "Anthrax hoax gets attention of State," *Washington Times*, February 10, 1999, p. A11, and "Anthrax Hoax Received at State Department," *Reuters*, February 9, 1999, 3:01 ET.

[751] Maria Elena Fernando, "Anthrax Hoaxes Are Sent in Mail," *Washington Post*, February 5, 1999, p. B8, Jack Warner, "Anthrax threat appears to be hoax," *Atlanta Constitution*, February 5, 1999, p. 1C, Jack Warner, "NBC Workers air complaints about showers," *Atlanta Constitution*, February 6, 1999, p. 2B.

[752] "Two More Anthrax Threats Arrive by Mail in D.C.," *Washington Post*, February 6, 1999, p. B2. The original story claimed that the threat was received at the D.C. Court of Appeals, but that was subsequently corrected to the U.S. Court of Appeals. "Corrections," *Washington Post*, February 10, 1999, p. A3.

[753] Laura Dunphy, "Capitol Police probe anthrax threats," *The Hill*, February 10, 1999, as found at the publications web site, *http://207.152.182.86*.

[754] "Boy petitioned to court over anthrax threat," *Buffalo News*, February 17, 1999, p. 5B, "East Aurora school shut after anthrax threat warning," *Buffalo News*, February 5, 1999, p. 4B, and "Success seen in meeting new standards," *Buffalo News*, February 12, 1999, p. 5B.

had been contaminated with anthrax. The telephone call was traced to a pay telephone and local police identified the perpetrators as two 14-year-old students of the Lackawanna Middle School.[755]

***Case 1999-13: Anthrax threat (against Cattaraugus County, New York, school), February 1999***

Three students at the West Valley Central School, Cattaraugus County, New York, were arrested on February 5, 1999, on charges of making an anthrax threat at their school. The students, two 13-years old and one 12, typed a message and placed it in the school. The County Sheriff's Department and the FBI arrested the three.[756]

***Case 1999-12: Anthrax threat (against Alden, New York, business), January 1999***

At 6:00 p.m. on January 25, 1999, someone called a business in Alden, New York, and claimed that there was anthrax in its building. Emergency crews responded to the threat, and took several hours to determine that no anthrax was present. The call apparently came from a pay telephone.[757]

***Case 1999-11: Anthrax threat (against grocery store), January 1999***

A Jubilee food store in East Aurora, New York, was closed on January 22, 1999, after an employee found a letter stuck in the store's back entrance supposedly contaminated with anthrax. The letter was opened when the first employees arrived at around 6:00 a.m., and the store and about one-third of the surrounding shopping center was cordoned off as authorities investigated. About ten people were kept in the building, including store employees and at least one delivery person who was present when the envelope was opened.[758]

***Case 1999-10: Anthrax threat (against Niagara County, New York, high school), January 1999***

On January 21, 1999, the assistant principal of the Newfane High School in Niagara County, New York, was given a note claiming that the school was threatened by anthrax. Initially, county sheriff's deputies quarantined the school, but eventually closed the school and allowed the students to go home. Two students were arrested in connection with the incident, one 13 and the other 14. Federal officials recommended that the two be tried under state laws for falsely reporting a threat, which is a misdemeanor under New York law.[759]

***Case 1999-09: Anthrax threat (against West Seneca, New York, town hall), January 1999***

On January 21, 1999, an operator at the West Seneca, New York, town hall, received a telephone call during the lunch hour claiming that anthrax spores were in the building's ventilation system. There were 43 people in the building at the time. Eventually, the threat was discounted, because the building uses a hot water heating system. Nevertheless, the town hall was closed until 6:00 p.m. while the threat was being evaluated. Some people working in the building were shifted to a nearby hockey rink in the middle of the afternoon, but remained quarantined.[760]

***Case 1999-08: Anthrax threat (against Erie County, New York, middle school), January 1999***

On January 19,1999, the Iroquois Middle School in Elma, New York, located in Erie County, received a letter with a handwritten note that read, "Anthrax may be in the building—this is a warning not a threat." The note was read around 8:30 a.m., and school officials promptly notified authorities. The middle school was quarantined. This meant that about 700 students were kept in the school, including some students from the connected intermediate school who were holding classes in the middle school. A hazardous materials team searched for evidence of anthrax in the ventilation system, but came up empty. Ultimately, the students were allowed to leave at around 6:20 p.m.[761]

---

[755] "Boys' anthrax threat prompts warning," *Buffalo News*, February 3, 1999, p. 4B.

[756] "3 more held in anthrax threats," *Buffalo News*, February 6, 1999, p. 5C.

[757] Peter Simon and Thomas J. Prohaska, "Student at Iroquois High Charged in Anthrax Scare," *Buffalo News*, January 26, 1999, p. 5B.

[758] Mike Levy and Elmer Ploetz, "Anthrax Letter Threat Closes Jubilee Foods Store," *Buffalo News*, January 22, 1999, p. C4.

[759] Mark Levy and Elmer Ploetz, "2 Students Arrested in Anthrax Threat at Newfane High," *Buffalo News*, January 22, 1999, p. 4C.

[760] Mark Levy and Elmer Ploetz, "2 Students Arrested in Anthrax Threat at Newfane High," *Buffalo News*, January 22, 1999, p. 4C, and Mike Levy and Elmer Ploetz, "Anthrax Letter Threat Closes Jubilee Foods Store," *Buffalo News*, January 22, 1999, p. C4.

[761] Elmer Ploetz, "Anthrax Scare Forces School to Isolate Students," *Buffalo News*, January 21, 1999, p. 1B.

The next week a 15-year old tenth grade student was arrested in connection with the incident. He told authorities that he wanted to get out of classes. The case was handled in juvenile court given the defendant's age, but authorities planned to ask restitution to cover the costs of the incident and intended to seek the maximum criminal penalty possible. The student pleaded guilty to the charge.[762] He was placed on probation for one year, required to perform 25 hours of community service, and ordered to pay the school district $1,500 as restitution.[763]

***Case 1999-07: Anthrax threat (against California hospital), January 1999***

On January 21, 22, and 23, an unidentified man made a series of telephone threats against the Arcadia Methodist Hospital in Sierra Madre, California. The called claimed that anthrax would be disseminated into the hospital's air handling system. One call claimed, "in five minutes a bomb will go off in one of the units, and anthrax is in the system." On January 23, the calls were traced to a home in Sierra Madre. The next day, Christopher J. McCoy, the 24-year-old son of the house's owners, was arrested on charges of threatening to use a weapon of mass destruction. According to authorities he denied having made the threats, and told FBI agents, "I don't have the technology. It was only words."[764]

***Case 1999-06: Anthrax threat (against Riverside County, California, restaurant), January 1999***

On January 19, 1999, a Pizza Hut in Palm Desert, a town in Riverside County, California, received a telephone threat claiming that the restaurant had been contaminated with anthrax. Firefighters investigated the threat and found no evidence of contamination.[765]

***Case 1999-05: Anthrax threat (against U.S. Attorney's Office, Buffalo, New York), January 1999***

On January 14, 1999, the U.S. Attorney's Office in Buffalo, New York, located in the Federal Center in the downtown area, received a letter claiming to have been contaminated with anthrax. According to authorities, the letter, which was postmarked in Rochester, New York, was smeared with an unknown substance and had a message written on it indicating, "You have just been exposed to anthrax." There was no indication that the letter was tied to any ideological grievance, although it may have been tied to two letters previously sent to the U.S. Attorney's office in Rochester.

Firefighters began responding to the threat at 12:22 p.m., and deployed around a dozen fire trucks and other emergency response vehicles to the scene. In addition to the Buffalo fire department, the Buffalo police department, the Erie County hazardous materials team, and medical personnel from the Erie County Medical Center were sent to the scene. In all, about 100 people were involved in the response.

Authorities closed off the area around the building and about 200 people in the building were detained for several hours. Only the 4 people who came into direct contact with the open letter were decontaminated. Tests performed at the Erie County Medical Center determined that the letter was not contaminated with anthrax.[766]

***Case 1999-04: Anthrax threat (against Cathedral City, California, store), January 1999***

At 5:10 p.m. on January 14, 1999, an employee of Cathedral City, California, Target store notified police that the store had received a telephone call claiming that the building was contaminated with anthrax. The building was evacuated and searched, but authorities found no evidence of anthrax and identified no suspicious containers. The store was reopened at 7:00 p.m. The Cathedral City police and fire departments were investigating the incident, as was the Federal Bureau of Investigation.[767]

---

[762] Peter Simon and Thomas J. Prohaska, "Student at Iroquois High Charged in Anthrax Scare," *Buffalo News*, January 26, 1999, p. 5B, "Teen in Kin's Custody after Denying Anthrax Scare," *Buffalo News*, January 27, 1999, p. 5B, and "Sentencing Set for Student in Iroquois Anthrax Scare," *Buffalo News*, February 12, 1999, p. 5B.

[763] Matt Gryta, "Teen sentenced in school anthrax scare," *Buffalo News*, June 2, 1999, p. 4B.

[764] "Man Charged in Anthrax Phone Calls to Hospital," *Los Angeles Times*, January 28, 1999, as found in the newspaper's World Wide Web site, *http://www.latimes.com*.

[765] "Bogus anthrax call clears pizza store," *Press-Enterprise* (Riverside, California), January 20, 1999, p. B3.

[766] Lou Michel, "U.S. Office is Threatened with Anthrax," *Buffalo News*, January 15, 1999, p. 1C, Dan Herbeck, "Federal Office here hit by Anthrax Threat," *Buffalo News*, January 16, 1999, p. 1C, Dan Herbeck, "No Anthrax Found on Letter to Federal Facility," *Buffalo News*, January 19, 1999, p. 1B.

[767] "Store evacuated after phoned-in anthrax threat," *Press-Enterprise* (Riverside, California), January 15, 1999, p. B3.

***Case 1999-03: Anthrax threat (against U.S. Attorney's Office, Rochester, New York), January 1999***

On January 14, 1999, two employees at the U.S. Attorney's Office in the Kenneth B. Keating Federal Building in Rochester, New York, opened letters that contained messages claiming that the letters were contaminated with anthrax. The two employees were taken to the decontamination unit of the Rochester General Hospital and given antibiotics. The letters were postmarked in Rochester.[768]

***Case 1999-02: Anthrax threat (against Oregon library), January 1999***

At about 3:00 p.m. on January 13, 1999 the switchboard at the Tualatin, Oregon, City Hall received a telephone call claiming that anthrax had been released in the Tualatin Public Library. The library was in the City Hall building, and as a result the library and city offices were evacuated and closed until January 15. The hazardous material team of Tualatin Valley Fire and Rescue took environmental samples, which failed to indicate the presence of anthrax. The FBI was called in to investigate the threat.[769]

***Case 1999-44: Anthrax threat against auto dealership, Los Angeles, California, January 1999***

At 7:00 a.m. on January 11, 1999, Los Angeles police received a report that anthrax had been released at an auto dealership on Wilshire Boulevard in Los Angeles, California. Authorities blocked off the street for 90 minutes while evaluating the threat. The incident was declared a hoax.[770]

***Case 1999-43: Anthrax threat against Ocala Regional Medical Center, Florida, January 1999***

On January 3, 1999, a telephone caller claimed that the emergency room of the Ocala Regional Medical Center had been contaminated with anthrax. The call, which was received at 1:00 p.m., led officials to close the emergency room for four hours and divert all emergency cases to the Munroe Regional Medical Center. Although the FBI, the Centers for Disease Control and Prevention, and the local public health department assessed that the threat was a hoax, the hospital implemented emergency response plans for the emergency department. The rest of the hospital was not affected.[771]

***Case 1999-50: Anthrax vial (Far North Dallas, Texas), January 1999***

On January 10, 1999, a man walking on a sidewalk in Far North Dallas, Texas, discovered a vial with a sticker with writing that suggested the vial contained anthrax. According to the man who picked up the vial, the sticker contained a message stating, "This is not a joke. Do not open this. This bottle contains anthrax."[772]

***Case 1999-01: Anthrax threat (against Orange County, California, High School), January 1999***

An anthrax threat was directed against Gilbert-East High School in Anaheim, California, on January 4, 1999. A telephone call was received at the school just before noon claiming that anthrax had been released into the ventilation system. Additional calls were sent to the school. According to an Anaheim Police officer, the person making the call "did sound young, and we'll be looking at whether he is a student." Police and Fire Department hazardous materials personnel sealed off the area around the school for nearly three hours. About 20 students and 100 school employees were at the school at the time. A threat assessment determined that "the threat lacked credibility." Authorities searched the building, and found nothing.[773]

---

[768] "2 at federal building treated after opening 'anthrax' letters, *Democrat and Chronicle* (Rochester, New York), January 14, 1999, as found at the newspaper's World Wide Web site, *http://www.rochesternews.com.*

[769] "Library closes after anthrax threat," *Oregonian*, January 14, 1999, as found at *http://oregonlive.com*, and "Anthrax "threat at Tualatin City Hall," *Associated Press*, January 15, 1999, 3:39 a.m. EST.

[770] "Anthrax," *City News Service*, January 11, 1999, and Donna Kelley and Charles Feldman, "Anthrax Hoaxes Causing Very Real Problems for Authorities," *CNN Today*, January 12, 1999, 1:39 p.m. Eastern Time, transcript number 99011208V13. I am grateful to Jason Pate, Monterey Institute for International Studies, for calling my attention to this incident.

[771] Carlos E. Medina, "Anthrax threat shuts down ORMC emergency room," *Star-Banner* (Ocala, Florida), January 4, 1999, as found at *http://www.starbanner.com*. "Threatens biological attack," *United Press International*, January 4 ,1999, pus the incident at the Munroe Regional Medical Center. I am grateful to Jason Pate, Monterey Institute for International Studies, for calling my attention to this incident.

[772] Jason Sickles, "Containing dangerous rumors," *Dallas Morning News*, March 1, 1999, as found at the newspaper's World Wide Web site, *http://www.dallasnews.com.*

[773] H.G. Reza, "1st O.C. Anthrax Hoax Quarantines Anaheim School," *Los Angeles Times*, January 5, 1999, as found at the newspaper's World Wide Web site, *http://latimes.com*, and Marla Jo Fisher, "Scare highlights busing problem," *Orange County Register*, January 5, 1999, as found at the paper's web site, *http://www.ocregister.com.*

***Case 1999-39: Anthrax threat (against Victorville, California, Wal-Mart), January 1999***

A telephone caller told a 911 dispatcher that anthrax was present in a Wal-Mart in Victorville, California. The call, made at 7:25 a.m. on January 2, 1999, caused the store to be evacuated while the local hazardous materials team evaluated the threat. The store was reopened about 9:30 a.m., after an investigation failed to identify the presence of anthrax.[774]

***Case 1998-44: Anthrax threat (against Rochester, New York, U.S. Attorney's office), December 1998***

On December 31, 1998, an employee at the U.S. Attorney's office, located in the Rochester, New York, federal building, opened a letter that allegedly contained anthrax. According to the Chief U.S. District Judge, the letter claimed, "You have now been infected by the anthrax virus, smile." The woman was taken to the Rochester General Hospital, where she went through the decontamination unit and was treated with antibiotics. The Monroe County health department sent the letter to another hospital for testing. No anthrax was detected.[775]

***Case 1998-43: Robert Peterson (anthrax threat), December 1998***

At 1:30 p.m. on December 29, 1998, the 911 operators at the Newark, California, police department received a 911 emergency telephone call from WorldPac, a local auto parts shipping company, claiming, "There's 400 people here in this building, and anthrax has been released." The telephone call was taped, which was turned over the Bay Area Counter-Terrorism Task Force, a combined operations force drawn from federal, state, and local law enforcement agencies in the San Francisco area. Hazardous materials teams were sent to the company's warehouse, and no evidence of anthrax was discovered. Law enforcement officials played the tape for company management, who identified the caller as Robert Alinea Peterson, a 43-year old employee. Peterson reportedly was considered an erratic worker, had made threats against a fellow employee earlier in the year, and also had stated that he wanted to kill one of his supervisors. According to a co-worker, he asked about how to obtain anthrax the day before allegedly making the threatening telephone call. Law enforcement officials claim that he admitted making the call, apparently so that he could go home to get heart medicine. Peterson was arrested on December 29. On December 31, a U.S. Magistrate decided that Peterson could remain free on a $50,000 personal recognizance bond. He was scheduled for arraignment on January 19, 1999 in Oakland, California. He was represented by a public defender.[776]

***Case 1998-42: Anthrax threat (against Palmdale, California, grocery stores), December 1998***

The Lancaster station of the Los Angeles County Sheriff's office received a telephone call at 2:40 p.m. on December 26, 1998 threatening to release anthrax into the ventilation system of a building in Palmdale (also in Los Angeles County). At 4:55 p.m. a second call claimed that the intended target was the Ralphs grocery store in Palmdale. A third call was received at 5:20 p.m. alleging that an Albertson's grocery store was targeted. All the telephone calls apparently were made by the same man, and originated at pay telephones. Sheriff's deputies responded to both threats, along with fire and other emergency personnel. Customers in the stores were given a hazardous agent exposure pamphlet.[777]

***Case 1998-41: Anthrax threat (against Wal-Mart), December 1998***

At 7:44 p.m. on December 28' 1998, the California Highway Patrol received a telephone call claiming that anthrax had been released at 4:00 p.m. in a La Quinta, California, Wal-Mart store. Approximately 200 people were in the store at the time, but authorities estimated that 2,000 people had passed through the store since the time of the claimed release. People in the store were detained in the garden section for around ?_ hours. They were not decontaminated, but were advised of the symptoms of anthrax and were told to shower

[774] "Victorville: Anthrax empties store," *Press-Enterprise* (Riverside, California), January 4, 1999, p. B2.

[775] Jon Hand, "Secretary treated after anthrax scare," *Democrat and Chronicle* (Rochester, New York), January 1, 1999, as found at the paper's World Wide Web site, *http://www.RochesterNews.com*, "Letter Claims to Contain Lethal Anthrax Bacteria," *New York Times*, January 1, 1999, as found at *http://proquest.umi.com*, and "Anthrax Scare a Hoax," *WHEC-TV*, Rochester, New York, from *http://www.msnbc.com.*

[776] E. Mark Moreno, "Worker in court over anthrax call," *San Jose Mercury News*, January 1, 1999, as found at the newspaper's World Wide Web site at *http://www.mercurycenter.com*, and Bill Wallace, "Hayward Man Charged in Anthrax Scare," San Francisco Chronicle, January 1, 1999, p. A13, as found in the newspaper's World Wide Web site, *http://www.sfgate.com.*

[777] Don Jergler, "Series of anthrax scares hits Valley," *Antelope Valley Press*, December 29, 1998, as found at the newspaper's World Wide Web site at *http://www.avpress.com.*

and wash their clothes. No evidence of anthrax was discovered, and at 8:45 a.m. the next morning Riverside Sheriff's Department declared the incident a hoax.[778]

***Case 1998-40: Anthrax threat (against Palm Desert department store), December 1998***

At 10:20 a.m. on December 24, 1998, a telephone caller to the Mervyn's Department Store in Palm Desert, California, claimed that the store had been contaminated with anthrax. The response involved the Riverside County Sheriff's Department, Fire Department, Hazardous Materials Team, and the county's Department of Environmental Health. The Corona Hazardous Materials Team and the FBI supported them. In response, the people in the store were quarantined and decontaminated by the Riverside County Hazardous Materials Team. Some 229 people, including shoppers and store employees, were decontaminated. At the same time, environmental samples were taken to determine if anthrax was present in the store.[779]

***Case 1998-38: Anthrax threat (against Pomona, California, dance club), December 1998***

At 11:50 p.m. on Saturday, December 26, 1998, an unidentified man called the Pomona Police Department and claimed that a "significant quantity" was about to be disseminated into a dance club. Authorities closed off the club, and kept 800 employees and patrons in the building for four hours while the Los Angeles County Fire Department's hazardous materials team and personnel from the FBI's Domestic Terrorism Task Force checked for indications of anthrax. Tests were completed by the following Monday, and revealed no signs of anthrax.[780]

***Case 1998-37: Anthrax threat (against office building), December 1998***

At 10:15 a.m. on December 23, 1998, a telephone caller threatened to release a "biological agent" in a Time Warner Cable Company building in Chatsworth, California. About 200 people were evacuated from the building and detained until 4:15 p.m. when they were permitted to go.[781]

***Case 1998-36: Anthrax threat (against Van Nuys courthouses), December 1998***

Just after 11:00 a.m. on December 21, 1998, an unidentified caller told a 911 operator, "I have something to tell you—anthrax has been released in the Van Nuys courthouse." Authorities sealed off two courthouses, the old and new Superior Court buildings, and evacuated some 1,500 to 2,000 people from the buildings. The Presiding Superior Court Judge ordered a court emergency, and closed down the operations of the court until December 23. Los Angeles County Health Department officials detained the evacuated individuals outside the courthouses. FBI agents and other Health Department officials searched the buildings to take biological samples. The samples were taken to the county's public health laboratory, which failed to identify the presence of anthrax. By 4:00 p.m., authorities concluded that the threat was a hoax, and the people evacuated from the building were released. Nevertheless, they were advised to take simple precautions, including watching for signs of flu, which might be early symptoms of inhalation anthrax, and to take showers to remove any possible contamination.[782]

---

[778] Marlowe Churchill, "Taking anthrax threats in stride," *Press-Enterprise* (Riverside, California), December 28, 1998, as found at the newspaper's World Wide Web site, *http://www.press-enterprise.com*, and "Another anthrax threat," *Press-Enterprise*, December 30, 1998, and "Region's eighth anthrax threat this month also turns out to be a hoax," Associated Press, December 29, 1998, 00:00 PST.

[779] Jacquie Paul, "Anthrax scare declared hoax," *Press-Enterprise* (Riverside, California), December 28, 1998, as found at the newspaper's World Wide Web site, *http://www.press-enterprise.com*, and Jacquie Paul, "Anthrax threat forces Wal-Mart evacuation," *Press-Enterprise* (Riverside, California), December 29, 1998, p. B3.

[780] "Anthrax Scare Disrupts Club," *Washington Post*, December 28, 1998, p. A12, as found at *http://www.washingtonpost.com*, and "Nightclub Anthrax Threat Proves to Be Another Hoax," *Los Angeles Times*, as found at *http://www.latimes.com*, and "Another Anthrax Scare in California," *Associated Press*, December 28, 1998, 0932EST.

[781] Andrew Blankstein and Solomon Moore, "Anthrax Threat Forces Evacuation," *Los Angeles Times*, December 24, 1998, and "Nightclub Anthrax Threat Proves to be Another Hoax," *Los Angeles Times*, December 29, 1998, as found in the newspaper's World Wide Web site, *http://www.latimes.com*. The two sources disagree on the number of people evacuated. The figure used came from the more recent article.

[782] Andrew Blankstein, "Anthrax Scare Forces Evacuation of Courts," *Los Angeles Times*, December 22, 1998, as found at the newspaper's World Wide Web site, *http://www.latimes.com*, and "Anthrax Scare forces Quarantined," *Associated Press*, December 21, 1998, 8:25 a.m. EST.

***Case 1998-35: Anthrax threat (against federal courthouse), December 1998***

Around 1:30 p.m., on December 18, 1998, a clerk of the court at the U.S. Bankruptcy Court in Woodland Hills, California, received a telephone call claiming that the building had been contaminated with anthrax. The U.S. Marshal's Office contacted the Los Angeles Fire Department at 2:10 p.m., initiated a substantial response involving more than 100 people from the fire and police departments. Burbank Boulevard was shut down, causing serious traffic problems. Tests determined that no anthrax was present.[783]

***Case 1998-33: Anthrax threat (against former wife), December 1998***

Around 10:30 a.m., December 18, 1998, an employee at the Westwood Village, California, offices of the Executive Parking Company opened an envelope containing a letter with a message claiming that the paper had been contaminated with anthrax. According to one press report, a woman received a letter from her ex-husband with the message, "You have been exposed to anthrax."[784]

A response effort consisting of FBI, Los Angeles County, and Los Angeles City officials responded to the incident, including both fire and public health officials. Portions of the building were evacuated, its ventilation system was turned off, and the employees in the office suite where the letter was delivered were decontaminated and quarantined. They were initially decontaminated in the basement by a hazardous materials team drawn from the county health department. When tests made on the site failed to show the presence of anthrax, around 1:00 p.m., the employees were taken to the UCLA Medical Center. At the medical complex, they were decontaminated again and given medical treatment. They were quarantined there for a period.

According to a spokesman for the Los Angeles Police Department, the response involved about 150 people and cost $500,000.[785]

***Case 1998-32: Anthrax threat (against Perris School District), December 1998***

On December 14, 1998, the director of special education of the Perris School District, located in southern California, opened a letter that contained the message, "You've been exposed to anthrax." Inside the envelope was a piece of gauze cloth with brown flakes on it. Initially, those present at the site were quarantined, and several hours later they were decontaminated. It appears that 21 people were decontaminated as a result of the threat, including 18 school district employees, two firefighters, and a mail carrier. Five employees were sent to the Riverside County Regional Medical Center for treatment. Sheriff's deputies from Riverside County, the county's hazardous materials team, FBI agents, and postal inspectors conducted the initial response.[786]

***Case 1998-29: Anthrax threat (Texas post office), December 1998***

At 12:45 a.m. on December 4, 1998, a postal worker at the Coppell, Texas, U.S. Postal Service bulk mail center discovered a 4-inch long vial with the phrase, "You have just been contaminated by anthrax," written on it. Although there were 450-500 employees at the facility, only six were in the area where the vial was discovered. The vial was discovered inside an all-purpose container located in an area closed to the public. The vial did not appear to have been prepared for mailing, but it could have originated in a mailbox. The facility contacted 911, and members of the FBI's regional terrorism task force responded. The vial was removed and the arms and hands of the six employees were washed with bleach and water. Authorities doubted

---

[783] Sue Fox and Scott Glover, "Anthrax Scare Forces Building to Be Evacuated," *Los Angeles Times*, December 19, 1998, as found at the newspaper's World Wide Web site, *http://www.latimes.com.*, and "91 People Held After Anthrax Scare," *Associated Press*, December 19, 1998, 7:37 p.m. EST.

[784] Josh Meyer and Matea Gold, "Anthrax Hoax Alarms Workers in Westwood," Los Angeles Times, December 18, 1998, as found at the newspaper's World Wide Web site, *http://www.latimes.com*. See also, "Another anthrax hoax frightens office," Sacramento Bee, December 18, 1998, as found at the newspaper's World Wide Web site, *http://www.sacbee.com*, and a December 17, 1998, news report, "Westwood Anthrax Scare Phone, Says FBI," Channel 2, the CBS affiliate in Los Angeles, California, at *http://www.channel2000.com/*.

[785] Sue Fox and Scott Glover, "Anthrax Scare Forces Building to Be Evacuated," *Los Angeles Times*, December 19, 1998, as found at the newspaper's World Wide Web site, *http://www.latimes.com.*.

[786] Steve Fetbrandt, "Anthrax threat holds 21 in Perris," Press-Express (Riverside, California), December 15, 1998, as found at the newspaper's World Wide Web site at *http://www.inlandempireonline.com*. See also "Anthrax Threat Received; 20 People Quarantined," *Los Angeles Times*, December 15, 1998, as found at the newspaper's World Wide Web site, *http://www.latimes.com*. See also the December 14, 1998, news report, "21 Decontaminated After Anthrax Scare," the Channel 2, the CBS affiliate in Los Angeles, California, at *http://www.channel2000.com/*.

that the vial contained anthrax even before testing it, but the vial was sent to an FBI laboratory in Washington, D.C., for testing.[787]

***Case 1998-28: Anthrax threat (against anti-abortion activist), November 1998***

On November 23, 1998, Jeff White, the director of Operation Rescue California, an anti-abortion group, received a letter with the message "You have been exposed to anthrax." White, who operates from his home in Twin Peaks, California, phoned 911 after reading the message. He apparently also called the FBI. Subsequently, White told reporters, "I wasn't too concerned about it. (Investigators) didn't walk in the masks. The FBI said they were 100 percent confident" that there was no anthrax in the letter. There was no powder in the envelope. The FBI took custody of the letter as part of their investigation.[788]

***Case 1998-27: Anthrax Threat (at Pembroke Pines, Florida, post office), November 1998***

On November 21, 1998, a mail sorter working in a Pembroke Pines, Florida, discovered an envelope with a threatening phrase, "Congratulations, you have been exposed to anthrax," written on it. The Pembroke Pines Police Department, the Broward County Sheriff's Office, the Broward County Hazardous Materials Response Team, and the FBI responded. Authorities evacuated the building, and three postal workers were taken to a hospital. The threat proved to be a hoax.[789]

***Case 1998-26: Anthrax Threat (against Virginia Beach school), November 1998***

On November 13, 1998, the Tallwood High School in Virginia Beach, Virginia, received a telephone threat claiming, "There will be an anthrax bomb on Monday at Tallwood High School." The message indicated that, "People will die. That is all." It concluded with obscenities. The caller left the message on an automated answering system sometime between 3:00 p.m. and 4:00 p.m., but no one listened to it until 7:30 p.m. School administrators contacted police, who arrived at the school at about 8:00 p.m. Soon thereafter the local fire department arrived. Over one hundred people watching a play were evacuated from the school. A search of the building was started, which was expected to continue until the next morning.[790]

***Case 1998-25: Anthrax Threat (against Virginia antiabortion activist), November 1998***

On November 13, 1998, an antiabortion activist in Chesapeake, Virginia, was the recipient of an anthrax threat letter. According to a press account of the incident, the man picked up the envelope from his post office box, and opened it outside the post office. After reading the note inside, he contacted the local fire department, which also informed the FBI and the Virginia Department of Emergency Services. The FBI refused to indicate whether any substance was contained in the envelope, but did state that there was no exposure to a dangerous substance.[791]

***Case 1998-24: Anthrax Threat (against Miami Beach magazine), November 1998***

On November 18, 1998, a receptionist at a Miami Beach magazine, Ocean Drive, opened a letter containing an anthrax threat and a white powder. According to the magazine's publisher, "It says 'if you've opened this, you've been exposed to anthrax' and then a four letter word I am not going to repeat."[792]

The letter was delivered to the office at 10:30 a.m., but was not opened until 1:30 p.m. A white, granular substance, apparently similar to salt, poured out of the envelope onto the lap of the receptionist.

---

[787] Domingo Ramirez, Jr., "Anthrax threat hits postal hub," *Star-Telegram* (Fort Worth, Texas), December 4, 1998, as found at the newspaper's World Wide Web site, *http://www.star-telegram.com*, and Jason Sickles, *Dalles Morning News*, December 5, 1998, as found at the newspaper's World Wide Web site, *http://www.dallasnews.com*.

[788] Ryan Slattery, "Anthrax threat hits anti-abortion activist," *Press-Express* (Riverside, California), November 24, 1998, as found at the newspaper's World Wide Web site, *http://www.inlandempireonline.com*. This incident was also mentioned in the California headlines produced by the States News Service, as found on November 24, 1998 at *http://dailynews.yahoo.com*.

[789] "Anthrax scare disrupts postal facility in Pines," *Miami Herald*, November 22, 1998., as found in the newspaper's World Wide Web site, *http://www.herald.com*, and "Another anthrax scare in South Florida," undated report, as found at *http://www.msnbc.com/*, on November 22, 1998.

[790] Steve Stone, "100 evacuated from Tallwood High after anthrax threat," *Virginian-Pilot* (Norfolk, Virginia), November 14, 1998, p. B3.

[791] "Anthrax exposure threat sent to Chesapeake post office box," *Virginian-Pilot* (Norfolk, Virginia), November 13, 1998, p. B9, and Steve Stone, "100 evacuated from Tallwood High after anthrax threat," *Virginian-Pilot* (Norfolk, Virginia), November 14, 1998, p. B3..

[792] Jim Loney, Miami Beach anthrax scare was a hoax," *Reuters*, November 18, 1998, 11:53 Eastern Time.

Accompanying it was a handwritten note with the anthrax threat. The receptionist called the emergency 911 number, but the operator told them to contact the Dade County's hazardous waste department. Because they were unable to find a number for that office, someone else called the Center for Disease Control and Prevention (CDC) in Atlanta, Georgia. CDC referred the matter to the FBI, and within a few minutes an FBI agent was on the scene. Soon after, local police and fire personnel arrived. Nineteen people who worked in the office, along with 7 response personnel, were taken to the Mount Sinai Medical Center for decontamination. After consultations with Army and FBI officials, the hospital treated the victims with ciprofloxacin, an antibiotic that the military recommends for treatment of anthrax. Officials from the Miami-Dade County Health Department recorded the identity of the individuals treated so that they could be contacted and given follow-on treatment if it was determined that they had been exposed to anthrax. By 9:00 p.m., the FBI was confident that the substance was not anthrax.[793]

According to the FBI, this was the 19th anthrax hoax in the past six months.[794]

***Case 1998-23: Anthrax threat (against Alexandria Middle School), November 1998***

According to press reports, two 14-year-old students at the Alexandria Middle School, located in Alexandria, Indiana, a small town outside Indianapolis, attempted to perpetrate an anthrax hoax. They reportedly put cinnamon in an envelope and enclosed a note claiming that the recipient had been exposed to anthrax. The two boys apparently wanted to shut down the school. According to the Assistant Superintendent, "They wanted to see the firemen in the special suits and the helicopters overhead." The words "anthrax" and "exposed" were misspelled in the note, reducing its credibility. Based on advice from FBI, school administrators and local police decided not to shut down the school. According to school officials, one of the perpetrators might be expelled for one year and the other suspended for at least five days.[795]

***Case 1998-22: Anthrax Threat (against Shelbyville Middle School), November 1998***

On November 13, 1998, three students allegedly placed an envelope supposedly containing anthrax on the desk of a teacher at the Shelbyville Middle School in Shelbyville, Indiana. The students apparently emptied a medicine capsule into the envelope, and included a message that said the material was anthrax. A teacher discovered the envelope at 8:50 a.m. Students in the classroom were quarantined, along with a fireman who examined the envelope, while most of the others were sent to the school gymnasium while the incident was being investigated. According to the local emergency management director, authorities believed the threat was a hoax, because the purported anthrax did not have the expected consistency. The three students allegedly responsible for the incident were arrested. One of them reportedly admitted to participation in what was intended as a joke.[796]

***Case 1998-21: Anthrax Threat (against Bloomington, Indiana, courthouse), November 1998***

On November 12, 1998, the court clerk's office at the Justice Building in Bloomington, Indiana, received a threatening letter that purportedly contained anthrax. The building was evacuated for over an hour. The material was taken to the Bloomington Hospital, which determined that it was not anthrax.[797]

***Case 1998-20: Anthrax Threat (against bank branch, Indianapolis), November 1998***

Around 4:30 p.m. on November 10, 1998 a piece of paper referring to anthrax was discovered at a branch of Bank One in Indianapolis. No suspicious substances were seen. The building was evacuated, and then searched by the Indianapolis Fire Department. Around 6:00 p.m. the Fire Department declared the building safe.[798]

---

[793] Luisa Yanez, Dana Calvo, and Deborah Ramirez, "Anthrax hoax at magazine sends 26 to hospital, snarls South Beach," *Sun-Sentinel* (Ft. Lauderdale), December 18, 1998, as posed on the newspaper's World Wide Web site, *http://www.sun-sentinal.com/.*

[794] Yanez, Calvo, and Ramirez, "Anthrax hoax at magazine," *Sun-Sentinel* (Ft. Lauderdale), December 18, 1998.

[795] Diane Frederick, "Boy could be suspended r a year for anthrax hoax," Indianapolis Star/News, November 17, 1998, as found at the newspaper's World Wide Web site, *http://www.starnews.com.*

[796] Michael Stone, "3 students suspected in threat at school," *Shelbyville News* (Indiana), November 13, 1998, and John Clark, "Middle schoolers angry over threat," *Shelbyville News* (Indiana), November 14, 1998, as found at the newspaper's World Wide Web site, *http://www.shelbtnews.com.*

[797] Jodi Burck, "Juvenile charged in hoax at school," *Herald-Times* (Bloomington, Indiana), as found at the newspaper's World Wide Web site, *http://www.hoosiertimes.com.*

[798] John Masson and John R. O'Neill, "FBI pleads for an end to anthrax hoaxes," *Indianapolis Star-News*, November 11, 1998, as found at the newspaper's World Wide Web site, *http://www.starnews.com.*

***Case 1998-19: Anthrax Threat (against Warren Central High School), November 1998***

At 9:00 a.m. on November 11, 1998, a letter was delivered to the Warren Central High School in Warren Township, Indiana, which according to the school superintendent, "appears to be an anthrax threat." The hazardous materials team from the Warren Township Fire Department removed the envelope and sealed it. The school was not evacuated.[799]

***Case 1998-18: Anthrax Threat (against Bloomington High School), November 1998***

Around noon on November 10, 1998 a teacher at Bloomington High School South in Bloomington, Indiana, discovered a letter on the floor outside the main office. It was addressed to the school principle. The words "Open ASAP" also were written on the envelope. Inside the envelope were white crystals, purportedly anthrax. The threat was written on notebook paper. The letter was tested by Bloomington Hospital, which determined that anthrax was not present.[800] On November 12, a 16-year old student was arrested in connection with the incident. He was charged with intimidation and false reporting.[801]

***Case 1998-17: Anthrax Threat (against Seymour, Indiana, Wal-Mart), November 1998***

An anthrax threat letter was delivered on November 10, 1998, to a Salin Bank branch located in a Wal-Mart store near Seymour, Indiana. According to a press report, dozens of people were evacuated from the store. The Seymour Fire Department responded to the threat.[802]

***Case 1998-16: Anthrax Threats, November 1998***

On November 10 and 11, 1998, a number of churches and anti-abortion organizations or individuals received letters postmarked in Fort Worth, Texas, on 5 or 6 November claiming to contain anthrax.[803]

One of the letters was sent to the office of Saint Matthew's parish in Washington Township, Indiana. According to the Catholic Archdiocese of Indianapolis, the letter stated, "You have been exposed to anthrax." Six people working in the offices were quarantined, decontaminated by firefighters and transported to Wishard Memorial Hospital in Indianapolis. At the hospital, they were decontaminated again and then treated with antibiotics. Authorities also ordered the evacuation of 481 students and teachers from the adjacent Saint Matthew's Catholic School. No powder was detected in the envelope, leading authorities to doubt that the threat was credible. Nevertheless, FBI officials, who took custody of the letter, indicated that it would be sent to a laboratory to determine if anthrax was present.[804]

A second letter was sent to Pro-Life Action League, an anti-abortion group located in Chicago, Illinois. Although there were seven people in the office when the letter arrived, none were decontaminated or treated. The envelope had a Texas postmark, as did the one sent to Indiana.[805]

On November 11, 1998, a similar letter was delivered to the Redeemer Lutheran Church in Rochester, New York. The pastor opened the letter at 11 a.m., but only notified police at 6:45 p.m. Two other people handled the letter in the intervening period. The police notified the Rochester Fire Department's hazardous materials team, which went to the church and picked up the letter. The three people who came into contact with the letter were taken to the Rochester General Hospital, where they were decontaminated, quarantined in an

---

799 John Masson and John R. O'Neill, "FBI pleads for an end to anthrax hoaxes," *Indianapolis Star-News*, November 11, 1998, as found at the newspaper's World Wide Web site, *http://www.starnews.com.*

800 John Masson and John R. O'Neill, "FBI pleads for an end to anthrax hoaxes," *Indianapolis Star-News*, November 11, 1998, as found at the newspaper's World Wide Web site, *http://www.starnews.com.*

801 "Authorities arrest teen-ager in phony anthrax threat," *Associated Press*, November 12, 1998, and Jodi Burck, "Juvenile charged in hoax at school," *Herald-Times* (Bloomington, Indiana), as found at the newspaper's World Wide Web site, *http://www.hoosiertimes.com.*

802 John Masson and John R. O'Neill, "FBI pleads for an end to anthrax hoaxes," *Indianapolis Star-News*, November 11, 1998, as found at the newspaper's World Wide Web site, *http://www.starnews.com.*

803 "Letters from FW test negative for anthrax," Dallas Morning News, November 15, 1998, p. 42A, and Jason Sickles, "Threats were sent from FW," *Dallas Morning News*, November 11, 1998, p. 40A. I am indebted to Jason Pate, Monterey Institute for International Studies, for bringing these references to my attention.

804 Thomas P. Wyman, "For 2nd time in 11 days, letter claims to contain anthrax," *Indianapolis Star-News*, November 10, 1998, as found at the newspaper's World Wide Web site, *http://www.starnews.com.* and John Kelly, "Anthrax Threat Clears Ind. School," *Associated Press*, November 9, 1998, 8:36 p.m.

805 John Kelly, "Anthrax Threat Clears Ind. School," *Associated Press*, November 9, 1998, 8:36 p.m.

isolation ward, and treated with antibiotics. The church was sealed off pending the completion of tests to determine if anthrax was present.[806]

Another letter, also mailed from Texas, was sent to a Carrollton, Georgia anti-abortion activist Neal Horsley. Horsley had gained notoriety for maintaining a World Wide Web site that identifies physicians who provide abortion. Some pro-abortion activists believe it served as a hit list for militant anti-abortion activists, and the FBI was investigating Horsley's activities. According to Horsley, the letter included the words, "You have been exposed to anthrax," and identified the strain of anthrax allegedly contained in the envelope. Horsley immediately resealed the envelope and took it to the Carrollton Police Department. The police triple-wrapped the envelope without looking at and contacted the FBI. Horsley was taken to the Tanner Medical Center, where the West Georgia Regional Hazardous Materials Team decontaminated him.[807]

An anthrax threat letter arrived on November 10, 1998 at the offices of the Kansas Area United Methodist Foundation in Wichita, Kansas.[808] Another letter arrived that same day at the Ridgeview Baptist Church in Knoxville, Tennessee. Two people were given antibiotic treatment as a precaution.[809] An unidentified organization in Boston also was the recipient of one of the letters on 10 November.[810]

***Case 1998-14: Anthrax Threats (Against Abortion Clinics), October 1998***

On October 30 and 31, 1998, eight abortion clinics in Indiana, Kansas, Kentucky, and Tennessee received threatening letters claiming that a powdery substance found in the envelopes was anthrax. Three of the clinics were in Louisville, Kentucky. Three Indiana clinics were targeted: in Indianapolis, New Albany, and Scottsburg. The other clinics were in Knoxville, Tennessee, and Wichita, Kansas. All the letters were sent from Cincinnati, Ohio, and contained no return address.[811]

Around 1:00 p.m. on October 30, an employee of a Planned Parenthood clinic in Indianapolis, Indiana, opened an envelope that reportedly contained a letter and a brown powder. According to press reports, the short letter claimed, "You have just been exposed to anthrax." Upon reading the letter, the clinic employee resealed the envelope, while another placed it into a biohazard bag. They then placed an emergency call to 911, initiating a massive response process. Two police officers responded to the call. They were followed by Indianapolis police officers, who cordoned off the area around the clinic, and fire department personnel, including paramedics with ambulances and approximately a dozen members of the fire department's hazardous materials response team. The clinic and the people in it, which included staff and patient, were quarantined. In addition, stores in the shopping center where the clinic is located were closed by authorities. A sample of the substance in the envelope was taken to an Indiana Public Health Department laboratory for testing, but up to 72 hours were needed to culture the sample to determine if it contained anthrax.[812]

Reportedly, authorities believed that 31 people might have been exposed, including two policemen, two firefighters, the mail carrier, approximately 11 clinic employees, and clinic patients. The hazardous materials response team set up a decontamination tent in the parking lot of the shopping center. People were told to undress and place their belongings in plastic bags, were then given a ten minute shower in the decontamination tent, and were then dressed in surgical scrubs. They were then transferred to one of three area hospitals for treatment. Another decontamination line was set up in the ambulance bay at Wishard Memorial Hospital, where 13 people were taken for treatment. The patients were given another shower and were dressed in hospital gowns and booties, sheets, and blankets. They were then transported by security vehicles to another part of the hospital, where they were treated with antibiotics. They were not moved through the hospital to minimize chances of secondary contamination.[813]

---

[806] Alan Morrell and Jilaine Burley, "'Anthrax' letter sent to church in the city," *Democrat and Chronicle* (Rochester, New York), November 11, 1998, as found at the newspaper's World Wide Web site, *http://www.rochesternews.com.*

[807] Diane Lore, "Abortion foe reports anthrax threat," Atlanta Journal-Constitution, November 11, 1998, ass found at the newspaper's World Wide Web site, *http://www.accessatlanta.com.*

[808] "FBI probes another threat of anthrax contamination," *Wichita Eagle*, November 11, 1998.

[809] "Anthrax may have tainted letter," *Chattanooga Times*, November 12, 1998, p. B4. I am indebted to Jason Pate, Monterey Institute for International Studies, for bringing this incident to my attention.

[810] Jason Sickles, "Threats were sent from FW," *Dallas Morning News*, November 11, 1998, p. 40A. I am indebted to Jason Pate, Monterey Institute for International Studies, for bringing this reference to my attention.

[811] Rick Callahan, "Feds Seek Bomb Threat Letter-Sender," *Associated Press*, November 2, 1998, 4:01 a.m. EST.

[812] Stephen Beaven, "Anthrax threat probed," *Indianapolis Star-News*, October 31, 1998, as found at the newspaper's World Wide Web site, *http://www.starnews.com.*

[813] Beaven, "Anthrax threat probed," *Indianapolis Star-News*, October 31, 1998, and Jenny Labalme and John Masson, "FBI says anthrax threat was hoax," *Indianapolis Star-News*, November 1, 1998.

Two clinics in Louisville, Kentucky, received envelopes on October 30. A third clinic received a letter the next day. After reading the letter on October 30, an employee at the Women's Health Service Clinic sealed the letter into a container. The worker, and the postal employee who delivered the envelope, were taken to the University of Louisville Hospital, and one of them—probably the clinic worker— received antibiotic treatments. Tests on the material in the envelope were conducted at the University of Louisville Hospital indicated that the material was not anthrax. Reportedly, the samples were sent to the U.S. Army Medical Research Institute for Infectious Disease, Fort Detrick, Maryland, for additional analysis.[814] The third envelope was delivered to the EMW Women' Surgical Center. The letter was placed on the desk of the clinic's executive director, who notified the FBI and postal inspectors when she noted that it fit the profile of the threatening letters highlighted in press reports the previous day. FBI agents packaged the envelope in a bag designed to handle hazardous materials and removed it.[815]

The Knoxville Center for Reproductive Health received one of the envelopes in the mail around noon on October 30. The clinic apparently contacted the E-911 center after opening and reading the letter. What happened next is unclear, but press reports suggest that Knoxville's police chief was dissatisfied with the handling of the case, and ordered an investigation into the procedures followed in responding to the threat. Initial reports do not indicate whether the clinic reported the anthrax threat in its initial report, or if the E-911 employees passed on the nature of the threat, or if the police officer sent to investigate the threat was aware of the alleged anthrax contamination. It appears that the responding officer did not appreciate the nature of the threat, because no steps were taken at the time to notify federal authorities. The letter was confiscated by the police, and was sealed at the clinic by a crime scene technician. It was not until 7:15 p.m., however, that the clinic was sealed off, when Knoxville Fire Department's Hazardous Materials Team was asked by the FBI to "put up crime scene tape." Knoxville police assisted the fire personnel in posting warning notices. It is unclear what steps were taken to provide medical treatment to people who may have been exposed to the suspected anthrax. The FBI sent the envelope to its Hazardous Materials Response Unit laboratory in Quantico, Virginia, for analysis. The unit did not expect to have results until sometime on the afternoon of November 2.[816]

Postal workers found a similar letter addressed to a Planned Parenthood clinic in New Albany, Indiana, and confiscated it before it could be delivered. The material in the envelope was analyzed on the evening of October 31 by the University of Louisville Hospital, which determined that it was not anthrax. In addition, there were concerns that one of the envelopes was sent to a clinic in Bloomington, Indiana, but subsequent investigation determined that it was an ordinary business envelope.[817]

A Wichita, Kansas, clinic received an envelope with a Cincinnati postmark on October 31. An alert clinic employee, aware of the threatening letters received at the other clinics the previous day, did not open the letter and called 911. The fire department's hazardous materials team and the Wichita police responded. The local authorities contacted the FBI. According to an FBI agent, "It wasn't opened at all. Just looking at it through back lighting, it does not look like there is any type of powder in there at all." The letter was sent to a laboratory in Washington to be opened.[818]

Initial tests conducted October 30 on several of the envelopes indicated that the threats were a hoax. Additional tests, completed by the afternoon of Saturday, October 31, were conducted at the U.S. Army Medical Research Institute for Infectious Diseases (USAMRIID) and confirmed that at least four of the envelopes contained no infectious diseases. The results of tests on the remaining envelopes were expected at the beginning of the next week.[819] According to an FBI official, "We now know that these letters appear not to be what they're claiming to be, but just because it's not anthrax doesn't mean it's not a crime. It's a crime nonetheless to threaten to use a weapon of mass destruction."[820]

---

[814] Thomas Nord, "Abortion clinics sent anthrax threat," Courier-Journal (Louisville), October 31, 1998, as found at the newspaper's World Wide Web site, *http://www.courier-journal.com.*

[815] Grace Schneider, "FBI: Anthrax threat to clinics was a hoax," *Courier-Journal* (Louisville), November 1, 1998.

[816] Jamie Satterfield, "Keith orders probe into response to anthrax threat," *Knoxville News-Sentinel*, November 1, 1998, as found at the newspaper's World Wide Web site, *http://www.knoxnews.com.*

[817] Nord, "Abortion clinics sent anthrax threat," *Courier-Journal* (Louisville), October 31, 1998.

[818] Robert Short, "Tiller's clinic receives threat of anthrax contamination," *Wichita Eagle*, November 1, 1998, as found at the newspaper's World Wide Web site, *http://www.wichitaeagle.com.*

[819] Press accounts indicated that tests were conducted at the University of Louisville Hospital and by the Indiana State Department of Health. In addition to the tests at USAMRIID, press accounts suggested that the FBI laboratory in Quantico, Virginia, also would be conducting tests to determine the nature of the substance.

[820] Rick Callahan, "Feds Seek Bomb Threat Letter-Sender," *Associated Press*, November 2, 1998, 4:01 a.m. EST.

On November 2, a similar envelope was delivered to the Center for Choice, an abortion clinic located in downtown Toledo. The owner of the clinic identified the envelope at 4:15 p.m., placed it in a plastic bag, put the bag on the sidewalk outside the clinic, and contacted authorities. It appears that she did not open the letter. The people who came into contact with the letter, including the clinic owner and two employees, were taken to the St. Charles Mercy Hospital for decontamination and treatment. No evidence of contamination was detected on those individuals. The streets around the clinic was closed off for four hours until the letter was recovered by the Toledo Fire Department's hazardous materials unit. The letter was taken by the FBI for further analysis.[821]

Another Knoxville abortion clinic, the Volunteer Medical Center, also received one of the letters on November 2. According to an FBI spokesman, "From the outward appearance [it] appeared to have originated from the same source." The letter was turned over to the FBI, and was sent to USAMRIID for analysis.[822] Following the anthrax threats, the Justice Department organized a multi-agency federal task force to investigate recent attacks on abortion clinics, including the anthrax threats as well as the murder of a doctor who performed abortions and 22 incidents in which someone released a chemical irritant, butyric acid, at clinics in the South.[823]

According to press reports, response personnel in both Louisville, Kentucky, and Indianapolis, Indiana, had recently received training in responding to incidents involving chemical and biological agents.[824]

As a result of the earlier scares, the U.S. Postal Service warned its mail handlers to look for suspicious packages. At 9 a.m. on Saturday, October 31, a postman in Shelbyville, Indiana, discovered that a package addressed to the W.S. Major Hospital was covered by a brown stain that appeared to result from a leak.[825] Although the package was mailed in Shelbyville, and did not fit the profile of the anti-abortion letters, the postman notified his superiors about the suspicious package. Concerned that the package also might contain anthrax, the post office activated its crisis management plan and evacuated the 31 postal employees working in the building. The postal authorities notified the local fire department, which in turn notified the hazardous materials team from nearby Columbus, Ohio, the FBI, the Shelbyville police, and the state fire marshal's office. Ambulances were readied in case they might be needed.

In the meantime, the postal employees, tired of waiting outside in the cold. Went to the nearby Knights of Columbus hall to wait out events. Authorities, concerned that any contamination might have spread to the hall, quarantined the postal employees and ten people who were in the Knights of Columbus hall, either working there or eating the hall's breakfast buffet. One person who left the hall before it was quarantined was tracked down and warned not to have contact with anyone else.

The post office was sealed off for five hours until authorities determined that the stain was caused by coffee. The package was an invoice sent from a local Holiday Inn to the hospital.

***Case 1998-30: Anthrax threat (against teacher), October 1998***

On October 21, 1998, Stacy Johnson, an elementary school teacher in Riverside, California, received a package similar to those sent to three families in Colorado at about the same time. The envelope was postmarked in Oxnard, California, and contained a thank you card. The front had the words "Thank You." On the inside were the words, "An agent will contact you about this anthrax sample." Enclosed was an unopened moist towelette packet. Johnson contacted the FBI when she received the package, who put her in touch with the U.S. Postal Inspection Service. The material was turned over to the postal inspectors, who told her that it contained nothing but a damp towelette. Neither Johnson nor her husband have any involvement with abortion

---

[821] Ignazio Messina, "Abortion-clinic threat appears to be a hoax," *Blade* (Toledo, Ohio) November 3, 1998, as found at the newspaper's World Wide Web site, *http://www.toledoblade.com*.

[822] Randy Kenner, "Knox women's clinic gets fake bomb in mail," *Knoxville News-Sentinel*, November 3, 1998.

[823] Blaine Harden and Roberto Suro, "FBI Seeks Man in Buffalo Sniper Case," *Washington Post*, November 5, 1998, p. A3.

[824] The Indianapolis hazardous materials response team took part in an exercise simulating an anthrax release only three weeks before. See Labalme and Masson, "FBI says anthrax threat was hoax," *Indianapolis Star-News*, November 1, 1998. The Louisville-Jefferson County Crisis Group had spent "several months" discussing how to respond to chemical and biological terrorism. See Andrew Melnykovych, "Louisville crisis team was prepared for threat like 'anthrax' letter," *Courier-Journal* (Louisville), November 1, 1998.

[825] The account of this incident is based on John Silcox, "Post Office exercises caution with letter," *Shelbyville News* (Indiana), November 2, 1998, as found at the newspapers World Wide Web site, *http://www.shelbynews.com*, Tanya Bricking, "Workers endure anthrax scare," *Cincinnati Enquirer*, November 1, 1998, a found at the newspaper's World Wide Web site, *http://enquirer.com*, and Labalme and Masson, "FBI says anthrax threat was hoax," *Indianapolis Star-News*, November 1, 1998.

or anti-abortion groups. The incident is being investigated by the Postal Inspection Service under laws that prohibit the mailing of threatening communications.[826]

***Case 1998-13: Unknown perpetrator, October 1998***

On Monday, October 12, 1998, a woman living in Highlands Ranch, Colorado, told the Douglas County sheriff's office that on the previous Saturday she had received a letter claiming that a moist towelette packet in the envelope was contaminated with anthrax. The family was told to go to their family physician for antibiotic treatment, and the family's house and car were ventilated by the Arapahoe-Douglas County hazardous materials response team to minimize the chances of contamination.[827] The previous week two other families living in Colorado Springs received similar letters.[828] According to a U.S. Postal Inspector, the three envelopes were mailed on the same day in early October from a small town in central California. On October 15, three members of the FBI's Hazardous Material Response Unit flew to Denver to examine the packets.[829] Tests of the packets indicated that they were not contaminated with anthrax. They were transported to the FBI laboratory in Quantico, Virginia, for additional analysis.[830]

The case is being investigated by the FBI and U.S. postal inspectors. The county sheriff's department, the Colorado Department of Public Health and the Tri-County Health Department also were involved in responding to the letters.[831]

***Case 1998-49: Anthrax threat (in Amarillo, Texas), October 1998***

Sometime in October 1998 an unidentified woman in Amarillo, Texas, received an anthrax threat in a letter with a California postmark.[832]

***Case 1998-48: Anthrax threat (against Catholic Church, Cheektowaga, New York), November 1998***

A third letter was sent to the Queen of Martyrs church in Cheektowaga, New York, a suburb of Buffalo. A hazardous materials team decontaminated seven people who were in the rectory, along with a policeman and postal deliveryman. The potentially exposed individuals were treated with antibiotics. The church was quarantined pending the results of tests of the letter by the U.S. Army Medical Institute for Infectious Diseases (USAMRIID). Unlike the other envelopes, this one had an Illinois postmark.[833]

***Case 1998-45: Anthrax threat (in San Diego, California, hotel), August 1998***

In August 1998, an anthrax threat was left beside a pay telephone in the lobby of the Sheraton Harbor Island Hotel in San Diego, California. The note claimed, "This phone has been infected with anthrax." A service worker at the hotel discovered the note and notified the Harbor Police. A coordinated response was mounted through the local antiterrorism team, and included the local police, fire department and hazardous materials team, under the leadership of the FBI.[834]

---

[826] Tina Dirmann, "Riverside Teacher Target of Anthrax Mail Hoax," *Los Angeles Times*, December 4, 1998, as found at the newspaper's World Wide Web site, *http://www.latimes.com*, and Mark Acosta, "Anthrax hoax puzzles Riverside teacher," *Press-Enterprise* (Riverside, California), December 2, 1998, as found at the newspaper's World Wide Web site at *http://www.inlandempireonline.com*.

[827] Marilyn Robinson, "Letter with 'anthrax' alarms area family," *Denver Post*, October 13, 1998, p. B-3.

[828] Hector Gutierrez, "Two more families get mailed anthrax threat," *Rocky Mountain News* (Denver), October 14, 1998, p. 12A, and Ardy Friedberg, "FBI probes anthrax scare," *Gazette* (Colorado Springs), October 15, 1998, as found at the newspaper's World Wide Web site, *http://www.gazette.com*.

[829] Mike McPhee, "FBI arrives to take over anthrax letter probe," Denver Post, October 15, 1998, p. B-3.

[830] "Letter didn't have anthrax," *Denver Post*, October 16, 1998, p. B-3, and Ardy Friedberg, "FBI Finds No Traces of Anthrax, Despite Note Sent to Colorado Families" *Gazette* (Colorado Springs), October 16, 1998.

[831] Robinson, "Letter with 'anthrax' alarms area family," *Denver Post*, October 13, 1998, p. B-3.

[832] Laura Vozzella, "Threat mail handled in Fort Worth," *Fort Worth Star-Telegram*, November 11, 1998, p. 1. . I am indebted to Jason Pate, Monterey Institute for International Studies, for bring this incident to my attention.

[833] John Kelly , "N.Y. Church Gets Anthrax Threat," *Associated Press*, November 10, 1998, 4:50 a.m., and "Anthrax scare closes rectory," *Newsday*, November 11, 1998, p. A19, as found at the newspaper's World Wide Web site, *http://www.newsday.com*.

[834] Cheryl Clark, "Alarm Sounded for silent disaster," *Union-Tribune* (San Diego), February 28, 1999, as found at the newspaper's World Wide Web site, *http://www.uniontrib.com*. Interviews, March 2, 1999, with FBI Special Agent John A. Sylvester and Dr. Michele Ginsberg, San Diego County Health and Human Services Agency.

***Case 1998-12: Brothers for the Freedom of Americans, August 1998***

According to press reports, during the morning of August 18, 1998 someone spread a white powder in the Finney State Office Building in Wichita, Kansas, and left a note claiming that it was anthrax. Initial tests suggested that it was not anthrax or any other toxic material. According to eye witnesses, the material looked like baking soda or dry carpet cleaner. Law enforcement officials were investigating to determine who was responsible for the apparent hoax.[835]

The presence of the material was first noted at about 11 a.m., when it was discovered in several elevators and spread over several floors. In response to the danger, 200 people working in the building were evacuated and a four-block area around the building was cordoned off. Around 100 people might have been exposed to the substance. People who had minimal exposure were kept isolated for about three hours, and were then allowed to leave. They were told to shower and put their clothes into a plastic bag after returning home.[836] In addition, about 15 people who came into direct contact with the substance were decontaminated by a team from McConnell Air Force Base, which set up a decontamination tent outside the building.[837] The building was reopened on August 20. According to law enforcement officials, the perpetrator can be charged under state law for making a criminal threat, which can result in probation for someone who has no previous criminal record.[838]

According to an FBI official, "handfuls" of the substance were spread in the building. Indicating that it was a widely available substance often found in households, he refused to specifically identify it. He did add, "It is non-toxic, non-hazardous, and it could be found in any house."[839]

The following day, a bomb threat was sent to Wichita's main library. According to a city police official, the note sent to the library was similar to the one found in the state office building. However, the official refused to confirm a possible relationship between the two cases.[840]

Copies of the threat letter left at the Finney State Office Building were mailed to a number of news organizations. On August 21, a local Wichita television station, KWCH (channel 12) received a copy of the letter, as did a national radio talk show host, Art Bell. According to Bell, the package he received contained a cover page and what was purported to be a duplicate of the original threat letter left in the building. It appears that the television station received an identical package. Bell originally posted the letter on his World Wide Web site, but removed it at the request of the FBI. Some details of the letter received by KWCH were reported in the Wichita Eagle, and Bell described it during his August 21 radio broadcast.[841]

According to Bell, the cover letter claimed that it was being sent to selected media outlets, including CNN and the BBC. The letter said that a group called the Brothers for the Freedom of Americans (or BFA) orchestrated the incident. According to the letter, the group was organized by people who broke away from the Kansas militia movement and Operation Rescue because of the perceived cowardice of the existing organizations. It claimed to be affiliated with the Christian Identify Movement, but also included two members who came from Belfast, Northern Ireland. According to an FBI official, investigators were attempting to determine whether this previously unknown organization actually existed, or whether it was another hoax.[842]

According to press reports, the FBI put together a task force consisting of 20 agents to pursue 160 leads. Larry McCormick, the FBI Special Agent responsible for Kansas and western Missouri, told reporters that the focus of the investigation was the threat letter. He said that the letter "just sort of rambles on about their anti-government beliefs." In an interview with the *Wichita Eagle*, Bell confirmed this depiction.[843]

---

835 Scott Rothschild, "Unknown substance leads to evacuation," *Wichita Eagle*, August 19, 1998, as found at *http://www.wichitaeagle.com.*

836 Roxana Hegeman, "FBI rules out deadly anthrax in building," *Associated Press*, August 19, 1998, 12:10 EDT, and Rothschild, "Unknown substance leads to evacuation," *Wichita Eagle*, August 19, 1998.

837 "Anthrax Note Evacuates Kan. Office," *Associated Press*, August 18, 1998, 9:18 p.m.

838 Lori Lessner, "Threatening notes similar in evacuations," *Wichita Eagle*, August 20, 1998.

839 Hurst Laviana, "20 FBI agents on hoax case," *Wichita Eagle*, August 27, 1998.

840 Lori Lessner, "Threatening notes similar in evacuations," *Wichita Eagle*, August 20, 1998.

841 Lori Lessner, "Groups takes credit for prank at building," *Wichita Eagle*, August 21, 1998, Hurst Laviana, "20 FBI agents on hoax case," *Wichita Eagle*, August 27, 1998, and Art Bell's World Wide Web site, *http://artbell.com.*

842 Lori Lessner, "Groups takes credit for prank at building," *Wichita Eagle*, August 21, 1998, and Art Bell's August 21 radio broadcast, found at *http://artbell.com.*

843 Hurst Laviana, "20 FBI agents on hoax case," *Wichita Eagle*, August 27, 1998.

***Case 1998-05: Rental car in San Antonio, March 1998***

On March 6, 1998, a canister marked "anthrax" was discovered inside a rental car parked in East San Antonio. The report turned out to be a hoax.[844] The motivation of the perpetrator is not explained in the available accounts.

***Case 1998-03: Lawrence Edward Pagnano, March 1998***

About noon on March 10, 1998, the employees at Recovery Technologies, a collection agency in Phoenix, Arizona, opened an envelope that contained a mail order made out to $53.99 and a handwritten letter claiming that the recipients had been exposed to biological agents. According to press reports, the letter claimed, "You S.O.B.!!!! You have just been exposed to anthrax spores prepare to die." In addition, the note reportedly asserted, "Also a standard pestelence [sic] has been put on you and your family and your organization and everybody associated with Smiths grocery stores." A "black and white speckled powdery substance" was found in the envelope.[845]

In response to the threat, Phoenix police and fire officials closed Thomas Road, the street where Recovery Technologies had its offices, from 32nd to 38th Streets. In addition, people were evacuated from the Sunshine Square shopping center and other nearby business concerns. Emergency personnel immediate quarantined nine employees of Recovery Technology and the Phoenix policeman who responded to the call. The ten people were undressed, hosed down to decontaminate them, and then transported to the Good Samaritan Hospital. At the hospital they were taken to an isolation room, given a medical examination, and given antibiotics. They were released after being interviewed by FBI agents.[846]

According to an official of the Phoenix Fire Department, the incident cost his department in excess of $7,000. In addition, other government agencies had to cover the cost of the police security at the crime scene, laboratory tests, and the criminal investigation.[847]

The FBI discovered that the envelope contained a name and return address. Based on this information, the FBI addressed Lawrence Pagnano at his house at 11 p.m. that evening. The next day, a federal grand jury indicted him on charges of threatening to use a weapon of mass destruction and for mailing a threatening communication. The first charge could result in life imprisonment, while the second charge could lead to a maximum fine of five years in prison and a $250,000 fine.

As of March 12, authorities had not yet determined if anthrax was present in the envelope, although police and fire officials indicated that they were skeptical that the organism would be found. Jim Topping, director of the Maricopa County Public Health Laboratory, indicated, "In my opinion, this is a really good hoax."[848]

On March 13, 1998, a spokesman for the FBI's Phoenix field office reported that the powder in the envelope was not anthrax. According to Wesley Press, the quality assurance manager for the state laboratory operated by the Department of Health Services, "It was one organism that can be found on any desktop or surface of paper. We believe this organism could have been living very happily on the envelope before he even started working with it."[849]

***Case 1997-10: Anthrax threats against U.S. cities, July 1997***

On July 15, 1997, a fax was sent to numerous U.S. cities claiming that terrorists intended to contaminate the water supplies of 36 cities with "germ warfare", including anthrax and botulinum toxin. The fax was sent by a retired army officer, Colonel James Ammerman, who was the head chaplain at the Full Gospel Military Chaplains, located in Dalles, Texas. Ammerman reportedly obtained the information from unidentified sources in Phoenix, Arizona. Among the cities to receive the threat were Tampa, Florida, Atlanta,

---

[844] "Anthrax scare prompts preparedness concerns," *Associated Press*, March 17, 1998, as found at *http://lasvegassun.com*. The article cites as its source Major General Paul Carlton, USAF, commander, Wilford Hall Medical Center, Lackland Air Force Base, Texas. In addition, the incident is described in an undated report produced by News 4 in San Antonio, Texas, Randy Escamilla, "Rapid response team formed," and retrieved from *http://www.msnbc.com* on March 17, 1998.

[845] Susie Steckner, "Arrest in anthrax threat: Collection agency got 'tainted' letter," *Arizona Republic*, March 12, 1998. All references from the *Arizona Republic* were taken from the newspaper's web site at *http://www.azcentral.com*.

[846] Susie Steckner and Eric Miller, "Anthrax scare sends 10 to showers, hospital: Officials respond quickly at collections agency," *Arizona Republic*, March 11, 1998, and Susie Steckner, "Arrest in anthrax threat: Collection agency got 'tainted' letter," *Arizona Republic*, March 12, 1998.

[847] Christina Leonard, "Letter threatening anthrax called hoax," *Arizona Republic*, March 14, 1998.

[848] Susie Steckner, "Arrest in anthrax threat: Collection agency got 'tainted' letter," *Arizona Republic*, March 12, 1998.

[849] Christina Leonard, "Letter threatening anthrax called hoax," *Arizona Republic*, March 14, 1998.

Georgia, and Dallas, Texas. Security was strengthened at water systems in the threatened cities. An FBI official indicated, "We've evaluated the threat and we believe it to be not credible. But we notified the police department, mayor's office and all the appropriate people."[850]

***Case 1992-02: Henry D. Pierce, March 1992***

On March 2, 1992, Henry D. Pierce was arrested and charged with malicious wounding after he sprayed ten people, including his roommates and some guests, with a liquid that he claimed was anthrax.[851] According to press accounts, Pierce became intoxicated during a party at the house he shared in Vienna, Virginia, and began acting in a belligerent manner. At around 10:00 p.m., he brought a small glass vial and a machete from his bedroom. He then said that the vial contained anthrax and that "If I break this, we all die in 48 hours." At that point, he broke open the vial with the machete, and began spraying the liquid in it on the other people in the room. One of the victims then called 911, and police officers were sent to the house to investigate. Pierce was confrontational with the police, and an electric stun gun was used to incapacitate him.

The Fairfax County Fire and Rescue Department decontaminated the people in the house at that location before sending them to the hospital. They were kept overnight at the Fairfax Hospital and received treatment for anthrax exposure. In addition, nine other people living in the neighborhood also went to the Fairfax hospital for treatment. The substance was sent to USAMRIID, Ft. Detrick, Maryland, for analysis, which showed that it was not anthrax.

---

[850] Manuel Mendoza, "Channel 8's anthrax report stirs the waters," *Dallas Morning News*, July 18, 1997, p. 36A, "Tampa warned f germ warfare," *Tampa Trib*une, July 16, 1997, p. 2, Alfred Charles, "Security scare for city water; FBI discounts threat as hoax," *Atlanta Journal and Constitution*, July 17, 1997, pp. B6; B4. I am grateful to Colonel Edward Eitzen for bringing this incident to my attention. According to Federal Bureau of Investigation, *Terrorism in the United States 1997*, no date, as found at the FBI's web site, *http://www.fbi.gov*, includes the following comments:

> In the summer of 1997, a group of individuals in Florida issued a warning that the water supplies of 27 major cities would be poisoned at a later date. Upon investigation, law enforcement identified no capability or apparent intent by the individuals to commit the acts; the threat was assessed as a hoax.

There are differences between this account, and the one described by press reports. The FBI report refers to only 27 "major cities" and the source of the report is placed in Florida, while press accounts mention 36 cities and identify the source as someone in Texas.

[851] Steve Bates, "Fairfax man accused of anthrax threat," *Washington Post*, March 3, 1992, p. C3, "No anthrax in Tysons Corner assault," *Washington Post*, March 5, 1992, p. C5, and Patrick Boyle and Maria Koklanaris, "Party guests fear host practiced germ warfare," *Washington Times*, March 3, 1992, p. B3.

# Chapter 7: Possession

## Confirmed Possession

This chapter includes cases in which authoritative sources confirmed that the alleged perpetrators possessed biological agents. In these cases, no attempts or threats to use these were made.

***Case 1996-02: Missing Botulinum Toxin, March 1996***

A vial containing botulinum toxin was stolen from a laboratory at Florida Institute of Technology on March 21 or 22, 1996. According to press accounts, the vial was stolen during a burglary, and apparently was not the objective of the crime. The material had been stored in the laboratory in a locked cabinet for almost 25 years. Several days after the theft, police found it in a library book return box following an anonymous tip that it had been deposited there.[852] There is no evidence that the toxin was stolen for criminal purposes, and its subsequent return tends to suggest that the thief had no interest in it.

***Case 1995-03: Dr. Ray W. Mettetal, August 1995***

In August 1995, Dr. Ray W. Mettetal, a neurologist who trained at the University of Virginia, was arrested in Nashville, Tennessee, for attempting to murder Dr. George S. Allen. Allen was Mettetal's supervisor as head of neurosurgery at the Vanderbilt University Medical Center in the 1980s while Mettetal was a resident. Allen rated Mettetal poorly during his residency, which led Mettetal to resign from the program. Because Mettetal was unable to become a neurosurgeon, he harbored a grudge against Allen.[853] At the time of his arrest, Mettetal was near a parking space once assigned to Allen wearing a clumsy disguise that attracted the attention of university security guards. In his possession was a large hypodermic needle filled with boric acid and saltwater that he apparently allegedly intended to use to kill Allen.[854]

Subsequent investigations revealed that Mettetal had acquired ricin, which he kept in a storage unit in Harrisonburg, Virginia. A federal case was brought against Mettetal, according to a state law enforcement official, because the antiterrorism legislation "is probably easier to try since they're not dealing with such complicated issues." If convicted of the federal crime, Mettetal could receive up to life imprisonment and a fine of up to $250,000, while if convicted in Tennessee courts of attempted murder he would receive no more than a 25-year sentence.[855]

Other reports claimed that Mettetal's notebooks contained notes suggesting that he considered soaking the pages of a book with a mixture of ricin and a solvent intended to promote movement of the toxin through the skin.[856] Federal investigators discovered that he possessed copies of *Poisoner's Handbook*, *Silent Death*, *Kill Without Joy*, and *Assorted Nasties*.[857] A passage in one of the books that called ricin an excellent poison because it was so hard to detect was checked, circled, and starred.[858]

Mettetal's case came to trial on July 27, 1998 at the U.S. District Court in Harrisonburg, Virginia. The prosecution presented evidence that Mettetal stalked Dr. Allen, and that he created several false identities. An

---

[852] "Botulism-causing powder stolen from lab," *Miami Herald*, March 25, 1996, p. 1B, Laurin Sellers, "Botulism toxin vial apparently returned," *Orlando Sentinel*, March 26, 1996, p. D1, "Melbourne School: Please Return Toxin," *Orlando Sentinel*, March 25, 1996, p. C1, and "Thieves grab toxic powder during school burglary," *Orlando Sentinel*, March 23, 1996, p. D3.

[853] Carlos Santos, "Neurologist to stand trial first in Virginia," *Richmond Times-Dispatch*, September 20, 1996, p. B4.

[854] Kirk Loggins, "Doctor accused of murder plot due federal trial," *Tennessean*, September 7, 1996, p. 1A.

[855] Kirk Loggins, "Doctor accused of murder plot due federal trial," *Tennessean*, September 7, 1996, p. 1A.

[856] Alan Bavley, "Castor-oil plant packs toxic punch," *Kansas City Star*, December 12, 1995.

[857] Lucas Wall, "Scientist says poison found in search could kill 3,900," *Richmond Times-Dispatch*, July 29, 1998.

[858] Lucas Wall, "Neurologist found guilty in toxin case, Charge included intent to kill man," *Richmond Times-Dispatch*, August 1, 1998.

FBI official confirmed the discovery of ricin, and claimed that Mettetal had enough to kill 3,900 people.[859] After the prosecution rested, Mettetal took the stand in his own defense. He conceded that he had produced the ricin, and that he had practiced extracting the substance since 1984. When asked why he produced the material, he told the court, "I was just trying to see if I could make it… It seemed to satisfy some sort of emotional outlet."[860] He also claimed, "I never intended to use that ricin on Dr. Allen or anybody. It was purposeless, as strange as that sounds."[861]

Mettetal was convicted of the charges.[862] On December 21, 1998, he was given a 10 year prison sentence. He could have received a life sentence. Mettetal also faces attempted murder charges in Tennessee.[863]

***Case 1995-01: Larry Wayne Harris, May 1995***

On May 12, 1995, about twenty law enforcement agents and firefighters raided the house of Larry Wayne Harris. In the glove compartment of his car were three vials of freeze-dried Yersinia pestis, the pathogen that causes bubonic and pneumonic plague. Harris had spent $300 to acquire the material from the American Type Culture Collection in Rockville, Maryland. He was arrested for acquiring the *Y. pestis* using falsified documents.

Investigators discovered a document that identified Harris as a lieutenant in the Aryan Nations. He told reporters that he belonged to the Christian Identity Church, a religious group that preaches white supremacy. He reportedly admitted these affiliations to his colleagues at Superior Labs, his place of employment.[864] However, his attorney indicated that Harris dropped his affiliation with the Aryan Nation following his arrest.[865]

Harris claimed that he acquired the culture in order to develop a cure for plague. According to his lawyer, "He wanted to write a book on antibiotics that can be used by average citizens against a germ warfare attack." He subsequently published a 131-page book, *Bacteriological Warfare: A Major Threat to North America*.[866]

In November 1995, Harris accepted a plea bargain agreement offered by federal prosecutors. The prosecutors agreed to drop all the charges, except one count of wire fraud. In return, Harris was to get a sentence of no more than six months in jail. A U.S. District Judge, however, rejected the agreement. Therefore, Harris was tried.[867] On April 22, 1997, he was convicted of fraud concerning the acquisition of the *Y. pestis* from ATCC. He was sentenced to 18 months probation and 200 hours of community service.[868] Under terms of the plea bargain agreement, Harris was not allowed to acquire pathogens except in connection with employment at an approved laboratory, and he was ordered to stop claiming that he was a one-time CIA employee.[869]

In February 1998, Harris was arrested as a result of allegations that he possessed anthrax for use as a weapon. (The details of that case can be found on 167.) After Harris' arrest, the Justice Department convinced a U.S. magistrate in Las Vegas that Harris had violated his parole agreement and that there was a danger that Harris might not show up for a court hearing in Ohio. The magistrate rejected arguments that Harris represented a threat to the community. On March 6, Assistant U.S. Attorney Dana M. Peters presented the government's case to a federal magistrate. Peters argued that there were four violations of the parole agreement. Harris possessed and experimented on pathogens. He boasted of possession of sufficient anthrax to kill everyone in Las Vegas. He misrepresented his credentials in violation of the parole agreement by claiming a one-time affiliation with the CIA. Finally, he failed to keep his parole officers informed of his location as

---

859 Lucas Wall, "Scientist says poison found in search could kill 3,900," *Richmond Times-Dispatch*, July 29, 1998.

860 Lucas Wall, "Neurologist testifies he stalked man," *Richmond Times-Dispatch*, July 31, 1998.

861 David Reed, "Neurologist calls plot to poison harmless," *Washington Times*, July 31, 1998, p. C7.

862 Lucas Wall, "Neurologist found guilty in toxin case, Charge included intent to kill man," *Richmond Times-Dispatch*, August 1, 1998.

863 Carlos Santos, "10-year term given in poison possession," *Richmond Times-Dispatch*, December 22, 1998.

864 Robert Ruth, "Deal may be dropped in plague case," *Columbus Dispatch*, April 2, 1996, p. D1. "Man suspected of buying plague bacteria," *St. Louis Post Dispatch*, May 17, 1995.

865 Karl Vick, "Plea Bargain Rejected in Bubonic Plague Case," *Washington Post*, April 3, 1996, p. A8.

866 Robert Ruth, "Bubonic plague case trial set," *Columbus Dispatch*, March 12, 1997, p. B1.

867 Robert Ruth, "Bubonic plague case trial set," *Columbus Dispatch*, March 12, 1997, p. B1.

868 Robert Ruth, "Suspect in germ case won't go to jail," *Columbus Dispatch*, April 23, 1997, p. 1A.

869 Carri Geer, "Harris will stay in jail, judge rules," *Las Vegas Review-Journal*, February 25, 1998, at *http://www.lvrj.com.*

required when he moved hotels during his Las Vegas visit. The magistrate rejected the first two arguments, but accepted the last two. He then freed Harris pending a hearing before U.S. District Judge Joseph P. Kinneary, who had sentenced Harris in 1997.[870] Harris could have received between three and nine months of jail time if the judge determines that he violated his parole.[871]

Ultimately, Judge Kinneary only extended Harris' probation time by five months, ordered him to perform 50 hours of community service, and required him to report in person to a probation officer every Monday morning. In addition, the judge reiterated the earlier prohibition against Harris claiming any affiliation with the CIA.[872]

***Case 1993-02: John Gunnar Linner, Texas, April 1991***

In May 1991, John Gunnar Linner, a scientist working at the Cryobiology Research Center in The Woodlands, Texas, a community about 25 miles north of Houston, was accused of attempting to poison a subordinate by placing a known carcinogen, beta-propiolactone, into an Afrin Nasal Spray bottle.[873] In addition, the victim believed that his telephone and doorknob were coated with the material. When the police searched the alleged perpetrator's home and office, they reportedly discovered in his possession canisters of two poisons: tetrodotoxin and diisopropylfluorophosphate. They also found a recipe in his briefcase for production of botulinum toxin.[874]

According to Peter Speers, the district attorney in Montgomery County, Texas, "He is not your ordinary fellow. He's eccentric to say the least. He had a fascination with poisons generally." Linner reportedly kept two books on poisons on his desk, *Silent Death* and *The Poisoner's Handbook*. A detective for the local sheriff's department reported that Linner was suspected of involvement in other poisonings. The detective was investigating allegations that Linner boasted about poisoning a former roommate and apparently claimed that he laced a colleague's lab coat with a substance believed to cause cancer.[875]

A grand jury handed down an indictment against Linner on August 8, 1991 on a charge of attempted murder.[876] Linner was acquitted of attempted murder after a jury trial held in Conroe, a town 40 miles north of Houston.[877]

***Case 1993-01: Thomas Lavy, April 1993***

On April 8, 1993, Thomas Lewis Lavy, an electrician working in Valdez, Alaska, for an oil pipeline company, was driving from Alaska to Arkansas. When he left Alaska, Canadian Customs became suspicious of his behavior and searched his possessions. They found 4 guns, 20,000 rounds of ammunition, $89,000 in U.S. currency, various publications, and a plastic bag with 130 grams of a white, powdery substance. According to one account, the publications included two books, *The Poisoner's Handbook* and *Silent Death*. Another account suggests that he had neo-Nazi literature as well. According to U.S. officials, Lavy told the Canadians that the bag contained a deadly poison, ricin, which he claimed to have stolen from the U.S. Army.[878]

Robert Bundy, the U.S. Attorney in Anchorage, Alaska, later told a reporter, "He told two stories of why he had the poison—one about protecting his chickens and the other about preventing people from stealing his property. He said if a thief came onto his property, the thief would probably steal the ricin—thinking it was cocaine. And then the ricin would kill the thief."[879] Lavy also said that he intended to use the poison to kill

---

[870] Robert Ruth, "Harris free; 2 charges dismissed," *Columbus Dispatch*, March 7, 1998, at *http://www.dispatch.com*.

[871] Frank Hinchey, "Anthrax criminal case dissolves," *Columbus Dispatch*, March 15, 1998.

[872] Robert Ruth, "Harris pleads guilty, is free: Anthrax case," *Columbus Dispatch*, March 25, 1998.

[873] J. Michael Kennedy, "Scientist Accused of Plot to Kill Colleague," *The Los Angeles Times*, May 3, 1991, p. A4.

[874] David McLemore, "Scientist reportedly spoke of poisonings," *Dallas Morning News*, May 4, 1991, p. 18B, and Scott McCartney, "Researcher Awaits Fate in 'Mad Scientist' Case," *Los Angeles Times*, July 14, 1991, p. A8. McLemore identifies the two poisons as tetrodotoxin and disopropylflourophosphate. McCartney mentions two substances (which he calls nerve agents): tetrodotoxin and DFP.

[875] Scott McCartney, "Researcher Awaits Fate in 'Mad Scientist' Case," *Los Angeles Times*, July 14, 1991, p. A8.

[876] "Scientist charged in nasal-spray case," *Dallas Morning News*, August 9, 1991, p. 25A.

[877] "Scientist acquitted of poisoning colleague at Houston-area lab," *Dallas Morning News*, May 9, 1992, p. 1A.

[878] John Kifner, "Antiterrorism Law used in poison smuggling case," *New York Times*, December 23, 1995, Mark Hume, "Smuggler's lethal secret buried with him" *Vancouver Sun*, January 20, 1996, p. B1, and "Jailed man who hanged self defended," *Dallas Morning News*, December 30, 1995, p. 22A.

[879] Michael Dorman, "Deadly poison, fatal mystery," *Newsday*, January 7, 1996, p. A10.

coyotes that might try to kill his chickens, an explanation most law enforcement officials found difficult to accept.

Lavy had neglected to fill out documents required to bring a large amount of money into Canada, and the Canadian Customs officials refused to let him cross the border. They also seized the plastic bag with the white material.

Nothing further was done about the ricin during the next two years. It was only in the spring of 1995 that law enforcement officials began to take a serious interest in the case. According to some accounts, this reflected the involvement of an FBI agent, Thomas Lynch, who had been involved in the earlier investigations of the Minnesota Patriots Council, a militia group accused of plotting to kill law enforcement officials using ricin. In the fall of 1995, Lynch heard about the case after being transferred to the FBI's Anchorage field office. The case was brought before a federal grand jury in Anchorage, which indicted Lavy on December 12, 1995, for violating the Biological Weapons Anti-Terrorism Act of 1989.

On December 20, 1995, a law enforcement team consisting of FBI agents, including six members of the Hostage Rescue Team, and the local sheriff arrested Lavy at his farm in Arkansas. U.S. Army and Navy personnel with expertise in chemical and biological agents supported them. According to one Justice Department official, as quoted in press accounts, the investigation found no identifiable link with any terrorist group, and Lavy had no poison in his possession at the time of his arrest. They found three books describing how to make ricin, as well as a small quantity of castor beans.[880]

At the time of his arrest, Lavy provided some additional information on his interest in ricin. According to one federal official, Lavy "admitted making the ricin. He even told Lynch how he made it and deviated from the cookbook to improve the procedure."[881]

When Lavy realized that he could be given a life sentence, he apparently became despondent. On December 23, 1995, he committed suicide in the Pulaski County Jail in Little Rock, Arkansas. According to the U.S. Magistrate, Jerry W. Cavaneau, the government presented no evidence to him that Lavy had any intent to use the ricin illicitly.[882] Lavy's lawyer claimed that the material was only seven per cent pure.[883]

It is unclear why it took more than two years for a criminal investigation to unfold after the Canadians seized the ricin. U.S. officials told reporters that the Canadian Customs informed U.S. Customs about the ricin at the time of its seizure. The Canadians also claimed to have asked U.S. Army officials in Alaska about the ricin, who denied any knowledge of the toxin. A Canadian Customs official told a journalist, "We didn't know what it was. We treated it as a suspected narcotic." They handled it using gloves and filtered facemasks, and stored it in a locked container. According to one account, the Canadians took several weeks to understand the danger posed by the ricin, and then a long search was needed to find someone willing to dispose of the material. Another account, however, suggests that it took the Canadians a month to understand that the ricin was dangerous, and that only at that point did they put the ricin into a container designed for hazardous materials. The material then remained in storage for nearly two years, forgotten, until the locker it was kept in was cleaned out. At that time, a Canadian military doctor identified the material, and the Canadian government got into contact with the United States. The ricin was transferred to the United States as evidence in Lavy's criminal prosecution and reportedly was stored at Ft. Detrick. Once Lavy committed suicide, the material was sent back to Canada for destruction.[884]

## Probable or Possible Possession

There is no authoritative confirmation that the perpetrators ever possessed biological agents in these cases. In these cases, no attempt was made to use or threaten use of the agents.

### *Case 1998-46: PKK possession of cobra toxin, June 1998*

According to a Turkish newspaper report, the Workers Party of Kurdistan (PKK) was in possession of 1,500 glass tubes with cobra poison. Reportedly, 960 of the vials, each worth $2,000, were seized from three

---

[880] William C. Lhotka, "Suicide leaves questions in poison case," *St. Louis Post-Dispatch*, December 31, 1995, p. E1, and "Jailed man who hanged self defended," *Dallas Morning News*, December 30, 1995, p. 22A.

[881] Richard Mostyn, "Stopped at border, man carried lethal toxin," *Yukon News*, February 23, 1996, as taken from *http://www.yukonweb.wis.net.*

[882] "Inmate in toxin case is dead," *Kansas City Star*, December 24, 1995. Taken from *http://www.kcstar.com.*

[883] William C. Lhotka, "Suicide leaves questions in poison case," *St. Louis Post-Dispatch*, December 31, 1995, p. E1.

[884] Mostyn, "Stopped at border, man carried lethal toxin," *Yukon News*, February 23, 1996, as cited in footnote 881 on page 154.

PKK operatives who was attempting to sell the material. The suspects were arrested as a result of a sting operation conducted by the Gendarmerie Regiment Command Headquarters in Istanbul Province. The material was smuggled into Turkey from Nakhichevan, and at least some was sold to an unidentified buyer based in Vienna, Austria. Turkish authorities believe that the PKK was conducting the operation to raise revenue.[885]

***Case 1997-03: James Dalton Bell, February 1997***

In May 1997, the Internal Revenue Service arrested James Dalton Bell for allegedly violating at least two federal laws, including impeding the administration of the tax code by harassing IRS personnel and using false social security numbers to evade income taxes. Bell, a 38-year old man living in his parent's house in Vancouver, Washington, has a bachelor's degree in chemistry from MIT.

Bell became a focus of IRS attention because of the February 20, 1997 seizure of his car for unpaid taxes. Among the items discovered in the car was a document, entitled "Assassination Politics", lists of the names and addresses of IRS employees, material on making improvised explosives (including accounts of the Oklahoma City bombing), and militia literature. "Assassination Politics" outlines a scheme which "would be awarding a cash prize to somebody who correctly 'predicted' the death of one of a list of violators of rights, usually either government employees, officeholders, or appointees." The scheme envisioned using encrypted messages and anonymous electronic cash to make it possible to pay someone for carrying out assassinations.[886]

The IRS also discovered that Bell was involved in the "Multnomah County Common Law Court," a group that was holding "trials" of IRS and other federal officials for various alleged infringements of U.S. law.

Following a review of this material, the IRS obtained search warrants to gain entry into the homes of Bell and a close friend of his, Robert East. Bell had various schemes for harassing the IRS. He believed it would be possible to destroy computers by putting small nickel-coated carbon fibers in the air ducts of buildings. Among the targets that Bell discussed were the Portland offices of the 911 emergency service. East told authorities that the two men talked about "putting the fibers down the air vents of a federal building."[887]

Evidence collected during the searches indicated that East and Bell also explored bioterrorism. According to someone friendly with both East and Bell, Bell had "hypothetical" conversations concerning contamination of water. In addition, Bell apparently tried to manufacture botulinum toxin in the late 1980s. At that time, the informant was shown containers that Bell was using in his closet in an effort to make the toxin using green beans.[888]

On February 15, 1997, East sent Bell an e-mail discussing an article on biological terrorism. He also commented, "I believe it might be worth looking for a source of castor beans for some experiments. I'm sure that a nefarious soul could find a buyer for some of that nasty stuff." East followed this up with some comments in a March 7 e-mail asking Bell, "Why don't you see what you can find on ricin? I'm really curious about how to extract that toxin."[889]

According to press reports, when the IRS executed the search warrant for East's house they expected to find sarin and anthrax.[890] Federal officials were told that Bell had manufactured small quantities of sarin.[891]

It is unclear whether Bell and East intended to implement their plans. Bell claimed that his essay, "Assassination Politics", was "hypothetical," and said that federal agents were "overreacting in the same way

---

[885] "PKK's Attempt to Sell Cobra Poison Obstructed," *Istanbul Turkiye* (Ankara edition), 9 June 1998, p. 17, as translated from the original Turkish by Foreign Broadcast Information Service. I am indebted to Jason Pate at the Monterrey Institute for International Studies for bring this incident to my attention.

[886] Affidavit, Jeffrey Gordon, Inspector, Internal Revenue Service, March 28, 1997, requesting permission from a U.S. magistrate for a search warrant. This copy of the document was taken from the World Wide Web site of the *Columbian*, *http://www.columbian.com*. See also John Branton, "Affidavit: Internet essay solicits murder," *Columbian*, April 3, 1997, also taken from the newspaper's web site.

[887] John Painter, Jr., "IRS says suspect discussed sabotage," *Oregonian*, May 20, 1997, Metro Section, p. P-1.

[888] Taken from United States v. James Dalton Bell, Complaint for Violation, May 16, 1997, Magistrate's Docket Case No. 97-5048M, drafted by Philipp Scott, Inspector, Internal Revenue Service. The text of the document was taken from *http://www.jya.com/jimbell3.htm* on July 3, 1997. See also John Painter, Jr., "IRS says suspect discussed sabotage," *Oregonian*, May 20, 1997, Metro Section, p. P-1.

[889] Complaint for Violation, May 16, 1997, identified in footnote 888 on page 155.

[890] John Branton, "Feds were looking for nerve gas and anthrax," *Columbian*, May 18, 1997, as shown on the newspaper's web site

[891] Taken from the criminal complaint filed by Scott, May 16, 1997, mentioned in footnote 888 on page 155.

they did eight years ago" during the Waco and Ruby Ridge incidents.[892] East claims that Bell was "a talker, not a doer," and Bell says that he is a "man of ideas, not action."[893]

On July 18, 1997, Bell entered into a plea agreement. He admitted that he tried to intimidate IRS employees and that he was responsible for the release of the stink bomb at the IRS's Vancouver office. He also admitted to the use of false Social Security numbers.[894] On December 11, 1997, a Federal District Judge sentenced Bell to 11 months in jail. He also received two to three years of probation.[895] He could have received up to eight years and $500,000 in fines. In addition, the probation terms included more than two dozen stipulations. During probation he was prohibited from using computers or the Internet, from fraternizing with common-law courts or militia groups, or from coming within 200 yards of any government official's residence.[896] He was released from prison in April 1998.[897]

***Case 1996-06: Aryan Republican Army, December 1996***

According to press reports, members of the Aryan Republican Army have claimed that they could gain access to radioactive isotopes and biological weapons. Law enforcement authorities have discovered no such items in the possession of any of the group's arrested members.[898]

***Case 1983-02: "Two Brothers in Massachusetts," 1983?***

According to Douglass and Livingstone, sometime in 1983 or 1984 the FBI seized an ounce of almost pure ricin that two brothers living in Springfield, Massachusetts, had produced and were storing in a 25-mm film canister. They further claim that an informer tipped off the FBI about the ricin cache, and that the FBI agents, working with someone from the EPA, took the material to MIT in a paint can. Once the FBI understood what they had found, it was taken to the U.S. Army laboratories at Ft. Detrick, where it was destroyed.[899] No information is provided on the disposition of the case. Nor is it indicated why the two acquired the ricin.

Richard Danzig, a former Undersecretary of the Navy who had considerable interest in biological warfare issues, described a similar incident. In a July 1995 presentation, Danzig said, "We recently had an example where a State highway patrol system is reported to have encountered ricin." The ricin "was carried around in the back of a police car, as I understand it, for a couple of days before it was brought in and a fairly elaborate chain led to its analysis." He also noted that this incident "was associated with a warfare between two drug gangs. One of them was producing this as a weapon to be used in this context."[900]

Danzig suggests that this incident happened relatively recently, implying that it might be a different incident than the one described by Douglass and Livingstone. Given the limited amount of information provided by Danzig, however, it is impossible to identify the incident by date or location.

***Case 1980-01: Red Army Faction, Paris, November 1980***

In November 1980, a West German prosecutor, Kurt Rebmann, told reporters that individuals associated with the Red Army Faction (RAF), a leftist terrorist group, were experimenting with biological agents. According to Rebmann, in October 1980 the French police discovered a culture of *C. botulinum*, laboratory equipment, and notes on biological agents in a Paris apartment used by members of the group. The

---

[892] John Branton, "Federal agents 'overreacting' says target of raid," *Columbian*, April 2, 1997, as taken from the newspaper's web site.

[893] John Painter, Jr., "IRS says suspect discussed sabotage," *Oregonian*, May 20, 1997, Metro section, p. P-1.

[894] "Guilty plea over IRS threats," *Seattle Times*, July 19, 1997, p. A6.

[895] Marcia Wolf, "'Assassination Politics' Author Gets 11 Months," *Columbian*, December 12, 1997, p. A1.

[896] Michael Zuzel, "Is this just a misfit in our midst?" *Columbian*, December 16, 1997, p. B9.

[897] John Branton, "Bell is returning home on probation," *Columbian*, April 15, 1998, p. B15.

[898] Bill Morlin, "The War Within," *Seattle Spokesman-Review*, December 29, 1996, from the web site *http://www.spokane.net/*.

[899] Douglass and Livingstone, *America the Vulnerable*, pp. 31-32. At one point (p. 31), the authors say the incident took place in 1983, but later (p. 186) give the date as "1983/4, Spring." In addition, on p. 186 they also state that the ricin was taken "from an individual."

[900] Richard Danzig, "Biowarfare: Making a Big Problem Smaller," pp. 1-14–1-15, in U.S. Public Health Service, Office of Emergency Preparedness, *Proceedings of the Seminar on Responding to the Consequences of Chemical and Biological Terrorism*, July 11-14, 1995, Unformed Services of Health Sciences, Bethesda, Maryland.

notes were written in the hand of Silke Maier-Witt, a leading member of the RAF. Rebmann also indicated that there was no indication that the group was planning to mount any attacks.[901]

A French newspaper, *Le Figaro*, published additional details relating to this incident, based on a report that originally appeared in *Neue Revue Illustrierte*, a publication that originated in Hamburg, Germany. According to this account, French and German police raided a two-room apartment located on the sixth floor of 41A Chaillot Street in Paris, France, and discovered a biological laboratory at the site. They allegedly discovered a culture of *clostridium botulinum*, the organism that produces the botulinum toxin. The culture was contained an anaerobic retort to protect the organism from oxygen.

The *Le Figaro* account claims that police seized "typed sheets referring to bacterial pathology" and "publications dealing with the struggle against bacterial infection." Writing on the margins of the typed pages apparently was identified as belonging to Silke Maier-Witt, a known member of the RAF. According to this account, Maier-Witt was trained as a medical assistant and "therefore possessed knowledge which is indispensable for the manufacture of microbes." This account further claims that the apartment was rented the previous May by a Belgian named Jan Derek. The rent was paid three months in advance. The landlady reported the matter to the police after noticing no activity in the apartment.

The same newspaper provided additional details, apparently from their own sources of information. This report differed in some respects from the previous account. According to this account, the "police headquarters in Paris" confirmed that on October 14, 1980, a police unit "entered" an apartment at 41A Chaillot Street. In this version, the police were invited into the apartment when the tenant returned from a trip and could not find the Belgian to whom he had sublet the apartment. Although the Belgian called himself Jan Derek, police determined that he was really Ralf Baptiste Fridrich, a known member of the RAF. They discovered a suitcase and five cartons in the apartment. The French police turned this over to the Germans, but never took an inventory of the contents.[902]

Joseph Douglass and Neil Livingstone give a slightly different account of the incident. They claim that the raid took place on October 14, 1984. Moreover, in their version, the police found medical publications relating to infectious diseases and "a bathtub filled with flasks containing cultures of *Clostridium botulinum*." The authors do not cite the source of their information, but it apparently came from intelligence sources.[903]

A recent study by Terence Taylor and Tim Trevan examines the episode in considerable detail, and casts doubt on the accuracy of the initial press reports of this incident. According to Taylor and Trevan, there is no corroborating evidence that Maier-Witt had a medical background. Moreover, German authorities told them that they had "no evidence whatsoever that members of the 'RAF' had planned or prepared an attack using biological agents." Finally, Taylor and Trevan assert that use of mass casualty agents would not be consistent with RAF's usual methods of operation.[904]

Unfortunately, the Taylor and Trevan critique fails to completely discredit the original account. First, there is nothing to suggest that the botulinum toxin was being produced to inflict mass casualties. It is equally plausible to believe that the intent was assassination. Second, the statement they quote by the German authorities does not deny the possibility that RAF experimented with biological agents, but only that RAF had no evident plans to use it. Finally, the authors never followed up the *Reuters* report about the press conference that it says was given by the German prosecutor Kurt Rebmann.

### *Case 1945-01: DIN (Judgement), early 1945*

There are several English-language accounts of a Jewish resistance group that intended to use biological agents or poisons against Germans after the end of war in Europe. Michael Elkins, a long-time BBC correspondent in Israel, gave the first account. Michael Bar-Zohar, an Israeli novelist and popular historian wrote the other. More recently, Ehud Sprinzak and Idith Zertal provide a detailed account that differs in significant respects from the others.

Elkins indicates that in early 1945 a group of Jewish resistance fighters operating in central Europe organized a group to exact revenge on German officials involved in the mass murder of Jews. They called their

---

[901] "W. German Terrorists Said to Test Bacteria," *International Herald Tribune*, November 8-9, 1980, p. 2. This is a *Reuters* report.

[902] *Le Figaro* (Paris), November 8-9, 1980, p. 7. A translation of this story was provided by Bruce Hoffman from the archives of *the RAND-St. Andrews Terrorism Chronology*. It appears to have originated with the Joint Publication Research Service.

[903] Douglass, Jr., and Livingstone, *America the Vulnerable*, p. 29. Purver, *Chemical and Biological Terrorism*, pp. 36-37, located six sources that described what he believes is the same incident, including the Douglass and Livingstone version. One account, written by the House Armed Services Committee, dates it to 1989.

[904] Terence Taylor and Tim Trevan, "The Red Army Faction (1980)," pp. 107-113, in Jonathan B. Tucker, *Toxic Terror: Assessing Terrorist Use of Chemical and Biological Weapons* (Cambridge, Massachusetts: MIT Press, 2000).

organization *Dahm Y'Israel Nokeam*, a biblical phrase from the Hebrew meaning "The blood of Israel will take vengeance." The words formed the acronym DIN, which is Hebrew for judgment. During most of 1945, the group was involved in a variety of schemes to murder former Nazi officials. Reportedly, they killed more than 100 people during this period.[905]

Sometime in late 1945, the group conceived what they called *Tochnit aleph*, meaning Plan A. The objective of the plan was to kill one million Germans. To accomplish this, they decided to contaminate the water supply of several major German cities. According to Elkins' account, those responsible for creating the plan stopped the operations of DIN. Most of the members of the organization were told that it was disbanding because its job was being taken over by the Allied war crimes tribunals. Only the most ruthless and trustworthy members were brought into the new plot.

The group attempted to place some of its members in the water treatment facilities of five major German cities: Berlin, Hamburg, Munich, Nuremberg, and Weimar. They were able to place people only in Munich and Nuremberg. At the same time, they researched methods for mass murder, looking for something that was odorless, colorless, tasteless, and capable of retaining virulence in the water. After researching the possibilities, they decided to inject pathogens into the water systems. Lacking anyone with the required expertise for culturing microorganisms, the group's leader went to Palestine to enlist the services of scientists there.

Elkins claims that the leader approached Chaim Weizman, who was to become the first President of Israel, and received his blessing on the project. Using his support, the group managed to obtain a quantity of some unspecified pathogen. The leadership of the *Haganah* was horrified when they were told of the plan. According to this account, *Haganah* supplied the resistance figure with false identity papers that would allow him to take a British troop ship back to Europe. The *Haganah* then informed the British authorities that the man was a suspicious character, which led to his arrest. The *Haganah* subsequently sent operatives to Europe who informed the other members of the group that the mission was cancelled.

Bar Zohar gives a different version of the story, based on accounts of former participants.[906] The group, which he refers to as *Nakam* (Hebrew for vengeance), was formed in July 1945. It included 50 people, divided into several sections. One section was charged with organizing its European operations. Another was responsible for fund raising, and resorted to smuggling and theft. Bar-Zohar was told that *Nakam* had three plans (known as A, B, and C). Plan B was the primary plan, and focused on killing former members of the SS and other "prominent Nazis" who were being held by the Allies in internment camps. Plan B apparently was actually carried out, and involved poisoning of bread with arsenic that was served to Germans held in an internment camp near Nuremberg. Plan C focused on finding and killing individual Nazis, since it was assumed that the Allies eventually would release most of the Nazis then in custody.

Finally, there was plan A. Bar-Zohar's source told him the following about the plot:

> The *Nakam leaders* evolved a scheme which was disclosed to only a very few people. Much time and money went into the preparations. We knew that if we succeeded, no other action would be necessary. Looking back, it could be called a diabolical scheme. It was designed to kill millions of Germans. Yes, millions, and all at the same time, men, women and children, old and young. The main difficulty was that we wanted to kill only Germans, and at that time there were large Allied armies and thousands of displaced persons of all nationalities still in Germany. Besides some of us were loath to commit such a terrible deed, even against Germans.
>
> That's why we concentrated on plan B.[907]

About two months after executing plan B on April 15, 1946, members of the group revived the dormant plan A. The plans did not get very far, because *Haganah* was concerned about *Nakam's* operations. According to what Bar-Zohar was told, seized the remaining *Nakam* operatives and thus shut down its operations.[908]

Bar-Zohar also recounts another operation, which he claims was totally separate from *Nakam's*.[909] This other group, composed mainly of non-Jews, planned to contaminate the water systems of large German cities. They apparently investigated contaminating the water supplies of Berlin, Munich, Nuremberg,

---

[905] Michael Elkins, *Forged in Fury: A true story of courage, horror ... and revenge* (London: Piatkus, 1996), pp. 168-169, 194-210.

[906] Michael Bar-Zohar, *The Avengers* (New York: Hawthorn Books, 1967), pp. 40-50.

[907] Bar-Zohar, *The Avengers*, p. 47.

[908] Bar-Zohar, *The Avengers*, pp. 55-56.

[909] Bar-Zohar, *The Avengers*, pp. 56-57.

Hamburg, and Frankfurt. Eventually, they focused on Nuremberg. Some of their members went to work for the city's water system, and obtained detailed information on its operations. The plot called for shutting down parts of the water system serving either the barracks of Allied troops or districts that were primarily inhabited by non-Germans.

The group found "a scientist living overseas" who agreed to provide them with an unspecified poison. The poison was to be brought to France by ship. The courier was a soldier who would carry the poison in his knapsack. Unfortunately, the ship's captain arrested the courier once the transport entered French waters. The knapsack was thrown over the ship's side to prevent discovery.

The group continued its efforts, and a new poison was identified. In the end, however, the project was abandoned. Bar-Zohar heard three different explanations for the cancellation of the project: (1) the group was concerned that too many non-Germans would be victimized by the attack; (2) German authorities got word of the operation; and, (3) the "Resistance" (*Haganah*?) heard about the operation and forced them to shut it down. Bar Zohar's account is remarkably similar in many respects to the operation that Elkins associated with DIN and treated as Plan A, suggesting that they in fact refer to the same incident.

Finally, Sprinzak and Zertal provide the most recent account of DIN, and the only one of the three that is documented. Drawing on Hebrew language printed sources and on some interviews, this account provides a substantially different version of events.[910]

First, they contend that Plan A always involved use of chemical poisons, although the basis for that claim is unclear. Second, they cite a source that contends that Weizman was told about Plan B, not Plan A. They rely on the same source for a report that arsenic was obtained in Palestine, not a biological agent. Finally, Sprinzak and Zertal interviewed someone who knew the scientist who allegedly produced the poison DIN acquired arsenic in Palestine. This individual contends that the scientist in question did not have the expertise to produce a biological agent, lending credence to the suggestion that a chemical poison was involved.

Thus, the third account claims that DIN never considered using a biological agent, and never acquired any.[911]

---

[910] Ehud Sprinzak and Idith Zertal, "Avenging Israel's Blood (1946)," pp. 17-41, , in Jonathan B. Tucker, editor, *Toxic Terror: Assessing Terrorist Use of Chemical and Biological Agents* (Cambridge, Massachusetts: MIT Press, 2000).

[911] Although the Sprinzak and Zertal version of DIN is the best-documented and most thorough account available in English, it fails to resolve the question of DIN's potential interest in biological agents. They state, "Some analysts have speculated that Bergman supplied Kovner with a biological agent rather than a chemical agent," and then make an argument supporting the involvement of chemical agents. Unfortunately, they never directly address the evidence from Elkins' account, which does specifically a bacterial agent was being sought and strongly implies (although does not specifically state) that it was obtained. Moreover, Elkins goes into great detail about the thinking that went behind Plan A and states very explicitly that DIN's leaders concluded that only a biological could achieve the effects that they were interested in.

According to Sprinzak and Zertal, DIN acquired only 50 kilograms of arsenic in Palestine, a quantity totally inconsistent with Plan A. Such an amount is consistent with Plan B. However, DIN had no need to go to Palestine to acquire a common industrial poison. After all, according to their version of events, Plan B eventually involved 18 kilos of arsenic, which DIN obtained in Europe. The notion that a major city water supply could have been affected in any serious way with such a small quantity of agent is absurd, and Elkins' argues that DIN understood that. He also claims that they had thought about the issue, had consulted scientific experts, and had come to conclusion that biologicals were the only way to inflict mass casualties. The rationale that Elkins describes for adopting biologicals is so overwhelmingly convincing that it impossible to believe the DIN leadership could have seriously believed that 50 kilos of arsenic would have caused mass deaths if distributed through a water system.

Thus, the weight of evidence appears to support the thesis that Plan A almost certainly involved a biological agent, but there is no direct evidence that DIN ever acquired a biological agent. In contrast, there is at least some evidence to suggest that DIN acquired arsenic in Palestine.

# Chapter 8: Other

## Possible Interest in Acquisition (No Known Possession)

These are cases in which the perpetrators expressed an interest in acquiring biological agents, but never actually acquired the agent. In some cases, the interest was slight, while in other cases the perpetrators actually attempted to acquire the agent. In these cases, the perpetrators also never made threats to employ biological agents.

***Case 1998-09:North American Militia of Southwest Michigan, 1998***

In March 1998, agents of the Bureau of Alcohol, Tobacco, and Firearms (ATF), the FBI, the IRS, Michigan State Police, and local law enforcement agencies arrested three men belonging to a group calling itself the North American Militia. According to federal prosecutors, the group obtained information on the manufacture of ricin. There was no evidence that they ever attempted to acquire ricin.[912]

***Case 1998-11: Algerian Armed Islamic Group (GIA), March 1998***

On May 26, 1998, a Belgian radio station issued a report claiming that sometime in March 1998 Belgian authorities searched a building associated with the Algerian Armed Islamic Group in Brussels Ixelles district of, also known as GIA (based on its name in French). According to this report, the police discovered isolation boxes containing biological cultures "which can lead to botulism". Presumably, this refers to *C. botulinum*, the organism that produces the toxin responsible for botulism. In addition, the report claimed that an address book was discovered that listed a laboratory in Brussels that might have been the source of the culture.[913]

The next day, a French language Belgian newspaper, *La Libre*, issued a report that contradicted many elements of the earlier report, but confirmed others. *La Libre* claimed that both the Brussels public prosecutor and the Gendarmerie denied the report. It claimed that a search related to the GIA was made on March 5, and that an address book was seized at that time. The further newspaper reported that one of the investigators told it, "the only discovery made during the operation in the Rue Wery connected with botulism are instructions enabling the production of a toxin of this kind."[914]

***Case 1998-04: Unknown "amateur scientist", March 1998***

According to press reports, the police in Lansing, Michigan, in early March 1998 considered filing charges against an unnamed "amateur scientist" who attempted to culture anthrax from dirt taken from a cow pasture.[915] The Ingham County health department was considering fining the man for health code violations.

According to the Ingham County Medical Director, Dr. Dean Sienko, the man was an "overzealous microbiology student" with an interest in pathogens, but "no intent to do harm." The man had taken courses at a community college. According to Sienko, "There was no anthrax," and the man had acted "more out of curiosity about what he could do rather than malicious intent."

---

[912] Lisa Singhania, "Militia member admits his role in bomb plot," *Associated Press*, June 2, 1998, as found at the World Wide Web site of the *Detroit News*, http://www.detnews.com. In a June 11, 1998 telephone interview, Lloyd Meyer, Assistant U.S. Attorney in the Office of the U.S. Attorney for the Western District of Michigan, stated that the court was informed that the group possessed a video tape prepared by Kurt Saxon on the manufacture of ricin.

[913] Brussels *La Une* Radio Network, 1200 GMT, May 26, 1998, as translated from the French by Foreign Broadcast Information Service and obtained from the service's on-line repository.

[914914] P.D.G. and F.H., "Fourteen Searched in Belgium without Arrests," *La Libre*, May 27, 1998, p. 8, as translated from the French by Foreign Broadcast Information Service and obtained from the service's on-line repository.

[915] This account is based on "Amateur Scientist Tries to Grow Anthrax," *United Press International*, March 11, 1998, as found at the web site of ABC News, *http://www.abcnews.com*, and in an updated form at *http://dailynews.yahoo.com*.

The incident started on Friday, March 6, when employees of a real estate company hired to sell a house discovered a laboratory in the basement. They notified police and public health officials, who investigated the report. According to Sienko, the laboratory had "some level of sophistication." However, the man's "methods were fairly crude." As of March 12, 1998, the Lansing police had not arrested anyone in connection with the case, and the FBI indicated that it did not intend to investigate.

***Case 1998-01: John Bernard Koch, February 1998***

At 9:40 a.m. on February 5, 1998, John Bernard Koch attempted to bring what appeared to be an explosive device into the Mecklenburg County Courthouse in Charlotte, North Carolina.[916] The device was contained in a plastic file box, and reportedly contained two small canisters. An FBI search of Koch's trailer revealed that he had in interest in biological and chemical weapons, including at least one book on the subject. As a result, it appears that law enforcement officials, including the explosive ordnance disposal personnel of the Charlotte-Mecklenburg Police, feared that the device might include chemical or biological agents.

Koch surrendered to police at 2:44 p.m., but it was not until 2:30 a.m. the following morning, the bomb squad disarmed the device. There was no immediate indication whether in fact the device contained chemical or biological agents.

The 31-year old man apparently was distraught over his divorce, and especially over a decision by a judge to award custody of their two sons to his former wife.

A bail hearing for Koch was held on February 16, and the Mecklenburg District Judge required him to pose a $2 million bond. At the hearing, Koch's attorney claimed that the device was incapable of detonating, pointing out that the wires in it were not connected.[917] Subsequently, the FBI reported that the device contained no pathogenic materials, but did not clarify earlier suggestions that Koch had an interest in chemical and biological weapons.[918]

On July 8, 1998, Koch was indicted by a federal grand jury on related charges, including one count of transporting an explosive device across state lines and three charges relating to violations of federal firearms laws. He could be fined up to $1 million and receive up to 60 years in prison if he is convicted of all the charges. Following the indictment, he was transferred from state to federal custody. In addition, Koch may be charged under state laws, including alleged possession of a weapon of mass destruction and possession of a weapon in a courthouse.[919]

***Case 1997-07: Osama bin Laden, 1997-1999***

According to a report that appeared in an Arabic language newspaper published in Paris, *Al-Watan al-'Arabi*, Dr. Hasan al-Turabi, the leading figure in the Sudanese Islamic government, hosted a meeting with several terrorist figures, including Osama bin Laden. Bin Laden is a wealthy businessman of Saudi origin who has became a major supporter of Islamic terrorist groups. Bin Laden is linked to a terrorist organization called Al Qaeda. According to the report, one of the issues discussed at that meeting was funding for a biological warfare facility.[920] The report listed a number of agenda items, including the following:

> Find the necessary financing to develop the chemical and bacterial weapons factory that the Sudanese Government has established in the Khartoum Bahri suburb of Kubar, in cooperation with the Iraqi Government, which smuggled special materials for this factory after the end of the Gulf War.[921]

---

[916] This account is based on Paul Nowell, "Bomb disarmed, standoff suspect in mental health facility," *Charlotte Observer*, February 6, 1998, and Diana Suchetka, "Extra precautions taken with device," *Charlotte Observer*, February 6, 1998, as taken from the newspaper's web site at *http://www.charlotte.com.*

[917] Gary L. Wright, "$2 Million Cash Bond for Koch," *Charlotte Observer*, February 17, 1998, p. 1C, and "Bond Set at $2 million in courthouse bomb," *News & Observer* (Raleigh, North Carolina), February 17, 1998, from the newspaper's web site at *http://www.news-observer.com.*

[918] Gary L. Wright, "FBI: Courthouse Bomb Nothing to Cause Disease," *Charlotte Observer*, February 20, 1998, p. 31.

[919] "Man indicted in bomb threat at courthouse," *Charlotte Observer*, July 9, 1998, as taken from the newspapers Web site.

[920] Al J. Venter, "North Africa faces new Islamic threat," *Jane's Pointer*, March 1998, p. 11. Based on an October 31, 1997 report that appeared in an Arabic language newspaper published in Paris, *Al-Watan al-'Arabi*.

[921] Jilad Salim, "Secrets of al-Manshiyah," *Al-Watan al-'Arabi*, October 31, 1997, pp. 22-24, as translated from the Arabic by FBIS.

On August 20, 1998, responding to the terrorist bombing of the U.S. embassies in Kenya and Tanzania, the United States launched cruise missiles at the Shifa Pharmaceuticals facility in north Khartoum.[922] According to an unidentified U.S. intelligence official, the United States believed that the Shifa facility was tied to bin Ladin.

> Even though he left Sudan in 1996, we know that Bin Ladin's businesses acquire restricted, high priced items for the Sudanese military including arms, communications, ***and dual use components for chemical and biological weapons***. [Emphasis added.][923]

Similarly, the George Robertson, Britain's Secretary State for Defence, made the following statement on August 23, 1998.

> We have independent evidence ourselves that Bin Laden and others were seeking to acquire chemical and biological weapons in order to prosecute the kind of campaign that we know they were involved in.[924]

Although these comments appear to confirm allegations of interest by Bin Ladin in biological agents, they do not suggest an association between the Shifa facility and a possible biological weapons program.[925]

U.S. government officials have released additional information suggesting that bin Laden and Al Qaeda had an interest in nuclear and chemical weapons. According to a criminal complaint filed against Mamdouh Mahmud Salim, a senior aide to bin Laden, sometime in 1993 the group tried to acquire highly enriched uranium "for the purpose of developing nuclear weapons"[926] In addition, the criminal complaint, which was written by an FBI Special Agent, made the following claim:

> While al Qaeda was located in the Sudan, CS-1 [confidential source 1] advises that al Qaeda and the NIF had a close working relationship in the Sudan, working together to obtain weapons and explosives and in an effort to develop chemical weapons.[927]

In June 1998, U.S. officials again renewed allegations that bin Laden was developing chemical and biological weapons capabilities. According to a report by ABC News, he has acquired materials needed for production of biological ad chemical agents from sources in the former Soviet Union. The same report claimed that bin Laden had laboratories supporting his chemical and biological weapons programs at two locations in Afghanistan, one near Khoust and the other near Jalalabad.[928]

### *Case 1991-03: Hamas, 1991-1993*

According to Congressional testimony of Steven Emerson, an investigative journalist who focuses on Islamic terrorist groups, the Palestinian group Hamas wanted to acquire chemical and biological weapons capabilities. As evidence of this interest, he cites Israeli documents that record the interrogation of a senior Hamas official, Muhammad Salah. In material submitted to a U.S. court, Salah is quoted as making the following statements:

> My task was to collect names of brothers ... together with the following details: Their fields of study, the date when they completed their studies, date of return to the occupied lands, their ability to express them selves, military activity, and the ability to work with chemical materials ... such as remote control activation, agricultural pesticides and basic chemical materials for the preparation of

---

922 James Bennet, "U.S. Cruise Missiles Strike Sudan and Afghan Targets Tied to Terrorist Network," *New York Times*, August 21, 1998, pp. A1, A10, and Barton Gellman and Dana Priest, "U.S. Attacks Sites in Afghanistan, Sudan," *Washington Post*, pp. A1, A10.

923 Background briefing on "Terrorist Camp Strikes," August 20, 1998, as found at *http://www.defenselink.mil.*

924 "Britain Has Bin Laden Evidence," *Associated Press*, August 23, 1998,11:00 a.m. EDT.

925 Considerable criticism has been directed at Clinton Administration claims that the facility at al-Shifa was tied to bin Laden and that the al-Shifa Pharmaceutical Factory was used by Sudan's reported chemical weapons program. For a careful review of the evidence, see Michael Barletta, "Chemical Weapons in the Sudan: Allegations and Evidence," *Nonproliferation Review*, Fall 1998.

926 Michael Grunwald, "U.S. Says Bin Laden Sought Nuclear Arms," *Washington Post*, September 26, 1998; p. A19.

927 United States of America v. Mamdouh Mahmud Salim, Sealed Complaint, Violation of Title 18, United States Code, Sections 2332 and 2332a, September 14, 1998. Similar language appears in an indictment of four bin Laden supporters. See United States v. Wadih el Hage, et al., Indictment, October 7, 1998, filed by the U.S. Attorney, Southern District of New York. David K. Schenker, now a Research Fellow at the Washington Institute for Near East Policy, provided me with a copy of these documents.

928 John McWethy, "Bin Laden Set to Strike Again?," *ABC News*, June 16, 1999, as found at *http://www.abcnews.go.com* on June 17, 1999. For a report that U.S. officials believe that bin Laden was acquiring chemical and biological weapons, see David Cloud and Carla Anne Robbins, "U.S. Intelligence Suggests Bin Laden May Strike Again," *Wall Street Journal*, June 17, 1999.

bombs and explosives ... and in the use of instruments to jam telephone conversations, and watches to activate explosive charges...

[We chose them] also according to their expertise, which were chemistry, physics, poisons, military material, and computers.... For example, in chemistry we asked him what is your specialization? Or what is your level [in] ... toxins chemistry? Can you prepare poisons?[929]

Although the statement clearly suggests an interest in chemical poisons, which could mean chemical agents, it is less clear that biological agents are mentioned. The references to toxins appear in the context of chemistry, and the context implies that the term was being used to refer to poisons.

***Case 1991-01: Doug Gustafson, 1991***

In October 1990, Doug Gustafson and a companion shot at a passing automobile from their own vehicle, killing one of the occupants of the other car. Gustafson was convicted of second-degree murder, and sentenced to 65 years in prison. Before his conviction, Gustafson plotted to kill a prosecution key witness, George Kerr. Gustafson recruited both his brother and sister in this plot. He and his sister discussed using ricin to poison Kerr. According to Gustafson, his sister attempted to acquire some castor bean plants from local nurseries, but found that the plants could only be obtained by special order. Accordingly, they resorted to a letter bomb instead, which killed Kerr's father when he opened it. Gustafson was convicted of the letter bombing and sentenced to life imprisonment. His sister received a 24-year sentence and his brother a 21-year sentence for their roles in the bombing plot.[930]

***Case 1985-01: Michael Swango, 1985***

On October 26, 1984, the police in the small town of Quincy, Illinois, arrested Dr. Michael Swango on a charge of aggravated assault for allegedly attempting to poison some of his fellow paramedics. In the month before the arrest, several of Swango's colleagues had become ill, and some of them were suspicious that he was responsible. One of them detected a strange sweetness in the tea that he had poured from the pitcher left standing on a table in the paramedic's room. When several of the paramedics began to feel ill after tasting some of the tea, someone had the presence of mind to save a sample of the liquid for later analysis. Laboratory tests proved that the tea had contained a lethal quantity of arsenic.

When police searched Swango's apartment, they discovered that he had collected considerable information on poisons. There were thirteen bottles of ant poisons, including one that proved to be chemically identical to the poison put into the tea. In addition, police discovered that Swango had books describing how to kill people, along with a collection of poison recipe cards. On those cards, he had extracted information on how to make several toxins, including ricin and botulinum toxin. Also discovered were castor beans, which are the source of ricin.[931]

On May 3, 1985, Michael Swango was convicted of attempting to kill six paramedics with arsenic. He was sentenced to five years in prison.[932] He could have been sentenced to a maximum of 60 years.[933]

The questions by the Quincy police about Swango's activities led to two additional investigations into his activities in Columbus, Ohio, one by Ohio State University and the other by the local district attorney. The Ohio State University report outlined some of Swango's suspicious activities during his neurosurgery residence from July 1983 to June 1984. These suspicious apparently played a role in the decision to release him from the program.

The Franklin County Prosecutor reported that there was circumstantial evidence linking Swango to several deaths at University Hospital, but that there was not enough evidence to warrant a prosecution.[934] The

---

[929] Steven Emerson, "Foreign Terrorists in America Five Years after the World Trade Center Bombing," February 24, 1998, a report submitted to the United States Senate, Judiciary Subcommittee on Terrorism, Technology and Government Information.

[930] Natalie Phillips, "Gustafson owns up to killing," *Anchorage Daily News*, November 27, 1995, p. C1.

[931] "Poison Packed Kitchen Shelves," *Newsday*, October 21, 1993, p. 129, Michael J. Berens, "Swango is suspect in new poisonings," *Columbus Dispatch*, June 8, 1989, p. 1A. According to "Ohio won't prosecute doctor: lack of evidence to tie him to patient deaths cited," *Chicago Tribune*, April 3, 1986, p. 4, the castor beans were discovered in Swango's Columbus, Ohio, apartment. For an extensive review of the case, see James B. Stewart, "Annals of Crime: Professional Courtesy," *New Yorker*, November 24, 1997, pp. 90-105. Stewart repeats the report that Swango was found to possess ricin, but also notes that he collected articles on the Markov case (see Case 1978-05 on page 58).

[932] "Poisoner of co-workers gets 5 years," *Chicago Tribune*, August 24, 1985, p. 3.

[933] "Sentencing delayed in poison trial," *Chicago Tribune*, June 13, 1985, p. 3 (Midwest Final edition).

[934] "Ohio won't prosecute doctor: lack of evidence to tie him to patient deaths cited," *Chicago Tribune*, April 3, 1986, p. 4.

Franklin County Prosecutor blamed the hospitals for failing to take appropriate steps following several suspicious deaths involving Swango. Because of suspicions that several patients who died may have been poisoned, seven autopsies were performed to look for signs of poisoning. While the pathologists unsuccessfully hunted for signs of poisons, they discovered that one patient died after a gauze pad was shoved down his throat. That death, which was then classified as homicide, occurred while Swango was on duty at the hospital.[935] According to a 1986-press report, the autopsy performed on an elderly woman suffering from leukemia who died during Swango's residency period appeared consistent with ricin intoxication.[936] Swango was never charged with any of these deaths.

It was after his dismissal from the program at Ohio State University, that Swango returned to work part time in his hometown of Quincy, Illinois, as a paramedic.[937] His medical license, however, was rescinded only after his 1985 conviction. After serving 30 months in prison, Swango was released. He apparently then moved to Newport News, Virginia, where he went to work at a medical employment agency in 1989. He was suspected of poisoning some of his coworkers, but was never charged.[938] Swango reappeared in 1992, when the University of South Dakota admitted him as a resident in internal medicine. He was suspended after four months when administrators learned of his tainted past through a cable television broadcast. After receiving the report of the Ohio State University investigation, Swango was dismissed from the program.[939]

In 1993, he was linked to several unexpected deaths at a Veterans Administration hospital while he was in a medical residency at State University of New York, Stony Brook. He was removed from the residency for failing to accurately fill out his application forms.[940] Swango then obtained a job in Zimbabwe, where he worked at a hospital. He was suspended from that position in 1995 on suspicions that he was involved in the deaths of some of the patients.[941] It is believed that he worked in Zambia and Namibia.[942] The government of Zimbabwe also accused him of murdering five people, and indicated that it was interested in extraditing him. No extradition treaty exists between the United States and Zimbabwe. According to an assistant U.S. attorney, such an agreement was on the verge of being signed.[943]

The FBI arrested Swango at Chicago's O'Hare airport as he was returning to the United States from South Africa. Although he used a false name in Zimbabwe, his U.S. passport was still under the name Swango. This meant that he had to use his real name when buying his airplane ticket, and federal authorities detected his name as a federal fugitive on the airplane's passenger list. After his arrest, Swango was charged with illegally prescribing narcotics to patients. This charge was based on the allegation that he had falsely obtained his position as resident, and thus had no right to prescribe narcotics.[944]

According to one account, FBI investigators believe that Swango may have been responsible for the death of dozens of people.[945] As of June 1999, authorities were still investigating Swango's activities, according to James Tatum, assistant U.S. Attorney for the Eastern District of New York. He told reporters that some bodies might be exhumed.[946]

---

[935] "Autopsy shows crash victim a homicide," *Chicago Tribune*, September 21, 1985, p. 3, "Autopsy done on Swango-treated hospital patient," *Columbus Dispatch*, November 10, 1993, p. 8D, and David Lore, "Trial set in OSU lawsuit: the hearing will be first involving tenure of Swango," *Columbus Dispatch*, October 17, 1993, p. 1B.

[936] "Ohio Won't Prosecute Doctor: Lack of Evidence to Tie Him to Patient Deaths Cited," *Chicago Tribune*, April 3, 1986, p. 4. This allegation is repeated with additional details in Stewart, "Annals of Crime: Professional Courtesy," *New Yorker*, p. 98.

[937] David Lore, "Swango is suspect in new poisonings," *Columbus Dispatch*, June 11, 1989, p. 4B.

[938] Robert Ruth, "Co-worker's tip to police started new Swango probe*," Columbus Dispatch*, June 10, 1989, p. 1A, Michael J. Berens, "Swango talks to police in poisoning probe," *Columbus Dispatch*, June 9, 1989, p. 1A, and David Lore, "Medical dragnet failed to snag the 'poison doctor'," *Columbus Dispatch*, November 7, 1993, p. 2C.

[939] The report appeared on a program called "The Justice Files." See "Swango says South Dakota probers were misled about his OSU residency,", *Columbus Dispatch*, December 27, 1992, p. 2C, and David Lore, "OSU needs Swango's approval to send files to medical school," *Columbus Dispatch*, December 10, 1992, p. 5C.

[940]. David Lore, "Medical dragnet failed to snag the 'poison doctor'," *Columbus Dispatch*, November 7, 1993, p. 2C.

[941] "Swango named in more deaths," *Columbus Dispatch*, January 12, 1998, at *http://www.dispatch.com.*

[942] Stewart, "Annals of Crime: Professional Courtesy," *New Yorker*, November 24, 1997, p. 105.

[943] "Swango named in more deaths," *Columbus Dispatch*, January 12, 1998.

[944] Robert E. Kessler, "New Charges for Poison Doctor," *Newsday*, September 13, 1997, p. A3.

[945] Stewart, "Annals of Crime: Professional Courtesy," *New Yorker*, p. 105.

[946] David Lore, "Jailed ex-doctor still under investigation," *Columbus Dispatch*, June 11, 1999, as found at the paper's web site, *http://www.dispatch.com.*

***Case 1980-03X: East German terrorist training, 1980s***

According to a report that appeared in a British newspaper, the *Independent*, the East Germany secret service, the *Stasi*, trained Iraqis, Palestinians, and others in the covert use of biological agents.[947] The story, reportedly based on an interview with a former member of the *Stasi*, claims that through 1985 the training was conducted at a secret facility outside Berlin. After that date, the training was given at camps in Iraq, Syria, and Yemen. The story claims that the students were given training in use of anthrax and yellow fever virus. Allegedly, they were taught to employ the agents in attacks on "wells, rivers and reservoirs or large areas of terrain." According to the former Stasi officer,

> They were trained extensively in the use of chemical and biological weapons and also the effects were explained in detail .... In particular they studied plans for terrorist attacks where people congregate, such as airports, railway stations and large public gatherings
>
> The importance of this was to achieve a demoralising effect of terrorising the population, throwing them off balance, and throwing into confusion the entire structure of the security forces in the individual countries.

The paper claims that the Iraqis were members of the Muhabarat secret police. The Iraqis and other foreigners were trained in groups of 15 to 20.

***Case 1974-01: The Symbionese Liberation Army, January 1974***

In January 1974, police raided a safehouse operated by the Symbionese Liberation Army (SLA) and discovered that the group possessed a volume on "Germ Warfare." Also discovered was a manual on "Anti-Aircraft Defenses," suggesting that the collection of materials may not have represented the types of capabilities the group intended to develop.[948] Although the group was known to coat its bullets with cyanide, there is no evidence to suggest that it ever developed any biological agent capability.[949]

***Case 1972-02: Unnamed Middle East terrorist organization, 1972***

According to the *RAND-St. Andrews Terrorism Chronology*, sometime in 1972 "A Middle East terrorist organization was reported to have established a scientific committee and assigned to it the task of purchasing and/or developing chemical and/or biological sabotage agents and the delivery systems for them."[950]

***Case 1970-03: Weatherman, November 1970***

In late November 1970, Jack Anderson wrote a story, reportedly based on an Customs Bureau intelligence report, claiming that the Weatherman faction, a radical leftist terrorist group associated with the Students for a Democratic Society, was attempting to acquire pathogens from the U.S. Army's biological warfare research facility at Ft. Detrick, Maryland.[951] According to Anderson, the Weatherman hoped to use an allegedly homosexual Army officer stationed at Ft. Detrick to gain access to information and materials. His story mentions two meetings in which this effort was discussed.

In the first meeting, described in a November 3, 1970 report, an informant to the Customs Bureau discussed a meeting with a drug dealer who allegedly associated with individuals in the Weatherman organization. According to the Customs informant, this Weatherman associate wanted "information on what kind of bacteria would be effective and would bypass the filtering system of a city and would incapacitate a population by infection for seven-to-ten days." According to the informant, this drug dealer "stated to me that he was merely engaged in a discussion with some SDS Weatherman as to the possibility of this." In addition, the informant reported that, "He asked me to contact the (homosexual) officer I know there and set him up for

---

[947] Harvey Morris, "Crisis in the Gulf: Saddam terrorists 'trained by *Stasi*'," *Independent*, January 30, 1991, p. 1. I am grateful to Cornelius G. McWright for bringing this article to my attention.

[948] U.S. Congress, House of Representatives, Committee on Internal Security, *Symbionese Liberation Army* (Washington, D.C.: U.S. Government Printing Office, 1974), p. 7. A less specific reference is Brian M. Jenkins and Alfred P. Rubin, "New Vulnerabilities and the Acquisition of New Weapons by Nongovernment Groups," p. 228, in Alona E. Evans and John F. Murphy, editors, *Legal Aspects of International Terrorism* (Lexington, Massachusetts: Lexington Books, D.C. Heath and Company, 1978), citing Lowell Ponte, KABC radio broadcast, Los Angeles, October 23, 1975.

[949] A discussion of the books discovered in the hideout of Patty Hearst makes no mention of any volumes relating to biological agents. See Philip Hager, "Guns and Bullets Among Patty's Effects, FBI Says," *Los Angeles Times*, September 30, 1975, pp. 3, 16.

[950] *The RAND-St. Andrews Terrorism Chronology.*

[951] Jack Anderson, "Weatherman Seeking BW Germs," *The Washington Post*, November 20, 1970, p. D15.

a discussion, and mentioned the possibility of the use of blackmail to induce the 'gay' officer in question to cooperate."

The second meeting between the drug dealer and the Customs informant took place several days later, was reported in a November 11 account. According to the informant, "He (the drug dealer) suggested that I obtain pictures and records that could be used to blackmail this officer into furnishing information as to the nature and character of a BW weapon that (1) is capable of infection, but not fatal infection, the entire population of a large city for seven-to-ten days, and (2) would pass through the water filtering plant of a large city and go directly into the homes of the population."

Following publication of the Anderson report, the U.S. Army confirmed that it had received reports that the Weatherman organization was plotting to acquire biological agents from Fort Detrick. The Army also indicated that the warning had been received from the Customs Bureau, and that it was based on information provided by an informant.[952]

***Case 1968-01: Arab Pharmaceutical Congress, September 1968***

According to the newspaper *Dagens Nyheter*, the Arab Pharmaceutical Congress indicated its support for the Palestine Liberation Organization (PLO) and advocated training in biological warfare.[953] It is unclear from this account whether the group was suggesting that the PLO undertake biological warfare training, or if that suggestion was directed at Arab states.

## False cases and hoaxes

These cases fall into several categories. First, there are some cases that never occurred, even though they are identified by some sources as examples of biological agent use. In some instances, it is unclear if the alleged event ever took place. In other cases, something may have happened, but if it did there is no indication that a biological agent, as defined by this study, was not involved. This includes instances in which law enforcement officials were unable to determine that alleged activities were in fact illegal.

***Case 1999-67: Feared use of West Nile Fever by Iraq, October 1999***

In October 1999, Richard Preston, a novelist and chronicler of disease outbreaks, published an article in *The New Yorker* magazine suggesting that the CIA was investigating whether Iraq was responsible for causing the outbreak of West Nile fever in the New York City area.[954] This account relied heavily on a story written by an Iraqi defector claiming that Saddam Hussein planned to use a strain of West Nile virus to mount biological weapons attacks. Preston drew on a story that appeared in the previous April in the London *Daily Mirror*.[955] That story was based on a book authored by the defector, Mikhail Ramadan, who supposedly served as a double for Saddam Hussein.[956]

According to the newspaper account, Saddam Hussein told Ramadan about plans to use a strain of the West Nile virus called SV1417 to stage biological warfare attacks. The newspaper story gave the following account of the episode.

> In 1997, on almost the last occasion we met, Saddam summoned me to his study. Seldom had I seen him so elated. Unlocking the top right-hand drawer of his desk, he produced a bulky, leather-bound dossier and read extracts from it. Immediately afterwards, I made coded notes of what he said. The dossier holds details of his ultimate weapon, developed in secret laboratories outside Iraq. That stage of Saddam's plan, Point One, was scheduled to be completed by mid-1998. Free of UN inspection, the laboratories would develop the SV1417 strain of the West Nile virus - capable of destroying 97 pc [percent] of all life in an urban environment. That would take two years, with another year to stockpile the virus. Saddam revealed that the virus could be released with impunity - the Iraqis would be safe. Plans were underway to distribute enough antidote to protect up to 30 million people. He said SV1417 was to be 'operationally tested' on a Third World population centre of not less than 100,000 and no more than 250,000 people, probably in the year 2000. The target had been selected, Saddam said, 'but that is not for your innocent ears'. Once sufficient stocks of

---

952 "Army Tells of Plot to Steal Bacteria From Ft. Detrick," *New York Times*, November 21, 1970, p. 34.

953 "Arab Plan for Chemical War," *Dagens Nyheter*, September 30, 1968, as cited in Roberta Wohlstetter, "Terror on a Grand Scale," *Survival*, May June 1976, p. 102.

954 Richard Preston, "West Nile Mystery," *The New Yorker*, October 17 & 25, 1999, pp. 90-108.

955 Mikhael Ramadan, "I Was Saddam's Double," *Daily Mail*, April 6, 1999, pp. 34-35.

956 Mikhael Ramadan, *In the Shadow of Saddam* (London: GreeNZone Publishing, 1999), pp. 317-319.

virus and antidote had been gathered, the news would be conveyed to the UN, followed by a series of ultimatums. The climax - Point Four in Saddam's dossier would be the releasing of SV1417 at strategic points in the world.[957]

The book's account of this episode is essentially similar, but gives slightly more detail and varies in a few important respects. The book places the fatality rate at only 90 percent, not 97 percent as claimed in the newspaper article.[958]

According to press reports, the CIA looked into the possibility that the outbreak resulted from deliberate introduction. According to an unnamed CIA official quoted by the *Washington Post*, "there's nothing we've found that would support the notion at all."[959] Subsequently, Peggy Hamburg, Assistant Secretary of Health in the Department of Health and Human Services, said, "The data did not indicate it was a result of terrorist action." She confirmed that the FBI and CIA had investigated the outbreak, even though there was skepticism about the possibility that it resulted from intentional acts.[960]

***Case 1999-63: Feared anthrax release (in Wichita, Kansas), December 1999***

On December 17, 1999, hazardous materials teams blocked off a considerable part of downtown Wichita, Kansas, after someone reported seeing a powder on the ground near the Finney State Office Building. Consequently, rush hour traffic was obstructed for two hours by the street closures. The teams identified the powder in more than 50 locations. Eventually, they discovered that the unknown substance was cooking flour used by a group of runners, the Hash Street Harriers, to mark their running paths. They use chalk and flour to mark the trails because they are environmentally friendly. According to a member of the group, "We've run downtown probably 30 times over the last three years."[961]

***Case 1999-74: Cobra venom smuggling, October 1999***

According to a press report, on at least two occasions Bangladeshi police seized illicit shipments of cobra venom. The cobra venom is collected for use in medical research. The newspaper claims that it is also misused as an illicit drug, apparently for its psychotropic effects.[962] There is no indication from the account that the people acquiring the cobra venom intended to use it to kill anyone.

***Case 1999-73: Stolen tuberculosis, June 1999***

According to press reports, a black overnight bag containing a vial of tuberculosis was stolen from the room of a researcher staying at the Cathedral Hill Hotel in San Francisco, California. According to police, the bag was taken during a daytime robbery. There is no evidence that the burglar knew that the tuberculosis was in the bag or had any interest in it.[963]

***Case 1999-69: "Nong Jaew", June 1999***

According to a Bangkok newspaper, police suspected that a 34-year-old woman identified as "Nong Jaew" was suspected of deliberately infecting policemen with HIV. According to these accounts, the woman's husband, a policeman, died of AIDS and infected her in the process. Apparently in revenge, she sought to infect other policemen with the disease. The reports suggest that she may have slept with as many as 20

[957] Mikhael Ramadan, "I Was Saddam's Double," *Daily Mail*, April 6, 1999, p. 35.

[958] Ramadan, *In the Shadow of Saddam*, p. 318.

[959] Vernon Loeb, "CIA Finds No Sign Virus Was An Attack," *Washington Post*, October 12, 1999. p. 2.

[960] "No evidence of bioterrorism in NY virus outbreak: official," *Agence France Press*, January 6, 2000.

[961] "Baking flour used to mark runners' route mistaken for anthrax," *Associated Press State and Local Wire*, December 18, 1999, AM cycle.

[962] "Snake Venom," *The Independent Emerging Markets Datafile*, October 29, 1999, as found in the *Lexis-Nexis* on-line database. This episode was brought to my attention by Gavin Cameron, Jason Pate, Diana McCauley, & Lindsay DeFazio, "1999 WMD Terrorism Chronology: Incidents Involving Sub-National Actors and Chemical, Biological, Radiological, and Nuclear Materials," *The Nonproliferation Review*, Summer 2000, p. 172.

[963] "Stolen TB vial is still out there," *San Francisco Examiner*, June 30, 1999, p. A5, Sabin Russell, "Stolen TB Vial Poses No Immediate Peril," *San Francisco Chronicle*, June 30, 1999, p. A15, and Jessie Seyfer, "Vial of virulent TB stolen from hotel room; police warn of health risks," *Associated Press State and Local Wire*, June 29, 1999, AM cycle. This episode was brought to my attention by Gavin Cameron, Jason Pate, Diana McCauley, & Lindsay DeFazio, "1999 WMD Terrorism Chronology: Incidents Involving Sub-National Actors and Chemical, Biological, Radiological, and Nuclear Materials," *The Nonproliferation Review*, Summer 2000, p. 170.

policemen, but it was not known if the allegation was accurate or if any had become infected with HIV. The woman was a nurse, and apparently died of AIDS on June 30, 1999.[964]

It is unclear over what period the alleged seductions are supposed to have occurred. This incident does not meet the case definition used in this study, because it involves the natural transmission of disease. It is reported here because it was included in another survey of bioterrorism incidents and because it is a relatively typical example of a type of crime that occurs more often than sometimes recognized.[965]

***Case 1999-72: Theft through threat of HIV exposure, March 1999***

A Cuban newspaper, *Tribuna de La Habana*, reportedly issued a story on March 21, 1999 that police had recently arrested two perpetrators, Manuel Basulto and Miguel Quevedo, who threatened to infect their victims with HIV contaminated blood by cutting themselves.[966] This method of dissemination does not meet the criteria for a bioterrorism or biocriminal case used by this study, but the incident is mentioned because of its mention in the other survey.[967]

***Case 1999-46: Feared anthrax threats (in New York), January 1999***

The Colonial Village Elementary School, located in the Niagara-Wheatfield school district in Niagara County, New York, was shut down on January 25, 1999, because of a "suspicious" package found shoved into the front door. Employees at an obstetrics/gynecology office in Lockport, New York, found an identical envelope. Although the envelopes were treated as hazardous, subsequent investigation determined that they were filled with advertisements from a collection agency in Amherst, New York.[968]

***Case 1998-47: Feared anthrax threat (in Providence, Rhode Island), November 1998***

On November 30, 1998, a Planned Parenthood of Rhode Island clinic received a suspicious package that was treated as a possible anthrax threat. The package, which was a little bigger than a shoe box, was delivered at about 1:00 p.m. Because it had no return address, employees at the clinic feared that it might be one of the anthrax threat packages being sent to Planned Parenthood clinics around the country. The package was taken outside the building, and authorities were notified. After being examined with bomb detection equipment, it was opened and found to contain return address labels for the clinic.[969]

***Case 1998-39: Anthrax scare (at hospital), December 1998***

On December 18, 1998, the Providence St. Joseph Medical Center in the Media District of Los Angeles County was closed for about an hour due to fears of possible anthrax contamination. At about 8:30 p.m. a woman suffering from flu-like symptoms arrived at the emergency room of the hospital. Medical providers initially thought that she had been in the Woodlands Hills Bankruptcy Court building, which had been the target of an anthrax threat. The hospital notified authorities and a Los Angeles city hazardous materials team was sent to the hospital. Further questioning, however, determined that the woman had not been in the court building but in one next to it, and there was no chance that she had been exposed to the anthrax.[970]

***Case 1998-15: Ricin scare in Jacksonville, Florida, November 1998***

About 8:00 a.m. on November 3, 1998 police officers at the Jacksonville's Sheriff's Office tested a white powder found in a small box seized in a vacant apartment to determine if the material was cocaine. When tested, the substance reacted in a way that suggested that it might be ricin. The box containing the

---

[964] "Infected wife targets men in uniform in AIDS vendetta," *Bangkok Post*, July 2, 1999, and "AIDS Vendetta: Embarrassed lawmen hounded by wives over widow," *Bangkok Post*, July 3, 1999.

[965] Gavin Cameron, Jason Pate, Diana McCauley, & Lindsay DeFazio, "1999 WMD Terrorism Chronology: Incidents Involving Sub-National Actors and Chemical, Biological, Radiological, and Nuclear Materials," *The Nonproliferation Review*, Summer 2000, p. 161.

[966] "Cuban police arrest muggers using AIDS as a weapon," *Agence France Presse*, March 21, 1999, 20:51 GMT.

[967] Gavin Cameron, Jason Pate, Diana McCauley, & Lindsay DeFazio, "1999 WMD Terrorism Chronology: Incidents Involving Sub-National Actors and Chemical, Biological, Radiological, and Nuclear Materials," *The Nonproliferation Review*, Summer 2000, p. 168.

[968] Peter Simon and Thomas J. Prohaska, "Student at Iroquois High Charged in Anthrax Scare," Buffalo News, January 26, 1999, p. 5B. I am grateful to Jason Pate at the Monterey Institute for International Studies for calling my attention to these incidents.

[969] Jonathan D. Rockoff, "Suspicious package prompts alert at Planned Parenthood," *Providence Journal-Bulletin*, December 1, 1998, p. 3B. I am indebted to Jason Pate, Monterey Institute for International Studies, for bring this incident to my attention.

[970] Leslie Simmons, "Anthrax scare at St. Joseph's," *Los Angeles Times*, December 26, 1998, as found at the newspaper's World Wide Web site, *http://www.latimes.com*.

suspected ricin powder was dropped on the loading dock of the Sheriff's Office as it was being removed from the building. As a result, nine people were exposed.

In response to the possible release of ricin, the Sheriff's Office was quarantined, and the Fire and Rescue Department's hazardous materials team was called to decontaminate the affected area. The material was taken to the Florida Department of Environmental Protection for testing. The nine affected employees were transported to the trauma center of the University Medical Center. The Sheriff's Office employees were decontaminated with a spray of bleach and water in a wash down area outside the trauma center. Other people coming to the hospital center was questioned to determine if they might have been exposed to the agent release at the Sheriff's Office. A similar process was followed at the Methodist Medical Center across the street.

The employees were kept in the University Medical Center's trauma unit for observation, and the unit was quarantined. The next day it was determined that the substance was not ricin, and the patients were released [971]

***Case 1998-02: Larry Wayne Harris and William Leavitt, February 1998***

On February 19, 1998, the FBI arrested two men, Larry Wayne Harris and William Leavitt, for alleged violations of the Biological Weapons Antiterrorism Act (Title 18, United States Code, Section 175). Specifically, the two were indicted on two counts. The first count charged them with conspiring to possess a biological agent for use as a weapon, while the second charged them with possessing a biological agent for use as a weapon.[972]

According to the criminal complaint, on February 18, a "citizen-informant" called the Las Vegas, Nevada, offices of the FBI and reported that at noon Harris and Leavitt claimed to possess "military grade" anthrax. The U.S. Attorney's office identified the informant as a "research scientist, specializing in cancer research." According to the criminal complaint, the informant had two extortion convictions, but that the FBI had no reason to suspect that he had any ulterior motive in providing this information. "It appears that his providing information to the FBI was done simply as a citizen performing his civic duty." Subsequent press reports indicate that the informant was Ronald George Rockwell, president of Rife Research Lab and Rockwell Research Company.

It appears that the informant must have called the FBI almost immediately after the meeting. At 3:15 p.m., Leavitt called the informant and set up a meeting at a restaurant for 7:00 p.m. that evening. The source met Leavitt and Harris in the parking lot of the restaurant, where they discussed the planned tests. According to press reports, the FBI recorded the conversation.

The FBI also identified another individual who encountered Leavitt and Harris at the Gold Coast Hotel. This informant claimed that Harris showed him a vial wrapped in cardboard that supposedly contained anthrax. Harris allegedly stated that the vial contained enough anthrax to "wipe out the city."

The vials suspected of containing anthrax were not removed from the automobile until the next day, February 19. They were securely packaged, and placed on an FBI aircraft that flew them to northern Virginia. The plane arrived at nearly midnight. The material was then flown to Ft. Detrick, Maryland, to the facilities of the U.S. Army Research Institute for Infectious Diseases (USAMRIID). Although the packages were delivered at 8:00 a.m., it was not until around noon that laboratory analyses were begun. The delay resulted in part from the need to handle the vials carefully so that evidence, such as fingerprints, was not disturbed. Analyses continued until the afternoon of February 21, by which time it was clear that the vials contained a non-pathogenic strain of anthrax used in veterinary vaccines.[973]

Based on the laboratory report, the Justice Department dropped the charges against both Leavitt and Harris. Leavitt was released from prison. Harris remained in jail because of claims by the Justice Department that he had violated the terms of his probation agreement.

---

[971] Kathleen Sweeney and Margie Mason, "Chemical scare taken seriously," *Florida Times-Union* (Jacksonville), November 4, 1998, and "Ricin scare ends; cause investigated," *Florida Times-Union* (Jacksonville), November 5, 1998, as found at the newspaper's World Wide Web site, *http://jacksonbille.com.*

[972] Details are taken from the Criminal Complaint, United States of America vs. Larry Wayne Harris and William Job Leavitt, U.S. District Court, District of Nevada, Case No. MAF-98-2042-M-RLH, February 19, 1998, found at the web site of the *Las Vegas Sun, http://www.lasvegassun.com.* Count two of the complaint accused that the two "knowingly possessed a biological agent and toxin, to wit: anthrax and anthrax precursors, for use as a weapon." The complaint never clarifies what toxin was involved. Nor does it clarify what was meant by "anthrax precursor." In addition, the second count in the criminal complaint accused the two of violating Title 18, United States Code, Section 2, for aiding and abetting. According to the code, "Whoever commits an offense against the United States or aids, abets, counsels, commands, induces or procures its commission, is punishable as a principal."

[973] Robert Suro and William Claiborne, "Caution Impeded Speed in Assessing Chemicals' Threat," *Washington Post*, February 24, 1998, p. A3.

The U.S. Attorney's office in Las Vegas indicated that it intended to continue its investigation into the incident. The next day, FBI agents exercised a search warrant to search Leavitt's home. A considerable amount of material was removed during the search. According to press accounts, not officially confirmed, a grand jury investigation into the case was initiated.

The FBI subsequently came under considerable criticism for its reliance on Rockwell. Although the FBI admitted that Rockwell had been convicted on extortion charges, some observers believed that they gave his allegations far too much credence.[974] Leavitt's lawyers claimed that Rockwell had a motive for making false allegations. They claimed, supported in part by documents, that Rockwell made the allegations against Leavitt and Harris only after negotiations between Leavitt and Rockwell collapsed. According to the attorneys, Rockwell wanted a $100,000 advance payment for the machine sight unseen. The talks fell apart over this issue, and, Leavitt's lawyers suggested, Rockwell then retaliated by going to the authorities with the story about the alleged activities of Leavitt and Harris.[975]

Questions also were raised concerning Rockwell's credentials as a cancer researcher. Rockwell was unknown to scientists who specialize in cancer, and appeared to have written no scientific articles.[976] Leavitt's attorneys also claimed that Rockwell attempted to involve their client in research on time travel and unidentified flying objects. According to the lawyers, Rockwell wanted Leavitt to finance this research.[977] Others who had encountered Rockwell confirmed these claims. One man who met Rockwell concluded that the man was "a total fruitcake" based on a fifteen-minute conversation. "He said he can build flying saucers any size you want. He said he has a plane the size of a 747 that extracts energy out of the air as it moves and flies for hours on one gallon of gasoline." Based on such statements, this individual concluded, "For the FBI to even listen to this man, I'm appalled."[978]

Finally, press reports suggest that Rockwell claimed on February 12, 1998, before he made the allegations about Leavitt and Harris, that he possessed anthrax obtained from the U.S. Army biological warfare research facility at Dugway Proving Grounds, Utah. Although Rockwell denied the allegation, a tape recording of the telephone conversation apparently exists.[979]

On March 3, Harris was returned to Ohio for a court hearing to determine if he in fact violated terms of his parole (see page 152 for details of the parole hearing).[980]

***Case 1998-07: Drug dealers and ricin, January 1998***

In January 1998, the Drug Enforcement Administration (DEA) sent a warning to law enforcement agencies about the potential use of ricin toxin by operators of drug laboratories manufacturing methamphetamine. According to the report, DEA was concerned that the ricin might be mixed in with illegal drugs and that the ricin could poison police officials raiding drug laboratories. According to Rodney Adams, a DEA spokesman, the warning originated in the agency's El Paso office. It was sent to other DEA offices, which then forwarded it to other law enforcement organizations. Adams denied that any specific information led to the alert, "We are taking this seriously, but we don't honestly believe there is any of this out there yet."[981]

The reports apparently are linked to the seizure of ricin by Customs Canada in 1993 from Thomas Lavy. (This episode is recounted starting on 153). Salt Lake County (Utah) sheriff's detective Dave Burdett, who reportedly looked into the story, was unable to find any instances in which drug dealers used ricin in this

---

[974] For example, see John L. Smith, "Too bad some clients of Rockwell didn't know a crock well," *Las Vegas Review-Journal*, February 25, 1988, and Jeff German, "FBI source's credibility muddles anthrax probe," *Las Vegas Sun*, March 7, 1998.

[975] Jeff German, "One man released after anthrax turns out to be harmless veterinary vaccine," *Las Vegas Sun*, February 21, 1998, and Jeff German, "FBI source made time travel, UFO research plans," *Las Vegas Sun*, February 23, 1998.

[976] Denise Cardinal and Art Nadler, "FBI informant's credibility probed in anthrax arrests," *Las Vegas Sun*, February 23, 1998

[977] Jeff German, "FBI source made time travel, UFO research plans," *Las Vegas Sun*, February 23, 1998.

[978] Steve Friess, "Credibility of FBI tipster comes under scrutiny," *Las Vegas Review-Journal*, February 24, 1998, as found at *http://www.lvrj.com*.

[979] Jeff German, "FBI tipster claimed he had anthrax," *Las Vegas Sun*, March 6, 1998.

[980] Robert Ruth, "Man in anthrax scare is returned," *Columbus Dispatch*, March 4, 1998, as found at the newspaper's web site, *http://www.dispatch.com*.

[981] J. Harry Jones, "DEA warns local police to beware of potent toxin," *San Diego Union-Tribune*, January 15, 1998, as found at *http://www2.uniontrib.com*.

way. Nevertheless, he told a journalist that, "It's definitely taken on a life of its own."[982] This was illustrated by the subsequent appearance of the report in Canada.[983]

***Case 1997-09: Israeli Intelligence, September 1997***

On September 25, 1997, two Israeli intelligence operatives attempted to assassinate Khaled Meshal, a political activist associated with Hamas, in a botched attack in Amman, Jordan. According to press accounts, the Israelis sprayed a synthetic opiate, Fentanyl, into his ear. Fentanyl is used as an anesthetic. The two agents involved in the attack were captured by Jordanian security, and the Israelis were forced to divulge the nature of the poison used in the attack. Meshal survived.[984] Some Arab sources speculated that the Israelis might have used ricin in the attack.[985]

***Case 1997-08: Shigella at Dartmouth-Hitchcock Medical Center, fall 1997***

According to press reports, seven laboratory technicians at the Dartmouth-Hitchcock Medical Center became infected with a strain of the shigella organism sometime in late September and early October of 1997. Two technicians were hospitalized. The first case was diagnosed on September 20, but the majority occurred during the first week of October.[986] The incident occurred at a time when vials of the organism were being transferred on a cart from a freezer that was not working. The two technicians moving the organisms became sick three days and seven days after moving the vials.[987] It appears that the subsequent victims were infected while using a vortex machine, which is used to shake the contents of test tubes.[988]

The incident was investigated by state public health officials, who invited the Centers for Disease Control (CDC) to assist.[989] The CDC investigators reportedly argued that it was possible that the infection resulted from deliberate spread of the disease. Investigators for the Centers for Disease Control looked into the cases in January, 1998, contended that the organism could only survive in the open for one day. Thus, they apparently believed that it was unlikely that other members of the staff could have become ill if the exposure were accidental during the move. Accordingly, CDC recommended that the hospital refer the case to the state's attorney general's office for further investigation. Apparently, the FBI also was brought into the case.[990]

A review of the case by the hospital's insurance company, American International Group, suggested, however, that there was "no demonstrable evidence to support a case of intentional conduct." Relying on advice from Dr. Leonard Mermel of Brown University and Dr. Donald Goldman of Harvard Medical School, the insurance investigator concluded that shigella can in fact live for days on dry surfaces and months in water. Moreover, the investigator noted that both of the technicians claimed that none of the vials was opened during the move, suggesting that the spread was accidental not intentional.[991]

***Case 1997-02: "Middle East" Terrorists in Ames, Iowa, February 1997***

On March 3 and 4, 1997, Steve Quayle, a survivalist who broadcasts a shortwave radio show known as "Blueprint for Survival," told his listeners that some Middle East terrorists posing as veterinary students at

---

[982] Tom Zoellner, "Urban Legend: Death-Drug Rumor Discredited, Cops Can Arrest Easier," *Salt Lake Tribune*, February 6, 1998, p. A1, as found at *http://archive1.sltrib.com*.

[983] Tom Godfrey, "Warning on Deadly Nerve Agent," *London Free Press* (Ontario, Canada), March 28, 1998, as found at *http://www.canoe.ca/LondonNews*. See also *http://snopes.simplenet.com/spoons/faxlore/ricin.htm* for a discussion of this story by the *Urban Legends Reference Pages*.

[984] Alan Cowell, "The Daring Attack that Blew Up in Israel's Face," *New York Times*, October 15, 1997, pp.. A1, A6.

[985] See, for example, the article that appeared in an Amman, Jordan, newspaper soon after the attack: "Paper Links Toxic Ricin to Mish'al Assassination Attempt," *al-Ra'y* (Arabic), September 30, 1997, pp. 1, 17, as translated by the Foreign Broadcast Information Service (FBIS) and retrieved from its World Wide Web site.

[986] Richard Saltus, "N.H. hospital probes bacteria outbreak," *Boston Globe*, December 3, 1997, p. B5.

[987] This account is based on "Investigation finds shigella outbreak at Dartmouth not Deliberate," *Associated Press*, April 22, 1998, 13:58 report, as found on the Boston Globe World Wide Web site, *http://www.boston.com/dailynews*.

[988] Richard Saltus, "N.H. hospital probes bacteria outbreak," *Boston Globe*, December 3, 1997, p. B5.

[989] Richard Saltus, "N.H. hospital probes bacteria outbreak," *Boston Globe*, December 3, 1997, p. B5.

[990] This account is based on "Investigation finds shigella outbreak at Dartmouth not Deliberate," *Associated Press*, April 22, 1998, 13:58 report, as found on the Boston Globe World Wide Web site, *http://www.boston.com/dailynews*.

[991] This account is based on "Investigation finds shigella outbreak at Dartmouth not Deliberate," *Associated Press*, April 22, 1998, 13:58 report, as found on the Boston Globe World Wide Web site, *http://www.boston.com/dailynews*.

Iowa State University had been arrested by government agents on February 1997.[992] According to Quayle, the alleged terrorists were in possession of seven vials containing anthrax, along with equipment needed to disseminate the agent into the air. Quayle told a journalist with the Ames *Daily Tribune* that the Federal Emergency Management Agency sent 48,000 doses of anthrax vaccine to Iowa. He also claimed that the story was first reported during a February 28 C-SPAN broadcast of a congressional hearing, although the subject was never mentioned at that hearing. Ultimately, a reporter who investigated the story believes that it may have originated with an article written by an official at the Iowa Department of Public Health that described a fictional biological attack on Des Moines, Iowa.

***Case 1989-02: The Breeders, November 1989***

In November 1989, a group calling itself the "Breeders" claimed that it was releasing fertile Mediterranean fruit flies (Medflies) in southern California. In a letter sent to Los Angeles Mayor Tom Bradley, other government officials, and several newspapers, the group claimed that it brought fertile Medflies into the region "and started breeding them here." Furthermore, the group said, "State officials have probably noticed an increased as well as an unusual distribution of Medfly infestation in Los Angeles County since March, 1989." The letter demanded a halt to aerial pesticide spraying or the group would release additional Medflies.[993] According to the letter, the Breeders planned to "make the Medfly 'problem' unmanageable and aerial spraying politically and financially intolerable." The group also stated that they could be reached with advertisements in the *Los Angeles Times*, but that "we are under no obligation to reply, and our position is absolutely non-negotiable. Every time the copters go up to spray, we'll go into virgin territory or old Medfly problem areas and release a minimum of several thousand blue-eyed Medflies. We are organized, patient and determined.[994]

The claim was given credence by an expert's panel convened on December 6, 1989. A U.S. Department of Agriculture (USDA) researcher asserted, "There are some peculiar things happening." The experts noted that they were able to identify few Medfly larvae, that most of the Medflies trapped were females, and that the Medflies were found in only one of three types of traps used to detect infestations. Moreover, many of the Medflies were trapped just outside previously sprayed areas. Nevertheless, the panel concluded, "We don't see any hard evidence [that the letter writer] has the wherewithal to do what he has threatened." The Chairman of the panel, an expert of the Medfly who worked for the USDA, concluded, "I have no explanation for it, except this may be just a string of improbable events."[995]

The letter was turned over to the Los Angeles Police's Criminal Conspiracy Section. The FBI also became involved in the investigation. An effort was made to contact the writer of the letter. The USDA inserted a classified ad in the *Los Angeles Times* with the following language: "Breeders if you're for real send one of your little friends. We want to talk. Call John at USDA."[996] It is not known if any reply was received.

This case is not included in the main list because it does not fit the definition for a biological agent used in this study.

***Case 1973-02: Naples cholera outbreak, 1973***

In a list of "C/B Incidents," Douglass and Livingstone include an episode, dated November 1974, described in the following terms: "Forty-eight people, including the head of the Naples Port Authority, tried on charges arising from a 1973 cholera outbreak."[997]

According to press accounts, however, the cholera outbreak resulted from contaminated mussels. Government officials were prosecuted for negligence in permitting mussels to be harvested from beds located in waters polluted by sewage.[998]

---

[992] "Anthrax in Iowa? There Just Isn't Any," *Omaha World Herald*, March 9, 1997, p. 1B.

[993] Stephanie Chavez and Richard Simon, "Mystery Letter Puts a Strange Twist on Latest Medfly Crisis," *Los Angeles Times*, December 3, 1988, p. B1 (Orange County edition).

[994] Ashley Dunn, "Officials Advertise to Contact Mystery Group Claiming Medfly Releases," *Los Angeles Times*, February 10, 1990, p. 3B.

[995] John Johnson, "Invasion of Pesky Medfly Defies Logic, Scientists Say," *Los Angeles Times*, December 30, 1989, p. B6.

[996] Ashley Dunn, "Officials Advertise to Contact Mystery Group Claiming Medfly Releases," *Los Angeles Times*, February 10, 1990, p. 3B.

[997] Douglass and Livingstone, *America the Vulnerable*, p. 183.

[998] "City officials in Naples sent to jail," *Times* (London), July 10, 1976, p. 4.

***Case 1970-02: CIA (against Cuba), March 1970***

On several occasions, the government of Cuba has alleged that it was the victim of biological warfare operations conducted by the United States. These allegations must be put in the context of the broader conflict between the United States and Cuba. On the one hand, there is a history of attempts by the United States to assassinate Cuban leaders and to destabilize the communist regime there.[999] On the other hand, Cuba is alleged by the United States to have an offensive biological weapons program (see page 29). This suggests that Cuba could be making these allegations to divert attention from its own activities.

In 1971, Cuba experienced a massive outbreak of African hog fever, which they claim was caused by the United States. According to Cuban estimates, nearly 500,000 hogs had to be killed as a result. The Cubans also assert, "According to the consensus of competent specialists who investigated the facts, there is no explanation for the epidemic except sabotage."[1000] The Cuban version of this event is reflected in one history of U.S. covert actions against Cuba, which recounts the following story. In March 1970, an anticommunist terrorist organization allegedly received a vial of "African swine fever virus" from a U.S. intelligence agent. According to this account, the virus was taken by a fishing boat to Navassa Island, and was then transferred to Cuba. The account continues, "Six weeks later Cuba suffered the first outbreak of the swine fever in the Western Hemisphere; pig herds were decimated, causing a serious shortage of pork, the nation's dietary staple."[1001]

In 1980, Cuba experienced a large outbreak of dengue fever. Cuban officials claim that an anti-Castro group known as Omega-7 was responsible for introducing mosquitoes into Cuba carrying the dengue virus. The Cubans further allege, "It is a well-known fact that no counterrevolutionary group has access to bacteriological weapons, which require not only special handling but also special knowledge and treatment, and that only the CIA or the U.S. Department of Defense can engage in thus type of action with White House approval."[1002] According to Cuban officials, 158 people were killed during the outbreak, including 101 children.[1003]

Dengue is a viral disease endemic to South Asia, Southeast Asia, Latin America, and the Pacific region. It affects mainly children. Recent outbreaks have occurred in Brazil, Columbia, Cuba, French Guiana, Nicaragua, Puerto Rico, Suriname, and Venezuela. A 1987 outbreak in Vietnam affected a reported 370,000 people. If not properly treated, fatality rates can reach 40–50 per cent. With appropriate treatment, the fatality rate drops to only 1–2 per cent.[1004]

When hemorrhagic conjunctivitis appeared in Cuba in 1981, the regime also alleged that the United States was responsible for its introduction. Indeed, the Cuban press asserted that an outbreak of the same disease that also appeared in Suriname could have been caused by the United States as well, "In order to justify its presence [the disease's presence] in the region and later introduce it into Cuba."[1005]

In May 1997, the Cuban government aired allegations that the United States deliberately spread thrips palmi, an insect that infects plants. According to the Cuban account, the United States flew a crop duster operated by the State Department over Cuba, and released the insects. The United States has denied the allegation. While U.S. agricultural experts discount the Cuban allegations, the United Nations has undertaken an investigation of the Cuban claims.[1006]

---

[999] For an example of this type of activity, see the assassination plots against Castro described on page 103.

[1000] *Havana International Service*, May 31, 1984, as translated from the Spanish in Foreign Broadcast Information Service, *Daily Report: Latin America*, June 4, 1984, p. Q2.

[1001] Warren Hinckle and William Turner, *Deadly Secrets: The CIA-Mafia War Against Castro and the Assassination of J.F.K.* (New York: Thunder's Mouth Press, 1992), p. 349.

[1002] *Havana International Service*, September 13, 1984, as translated from the Spanish in Foreign Broadcast Information Service, *Daily Report: Latin America*, September 14, 1984, p. Q6.

[1003] *Havana International Service*, September 12, 1984, as translated from the Spanish in Foreign Broadcast Information Service, *Daily Report: Latin America*, September 13, 1984, p. Q3, and *Havana International Service*, September 13, 1984, as translated from the Spanish in Foreign Broadcast Information Service, *Daily Report: Latin America*, September 14, 1984, pp. Q5-6.

[1004] Abram S. Benenson, editor, *Control of Communicable Diseases Manual*, Sixteenth edition (Washington, DC: American Public Health Association, 1995), pp. 131-133.

[1005] *Havana Domestic Service*, September 9, 1981, as translated from the Spanish in Foreign Broadcast Information Service, *Daily Report: Latin America*, September 11, 1981, p. Q1.

[1006] Craig Turner, "Cuba Accuses U.S. of Waging Bug Warfare," *Los Angeles Times*, August 26, 1997, p. A21, "Cuba Accuses U.S. of 'biological aggression'," *Reuters*, May 5, 1997, Havana *Tele Rebelde* and *Cubavision* Networks, 14 May 97, translated from the Spanish by Foreign Broadcast Information Service, May 14, 1997, as available at *http://fbis.fedworld.gov*.

***Case 1960-03X: Minutemen, date uncertain (1964-1969?)***

Robert DePugh, who founded the right-wing Minutemen organization, once discussed possible use of biological agents with a reporter. The journalist, J. Harry Jones, Jr., who followed the activities of the Minutemen for many years and interviewed DePugh on many occasions, gave the following account of this interview.

> I have not talked with him [DePugh] at length yet without his quite calmly and unexpectedly volunteering some incidental tidbit designed to alarm or chill me. While discussing the relative likelihood of nuclear or bacteriological warfare being used against the United States, DePugh, who regarded the latter as the more logical prospect, wrinkled his brow and with seeming seriousness said. "Do you realize that I could kill everyone in the United States except myself if I wanted to?"
>
> "Oh? How?"
>
> He explained he could do this with a virus developed in his own Biolab Corporation laboratory, a veterinary drug firm he heads in Norbonne, Missouri. After immunizing himself against it, he said, he could spread it throughout the country merely by coughing on enough outbound passengers at Kansas City's Municipal Air Terminal. In two weeks, DePugh said, everyone else in the nation would be dead.[1007]

Jones does not date the interview, and clearly did not take the statements seriously. Significantly, Jones provides no indication in his history of the Minutemen that DePugh ever attempted to develop a biological, or even that he considered acquisition of such a capability. Nor is there any reason to believe that DePugh's company had the capability to undertake the kinds of research that he discussed.

DePugh was arrested for his activities involving the Minutemen, and served three years in federal prison. He was arrested in September 1991 on charges of sexual exploitation of a minor. According to law enforcement officials, he was found to have taken nude pictures of young girls, ages 10 to 15, while pretending to be a fashion model.[1008] Following these allegations, DePugh was indicted by a federal grand jury on several weapons-related charges. Among the weapons he allegedly possessed were an 81mm mortar, a machinegun, handguns, rifles, rocket propellant, and antiaircraft ammunition. A jury convicted him on three of the four weapons charges on February 20, 1992.[1009]

***Case 1963-01: KGB (against Hugh Gaitskell), 1963***

Douglass and Livingstone claim that the British Labour leader, Hugh Gaitskell, was murdered by the Soviets in 1963. They allege that the food served to him during a function held "at the Soviet embassy" was contaminated with an unspecified biological agent that led to "an unusual illness and death."[1010]

Peter Wright, a former MI5 (British internal security) official who was involved in the investigation of Gaitskell's death, provides the following account of the incident.[1011] Wright knew the labor leader personally, and had heard about a month before Gaitskell's death about a trip that the labor leader planned to take to the Soviet Union.[1012] After Gaitskell died, Wright claims that MI5 was contacted by one of his

---

[1007] J. Harry Jones, Jr., *A Private Army* (Toronto, Canada: Collier Books, 1969), pp. 17-18. Jones was a correspondent for the Kansas City *Star* who closely followed the activities of the Minutemen from 1964. DePugh made similar statements to other journalists. He told one reporter that his group had "a number of our own physicians and bacteriologists working on the production of biological agents.... Most of this research goes on after hours in public and private institutions where they hold a regular job during the day and have an opportunity to moonlight a few hours in the evening on their own." He also told this reporter that his group was working on seven biological agents, and that they had undertaken "the selective breeding of various pathogens to increase or decrease their virulence and render them resistant to antibiotics." See Eric Norden, "The Paramilitary Right," Playboy Magazine, June 1969, pp. 103-104, 146, 242-246, as quoted in Milton Leitenberg, *Biological Weapons Arms Control*, Project on Rethinking Arms Control, Center for International and Security Studies at Maryland School of Public Affairs, University of Maryland at College Park, PRAC Paper No. 16, May 1996, pp. 52-53.

[1008] Bill Norton, "Head of rightist army charged in sex case," *Kansas City Star*, September 14, 1991, Diane Carroll and John T. Dauner, "Snapshots taken at area inn: Man who faces sex charge photographed girls in Independence," *Kansas City Star*, September 20, 1991, and Bill Norton and Joe Stephens, "DePugh: A trail of trusts betrayed, Failed businesses leave towns in a state of shock," *Kansas City Star*, September 20, 1991, as they appear on the newspaper's web site, *http://www.kcstar.com*.

[1009] John T. Dauner, "Grand jury indicts ex-leader of ultraright group," *Kansas City Star*, October 8, 1991, and Tom Jackman, "DePugh convicted on gun charges, Jury not swayed by testimony of son that the weapons were his," *Kansas City Star*, February 21, 1992, as they appear on the newspaper's web site, *http://www.kcstar.com*.

[1010] Douglass and Livingstone, *America the Vulnerable*, p. 85.

[1011] Peter Wright with Paul Greengrass, *Spy Catcher: The Candid Autobiography of a Senior Intelligence Officer* (New York: Viking, 1987), pp. 362-363.

[1012] According to press reports at the time, Gaitskell never took the Russia trip Wright mentions. See "Mr. Gaitskell puts off Moscow visit," *Times* (London), December 27, 1962, p. 6.

physicians, who had concerns about the manner of his death. The doctor told MI5 that Gaitskell died from what Wright calls "lupus disseminata," which the doctor told MI5 rarely appears in temperate regions. Based on this information, Wright met with a medical officer at Porton Down. According to this expert the cause of lupus was not known, some people thought that a fungus might be involved, and he had no notion about how someone might be infected with the disease.

MI5 also received a report from a high level KGB defector who had interactions with colleagues who worked for Department 13, which was responsible for assassinations (known as "wet affairs" to the Soviets). This defector had learned that the KGB intended to assassinate a senior West European politician so that someone favorable to the Soviet Union could take charge. This information naturally increased British suspicions that Gaitskell had been murdered, given that many officials in MI5 were hostile towards Gaitskell's Labour party successor, Harold Wilson.[1013]

The British asked for assistance from the CIA. According to Wright, the CIA discovered that one (and only one) scientific paper had appeared in the Soviet Union about lupus. It showed how a particular chemical (which Wright does not name, but other sources indicate was hydralazine) could produce lupus symptoms in rats, but only with enormous doses. Wright claims that this information ended the investigation. However, MI5 fruitlessly continued looking for additional cases of lupus among people who might be Soviet targets for several years thereafter.[1014]

Other sources pinpoint additional suspicious indications. According to one account, allegedly based on information provided by Wright, Gaitskell visited the Soviet consulate to apply for a visa for his upcoming visit to the Soviet Union. There was a lengthy delay in dealing with his application. While waiting for his meeting, Gaitskell was served coffee and biscuits. This account asserts that it was after this visit that Gaitskell became seriously ill.[1015]

Other accounts cast doubt on Wright's story. According to Walter Somerville, who was Gaitskell's consulting physician, the Labor leader did not die of Lupus. An autopsy failed to find any evidence of Lupus. Somerville reportedly told one investigator, "It was a condition like Lupus. What he actually had was what we call an immune complex deficiency. His immune system broke down as the cells degenerated." However, Somerville also recalled, "Somebody close to Gaitskell told me they feared a pill may have been dropped in his coffee while on a visit to Poland. They hadn't seen this happen—they were speculating … I don't know if somebody who had been with Gaitskell told MI5." Somerville denied that either he or the chief medical officer at the hospital where Gaitskell was treated ever approached MI5 about the case.[1016]

Wright interviewed Somerville after receiving the CIA-supplied article on hydralazine. Somerville cast doubt on the poisoning theory, noting that hydralazine was commercially available for the treatment of hypertension. Furthermore, "I told them there was nothing new in what they were saying. The side-effects of hydralazine had been well-known in the West for ten years." He also told Wright that to poison Gaitskell with hydralazine would have required repeated doses of the drug given over an extended period.[1017]

It also appears that others in MI5 were less inclined than Wright to believe that Gaitskell had been killed. Arthur Martin, who headed the Soviet counterintelligence branch of MI5, talked to a virus specialist familiar with Soviet research on Lupus, who totally discounted the possibility that the Soviets might have some poison capable of producing the disease.[1018]

Gaitskell's biographer, Philip Williams, provided the most thorough account of this episode. Based on wide ranging interviews, Williams determined that Gaitskell complained of "rheumatic pains" in early 1962 that made it difficult for him to work in the garden. On June 13, he blacked out. During the rest of the summer he was extremely fatigued, and by the fall was no longer able to drive because of shoulder pains. On December 7, he told friends that he was ill and had "picked something up in Paris." His condition deteriorated, and he

---

[1013] There are conflicting accounts of the role played by this defector, Anatoli Golitsin. For an account by someone highly skeptical of both Golitsin and his CIA and MI5 handlers, see David Leigh, *The Wilson Plot* (New York: Pantheon Books, 1988), pp. 79-86.

[1014] Wright, *Spy Catcher*, p. 363. Chapman Pincher, *Their Trade is Treachery* (New York: Bantam Books, 1982), p. 78, however, claims that the CIA discovered three articles. Pincher gives a slightly different spin on the subject. He writes, "Soviet medical researchers had published three academic papers describing how they had produced a drug that, when administered, reproduced the fatal heart and kidney symptoms." Leigh, *The Wilson Plot*, p. 82, claims that Wright was the source of Pincher's account.

[1015] Pincher, *Their Trade is Treachery*, p. 77.

[1016] As quoted in Leigh, *The Wilson Plot*, p. 82. Gaitskell arrived in Poland on August 31, 1962 and left on September 6, 1962, after meeting with the prime minister, foreign minister, and first secretary of the communist party. See, "Poles anxious, Mr. Gaitskell says," *Times* (London), September 6, 1962, p. 5, and "Mr. Gaitskell arrives in Poland," *Times* (London), September 1, 1962, p. 5.

[1017] As quoted in Leigh, *The Wilson Plot*, p. 85.

[1018] Leigh, *The Wilson Plot*, p. 83.

entered the hospital on December 15. He had a relapse soon after leaving the hospital on December 23, and was readmitted. Thus, it is evident that the condition that ultimately killed him did not suddenly appear after his visit to Poland in September or to the Soviet consulate in December.[1019]

Following publication of Wright's account, *The Times* (London) asked some poison experts (which it did not name) about the possibility that Gaitskell was poisoned by the Soviets during a trip to Poland. The newspaper identified hydralazine, a chemical used to treat high blood pressure, as the chemical known to induce symptoms similar to those of Systemic Lupus Erythematosus (SLE), the disease that killed Gaitskell. Based on its research, however, the newspaper concluded that "a single large dose of hydralazine causes vomiting, drowsiness and collapse, so that it would be a very risky way of murdering a visiting politician." Other chemicals capable of causing symptoms similar to SLE were also considered unlikely.[1020]

A review of this material suggests that it is unlikely that Gaitskell was murdered. Even if he was, however, there is no evidence to suggest that a biological agent was involved.

---

[1019] Philip M. Williams, *Hugh Gaitskell: A Political Biography* (London: Jonathan Cape, 1979), pp. 759-763.

[1020] "Red herring," *Times* (London), November 17, 1988, p. 15.

# Appendix A:
# List of Cases

| Case Number | Page | Perpetrator | Action | Date | Agents Involved | Type | Included in cases analyzed |
|---|---|---|---|---|---|---|---|
| **I. A.** | | **Confirmed Use** | | | | | |
| 1997-06 | 42 | New Zealand farmers | Illegal spreading of rabbit hemorrhagic disease virus in New Zealand. | August 1997 | Rabbit hemorrhagic disease (RHD) | Criminal | YES: Overwhelming evidence to support intentional introduction of prohibited pathogen. |
| 1996-05 | 43 | Diane Thompson | Used Shigella taken from a hospital laboratory to infect co-workers. | October 1996 | *Shigella* | Criminal | YES: Thompson pled guilty to the charges. |
| 1995-02 | 45 | Debora Green, MD | Poisoned husband with ricin. | August 1995 | Ricin | Criminal | YES: Perpetrator convicted. |
| 1994-04 | 47 | Richard J. Schmidt | Accused of injecting a former girlfriend with HIV-infected blood. | August 1994 | HIV | Criminal | YES: Convicted in jury trial. |
| 1993-03 | 47 | "Iwan E." | Accused of injecting lover with HIV-contaminated blood. | June 1993 | HIV | Criminal | YES: Convicted by Dutch judge. |
| 1992-05 | 76 | Brian T. Stewart | Deliberately injected his own son with HIV-contaminated blood. | February 1992 | HIV | Criminal | YES: Convicted in jury trial. |
| 1990-01 | 47 | Aum Shinrikyo | Allegedly attempted to use botulinum toxin and anthrax. | April 1990-March 1995 | *Bacillus anthracis*, Botulinum toxin, and other pathogens | Terrorist | YES: Numerous press reports, but no official indictment on these allegations. |
| 1984-02 | 50 | Rajneeshees | Used biological agent to make townspeople ill as test for plot to take over community. | August-September 1984 | *Salmonella typhimurium* | Terrorist | YES: Two members of group convicted in both state and federal courts for participation in plot. Other members admitted to participation, but never tried. |
| 1981-02 | 58 | "Dark Harvest" | Spread anthrax-contaminated soil to send political message. | October 1981 | *Bacillus anthracis* | Terrorist | YES: Press reports suggest that anthrax was found in at least one sample of dirt consistent with soil found on Gruinard Island. |
| 1978-04 | 58 | Bulgarian Secret Police | Attempt to assassinate Bulgarian dissident Georgi Markov. | September 1978 | Ricin | State | NO: State action. Official statements at time of incident support theory of Bulgarian use of ricin. Former KGB officials admit involvement in case. Subsequent reports consistent with original account. |
| 1978-03 | 60 | Bulgarian Secret Police | Attempt to assassinate Bulgarian defector Vladimir Kostov. | August 1978 | Ricin | State | NO: State action. Official statements at the time support the theory of Bulgarian use of ricin. Subsequent reports consistent with original account. |
| 1977-02M | 60 | Arnfinn Nesset | Convicted of using curacit, a curare derivative. | May 1977-November 1980 | *Curacit* | Criminal | NO: Medical case, although convicted of murdering 22 people by a Norwegian court. |
| 1970-01 | 61 | Eric Kranz, Ph.D. | Used animal parasite to infect roommates. | February 1970 | *Ascaris suum* | Criminal | YES: Defendant indicted and brought to trial for alleged use of parasite to |

| Case Number | Page | Perpetrator | Action | Date | Agents Involved | Type | Included in cases analyzed |
|---|---|---|---|---|---|---|---|
| | | | | | | | harm his roommates. |
| 1964-01 | 61 | Mitsuru Suzuki, MD | Physician used shigella and dysentery to infect up to 200 people. | December 1964-March 1966 | *Salmonella typhi* and *Shigella* | Criminal | YES: Defendant indicted and brought to trial for alleged use of pathogens. |
| 1952-02 | 63 | Mau Mau | Use of plant toxin to kill livestock. | 1950s | Toxin: African milk bush (*Synadenium grantii)* | Terrorist | YES: Confirmed by scientific studies of the incident. |
| 1939-01 | 65 | Kikuko Hirose | Contaminated pastry used to infect 12 people. | April 1939 | *S. typhi and S. paratyphi* | Criminal | YES: Accused convicted by Japanese court. |
| 1936-01 | 65 | Tei-Seburo Takahashi | Infected 17 people, killing 3, using food contaminated with *S. typhi.* | March 1936-November 1936 | *S. typhi* | Criminal | YES: Convicted by a Japanese court and sentenced to death. |
| 1933-01 | 65 | Benoyendra Chandra Pandey | Use of plague to murder. | November 1933 | *Yersinia pestis* | Criminal | YES: Defendants convicted in court of the offense. |
| 1932-01 | 67 | Japanese military | Fruit infected with cholera fed to League of Nations commission investigating the take over of Manchuria. | April-June 1932 | cholera | State | NO: State action. Statement by member of Japanese Imperial family is the primary source of the information, reflecting a document written by him in the 1940s. |
| 1916-01 | 67 | Arthur Warren Waite | Used various biological agents to murder in-laws. | 1916 | Various | Criminal | YES: Convicted of murder and executed. |
| 1915-01 | 69 | German intelligence | Sabotage operations conducted by German intelligence in neutral countries to kill animals being shipped to Allied countries or being used to support Allied operations. | 1915-1917 | Glanders (*Burkholderia mallei)* and *Bacillus anthracis* | State | NO: State action. Overwhelming evidence of these activities. |
| 1913-01 | 71 | Karl Hopf | Infected third wife with typhus-contaminated food. Acquired cholera for same purpose. Also probably killed first two wives and parents using arsenic. May have used *M. bovis* to kill two step-children | 1913 | *S. typhi*<br>*M. bovis?* | Criminal | YES: Convicted by German court for attempting to murder wife. Sentenced to death for other murders involving arsenic. |
| 1912-1 | 71 | Henri Girard | Used *Salmonella typhi* and poisonous mushrooms to murder people to get death benefits from life insurance policies. Killed two people. | 1912-1918 | *Salmonella typhi* and poisonous mushrooms | Criminal | YES: Girard died before trial. He allegedly admitted to crimes. Co-conspirators were convicted. |
| 1910-01 | 73 | O'Brien de Lacy and Vladimir Pantchenko | Use of diphtheria toxin to murder O'Brien de Lacy's brother-in-law. | 1910 | Diphtheria toxin and cholera endotoxin | Criminal | YES: Defendants convicted in Russian court for murder. |
| **I. B.** | | **Probable or Possible Use** | | | | | |
| 1994-03M | 76 | Orville Lynn Majors | Accused of murdering six hospital | 1994-1995 | Possibly | Criminal | NO: Medical case. Unclear that Majors |

| Case Number | Page | Perpetrator | Action | Date | Agents Involved | Type | Included in cases analyzed |
|---|---|---|---|---|---|---|---|
| | | | patients, but could be responsible for as many as 100 deaths. In addition to use of potassium chloride, press accounts allege that he may have employed epinephrine (adrenaline). | | epinephrine (adrenaline) in addition to potassium chloride. | | used biological agent; not yet convicted of any murders. |
| 1993-04 | 76 | Animal Liberation Front | Claimed to have put HIV into a bomb | 1993 | HIV | Terrorist | YES: ??? |
| 1992-06 | 76 | Marilyn Tan | Accused of injecting Con Boland with HIV-contaminated blood | 1992 | HIV | Criminal | NO: Judge acquitted Tan. |
| 1990-05X | 77 | Unidentified woman | Suicide attempt using HIV-infected blood | 1990? | HIV | Criminal | NO: As a suicide does not meet the case definition. |
| 1990-02 | 77 | Giardia in Scotland | Feces containing giardia put into apartment building water tank in Edinburgh | June 1990 | Giardia | Criminal | NO: No evidence that perpetrator knew that his actions would cause a disease outbreak. |
| 1989-04M | 77 | Efren Saldivar | Allegedly poisoned patients, including using morphine (a toxin) | 1989-1998 | Morphine | Criminal | NO: Medical case also allegations still under investigation and alleged perpetrator not formally charged with any crimes. |
| 1989-03 | 77 | Civilian Cooperation Bureau, Republic of South Africa | Allegedly contaminated water supply in refugee camp in Namibia | 1989 | Cholera, Yellow fever virus | State | NO: State action. No confirmation of this specific incident, but additional details about efforts to acquire biological materials for use in similar types of activities revealed in hearings by Truth and Reconciliation Commission. |
| 1988-01 | 78 | Unknown | Colonel Jean-Claude Paul, one-time commander of the elite Dessalines Battalion, was murdered by an unspecified poison. | November 6, 1988 | Unknown | Unknown | NO: Insufficient evidence to identify the type of poison involved. May have been a chemical. |
| 1987-01 | 79 | David Acer, DDS | Dentist infected with HIV either deliberately or accidentally infected six patients with HIV | December 1987-1990 | HIV | Criminal | NO: Never officially confirmed that Acer deliberately infected his patients. |
| 1985-02 | 80 | Unidentified Mexican workers | Allegedly spread parasite to protect jobs in screwworm eradication program. | 1985? | Screwworm | Criminal | NO: Only a single source, and account suggests perpetrators were never formally charged. |
| 1981-01 | 80 | Unknown | One-time double agent for CIA (Boris Korczak) allegedly attacked with contaminated pellet similar to one used against Markov and Kostov | September 1981 | Ricin? | State? | NO: Alleged state action. Medical accounts confirm that something happened to Korczak. |
| 1970-04X | 82 | Additional East Bloc bioassassinations | Numerous reported instances of assassination attempts using toxins | 1970s-1980s | Unknown | State | NO: Insufficient information. |
| 1979-02 | 83 | Zimbabwe terrorists | White government of Rhodesia claims that terrorists have spread anthrax, possibly killing 20 people. | November 1979 | *Bacillus anthracis* | Terrorist | NO: Insufficient information to support allegations. |

| Case Number | Page | Perpetrator | Action | Date | Agents Involved | Type | Included in cases analyzed |
|---|---|---|---|---|---|---|---|
| 1976-02 | 83 | Rhodesian Central Intelligence Organization | Allegations that the former government of Rhodesia deliberately spread anthrax and cholera in predominantly guerilla-controlled areas. | 1976-1980 | *Bacillus anthracis* | State | NO: Insufficient information to support allegations. |
| 1971-01 | 84 | KGB | Reported attempt to assassinate Alexander Solzhenitsyn using toxin-contaminated salve | August 1971 | Claimed to be ricin | State | NO: State action. Evidence marginal, but appears to originate with former KGB officials involved in the incident. |
| 1969-01 | 84 | John R. Hill. MD | Allegedly murdered wife with biological agents | 1969 | Probable multiple unknown | Criminal | NO: Insufficient evidence to support allegations of bioagent use. |
| 1966-01M | 86 | Mario Jascalevich, MD | Allegedly murdered patients at a hospital. | 1966 | Tubocurarine, a curare component. | Criminal | NO: Medical case plus no conviction in case. |
| 1961-01 | 86 | "J.L." | Hepatitis A virus contaminates food served at officer's mess | October 1961 | Hepatitis A virus | Criminal | NO: No evidence that perpetrator knowingly caused the outbreak. |
| 1957-01 | 86 | Brazilian Indian Protection Service (SPI), | Used of biological agents against aborigines in a campaign of genocide | 1957-1965 | Multiple | State | NO: Available information suggests that confirmed dissemination methods do not meet case definition. |
| 1949-01 | 87 | Toshima Hospital Outbreak | Allegation that unnamed intern contaminated food infecting 20 people | November 1949 | *S. Typhi* | Criminal | NO: Case never prosecuted, apparently due to lack of evidence. |
| 1947-01 | 87 | "Zionist" terrorists | Allegations that Jewish groups used cholera and other agents against Egypt and Syria | November 1947-May 1948 | *V. cholerae*, *S. typhi*, "dysentery" | Terrorist/ State | NO: Insufficient evidence on most credible part of allegations. |
| 1942-02 | 88 | Polish resistance | Use of pathogens to infect German soldiers during World War Two | December 1942-September 1943 | *Salmonella typhi* | Terrorist | NO: Insufficient information |
| 1942-01 | 89 | British intelligence (SOE) and Czech resistance | Allegation that botulinum was used in assassination attempt against Richard Heydrich | May 1942 | Botulinum toxin | State | NO: Available evidence does not support claim that botulinum toxin was used. |
| 1940-01X | 89 | Egyptian "gangster" | Used stolen S. typhi culture to murder victims in insurance scam | 1940s? | *S. typhi* | Criminal | NO: Insufficient information on incident. |
| 1930-02X | 90 | German doctor | Attempted to commit suicide by giving himself an injection of tetanus toxin | About 1930 | Tetanus toxin | Criminal | NO: Insufficient information to confirm that the case occurred as reported. |
| 1930-01X | 90 | "Hungarian artist" | Attempted to kill wife. | About 1930 | *V. cholerae* and *S. typhi* | Criminal | NO: Insufficient information to confirm that case occurred as reported. |
| 1917-01 | 90 | Unknown German sympathizers | Allegation that supplies of court plaster, used to cover wounds, were contaminated with tetanus by | July 1917 | Tetanus | Unknown | NO: Available evidence does not support claim that material was deliberately infected. |

| Case Number | Page | Perpetrator | Action | Date | Agents Involved | Type | Included in cases analyzed |
|---|---|---|---|---|---|---|---|
| | | | German agents. | | | | |
| 1910-02X | 90 | Pancho Villa | Alleged use of botulinum toxin to attack Federal troops during Mexican revolution | 1910s | Botulinum toxin | Terrorist | NO: Insufficient information. |
| 1909-01 | 91 | B. Clarke Hyde | Allegedly infected as many as 10 people with typhoid to cover up use of poisons. | November 1909 | *Salmonella typhi* | Criminal | NO: Suspect never convicted of alleged actions, despite three trials. |
| 1900-01X | 93 | Deaths in Malawi | Use of castor beans (containing ricin) to kill unwanted children. | Unknown | Ricin | Criminal | NO: Insufficient details of cases to permit analysis. |
| **II. A.** | **Threatened Use (Confirmed Possession)** | | | | | | |
| 1998-06 | 95 | Iraqi terrorism | Claimed plans by Iraq to use biological agents against UK | March 1998 | *B. anthracis* | State | NO: Insufficient information. |
| 1997-01 | 95 | Thomas Leahy | Possession of toxins with apparent intent to use them as weapons | January 1997 | Ricin and nicotine | Criminal | YES: Convicted in U.S. federal court. |
| 1996-04 | 98 | Michael Just, Ph.D. | Attempted extortion directed at British dairies | May 1996 | *Yersinia enterocolitica* | Criminal | YES: Defendants convicted in British courts. |
| 1993-05 | 99 | Dwayne Kuehl | Planned to use ricin to murder building inspector | March or May 1993 | Ricin | Criminal | YES: Defendant admitted to plot |
| 1992-03 | 99 | Minnesota Patriots Council | Planned use of ricin toxin to murder law enforcement officials | May 1992 | Ricin | Terrorist | YES: Several defendants convicted in federal court. |
| 1990-03 | 100 | Iraqi Terrorism | Claimed plans by Iraq to use biological agents in terrorism attacks at time of Gulf War crisis | August 1990-February 1991 | Unknown | State | NO: Insufficient information. |
| 1984-03 | 101 | Kevin T. Birch and James B. Cahoon | Use of pathogens to kill race horses | November 1984 | *Clostridium botulinum, and Clostridium tetani* | Criminal | YES: Defendants convicted in U.S. federal courts. |
| 1972-01 | 102 | RISE | Planned use of S. typhi to contaminate water systems | January 1972 | *Salmonella typhi* | Terrorist | YES: One defendant pled guilty to the offense. |
| 1960-02 | 103 | CIA | Plot to kill Lumumba | September 1960 | Unknown | State | NO: State action. Confirmed by official U.S. account. |
| 1960-01 | 103 | CIA | Multiple plots to kill Castro | 1960-1961 | Botulinum toxin | State | NO: State action. Confirmed by official U.S. account. |
| 1952-01 | 103 | MGB | Plot to assassinate Tito | Late 1952 | Plague | State | YES: Confirmed by official records. |
| 1944-01 | 104 | British SOE | Plot to assassinate Hitler | June 1944 | Anthrax | State | YES: Confirmed by official records. |
| **II. B.** | | **Threatened Use (No Confirmed Possession)** | | | | | |
| 2000-08 | 105 | Unknown | Two potteries threatened with biological agent | June 2000 | Unknown | Unknown | YES: Apparent threat intended to make people believe that they were subjected to biological attack. |
| 2000-07 | 105 | Unknown | Internet hoax involving supposed pathogen known as Klingerman virus | May 2000 | Nonexistent | Unknown | YES: People apparently believed in the existence of the danger, which led to |

| Case Number | Page | Perpetrator | Action | Date | Agents Involved | Type | Included in cases analyzed |
|---|---|---|---|---|---|---|---|
| | | | pathogen known as Klingerman virus | | | | real responses. |
| 1999-66 | 105 | James Kenneth Gluck | Threatened ricin use | September 1999 | Ricin | Criminal | YES: Made threat and apparently explored production of ricin. |
| 1999-77 | 106 | Diazien Hossencofft | Threatened to provide virus to China | September 1999 | Unknown virus | Criminal | YES: Perpetrator clearly wanted people to believe that he was capable of producing material in question |
| 1999-76 | 106 | Unknown | Threats against robbery victims with allegedly HIV contaminated syringes | August 1999 | Claimed HIV | Criminal | YES: Perpetrator intended robbery victims to believed HIV was present. |
| 1999-64 | 106 | World Islamic Front for Fighting Jews and Christians | Threatened use of biological agents against Israeli and U.S. targets | April 1999 | Unknown | Terrorist | YES: Intention to convince West that biological agents could be used. |
| 1999-71 | 107 | Chechens | Threats to obtain and use biological agents, coupled with Russian claims that Chechens possess agents | February 1999 | Claimed biological agents | Terrorists | YES: Multiple claims of possession or interest coupled with explicit threat to obtain and use. |
| 1999-68 | 107 | Unknown | Claim that milk was contaminated with biological agent | March 1999 | Unknown | Unknown | YES: Investigated by U.S. government agencies. |
| 1999-70 | 107 | Unknown Croatian thief | Robbery victims threatened with allegedly HIV contaminated syringe | January 1999 | Claimed HIV | Criminal | YES: Perpetrator intended victims to believe HIV was present. |
| 1999-75 | | Unnamed Christian Millenarian groups | Unspecified threats to use biological weapons in Israel | Throughout 1999 | Claimed acquisition of unspecified biologicals | Terrorist | NO: Despite claimed concern by U.S. government intelligence organizations, only one source available. |
| 1998-31 | 108 | Unknown | HIV threat against meat packing company | December 1998 | Claimed HIV | Unknown | YES: No agent used, but perpetrator intended recipients to believe HIV was present. |
| 1998-10 | 108 | Republic of Texas: Johnnie Wise, Jack Abbott Grebe, and Oliver Dean Emigh | Threatened to use biological agents against federal officials | June 1998 | Unknown | Terrorist | YES: Threat confirmed, even if no evidence of agent possession. |
| 1998-50 | 110 | Lawrence A. Maltz | Unspecified biological threats | April 1998 | Unknown | Criminal | YES: Threatened to use biological agents, although there is no evidence of possession. |
| 1998-34 | 108 | Unknown | Someone deliberately spread rumors that meat was contaminated with HIV | April 1998 | HIV | Criminal | YES: Effort to make people think that an actual incident occurred. |
| 1998-08 | 108 | Palestine Islamic Jihad | Threatened to use biological weapons against Israel | April 1998 | Unknown | Terrorist | NO: Insufficient evidence. |
| 1997-12 | 111 | Unknown | Extortion attempt involving claim that products of a bottling plant were contaminated with a biological agent. | March 1997 | Unknown | Criminal | YES: Threat ultimately assessed as a hoax, but perpetrator identified and convicted. |
| 1997-10 | 110 | Unknown | Threat against the water systems of 36 U.S. cities | July 1997 | Anthrax and botulinum toxin | Terrorist | YES: Threats ultimately deemed not credible, but were initially taken seriously by government officials in |

| Case Number | Page | Perpetrator | Action | Date | Agents Involved | Type | Included in cases analyzed |
|---|---|---|---|---|---|---|---|
| | | | | | | | threatened cities. Actual source of threat is unclear. |
| 1997-04 | 110 | PKK (Kurdish terrorist group) | Allegation that group was considering use of biological agents. | August 1997 | *E. coli* and *C. botulinum* | Terrorist | NO: All reporting from one source of uncertain reliability. |
| 1997-05 | 110 | Counter Holocaust Lobbyists of Hillel | False claim that anthrax was sent to B'nai B'rith headquarters in Washington, D.C. | April 1997 | *Bacillus cereus*, but claimed *Bacillus anthracis* | Terrorist | YES: Considerable publicity of event, but no prosecution. |
| 1996-03 | 111 | Tokiyuki Asaoka | Extortion attempt | August 1996 | Claimed *E. coli* | Criminal | YES: Only one press account, but based on official report. |
| 1996-07 | 112 | Hiroaki Chiku | Extortion attempt | August 1996 | Claimed *E. coli* | Criminal | NO: Case confirmed by Japanese police, but information received too late to be incorporated into analysis. |
| 1996-08 | 112 | Justice Department | Claimed that razor blades found in envelopes contained in letters were covered with HIV-infected blood | March 1996 | Claimed HIV | Terrorist | YES: Perpetrators wanted recipients to believe HIV was present. |
| 1996-01 | 112 | German Blackmailers | Extortion attempt | January 1996 | Claimed Snake venom | Criminal | YES: Multiple press accounts citing German police sources. |
| 1995-06 | 113 | Biological agent threats against Latin American cities | Threats | April 1995 | Claimed cholera, typhoid, malaria, and yellow fever | Terrorist | NO: Only a single source. |
| 1995-05 | 113 | Frank Riolfo | Extortion attempt | October 1995 | Claimed HIV | Criminal | YES: Defendant convicted in British court. |
| 1995-04 | 113 | Barry Dixon | Extortion attempt | November 1995 | Claimed *Bacillus cereus* | Criminal | YES: Defendant convicted in British court. |
| 1994-02 | 113 | Michael Norman and Alexander Taylor | Extortion attempt | January 1994 | Claimed HIV | Criminal | YES: Defendant convicted in British court. |
| 1994-01 | 114 | Animal Liberation Front | Mailing hypodermic needles allegedly contaminated with HIV | January 1994 | Claimed HIV | Terrorist | NO: Insufficient information. Incident not included on Animal Liberation Front list of its activities. |
| 1992-04 | 114 | "The Terminator" | Extortion attempt | September 1992 | Claimed HIV | Criminal | YES: Press reports only, but based on official reports. |
| 1992-01 | 114 | Animal Aid Association | Claim that food bars were infected with HIV | January 1992 | Claimed HIV | Terrorist | NO: Insufficient information. Incident not included on Animal Liberation Front list of animal rights terrorist activities. |
| 1991-02 | 114 | Threat against Kelowna, British Columbia water supply | Claim that water supply of Kelowna, BC was contaminated by a biological material | January 1991 | Unknown | Terrorist | NO: More information needed. |
| 1989-01 | 114 | Robin Smith | Extortion attempt | May 1989 | Claimed HIV | Criminal | YES: Defendant convicted by court. |

| Case Number | Page | Perpetrator | Action | Date | Agents Involved | Type | Included in cases analyzed |
|---|---|---|---|---|---|---|---|
| 1984-01 | 115 | Peter Vivian Wardrop | Prison inmate tries to force Queensland, Australia, authorities into instituting prison reform | January 1984 | Claimed hoof and mouth disease | Criminal | YES: Press coverage of incident cites official statements. |
| 1983-01 | 115 | Montgomery Todd Meeks | Attempted to acquire ricin to murder father | October 1983 | Ricin | Criminal | YES: Press reports indicate perpetrator convicted. |
| 1982-01 | 116 | William Chanslor | Attempted to acquire ricin to murder wife | April 1982 | Ricin | Criminal | YES: Press reports perpetrator convicted. |
| 1980-02X | 117 | Tamil guerrillas | Threat to use biological agents against Sinhalese and crops in Sri Lanka by Tamil group | 1983-1987? | Claimed *Schistosoma* worms, Yellow fever, Leaf Curl (against rubber plants), and unspecified agent against tea bushes | Terrorist | NO: Only one source of information on incident. |
| 1970-05X | 118 | Red Army Faction | Variety of claims of interest in biological agents | 1970s | Claimed *Bacillus anthracis* | Terrorist | NO: Insufficient information. |
| 1979-01 | 119 | Aliens of America | Threatened to contaminate U.S. consulate in Munich with Legionnaires disease, | July 1979 | Legionnaires | Terrorist | NO: Insufficient information. |
| 1978-02 | 119 | Tucson extortionist | Threatened to spread plague-infected fleas in Tucson, Arizona unless an extortion payment was made. | September 1978 | *Yersinia pestis* | Criminal | YES: Press reports cite official statements regarding incident. |
| 1978-01 | 120 | Tucson extortionist | Threatened to contaminate Tucson, Arizona water supply with typhoid unless extortion was made. | April 1978 | Typhoid | Criminal | YES: Press reports cite official statements regarding incident. |
| 1977-03 | 120 | Unknown | Claim that someone had discovered a bacteria that could contaminate water of nuclear-armed nations, | March 1977 | Unknown pathogen | Terrorist? | NO: Insufficient information. |
| 1977-01 | 120 | Extortionist | Unnamed extortionist threatened to contaminate Miami city water supply with botulinum toxin. | 1977 | Botulinum toxin | Criminal | NO: Insufficient information. |
| 1976-01 | 121 | Stephen Grant Morton | Threat to spread pathogen-containing ticks through the mails | June 1976 | Unspecified | Criminal | YES: Substantial press coverage citing official statements. Suspect arrested. |
| 1975-01 | 121 | Polisario | Explored using biological agents to contaminate water systems in major cities. | February 1975 | Cholera | Terrorist | No: Insufficient information. |
| 1974-03 | 121 | Middle East firm | Allegedly sought bacteria to contaminate Jordan River. | 1974 | Unknown | Terrorist | NO: Insufficient information. |
| 1974-02 | 122 | Legion of Nabbil Kadduri Usur | Threat to release bacteria if demands not met. | 1974 | Unknown | Terrorist | NO: Insufficient information. |

| Case Number | Page | Perpetrator | Action | Date | Agents Involved | Type | Included in cases analyzed |
|---|---|---|---|---|---|---|---|
| 1973-01 | 122 | German "mad scientist" | Threat to use botulinum toxin and anthrax against targets in Germany | November 1973 | Claimed *Bacillus anthracis* and botulinum toxin | Uncertain (either terrorist or criminal) | YES: Substantial press coverage, but evidence admittedly marginal. |
| 1970-06X | 122 | Poisoner of Los Angeles water supply | Threat to poison Los Angeles water supply with biological poison | No date | Unspecified | Uncertain (either terrorist or criminal) | NO: Insufficient information. |
| **II. C.** | | **Threatened Use (Anthrax hoaxes)** | | | | | |
| 2000-10 | 122 | Unknown | Anthrax threat against Cape Coral Industrial Park | November 2000 | Claimed *B. anthracis* | Unknown | YES: Perpetrator intended recipients to believe anthrax was present. |
| 2000-09 | 123 | Unnamed 19-year-old | Falsely identified jar | September 2000 | Claimed *B. anthracis* | None | YES: Perpetrator intended recipients to believe anthrax was present. |
| 2000-06 | 123 | Unknown | Anthrax threat against University of Pennsylvania Hillel | April 2000 | Claimed *B. anthracis* | Unknown | YES: Perpetrator intended recipients to believe anthrax was present. |
| 2000-05 | 123 | Unknown | Anthrax hoax at U.S. Post Office mailbox | March 2000 | Claimed *B. anthracis* | Unknown | YES: Perpetrator intended recipients to believe anthrax was present. |
| 2000-04 | 123 | Unknown | Threat against IRS Service Center in Utah treated as anthrax threat | | Claimed *B. anthracis* | Unknown | YES: Perpetrator intended recipients to believe anthrax was present. |
| 2000-03 | 123 | Student | Anthrax threat against Fredonia High School in New York state | | Claimed *B. anthracis* | Criminal | YES: Perpetrator intended recipients to believe anthrax was present. |
| 2000-02 | 123 | Micky A. Sauer | Anthrax threat against targets in Wisconsin | January 2000 | Claimed *B. anthracis* | Criminal | YES: Perpetrator intended recipients to believe anthrax was present. |
| 2000-01 | 123 | Unknown | Anthrax threat against abortion clinics in 21 states and District of Columbia | January 2000 | Claimed *B. anthracis* | Terrorist | YES: Perpetrator intended recipients to believe anthrax was present. |
| 1999-59 | 122 | Unknown | Anthrax threat against Bedford North Lawrence High School | December 1999 | Claimed *B. anthracis* | Unknown | YES: Perpetrator intended recipients to believe anthrax was present. |
| 1999-62 | 122 | Unidentified juvenile | Anthrax threat against Fredonia High School | November 1999 | Claimed *B. anthracis* | Criminal | YES: Perpetrator intended recipients to believe anthrax was present. |
| 1999-55 | 124 | Unknown | Anthrax threat against Department of Energy processing plant | November 1999 | Claimed *B. anthracis* | Unknown | YES: Perpetrator intended recipients to believe anthrax was present. |
| 1999-78 | 124 | Unknown | Anthrax threat against financial services office | October 1999 | Claimed *B. anthracis* | Unknown | YES: |
| 1999-53 | 105 | Unknown | Anthrax threat against Kentucky Educational Television in Lexington, Kentucky | October 1999 | Claimed *B. anthracis* | Unknown | YES: Perpetrator intended recipients to believe anthrax was present. |
| 1999-52 | 125 | Unknown | Anthrax threat against U.S. Post Office in Robinson, Pennsylvania | September 1999 | Claimed *B. anthracis* | Unknown | YES: Perpetrator intended recipients to believe anthrax was present. |

| Case Number | Page | Perpetrator | Action | Date | Agents Involved | Type | Included in cases analyzed |
|---|---|---|---|---|---|---|---|
| 1999-54 | 125 | Unknown | Anthrax threat against Truman Library | August 1999 | Claimed *B. anthracis* | Unknown | YES: Perpetrator intended recipients to believe anthrax was present. |
| 1999-60 | 125 | Unknown | Anthrax threat against Internet service provider in Seattle, Washington | August 1999 | Claimed *B. anthracis* | Unknown | YES: Perpetrator intended recipients to believe anthrax was present. |
| 1999-57 | 105 | Unknown | Anthrax threat against Proctor and Gamble | August 1999 | Claimed *B. anthracis* | Unknown | YES: Perpetrator intended recipients to believe anthrax was present. |
| 1999-56 | 125 | Unknown | Anthrax threat against grocery store | July 1999 | Claimed *B. anthracis* | Unknown | YES: Perpetrator intended recipients to believe anthrax was present. |
| 1999-58 | 125 | Unknown | Anthrax threat against Planned Parenthood office | July 1999 | Claimed *B. anthracis* | Unknown | YES: Perpetrator intended recipients to believe anthrax was present. |
| 1999-42 | 137 | Unknown | Anthrax threat against two Nassau County, New York, courthouses | June 1999 | Claimed *B. anthracis* | Unknown | YES: Perpetrator intended recipients to believe anthrax was present. |
| 1999-45 | 105 | Unknown | Two Planned Parenthood clinics in Cincinnati, Ohio, received anthrax threat letters | June 1999 | Claimed *B. anthracis* | Unknown | YES: Perpetrator intended recipients to believe anthrax was present. |
| 1999-51 | 105 | Unknown | Anthrax threat letters sent to Jesuit college and Catholic high school | May 1999 | Anthrax | Unknown | YES: Perpetrator intended recipient to believe anthrax was present. |
| 1999-41 | 126 | Unknown | Anthrax threat against Mentor, Ohio, high school | May 1999? | Claimed *B. anthracis* | Unknown | YES: Perpetrator intended recipients to believe anthrax was present. |
| 1999-38 | 126 | Unknown | Anthrax threat against Madison, Tennessee, library | May 1999 | Claimed *B. anthracis* | Unknown | YES: Perpetrator intended recipients to believe anthrax was present. |
| 1999-37 | 127 | Dead man | Anthrax hoax in Brooklyn, New York | May 1999 | Claimed *B. anthracis* | Unknown | YES: Perpetrator intended recipients to believe anthrax was present. |
| 1999-40 | 127 | Unknown | Anthrax threat against Sharonville, Ohio, anti-pornography group | April 1999 | Claimed *B. anthracis* | Unknown | YES: Perpetrator intended recipients to believe anthrax was present. |
| 1999-61 | 127 | Unknown | Anthrax threat against offices of Blackfeet tribal council | April 1999 | Claimed *B. anthracis* | Unknown | YES: Perpetrator intended recipients to believe anthrax was present. |
| 1999-36 | 127 | Unknown | Anthrax hoax against Lake Worth, Florida, law firm: powder in letter suspected of being anthrax | May 1999 | Suspected *B. anthracis* | Unknown | YES: It appears that perpetrator wanted recipient to believe that the powder was a dangerous substance. |
| 1999-35 | 127 | Unknown | Anthrax threat against Intel Corporation | April 1999 | Claimed *B. anthracis* | Unknown | YES: Perpetrator intended recipients to believe anthrax was present. |
| 1999-27 | 127 | Unknown | Anthrax threat against Dunkirk High School in New York | April 1999 | Claimed B. anthracis | Unknown | YES: Perpetrator intended recipients to believe anthrax was present. |
| 1999-34 | 127 | Two pranksters | Milk jugs labeled "anthrax" | April 1999 | Claimed *B. anthracis* | Unknown | YES: Perpetrators intended recipients to believe anthrax was present. |
| 1999-33 | 128 | Unknown | Suspicions that package was an anthrax threat | April 1999 | Claimed *B. anthracis* | Unknown | YES: Unclear whether the package was an anthrax hoax or not. |
| 1999-49 | 128 | Unknown | Suspected hazardous materials threat at Kansas City, Missouri, IRS | April 1999 | Anthrax | Unknown | NO: No evidence that anyone actually intended to threaten or imply a threat of |

| Case Number | Page | Perpetrator | Action | Date | Agents Involved | Type | Included in cases analyzed |
|---|---|---|---|---|---|---|---|
| | | | Service Center treated as potential anthrax threat | | | | biological agents. |
| 1999-48 | 128 | Unknown | Anthrax threat against Harrison County Courthouse, Biloxi, Mississippi | April 1999 | Anthrax | Unknown | YES: Perpetrator intended recipients to believe anthrax was present. |
| 1999-47 | 128 | Unknown | Anthrax threat letter sent to house in Lewisville, Texas | March 1999 | Anthrax | Unknown | YES: Perpetrator intended recipient to believe anthrax present. |
| 1999-65 | 106 | Unknown | Anthrax hoax at Hamburg Senior High School | March 1999 | Claimed *B. anthracis* | Unknown | YES: Perpetrator intended recipients to believe anthrax was present. |
| 1999-32 | 107 | | Woman put vials labeled anthrax and Ebola in brother's jacket, creating incident at Pittsburgh International Airport | March 1999 | Claimed *B. anthracis* and *Ebola* | Hoax | YES: Perpetrator intended recipient to believe anthrax and Ebola were present. |
| 1999-31 | 129 | Unknown | Offices of Southern Baptist Convention in Nashville, Tennessee, sent anthrax threat | March 1999 | Claimed *B. anthracis* | Unknown | YES: Perpetrator intended recipients to believe anthrax was present. |
| 1999-30 | 129 | Unknown | Anthrax threat against Lumberton, North Carolina, dialysis clinic | March 1999 | Claimed *B. anthracis* | Unknown | YES: Perpetrator intended recipients to believe anthrax was present. |
| 1999-28 | 129 | Unknown | Anthrax threat against offices of Latter-Day Saints in Salt Lake City, Utah | March 1999 | Claimed *B. anthracis* | Unknown | YES: Perpetrator intended recipients to believe anthrax was present. |
| 1999-26 | 105 | Unknown | Suspected anthrax threat against Planned Parenthood clinic in Chicago, Illinois | March 1999 | Claimed *B. anthracis* | Unknown | NO: Press reports do not indicate if an actual threat was included in the package. |
| 1999-29 | 129 | Unknown | Anthrax threat against Blanca, Colorado, town officials | February 1999 | Claimed *B. anthracis* | Unknown | YES: Perpetrator intended recipients to believe anthrax was present. |
| 1999-25 | 129 | Unknown | Anthrax threat against Department of Motor Vehicles office in Honolulu, Hawaii | February 1999 | Claimed *B. anthracis* | Unknown | YES: Perpetrator intended recipients to believe anthrax was present. |
| 1999-24 | 130 | Unknown | Letters threatening congressional offices with chemical and biological weapons | February 1999 | Unspecified | Unknown | YES: Perpetrators clearly wanted to threaten use of biological weapons. |
| 1999-23 | 130 | Unknown | Anthrax threat in Gwinnett County, Georgia | February 1999 | Claimed *B. anthracis* | Unknown | YES: Perpetrator intended recipients to believe anthrax was present. |
| 1999-22 | 130 | Unknown | Anthrax hoax at Spring Hills, Florida, car wash: someone left a milk bottle labeled "anthrax" | February 1999 | Claimed *B. anthracis* | Unknown | YES: Perpetrator intended someone to believe anthrax was present. |
| 1999-21 | 130 | Unknown | A package with powder was discovered at the loading dock of the U.S. Court of Appeals, Atlanta, Georgia | February 1999 | Suspected B. *anthracis* | Unknown | NO: Press reports do not indicate whether or not the incident involved a threat, or whether it was just a suspected threat. |
| 1999-20 | 131 | Unknown | Anthrax threats against 30+ abortion | February | Claimed *B.* | Unknown | YES: Perpetrator intended recipients to |

| Case Number | Page | Perpetrator | Action | Date | Agents Involved | Type | Included in cases analyzed |
|---|---|---|---|---|---|---|---|
| | | | clinics | 1999 | *anthracis* | | believe anthrax was present. |
| 1999-19 | 133 | Unknown | Terrorist group in Yemen makes anthrax threat | February 1999 | Claimed *B. anthracis* | Unknown | YES: Perpetrator intended recipients to believe anthrax was present. |
| 1999-18 | 134 | Unknown | Anthrax threat against *Los Angeles Times* | February 1999 | Claimed *B. anthracis* | Unknown | YES: Perpetrator intended recipients to believe anthrax was present. |
| 1999-17 | 134 | Unknown | Anthrax threat against State Department | February 1999 | Claimed *B. anthracis* | Unknown | YES: Perpetrator intended recipients to believe anthrax was present. |
| 1999-16 | 134 | Unknown | Anthrax threat against multiple targets, including government and press offices | February 1999 | Claimed *B. anthracis* | Unknown | YES: Perpetrator intended recipients to believe anthrax was present. |
| 1999-15 | 134 | Unknown | Anthrax threat against school in East Aurora, New York | February 1999 | Claimed *B. anthracis* | Student | YES: Perpetrator intended recipients to believe anthrax was present. |
| 1999-14 | 134 | Unknown | Anthrax threat against Lackawanna, New York, school | February 1999 | Claimed *B. anthracis* | Students | YES: Perpetrator intended recipients to believe anthrax was present. |
| 1999-13 | 135 | Unknown | Anthrax threat against school in Cattaraugus County, New York | February 1999 | Claimed *B. anthracis* | Students | YES: Perpetrator intended recipients to believe anthrax was present. |
| 1999-12 | 105 | Unknown | Anthrax threat against business in Alden, New York | January 1999 | Claimed *B. anthracis* | Unknown | YES: Perpetrator intended recipients to believe anthrax was present. |
| 1999-11 | 135 | Unknown | Anthrax threat against grocery store in East Aurora, New York | January 1999 | Claimed *B. anthracis* | Unknown | YES: Perpetrator intended recipients to believe anthrax was present. |
| 1999-10 | 135 | Two students | Anthrax threat mailed to Buffalo, New York, high school | January 1999 | Claimed *B. anthracis* | Criminal | YES: Perpetrator intended recipients to believe anthrax was present. |
| 1999-09 | 135 | Unknown | Anthrax threat called into West Seneca, New York, town hall | January 1999 | Claimed *B. anthracis* | Unknown | YES: Perpetrator intended recipients to believe anthrax was present. |
| 1999-08 | 135 | High school student | Anthrax threat sent to Erie County, New York, middle school | January 1999 | Claimed *B. anthracis* | Criminal | YES: Perpetrator intended recipients to believe anthrax was present. |
| 1999-07 | 136 | Unknown | Anthrax threat against Sierra Madre hospital | January 1999 | Claimed *B. anthracis* | Criminal | YES: Perpetrator intended recipients to believe anthrax was present. |
| 1999-06 | 136 | Unknown | Anthrax threat against Riverside, California, Pizza Hut | January 1999 | Claimed *B. anthracis* | Unknown | YES: Perpetrator intended recipients to believe anthrax was present. |
| 1999-05 | 136 | Unknown | Anthrax threat against U.S. Attorney's Office in Buffalo, New York | January 1999 | Claimed *B. anthracis* | Unknown | YES: Perpetrator intended recipients to believe anthrax was present. |
| 1999-04 | 136 | Unknown | Anthrax threat against Cathedral City, California, Target store | January 1999 | Claimed *B. anthracis* | Unknown | YES: Perpetrator intended recipients to believe anthrax was present. |
| 1999-03 | 137 | Unknown | Anthrax threat against U.S. Attorney's Office in Rochester, New York | January 1999 | Claimed *B. anthracis* | Unknown | YES: Perpetrator intended recipients to believe anthrax was present. |
| 1999-02 | 105 | Unknown | Anthrax threat against Oregon library | January 1999 | Claimed *B. anthracis* | Unknown | YES: Perpetrator intended recipients to believe anthrax was present. |
| 1999-44 | 137 | Unknown | Anthrax threat against auto | January 1999 | Claimed *B.* | Unknown | YES: Perpetrator intended recipients to |

| Case Number | Page | Perpetrator | Action | Date | Agents Involved | Type | Included in cases analyzed |
|---|---|---|---|---|---|---|---|
| | | | dealership in Los Angeles, California | | *anthracis* | | believe anthrax was present. |
| 1999-43 | 137 | Unknown | Anthrax threat against Ocala Regional Medical Center | January 1999 | Claimed *B. anthracis* | Unknown | YES: Perpetrator intended recipients to believe anthrax was present. |
| 1999-50 | 105 | Unknown | Vial marked anthrax found on sidewalk | January 1999 | Anthrax | Unknown | YES: Perpetrator intended recipient to believe anthrax was present. |
| 1999-01 | 137 | Unknown | Anthrax threat against Orange County High School | January 1999 | Claimed *B. anthracis* | Unknown | YES: Perpetrator intended recipients to believe anthrax was present. |
| 1999-39 | 138 | Unknown | Anthrax threat against Wal-Mart in California | January 1999 | Claimed *B. anthracis* | Unknown | YES: Perpetrator intended recipients to believe anthrax was present. |
| 31998-49 | 107 | Unknown | Anthrax threat against woman in Amarillo, Texas | October 1998 | Claimed *B. anthracis* | Unknown | YES: Perpetrator intended recipients to believe anthrax was present. |
| 1998-48 | 147 | Unknown | Anthrax threat against Catholic Church in Cheektowaga, California | November 1998 | Claimed *B. anthracis* | Unknown | YES: Perpetrator intended recipients to believe anthrax was present. |
| 1998-45 | 107 | Unknown | Anthrax threat at San Diego, California, hotel | August 1998 | Claimed *B. anthracis* | Unknown | YES: Perpetrator intended recipients to believe anthrax was present. |
| 1998-44 | 105 | Unknown | Anthrax threat against U.S. Attorney's office, Rochester, New York | December 1998 | Claimed *B. anthracis* | Unknown | YES: Perpetrator intended recipients to believe anthrax was present. |
| 1998-43 | 138 | Unknown | Anthrax threat against Newark, California, shipping company | December 1998 | Claimed *B. anthracis* | Unknown | YES: Perpetrator intended recipients to believe anthrax was present. |
| 1998-42 | 138 | Unknown | Anthrax threat against grocery stores in Palmdale, California | December 1998 | Claimed *B. anthracis* | Unknown | YES: Perpetrator intended recipients to believe anthrax was present. |
| 1998-41 | 138 | Unknown | Anthrax threat against Wal-Mart in La Quinta, California | December 1998 | Claimed *B. anthracis* | Unknown | YES: Perpetrator intended recipients to believe anthrax was present. |
| 1998-40 | 105 | Unknown | Anthrax threat against California department store | December 1998 | Claimed *B. anthracis* | Unknown | YES: Perpetrator intended recipients to believe anthrax was present. |
| 1998-38 | 139 | Unknown | Anthrax threat against California dance club | December 1998 | Claimed *B. anthracis* | Unknown | YES: Perpetrator intended recipients to believe anthrax was present. |
| 1998-37 | 139 | Unknown | Anthrax threat against California office building | December 1998 | Claimed *B. anthracis* | Unknown | YES: Perpetrator intended recipients to believe anthrax was present. |
| 1998-36 | 105 | Unknown | Anthrax threat against Van Nuys courthouses | December 1998 | Claimed *B. anthracis* | Unknown | YES: Perpetrator intended recipients to believe anthrax was present. |
| 1998-35 | 140 | Unknown | Anthrax threat against federal courthouse | December 1998 | Claimed *B. anthracis* | Unknown | YES: Perpetrator intended recipients to believe anthrax was present. |
| 1998-33 | 140 | Unknown | Anthrax threat against ex-wife | December 1998 | Claimed *B. anthracis* | Criminal | YES: Perpetrator intended recipients to believe anthrax was present. |
| 1998-32 | 140 | Unknown | Anthrax threat against employees of California school district | December 1998 | Claimed *B. anthracis* | Unknown | YES: Perpetrator intended recipients to believe anthrax was present. |
| 1998-30 | 108 | Unknown | Teacher received towelette allegedly containing anthrax | October 1998 | Claimed *B. anthracis* | Unknown | YES: No biological agent present, but perpetrator intended recipients to believe anthrax was present. May be |

| Case Number | Page | Perpetrator | Action | Date | Agents Involved | Type | Included in cases analyzed |
|---|---|---|---|---|---|---|---|
| | | | | | | | related to case 1998-13. |
| 1998-29 | 140 | Unknown | Anthrax threat at Coppell, Texas, postal facility | November 1998 | Claimed *B. anthracis* | Unknown | YES: No biological agent present, but perpetrator intended recipients to believe anthrax was present. |
| 1998-28 | 141 | Unknown | Anthrax threat against anti-abortion activist in Twin Peaks, California | November 1998 | Claimed *B. anthracis* | Unknown | YES: No biological agent present, but perpetrator intended recipients to believe anthrax was present. |
| 1998-27 | 141 | Unknown | Anthrax threat discovered at Pembroke Pines, Florida, post office | November 1998 | Claimed *B. anthracis* | Unknown | YES: No biological agent present, but perpetrator intended recipients to believe anthrax was present. |
| 1998-26 | 141 | Unknown | Anthrax threat against school in Virginia Beach, Virginia | November 1998 | Claimed *B. anthracis* | Unknown | YES: No biological agent present, but perpetrator intended recipients to believe anthrax was present. |
| 1998-25 | 141 | Unknown | Anthrax threat against antiabortion activist in Chesapeake, Virginia | November 1998 | Claimed *B. anthracis* | Unknown | YES: No biological agent present, but perpetrator intended recipients to believe anthrax was present. |
| 1998-24 | 141 | Unknown | Anthrax threat against Miami Beach, Florida, magazine | November 1998 | Claimed *B. anthracis* | Unknown | YES: No biological agent present, but perpetrator intended recipients to believe anthrax was present. |
| 1998-23 | 142 | Two students | Anthrax threat against Alexandria (Indiana) Middle School | November 1998 | Claimed *B. anthracis* | Criminal | YES: No biological agent present, but perpetrator intended recipients to believe anthrax was present. |
| 1998-22 | 141 | Three students | Anthrax threat against Shelbyville (Indiana) Middle School with envelope purportedly containing anthrax left on a teacher's desk | November 1998 | Claimed *B. anthracis* | Criminal | YES: No biological agent present, but perpetrator intended recipients to believe anthrax was present. |
| 1998-21 | 142 | Unknown | Anthrax threat against courthouse in Bloomington, Indiana | November 1998 | Claimed *B. anthracis* | Unknown | YES: No biological agent present, but perpetrator intended recipients to believe anthrax was present. |
| 1998-20 | 142 | Unknown | Note left at bank mentioning anthrax exposure | November 1998 | Claimed *B. anthracis* | Unknown | YES: No biological agent present, but perpetrator intended recipients to believe anthrax was present. |
| 1998-19 | 143 | Unknown | Letter purportedly containing anthrax sent to Warren Township High School, Indiana | November 1998 | Claimed *B. anthracis* | Unknown | YES: No biological agent present, but perpetrator intended recipients to believe anthrax was present. |
| 1998-18 | 143 | Student | Anthrax threat against high school, Bloomington, Indiana | November 1998 | Claimed *B. anthracis* | Criminal | YES: No biological agent present, but perpetrator intended recipients to believe anthrax was present. |
| 1998-17 | 143 | Unknown | Letter purportedly containing anthrax sent to branch bank in Wal-Mart | November 1998 | Claimed *B. anthracis* | Unknown | YES: No biological agent present, but perpetrator intended recipients to believe anthrax was present. |
| 1998-16 | 143 | Unknown | Letters purportedly containing | November | Claimed *B.* | Terrorist | YES: No evidence of biological agent, |

| Case Number | Page | Perpetrator | Action | Date | Agents Involved | Type | Included in cases analyzed |
|---|---|---|---|---|---|---|---|
| | | | anthrax sent to five locations | 1998 | *anthracis* | | but perpetrator(s) clearly wanted victims to believe anthrax was involved. |
| 1998-14 | 143 | Unknown | Letters allegedly containing anthrax mailed to ten abortion clinics | October 1998 | Claimed *B. anthracis* | Terrorist | YES: No evidence of biological agent, but perpetrator(s) clearly wanted victims to believe anthrax was involved. |
| 1998-13 | 146 | Unknown | Mailed letters allegedly containing anthrax-contaminated moist towelette packages | October 1998 | Claimed *B. anthracis* | Unknown | NO: No evidence of biological agent and no information on motivation of perpetrator. |
| 1998-12 | 143 | Brothers for the Freedom of America | Claimed to have spread anthrax in a state office building | August 1998 | Anthrax | Terrorist | YES: Confirmed by multiple sources, although the identity of the perpetrators still unknown. |
| 1998-03 | 110 | Lawrence Edward Pagnano | Claimed to have put anthrax into letter mailed to collection agency | March 1998 | *B. anthracis* | Criminal | YES: Effort made to make it appear a biological agent was in the letter. |
| 1992-02 | 150 | Henry D. Pierce | Claimed use of anthrax | March 1992 | Claimed *Bacillus anthracis* | Criminal | YES: Press reports only, but based on official reports. |
| **III. A.** | | **Confirmed Possession** | | | | | |
| 1996-02 | 151 | Unknown | Theft of botulinum toxin from university laboratory. Toxin returned to university after publicity over theft. | March 1996 | Botulinum toxin | Criminal | NO: No evidence that the perpetrator even knew that botulinum was in the stolen package. |
| 1995-03 | 151 | Ray W. Mettetal, MD | Contemplated murder using ricin toxin | August 1995 | Ricin | Criminal | YES: Under indictment by U.S. prosecutors. Not yet tried. |
| 1995-01 | 152 | Larry Wayne Harris | Illicitly obtained Yersinia pestis culture | May 1995 | *Yersinia pestis* | Uncertain | YES: No evidence to support intended terrorist intent, but he was convicted of fraud in connection with acquisition of the agent. |
| 1993-02 | 153 | John Gunnar Linner, Ph.D. | Scientist found in possession of several toxins, plus had recipe to make botulinum | April 1991 | Tetrodotoxin and botulinum toxin | Criminal | YES: Alleged perpetrator clearly had interest in poisons, but was never convicted of any criminal offense. |
| 1993-01 | 153 | Thomas Lavy | Arrested for possession of ricin toxin | April 1993 | Ricin | Uncertain | YES: Considerable evidence to support possession of agent, but no evidence to prove intent. |
| **III. B.** | | **Probable or Possible Possession** | | | | | |
| 1998-46 | 154 | PKK | Reportedly in possession of cobra toxin for resale. | June 1998 | Cobra toxin | Terrorist | NO: Only a single source. |
| 1997-03 | 154 | James Dalton Bell | Explored toxins as means to assassinate IRS and other government officials | February 1997 | Botulinum toxin and ricin | Terrorist | YES: Although never tried on these allegations, supporting evidence is contained in court documents. |
| 1996-06 | 156 | Aryan Republican Army | Claimed possession of radiological | September | Unspecified | Terrorist | NO: Insufficient evidence. |

| Case Number | Page | Perpetrator | Action | Date | Agents Involved | Type | Included in cases analyzed |
|---|---|---|---|---|---|---|---|
| | | | isotopes and biological agents | 1997 | | | |
| 1983-02 | 156 | "Two brothers in Massachusetts" | Allegedly possessed ricin | 1983 | Ricin | Criminal | NO: Insufficient information. |
| 1980-01 | 156 | Red Army Faction | Police reportedly raided a safe house in Paris, France, where a laboratory being used to make botulinum toxin | November 1980 | Botulinum toxin | Terrorist | YES: German prosecutor confirmed incident, but details remain scanty. |
| 1945-01 | 157 | DIN (Judgment) | Plot by former Jewish resistance fighters to put biological agents into water supply of major German cities. | 1945 | Unspecified pathogen | Terrorist | NO: Insufficient information to confirm allegation. |
| **IV. A.** | | **Possible Interest in Acquisition (No Known Possession)** | | | | | |
| 1998-11 | 161 | Algeria's Armed Islamic Group (GIA) | Allegedly trying to grow *C. botulinum*, but police only confirm possession of document on how to grow it. | March 1998 | *Botulinum toxin* | Terrorist | YES: Press accounts appear to confirm interest in biological agents. |
| 1998-09 | 161 | North American Militia of Southwestern Michigan | Possessed video tape describing techniques for manufacturing ricin. | March 1998 | *Ricin* | Terrorist | NO: No evidence that group had an serious interest in manufacturing ricin. |
| 1998-04 | 161 | "Amateur scientist" | Attempted acquisition of anthrax | March 1998 | *B. anthracis* | Unknown | NO: Never actually obtained anthrax and no indication of malicious intent. |
| 1998-01 | 162 | John Bernard Koch | FBI feared that he had put chemical or biological agents into bomb | February 1998 | Unknown | Criminal | NO: No evidence that a biological agent was in the bomb, and no evidence of intent to make it appear that a biological agent was involved. |
| 1997-07 | 162 | Osama bin Laden | Claims that terrorist groups lead by Osama bin Laden may be funding construction of chemical and biological warfare facility in Sudan | 1997 | Unknown | Terrorist | YES: Involvement of bin Laden confirmed by U.S. and British intelligence. |
| 1991-03 | 163 | Hamas | Alleged interest in biological weapons | ≈1991 | Unknown | Terrorist | NO: Insufficient evidence to suggest interest in biological rather than chemical agents. |
| 1991-01 | 164 | Doug Gustafson | Contemplated use of ricin | 1991 | Ricin | Criminal | YES: Admitted in interview considering use of ricin. |
| 1985-01 | 164 | Michael Swango, MD | Researched production of ricin and botulinum toxin, and possessed castor beans | 1985 | Ricin | Criminal | YES: Evidence seized in connection with investigation of crimes for which he was convicted. |
| 1980-03X | 166 | East German Stasi training | Provided training in covert employment of biological warfare to Iraqis, Palestinians, and others | 1980s | "anthrax and yellow fever virus" | Terrorist | NO: Insufficient information. Only one account available. |
| 1974-01 | 166 | Symbionese Liberation Army | Possessed book on "Germ Warfare" | January 1974 | Unknown | Terrorist | YES: Press accounts based on information released by law enforcement officials. |

| Case Number | Page | Perpetrator | Action | Date | Agents Involved | Type | Included in cases analyzed |
|---|---|---|---|---|---|---|---|
| 1972-02 | 166 | Middle East terrorist organization | Unnamed organization allegedly established a program to develop chemical and biological warfare agents. | 1972 | Unknown | Terrorist | NO: Insufficient Information. |
| 1970-03 | 166 | Weatherman | Attempted to acquire biological agents from Ft. Detrick | November 1970 | Unknown | Terrorist | YES: Press accounts based on information released by law enforcement officials. |
| 1968-01 | 167 | Arab Pharmaceutical Congress | Advocated training in biological warfare | September 1968 | Unknown | Terrorist? | NO: Insufficient information. |
| **IV. B.** | | **False Cases** | | | | | |
| 1999-67 | 167 | None | Claim that Iraq was planning to spread West Nile Valley virus, and may have been responsible for outbreak in New York City | October 1999 | Alleged West Nile Valley virus | False case | NO: No evidence to support allegation. |
| 1999-73 | 168 | Unknown | Stolen tuberculosis culture | June 1999 | Tuberculosis | Criminal | NO: No evidence that perpetrator even knew tuberculosis was included in stolen material |
| 1999-69 | 168 | Nong Jaew | Thai policemen | June 1999 | Transmission of HIV | Criminal | NO: Transmission means does not meet case definition for inclusion in this study. |
| 1999-63 | 167 | None | Flour used to mark a trail by has Street Harriers incorrectly thought to be anthrax | December 1999 | Suspected *B. anthracis* | False case | NO: No evidence that anyone intended to threaten or use anthrax. |
| 1999-72 | 169 | Manuel Basulto and Miguel Quevedo | Threatened robbery victims with exposure to HIV infected blood | March 1999 | Claimed HIV | Criminal | NO: Dissemination method does not meet case definition for inclusion in the study |
| 1999-46 | 167 | None | Authorities wrongly suspected envelopes of containing anthrax threats | January 1999 | Suspected *B. anthracis* | False case | NO: No evidence that anyone intended to threaten or use anthrax. |
| 1998-39 | 167 | None | Anthrax scare in California hospital | December 1998 | Claimed *B. anthracis* | Unknown | NO: Scare based on patient's ill-founded fears. |
| 1998-15 | 167 | None | Ricin scare in Jacksonville, Florida, when police officials incorrectly suspected that what was originally thought to be cocaine was actually ricin | November 1998 | Suspected ricin | Criminal | NO: No evidence of biological agent. |
| 1998-05 | 110 | None | Canister in rental car labeled "anthrax" in East San Antonio | March 1998 | Claimed *B. anthracis* | Unknown | NO: No evidence of biological agent and no information on motivation of perpetrator. Almost certainly a hoax. |
| 1998-02 | 167 | Larry Wayne Harris and William Leavitt | Allegedly possessed B. anthracis with intention to use as a biological agent | February 1997 | B. anthracis in veterinary vaccine (probably Sterne | Terrorist | NO: U.S. Justice Department dropped case |

| Case Number | Page | Perpetrator | Action | Date | Agents Involved | Type | Included in cases analyzed |
|---|---|---|---|---|---|---|---|
| | | | | | strain) | | |
| 1998-07 | 171 | Drug dealers and ricin | Claims that manufacturers of illicit drugs were contaminating material in their laboratories with ricin to poison law enforcement officials | January 1998 | Ricin | Criminal | NO: No evidence that anyone actually has acquired ricin for this purpose. |
| 1997-09 | 172 | Israeli intelligence | Failed assassination attempt against Hamas activist. | September 1997 | Alleged ricin, but probably Fentanyl, an artificial opiate | State | NO: State action, and no evidence a biological agent was involved. |
| 1997-08 | 172 | None | Fears of deliberate spread of Shigella at Dartmouth-Hitchcock Medical Center | October 1997 | Shigella | Unknown | NO: Investigation strongly indicates accidental contamination. |
| 1997-02 | 172 | "Middle East Terrorists" | Alleged biological agent attack on Ames, Iowa | February 1997 | Claimed *Bacillus anthracis* | Terrorist | NO: No evidence of any attack. |
| 1989-02 | 173 | The Breeders | Alleged release of Medflies in California | November 1989 | Claimed Medflies | Terrorist | NO: Not a biological agent. |
| 1973-02 | 173 | Naples cholera outbreak | Episode involving cholera outbreak in Naples | November 1974 | Claimed Cholera | Unknown | NO: No intentional use of a biological agent evident. |
| 1970-02 | 174 | CIA | Operations against Cuba | March 1970-March 1997 | Claimed African swine flu virus | State | NO: No evidence to support Cuban allegations. |
| 1960-03 | 175 | Minutemen | Claims that group was contemplating use of biological agents | 1964-1969 | Unknown | Terrorist | NO: No evidence to suggest that group had any real interest in biological agents. |
| 1963-01 | 175 | KGB | Allegations that KGB used a biological agent to assassinate Labor leader Hugh Gaitskell | 1963 | Unknown | State | NO: No evidence to support allegation, and likely agent is not biological. |

# Sources

This is a partial listing of the sources consulted in researching this study. Omitted are publications consulted that proved to have no information pertinent to the research. Also ignored are sites on the World Wide Web, except those included through mention of a newspaper consulted by viewing a web site. Many of the newspapers were used through on-line databases, such as NEXIS.

The secondary research was supplemented in a number of cases by primary research. Documents were consulted in several instances, but such material is referenced only in the specific case studies. In addition, people involved in investigating several of the cases were interviewed, and are noted in connection with the specific case study.

## Newspapers

*Advocate* (Baton Rouge, Louisiana)
*Anchorage Daily News*
*Antelope Valley Press* (Palmdale, California)
*Arizona Republic*
*Arizona Daily Star*
*Baltimore Sun*
*Blade* (Toledo, Ohio)
*Boston Globe*
*Brazil Times* (Indiana)
*Brownsville Herald* (Texas)
*Buffalo News*
*Charlotte Observer*
*Chicago Tribune*
*Cincinnati Enquirer*
*Columbian* (Vancouver, Washington)
*Columbus Dispatch* (Ohio)
*Courier-Journal* (Louisville)
*Daily Mail*(London)
*Daily Telegraph* (London)
*Dallas Morning News*
*Democrat and Chronicle* (Rochester, N.Y.)
*Denver Post*
*Deseret News* (Salt Lake City)
*Edmonton Journal*
*Egyptian Gazette* (Cairo)
*Florida Times-Union* (Jacksonville)
*Gazette* (Colorado Springs, Colorado)
*Gazette* (Montreal)
*Financial Times*
*Globe and Mail* (Toronto)
*Guardian* (London)
*Grand Forks Herald* (Minnesota)
*Herald-Times* (Bloomington, Indiana)
*Houston Chronicle*
*Houston Post*
*Independent* (London)
*Indianapolis Star-News*
*International Herald Tribune*
*Japan Times*
*Journal Sentinel* (Milwaukee, Wisconsin)
*Kansas City Star*
*Knoxville News-Sentinel*
*L'Aurore* (Paris)
*Le Figaro* (Paris)
*London Free Press* (Ontario, Canada)
*Los Angeles Times*
*Miami Herald*
*Milwaukee Journal Sentinel*
*New York Herald* (European Edition—Paris)
*New York Times*
*News & Observer* (Raleigh, North Carolina)
*Newsday*
*Omaha World Herald*
*Orange County Register*
*Oregonian* (Portland)
*Orlando Sentinel*
*Philadelphia Inquirer*
*Plain Dealer* (Cleveland)
*Press* (New Zealand)
*Press-Enterprise* (Riverside, California)
*Review-Journal* (Las Vegas)
*Richmond Times*
*Rocky Mountain News* (Denver)
*San Diego Union-Tribune*
*Southland Times* (New Zealand)
*St. Louis Post-Dispatch*
*St. Paul Pioneer Press*
*Salt Lake Tribune*
*San Antonio Express*
*San Diego Union-Tribune*
*San Jose Mercury News*
*Seattle Spokesman-Review*
*Shelbyville News* (Indiana)
*Star of India* (Calcutta)
*Star-Telegram* (Fort Worth, Texas)
*Star Tribune* (Minneapolis-St. Paul)
*Sun* (Las Vegas)
*Sun* (Vancouver)
*Sunday Times* (London)
*Tampa Tribune*

*Tennessean*
*Times* (London)
*Times* (Seattle)
*Tucson Citizen* (Arizona)
*Union-Tribune* (San Diego, California)
*Vancouver Sun*
*Virginian-Pilot* (Norfolk, Virginia)
*Washington Post*
*Washington Times*
*Wichita Eagle* (Kansas)
*Yukon News*

## Wire services, Television

*AAP*
*Agence France Presse*
*Associated Press*
*CNN*
*Deutsche Presse-Agentur*
*Reuters*
*Reuters North European Service*
*United Press International*

## Department of Defense Publications

Defense Science Board, 1997 Summer Study Task Force, *DoD Responses to Transnational Threats*, Volume I: *Final Report*, October 1997, Office of the Under Secretary of Defense for Acquisition and Technology, Washington, D.C.
Joint Publication 1-02, *DOD Dictionary of Military and Associated Terms*
Department of Defense. *Report of the Quadrennial Defense Review*, May 1997.
*Medical Management of Biological Casualties* (Fort Detrick, Frederick, Maryland: U.S. Army Medical Research Institute of Infectious Diseases, March 1996).
National Defense Panel. *Transforming Defense: National Security in the 21st Century*, December 1997.
Office of the Assistant to the Secretary for Nuclear, Biological, and Chemical Matters, and the U.S. Army Chemical and Biological Defense Command. *Assessment of the Impact of Chemical and Biological Weapons on Joint Operations in 2010*, November 1997.
Office of the Secretary of Defense. *Proliferation: Threat and Response*, November 1997.
Frederick R. Sidell, et al. *Medical Aspects of Chemical and Biological Warfare* (Washington, D.C.: Office of the Surgeon General, Department of the Army, 1997).

## Books

Alibek, Ken. *Biohazard* (New York: Random House, 1999).
Andrew, Christopher, and Oleg Gordievsky. *KGB: The Inside Story of its Foreign Operations from Lenin to Gorbachev* (New York: HarperCollins, 1990).
Bar-Zohar, Michael. *The Avengers* (New York: Hawthorn Books, 1967).
Barnaby, Wendy. *The Plague Makers: The Secret World of Biological Warfare* (London: VISION Paperbacks, 1997).
Benenson, Abram S., editor. *Control of Communicable Disease Manual*, 16th edition (Washington, DC: American Public Health Association, 1995).
Brackett, D.W. *Holy Terror: Armageddon in Tokyo* (New York: Weatherhill, 1996).
Burrows, William E., and Robert Windrem. *Critical Mass: The Dangerous Race for Superweapons in a Fragmenting World* (New York: Simon and Shuster, 1994).
Clark, Richard Charles. *Technological Terrorism* (Old Greenwich, Connecticut: Devin-Adair, 1980).
Davis, Shelton H. *Victims of the Miracle: Development and the Indians of Brazil* (New York: Cambridge University Press, 1977).
Davis, Wade. *The Serpent and the Rainbow: A Harvard Scientist's Astonishing Journey into the Secret Societies of Haitian Voodoo, Zombis, and Magic* (New York: A Touchstone Book published by Simon and Shuster, 1997).
Douglass, Jr., Joseph D., and Neil C. Livingstone. *America the Vulnerable: The Threat of Chemical and Biological Warfare* (Lexington, Massachusetts: Lexington Books, D.C. Heath and Company, 1987).
Edgerton, Robert B. *Mau Mau: An African Crucible* (New York: Free Press, 1989).
Elkins, Michael. *Forged in Fury: A true story of courage, horror ... and revenge* (London: Piatkus, 1996).

Ellenhorn, Matthew J., et al., editors. *Ellenhorn's Medical Toxicology: Diagnosis and Treatment of Human Poisoning*, 2nd Edition (Baltimore: Williams & Wilkins, A Waverly Company, 1997).
Ellert, H. *The Rhodesian Front War: Counter-insurgency and guerrilla war in Rhodesia 1962-1980* (Gweru, Zimbabwe: Mambo Press, 1989).
Farber, Myron. *Somebody Is Lying: the Story of Dr. X* (Garden City, N.Y.: Doubleday, 1982).
Foot, M.R.D. *SOE: An outline history of the Special Operations Executive, 1949-1946* (Frederick, Maryland: University Publications of America, 1986).
Gonzales, Thomas A., Morgan Vance, and Milton Helpern. *Legal Medicine and Toxicology* (New York: D. Appleton-Century Company, 1940).
Gunaratna, Rohan. *War and Peace in Sri Lanka* (Sri Lanka: Institute of Fundamental Studies, 1987).
Hall, W. Reginald, and Amos J. Peaslee. *Three Wars with Germany* (New York: G.P. Putnam's Sons, 1944).
Harris, Robert, and Jeremy Paxman. *A Higher Form of Killing: The Secret Story of Chemical and Biological Warfare* (New York: Hill and Wang, 1982).
Hellmann-Rajanayagam, Dagmar. *The Tamil Tigers: Armed Struggle for Identity* (Stuttgart: Franz Steiner Verlag, 1994).
Hickey, Eric W. *Serial Murderers and Their Victims*, 2nd edition (Washington: Wadsworth Publishing Company, 1997).
Hinckle, Warren, and William Turner. *Deadly Secrets: The CIA-Mafia War Against Castro and the Assassination of J.F.K.* (New York: Thunder's Mouth Press, 1992).
Inter-Parliamentary Union Geneva. *What Would Be the Character of a New War* (London: Victor Gollancz, 1933).
Irving, David. *Hitler's War* (New York: Viking Press, 1977).
Jenkins, Brian Michael. *Future Trends in International Terrorism*, RAND Paper P-7139, December 1985
Jenkins, Brian Michael. *The Future Course of International Terrorism*, RAND Paper P-7139, September 1985
Jones, Jr., J. Harry. *A Private Army* (Toronto, Canada: Collier Books, 1969).
Kalugin, Oleg. *The First Directorate* (New York: St. Martin's Press, 1994).
Kaplan, David E. and Andrew Marshall. *The Cult at the End of the World* (New York: Crown Publishers, 1996).
Leigh, David. *The Wilson Plot* (New York: Pantheon Books, 1988).
Leitenberg, Milton. *Biological Weapons Arms Control*, Project on Rethinking Arms Control, Center for International and Security Studies at Maryland School of Public Affairs, University of Maryland at College Park, PRAC Paper No. 16, May 1996.
Lifflander, Matthew. *Final Treatment: The File on Dr. X* (New York: W.W. Norton, 1979).
Livingstone, Neil C. *The War Against Terrorism* (Lexington, Massachusetts: Lexington Books, 1982).
MacDonald, Callum. *The Killing of SS Obergruppenführer Reinhard Heydrich* (New York: Collier Books, Macmillan Publishing Company, 1989).
Mann, John. *Murder, Magic, and Medicine* (New York: Oxford University Press, 1992).
Maloba, Wunyabari O. *Mau Mau and Kenya An Analysis of a Peasant Revolt* (Bloomington: Indiana University Press, 1993).
Nowak, Jan. *Courier from Warsaw* (Detroit: Wayne State University Press, 1982).
O'Ballance, Edgar. *The Cyanide War: Tamil Insurrection in Sri Lanka 1973-88* (Washington: Brassey's (UK), 1989).
Pauw, Jacques. *In the Heart of the Whore: The story of apartheid's death squad*s (Halfway House, South Africa: Southern Book Publishers, 1991).
Pincher, Chapman. *Their Trade is Treachery* (New York: Bantam Books, 1982)
Purver, Ron. *Chemical and Biological Terrorism: The Threat According to the Open Literature*, Canadian Security Intelligence Service, June 1995.
Roberts, Brad, editor. *Terrorism with Chemical and Biological Weapons* (Alexandria, Virginia: Chemical and Biological Arms Control Institute, 1997).
Rom, Mark Carol. *Fatal Extraction: The Story Behind the Florida Dentist Accused of Infecting His Patients with HIV and Poisoning Public Health* (San Francisco: Jossey-Bass Publishers, 1997).
Rothschild, J.H. *Tomorrow's Weapons* (New York: McGraw-Hill, 1964)
Rule, Ann. *Bitter Harvest: A Woman's Fury, A Mother's Sacrifice* (New York: Simon & Schuster, 1997).
Sifakis, Carl. *Encyclopedia of Assassination* (New York: Facts On File, 1991).
Simon, Jeffrey D. *Terrorists and the Potential Use of Biological Weapons: A Discussion of Possibilities*, RAND report R-3771-AFMIC, December 1989.
SIPRI. *The Problem of Chemical and Biological Warfare, Volume I: The Rise of CB Weapons* (New York: The Humanities Press, 1971).

Narayan Swamy, M.R. *Tigers of Lanka, from boys to guerrillas* (Delhi: Konark Publishers, 1994).
Tedeschi, C.G., William G. Eckert, and Luke G. Tedeschi, editors. *Forensic Medicine: A study in trauma and environment, Volume III: Environmental Hazards* (Philadelphia: W. B. Saunders, 1977).
Thompson, C.J.S. *Poisons and Poisoners: With Historical Accounts of Some Famous Mysteries in Ancient and Modern Times* (London: Harold Shaylor, 1940).
Thompson, Thomas. *Blood and Money* (Garden City, New York: Doubleday and Company, 1976).
Triplett, William. *Flowering of the Bamboo* (Kensington, Maryland: Woodbine House, 1985).
Uncle Fester. *Silent Death*, Revised and Expanded 2nd Edition (Port Townsend, Washington: Loompanics Unlimited, 1997).
Verdcourt, Bernard, and E.C. Trump. *Common Poisonous Plants of East Africa* (St. James's Place, London: Collins, 1969).
Williams, Philip M. *Hugh Gaitskell: A Political Biography* (London: Jonathan Cape, 1979).
Wilson, Colin, and Donald Seaman. *The Encyclopedia of Modern Murder 1962–1982* (New York: G.P. Putnam's Sons, 1985).
Watt, John Mitchell, and Maria Gerdina Breyer-Brankwijk. *Medicinal and Poisonous Plants of Southern and Eastern Africa* (London: E. & S. Livingstone, 1962).
Witcover, Jules. *Sabotage at Black Tom: Imperial Germany's Secret War in America, 1914-1917* (Chapel Hill, North Carolina: Algonquin Books of Chapel Hill, 1989).
World Health Organization. *Health Aspects of Chemical and Biological Weapons* (Geneva: World Health Organization, 1970).
Wright, Peter, with Paul Greengrass. *Spy Catcher: The Candid Autobiography of a Senior Intelligence Officer* (New York: Viking, 1987).

## Journal articles

"CDC Closes the Case of The Florida Dentist," *Science*, May 22, 1992, p. 1130.
"Deliberate spreading of typhoid in Japan," *Science Journal*, Vol. 2 (1966), pp. 2.11-2.76.
"Dirty Tricks and Dirtier Germs," *CovertAction Quarterly*, Winter 1998, p. 29.
"Possible Transmission of Human Immunodeficiency Virus to a Patient during an Invasive Dental Procedure," *Morbidity and Mortality Weekly Report,* July 27, 1990, p. 489-493.
Barr, Stephen. "The 1990 Florida Dental Investigation: Is the Case Really Closed?," *Annals of Internal Medicine*, January 15, 1996, pp. 250-254.
Barron, John. "Castro, Cocaine and the A-Bomb Connection," *Reader's Digest*, March 1990, p. 70
Breo, Dennis L. "The dental AIDS cases—Murder or an unsolvable mystery," *JAMA*, December 8, 1993, p. 2732.
Brickhill, "Zimbabwe's Poisoned Legacy," *CovertAction*, Number 43, Winter 1992-93, pp. 4-11+.
Brown, David. "The 1990 Florida Dental Investigation: Theory and Fact," *Annals of Internal Medicine*, January 15, 1996, pp. 255-256.
Christopher, George W., et al. "Biological Warfare: A Historical Perspective," *JAMA*, Vol. 278, No. 5 (August 6, 1997), p. 412.
Crompton, Rufus, and David Gall. "Georgi Markov--Death in a Pellet," *Medic-Legal Journal*, Volume 48 (1980), pp. 51-62.
Davies, J.C.A. "A Major Epidemic of Anthrax in Zimbabwe, part I," *Central African Journal of Medicine*, December 1982, pp. 292-298.
Davies, J.C.A. "A Major Epidemic of Anthrax in Zimbabwe, part II," *Central African Journal of Medicine*, January 1983, pp. 8-12.
Garrett, Benjamin C. "Ricin: A Case Study for the Treaty," *ASA Newsletter*, No. 92-2, April 3, 1992, pp. 1, 10.
Hoffman, Bruce. "Why Terrorists Don't Claim Credit," *Terrorism and Political Violence*, Vol. 9, No. 1 (Spring 1997), p. 4.
Horowitz, Leonard G. "Murder and cover-up could explain the Florida dental AIDS mystery," *British Medical Journal*, December 1994, p. 423-427.
Hugh-Jones, Martin. "Wickham Steed and German Biological Warfare Research," *Intelligence and National Security*, Vol. 7, No. 4 (1992), pp. 379-402.
Jenkins, Brian M., and Alfred P. Rubin. "New Vulnerabilities and the Acquisition of New Weapons by Nongovernment Groups," p. 228, in Alona E. Evans and John F. Murphy, editors, *Legal Aspects of International Terrorism* (Lexington, Massachusetts: Lexington Books, D.C. Heath and Company, 1978).
Jones, R.V. *Reflections on Intelligence* (London: Mandarin Paperbacks, 1990).

Joseph, P.R., Millar, J.D., and Henderson, D.A. "An Outbreak of Hepatitis Traced to food contamination," *New England Journal of Medicine*, July 22, 1965, pp. 188-194.
Knight, Bernard. "Ricin--a potent homicidal poison," *British Medical Journal*, February 3, 1979, p. 350.
Kolavic, S. A., et al. "An Outbreak of *Shigella dysenteriae* Type 2 Among Laboratory Workers Due to Intentional Food Contamination," *JAMA* (Journal of the American Medical Association), August 6, 1997, pp. 396-398.
Lambert, D.P. "The Pakur Murder," *Medico-legal and Criminological Review*, vol. 5, July 1937, pp. 297-302.
Laqueur, Walter. "Postmodern Terrorism," *Foreign Affairs*, September-October 1996, pp. 24-36.
McGeorge, Harvey. "Chemical Addiction," *Defense and Foreign Affairs*, April 1989, p. 17.
Meselson, Matthew, Jeanne Guillemin, Martin Hugh-Jones, Alexander Langmuir, Ilona Popova, Alexis Shelokov, and Olga Yampolskaya. "The Sverdlovsk Anthrax Outbreak of 1979," *Science*, Volume 266, Number 5188 (November 18, 1995), pp. 1202-1208.
Monaghan, Rachel. "Animal Rights and Violent Protest," *Terrorism and Political Violence*, Vol. 9, No. 4 (Winter 1997), pp. 106-116.
Morton, Julia F. "Poisonous and Injurious Higher Plants and Fungi," p. 1502, in C.G. Tedeschi, William G. Eckert, and Luke G. Tedeschi, editors, *Forensic Medicine: A study in trauma and environment, Volume III: Environmental Hazards* (Philadelphia: W. B. Saunders, 1977).
Nass, Meryl. "Anthrax Epizootic in Zimbabwe, 1978-1980: Due to Deliberate Spread?," *PSR Quarterly*, December 1992, pp. 198-209.
Nass, Meryl. "Zimbabwe's Anthrax Epizootic," *CovertAction*, Number 43, Winter 1992-93, pp. 12-18+.
Phills, James A., A. John Harrold, Gabriel V. Whiteman, and Lewis Perelmutter. "Pulmonary Infiltrates, Asthma and Eosinophilia due to *Ascaris Suum* Infestation in Man," *New England Journal of Medicine,* May 4, 1972, pp. 965-970.
Pile, James C., John D. Malone, Edward M. Eitzen, and Arthur M. Friedlander. "Anthrax as a Potential Biological Warfare Agent," *Archives of Internal Medicine*, Vol. 158 (March 9, 1998), pp. 429-434.
Pomerantz, Steve. "Counterterrorism in a Free Society," *Journal of Counterterrorism & Security International*, Spring 1998, p. 24.
Punte, Charles L. "Some Aspects of Particle Size in Aerosol Studies," *Armed Forces Chemical Journal*, March-April 1968, p. 28.
Ramsey, C.N., and J. Marsh. "Giardiasis due to deliberate contamination of water supply," *Lancet*, Vol. 336 (October 6, 1990), pp. 880-881.
Rauber, Albert, and Julia Heard. "Castor Bean Toxicity Reexamined: A New Perspective," *Veterinary and Human Toxicology*, Vol. 27 (December 1965), pp. 498-502.
Robertson, Andrew G. "From Asps to Allegations: Biological Warfare in History," *Military Medicine*, August 1995, pp. 370-371.
Root-Bernstein, Robert S. "Infectious Terrorism," *Atlantic*, May 1991, p. 48.
Rosenberg, Janice. "Attack of the killer shellfish, raspberries, hamburgers, milk, poultry, eggs, vegetables, potato salad, pork...," *American Medical News*, May 4, 1998, pp. 12-15.
S.J. "Homicide By Means of Plague Bacilli," *Bulletin of the New York Academy of Medicine*, September 1967, pp. 850-851.
Smith, G.D. "Militant Activism and the Issue of Animal Rights," Commentary Number 21, Canadian Security Intelligence Service, April 1992, found at *http://www.csis-scrs.gc.ca/eng/comment/com21e.html.*
Stern, Jessica Eve. "Will Terrorists Turn to Poison?," *Orbis*, Vol. 37, No. 3 (Summer 1993), pp. 393-410.
Stewart, James B. "Annals of Crime: Professional Courtesy," *The New Yorker*, November 24, 1997, pp. 90-105.
Thorold, P.W. "Suspected Malicious Poisoning," *Journal of the South African Veterinary Medical Association*, Volume 24 (December 1953), pp. 215-217.
Török, Thomas J., et al. "A Large Community Outbreak of Salmonellosis Caused by Intentional Contamination of Restaurant Salad Bars," *JAMA*, August 6, 1997, pp. 389-395.
Venter, Al J. "North Africa faces new Islamic threat," *Jane's Pointer*, March 1998, p. 11.
Watson, A., and D. Keir. "Information on which to base assessments of risk from environments contaminated with anthrax spores," *Epidemiology and Infection*, 113(1994), pp. 479-490.
Wohlstetter, Roberta. "Terror on a Grand Scale," *Survival*, May June 1976, p. 102.
Woker, G. "Chemical and Bacteriological Warfare," pp. 388-389, in Inter-Parliamentary Union, Geneva, *What Would Be the Character of a New War* (London: Victor Gollancz, 1933).
Zilinskas, Raymond Allan. "Iraq's Biological Weapons: The Past as Future?," *JAMA*, Vol. 278, No. 5 (August 6, 1997), p. 419.

Zilinskas, Raymond Allan. "Terrorism and Biological Weapons: Inevitable Alliance?," *Perspectives in Biology and Medicine*, Vol. 34, No. 1 (Autumn 1990), pp. 44-72.

# Index

# About the Author

W. Seth Carus is a Senior Research Professor Visiting Fellow at the Center for Counterproliferation Research, where he is working on biological warfare issues. Prior to joining the center, Dr. Carus worked at the Center for Naval Analyses (CNA), where he was a Research Analyst. While at the CNA, Dr. Carus directed a study on the implications of NBC weapons on a major regional contingency in Korea. In addition, he participated in other studies for the Commandant, U.S. Coast Guard, the Commander in Chief, U.S. Pacific Fleet, and the Commander in Chief, Naval Forces, Central Command.

From 1991 to 1994, Dr. Carus was a member of the Policy Planning staff in the Undersecretary of Defense for Policy, Office of the Secretary of Defense. Dr. Carus participated in the Clinton Administration's Nuclear Posture Review. Prior to joining OSD, he was a research fellow at the Washington Institute for Near East Policy.

Dr. Carus has published extensively on the proliferation issues. He has published several studies on chemical and biological weapons proliferation in the Middle East, including two monographs, *"The Poor Man's Atomic Bomb,"?: Biological Weapons in the Middle East* (January 1991) and *The Genie Unleashed: Iraqi Biological and Chemical Weapons* (July 1989). He also has published extensively on ballistic and cruise missile proliferation, including two monographic studies for the Center for Strategic and International Studies, *Cruise Missile Proliferation in the 1990s* (1992) and *Ballistic Missiles in the Third World: Threat and Response* (1990). He co-authored the first detailed description of Iraq's *Al-Husayn* missile program in 1990.

www.ingramcontent.com/pod-product-compliance
Lightning Source LLC
Chambersburg PA
CBHW080540170426
43195CB00016B/2624
*9781410100238*